War and Remembrance

AUSA Books

Series Editor: Joseph Craig

WAR *and* Remembrance

The Story of the American Battle Monuments Commission

THOMAS H. CONNER

FOREWORD BY JAMES SCOTT WHEELER

Copyright © 2018 by The University Press of Kentucky

Scholarly publisher for the Commonwealth,
serving Bellarmine University, Berea College, Centre College of Kentucky,
Eastern Kentucky University, The Filson Historical Society, Georgetown
College, Kentucky Historical Society, Kentucky State University, Morehead
State University, Murray State University, Northern Kentucky University,
Transylvania University, University of Kentucky, University of Louisville,
and Western Kentucky University.

All rights reserved.

Editorial and Sales Offices: The University Press of Kentucky
663 South Limestone Street, Lexington, Kentucky 40508–4008

www.kentuckypress.com

Cataloging-in-Publication Data available from the Library of Congress

ISBN 978-0-8131-7631-4 (hardcover : alk. paper)
ISBN 978-0-8131-7633-8 (pdf)
ISBN 978-0-8131-7632-1 (epub)

This book is printed on acid-free paper meeting
the requirements of the American National Standard
for Permanence in Paper for Printed Library Materials.

Manufactured in the United States of America

Member of the Association of University Presses

To Gene S. Dellinger,
and to the memory of my father, Norman H. Conner

Contents

Maps   viii

Foreword by James Scott Wheeler   xiii

Introduction: The Agency and Its Mission   1

1. Remembrance Begins, 1919–1923: From the End of the Great War to the Creation of the American Battle Monuments Commission   15
2. The New Commission Goes to Work, 1923–1938: Organizing and Implementing the Nation's Overseas Commemorative Program   52
3. Building the American Memorials in Europe, 1925–1933   83
4. The Completion of the ABMC's Original Mission and Looking toward an Uncertain Future, 1937–1938   117
5. The American Battle Monuments Commission and World War II, 1939–1945   143
6. Reopening the European Office and New Leadership for a Renewed Mission, 1944–1948   176
7. Building the World War II Memorials, 1945–1960   183

Conclusion: The ABMC Story Goes On, 1960–Present   222

Acknowledgments   235

Appendix: Text of President Roosevelt's Address, Broadcast by Radio, to the Dedication Ceremony at Montfaucon, France—August 1, 1937   239

Notes   241

Selected Bibliography   305

Index   315

Illustrations follow page 142

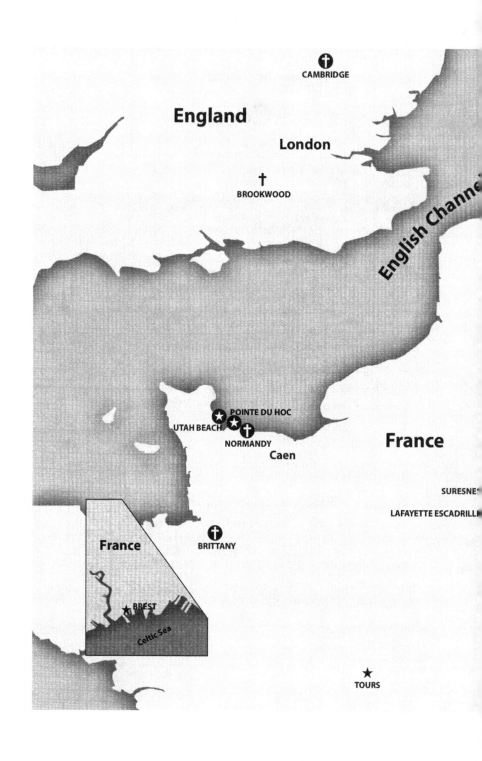

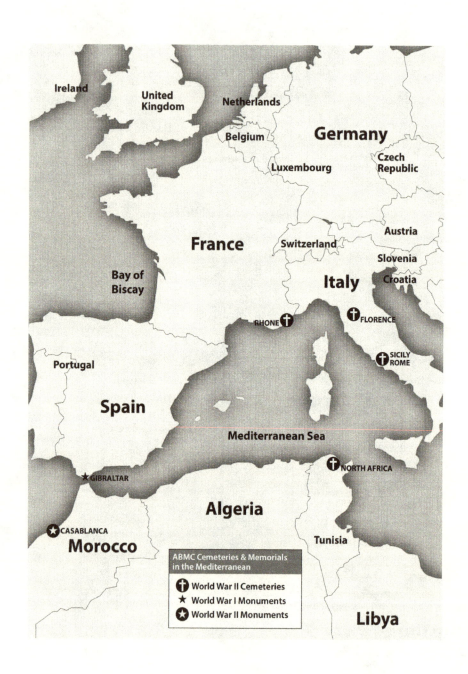

Foreword

Thomas H. Conner's *War and Remembrance* is a superb history of the American Battle Monuments Commission (ABMC). The ABMC was created in 1923 to deal with the bodies of Americans who died overseas during the First World War. The agency also was entrusted with the task of creating and maintaining the cemeteries and monuments in Europe to honor and memorialize the service and sacrifices of over one hundred thousand men and women who died in that war. Conner's well-documented book tells the fascinating story of how the commission dealt with the immediate tasks of designing and building the cemeteries in France, Belgium, and Great Britain for the bodies of those soldiers, sailors, marines, and airmen whose families chose to leave them in Europe to lie with their comrades-in-arms for eternity.

General John J. Pershing was the chairman of the commission from its creation in 1923 until his death in 1948. Pershing personally reviewed the plans for the cemeteries and visited them each summer until 1939. He usually spent most of each visit in the guest quarters in the Meuse-Argonne cemetery, northwest of Verdun, France. The Argonne, or Romagne, cemetery is the largest of the First World War cemeteries, with roughly fourteen thousand graves and an impressive chapel. Like the other cemeteries from that war, it is located on the battlefield on which so many Americans perished defending freedom.

Pershing's successor as chairman was General of the Army George C. Marshall, indicating the importance attached to the ABMC by Presidents Truman and Eisenhower. Following the Second World War, the ABMC was tasked by Congress to design, build, and operate new military cemeteries in the Philippines, Tunisia, Italy, France, Belgium, Great Britain, Luxembourg, and the Netherlands. This mission was in addition to the ABMC's mission of maintaining and operating the World War I cemeteries.

The commission also was entrusted with the task of designing and building a number of memorials outside of the cemeteries in Europe. The monuments of Montsec and Château-Thierry are examples of these monuments. As part of this mandate, the commission prevented unwanted or unsightly memorials from being built across the zone of the Great War's battlefields by individuals, units, or states, and it worked closely with the governments of the nations in which the cemeteries and memorials are located.

Conner's *War and Remembrance* makes the point that American cemeteries and monuments keep alive the memory of those who fell and also of those who fought to defend the world from regimes of unspeakable evil. Whenever one visits the US cemetery in Normandy, near Colleville-sur-Mer, he or she will see numerous groups of French school children visiting the graves of the men who helped liberate their nation over seventy years ago. Those graves are a constant reminder of the shared values of the Western democracies and of the commitment of our nation to defend those values. In many European cemeteries the local populations have adopted individual graves and regularly visit them.

I have visited most of the cemeteries which the ABMC operates in Europe, and Conner's narrative about how they came to be the beautiful places they are is interesting, well-documented, and touching. There is no other book like this one, and it will be the authority on the subject for decades.

James Scott Wheeler

Introduction

The Agency and Its Mission

The American Battle Monuments Commission (ABMC) was created by an act of Congress in 1923. For more than ninety years, the ABMC has been one of the smallest independent federal agencies. Its expenditures for Fiscal Year 2017, for example, were just over $75 million.[1] The agency has never been attached to any other part of the federal bureaucracy; rather, its leadership reports directly to the president of the United States and serves at his pleasure. Few Americans have heard of the commission; indeed, some of its most important current employees admit to having known nothing about it before they first sought to join its ranks.[2] As this book will endeavor to show, in any case, the commission has been entrusted with one of the nation's most important tasks: to honor and promote remembrance of the service and the sacrifice of American soldiers in foreign wars and to preserve the sites overseas where tens of thousands of them lie buried.

During the 1920s and 1930s, the commission beautified eight cemeteries in France, Belgium, and England already built by the Graves Registration Service of the US Army, and erected eleven monuments and two markers in France, Belgium, and Gibraltar as memorials to those who served and died in the Great War. After World War II, the commission built fourteen new cemetery memorials in eight countries worldwide and raised eight more monuments, three of which are in the United States, and three markers to the soldiers and sailors of the 1941–45 war. Additional monuments in Cuba (pertaining to the Spanish-American War); Belleau Wood, France (to the marines who fought there in 1918); Busan, South Korea (to the Korean War); Midway Island (World War II); and Dartmouth, England (also World War II) round out the federal sites within

ABMC's administration. Eight non-federal monuments erected outside the United States to specific units that fought in the Second World War are also maintained by the commission. Finally, a trio of memorials built by the ABMC in the nation's capital to the American Expeditionary Forces (World War I), the Korean War veterans, and the combined efforts of uniformed service personnel and the home front in World War II are now in the care of the National Park Service.

All told, the agency is responsible for the administration, operation, and maintenance of diverse commemorative sites in sixteen foreign countries or national dependencies, as well as the United States. At rest in the twenty-six overseas cemeteries under the commission's control (as of 2017) are nearly 139,000 of our dead—almost all of them from three wars, and all but 15,000 from the two world wars. Memorialized on "Walls of the Missing" in the twenty-two burial grounds from the 1917–18 and 1941–45 wars are the names of 60,314 fallen soldiers with no known graves.[3] The ABMC's work is administered principally out of two offices—one in Arlington, Virginia, and the other in Paris. The commission's work is done by 422 full-time equivalent employees, roughly 80 percent of whom are foreign nationals.[4] The agency's mission *does not* include the numerous "national cemeteries" situated throughout the homeland and is independent of the government departments that administer those sites. Unlike most of the latter cemeteries, furthermore, those of the ABMC—with the principal exceptions of the one in Panama and one in the Philippines—do not accept new burials.[5]

The American Battle Monuments Commission is also a second entity: a board of up to eleven civilians appointed by the president who serve without pay and oversee the agency's work. The commissioners elect from their own ranks a chairman, who has always been a high-ranking general,[6] and the president selects a secretary, who is effectively the chief executive officer of the agency. For much of the commission's history its members were appointed and retained without much regard to politics. Three of the original seven commissioners appointed in 1923, for example, including the first chairman, served continually through parts of five presidential administrations—three Republican and two Democratic.[7] All but the two most recent chairmen served at least two presidents.

Since the Second World War, however, it has become more common for incoming presidents to replace earlier appointees to the commission with people of their own choosing. Between the last meeting under the Truman administration and the first meeting under the Eisenhower administration, for example, eight of the commissioners were replaced by the newly elected president, although the chairman (George C. Marshall) and the secretary (Thomas North) remained in place.[8] In 1961, John F. Kennedy replaced five of the eleven commissioners he inherited from his predecessor, while again retaining the incumbent chairman (Jacob Devers) and secretary (North).[9] During the transition between Lyndon Johnson and Richard Nixon, the latter made nine new appointments, including a new chairman (Mark Clark), while retaining only two from the outgoing administration, plus the secretary (Andrew J. Adams).[10] It was fifteen months into President Clinton's first term before he addressed the composition of the ABMC, but when he did, he repopulated with his own selections the entire body that had been appointed by his predecessor, George H. W. Bush.[11]

At the beginning of the Obama administration, in an action without precedent in the history of the agency, all eleven commissioners, including the chairman, General Frederick M. Franks Jr., resigned on Inauguration Day 2009. Only the then-secretary of the commission, US Army general John W. Nicholson, was allowed to hold his position until Obama appointed former US senator Max Cleland to the post later in 2009, just ahead of the president's visit to the Normandy cemetery for the sixty-fifth anniversary of the D-Day landings.[12] But it took more than two years of appointing new commissioners at periodic intervals to fill all the vacancies, and the agency functioned without a chairman until retired US Air Force general Merrill A. McPeak assumed that position in May 2011. (As of December 2017, the new president removed General McPeak and did not immediately replace him.)

It is no exaggeration to say that some of the most famous soldiers in the past century of American history have chaired the commission. It is equally true that this is a little-known fact. John J. Pershing, who commanded the American Expeditionary Forces in World War I, was the first and remains the longest-serving chairman (from 1923 to 1948). In our entire national experience, Pershing is the only man besides George Washington to hold the exalted rank of "General of the Armies." While most of his biographers give little attention to Pershing's involvement with ABMC, Carlo D'Este wrote in his study of the life of General Dwight D. Eisenhower that Pershing's "most enduring legacy was the creation of the [American] Battle Monuments Commission in 1923."[13] General George

C. Marshall, army chief of staff throughout World War II, served for a decade as chairman after Pershing's death. His biographers pay similarly scant attention to his ABMC service.[14] President Truman, moreover, could not resist making light of his appointment of Marshall to the commission in October 1946. The manner in which Truman announced Marshall's appointment actually confirms two paradoxical realities: the prevalence of historically high-profile and famously accomplished military officers as leaders of the ABMC, and the commission's generally low profile and unfamiliarity among the public.

To illustrate the foregoing point, when President Truman announced General Marshall's appointment to the commission, he engaged in a bit of fun at the expense of the White House Press Corps by mentioning cryptically that he was about to give Marshall a new job, but not saying until the very last that it was with such a little-known agency. The reporters, who waited with rising excitement for the revelation of Marshall's new role, collectively groaned when Truman, "after an impressive pause," told them that the general was going to the American Battle Monuments Commission. The president, who played to the hilt his role in the ruse, made no effort to conceal his own amusement at the journalists' reaction. One newspaper account observed that "President Truman treated reporters yesterday to the vaudeville trick of the mammoth build-up followed by the anticlimactic blackout." Of the ABMC, the same reporter wrote: "It is an organization which exists principally in the pages of the Congressional Directory."[15] The fact still remains that Truman saw fit to entrust a man of Marshall's magisterial standing with the ABMC job. The general's incomparable leadership, moreover, was not wasted on the commission's work, for he led the agency throughout the construction of the World War II cemeteries and memorials, just as Pershing had done for the World War I sites.

In January 1960, following the death of Marshall the previous year, President Eisenhower appointed General Jacob Devers to the commission, and he was quickly elected the group's third chairman.[16] Devers had commanded the Sixth Army Group under Eisenhower in the final stages of World War II and was one of the most distinguished living army veterans when he joined the commission. General Mark Clark, who chaired the commission for four presidents between 1969 and 1984, three Republicans and one Democrat, had commanded the US Fifth Army during the Second World War.[17] Clark, whose tenure as chairman was the second-longest in ABMC history, wrote in a 1978 letter to President Carter that he considered "this position to be one of the highest honors bestowed upon me."[18]

The five ABMC chairmen since 1985 have served for shorter periods, largely because of the aforementioned intrusion of politics into the selection and retention of the commission's membership. Army general Andrew Goodpaster was the first of this latter group, and he held the chairmanship from 1985 until 1990. Marine corps general P. X. Kelley, appointed by President George H. W. Bush, was elected chairman in 1990 and served until President Clinton replaced him with army general Fred Woerner in 1994. General Kelley returned to the post in 2001, appointed by George W. Bush, and served until army general Frederick Franks assumed the office in 2005. Air force general Merrill McPeak, as already noted, took the position in 2011 after it had been vacant more than two years.

In the first annual report issued after he assumed chairmanship of the commission, General Franks wrote somewhat ruefully: "Our cemeteries and memorials are symbols of service and sacrifice, instilling patriotism, evoking gratitude, and teaching history to all who visit. But few Americans know of them—or visit them." He went on to assert that increasing public awareness of these commemorative sites would be a top priority for the agency under his leadership.[19] Fuller explanation of the mission of the American Battle Monuments Commission will be one of the recurring objectives of this book. For now, it suffices to establish that the commission is indeed the "guardian of America's overseas commemorative cemeteries and memorials,"[20] and to identify some of the most important implications of that fact. The ABMC's animating goal, perhaps best expressed in a motto selected by General Pershing himself, is that "time will not dim the glory of their deeds." To be faithful to these words, the commission and its personnel endeavor not only to maintain the sites entrusted to them in their most beautiful and unblemished state, but to honor "the service, achievements and sacrifices of the United States armed forces" through a variety of commemorative and educational activities.[21]

If ABMC cemeteries are the final resting place of well over a hundred thousand of the nation's overseas war dead, there is nothing "dead" about these grounds. Rather, they are *living* sites devoted to the daily remembrance of those who have served and fallen in America's wars. The cemeteries and memorials are open to visitors every day of the year but Christmas and New Year's, and untold numbers of people visit them from all over the world. Many come simply to pay their respects to the dead and to what they symbolize, or to enjoy a quiet walk amid the stunning beauty of the white marble headstones and the lush and meticulously manicured grass, trees, and shrubs. Others come as surviving relatives, friends, or acquaintances of the interred dead to mourn individuals with whom they had close relationships. In the broadest sense, the ABMC memorials are the scenes of innumerable acts of remembrance—official and private, rehearsed and unrehearsed, great and small. Heads of state—our own and those of host governments—and public officials of lesser rank come as well, making the cemeteries, in particular, venues for the continual expression and renewal of bilateral friendships and of the nation's most important international commitments.

Each member of the corps of cemetery superintendents, all of whom are Americans who have served in the military, relish stories of particularly memorable visits they have hosted. Three such stories stand out, all from recent years, as especially illustrative of the role that these places play in the whole panoply of national memory. At the Henri-Chapelle cemetery in Belgium, an elderly woman came from the United States in 2010 to pay homage to the grave of her twin brother who had died in World War II. It was the first time she had done so, and she brought with her a note that she had written to the departed twin she had not seen for more than sixty-five years. She placed the handwritten piece in a weatherproof plastic envelope and taped it to his headstone. After she had left the cemetery, the office staff retrieved the note, to keep it unopened in a safe place until some relative might visit again and provide them with an opportunity to pass along the heartfelt relic to a member of the same family.[22]

A similarly elderly American veteran visited the Lorraine cemetery, in the company of his son, to pay homage to members of the units in and alongside which he had fought in the region during the last year of the Second World War. His legs would not carry him around the expanse of our largest World War II cemetery in Europe, so the staff provided him with a wheelchair. At one particular grave, the man got out of the wheelchair, gripped the arms of the headstone cross with both hands, and prayed on his knees. Some moments later, when the small group was back in motion again, the assistant superintendent asked if the veteran had known personally the man at whose grave he had stopped. "No," he replied. "I did not know him. But I knew them all."[23]

Finally, a woman whose husband had died in action in World War II discovered, after thinking him missing for more than sixty years, that he was in fact buried at the Normandy American Cemetery. Having never remarried out of a singular and indivisible love for him, she has made the long trip from her home in Texas to visit and decorate his grave every year since learning where he had been laid to rest. Cemetery staff have told this story to so many visitors that the grave is decorated almost all the time by anonymous well wishers, so much so that the grass at the front base of the headstone can barely be kept green because it is so frequently covered with flowers.[24]

Without question, the Normandy cemetery, on the bluffs overlooking "Bloody" Omaha Beach in Colleville-sur-Mer, France, is the most visited and familiar of all the overseas sites, certainly on the part of Americans. Since 1978, all but one sitting president of the United States has visited there.[25] In addition to the extensive media coverage of such visits, Steven Spielberg's immensely popular movie *Saving Private Ryan,* whose opening and closing scenes were filmed at this cemetery, has had much to do with pushing annual visitation to this site to well over a million since the late 1990s. But the other memorials enjoy their own prominence as well and, in every case, serve as living reminders of the role Americans have played in the defense of freedom far from their own shores.

The relationship between the American sites and their local hosts constitutes one of the most compelling and least known aspects of the larger story of the ABMC. Not only do almost all of the employees who care for the cemeteries and monuments come from the local populations of the host countries, most visitors to the sites hail from those and neighboring countries as well. A 2003 study of visitors to the Normandy cemetery, for example, established that half of them were French and one in seven came from the United Kingdom. Only one in six came from the United States.[26]

Many Europeans, in particular, do not simply remember the Americans interred in their soil as the lost from two great wars, but as their defenders and their liberators. At the ceremonies held every year in the American cemeteries on Memorial Day, and on special anniversaries like D-Day and Armistice Day, hundreds and often thousands of local citizens crowd onto the sites, enduring whatever the weather conditions might be and whatever lengthy distances from remote parking sites they might be obliged to walk to take their part in the collective acts of remembrance. Local dignitaries always join American officials in speaking at such occasions, and their words typically aim not only to evoke memory of the fallen, but to express gratitude to the young soldiers from far away who paid with their lives so that freedom might be restored to people whom the warriors would likely never even meet. During the Memorial Day ceremony at Normandy in May 2011, for example, one of the local mayors referred with evident emotion to the Americans buried there as "soldiers of liberty" and vowed that "France will never forget them."[27] Indeed, if most Americans will never see these distant outposts of honor and memory—and some will never even hear of them—all of our countrymen can take deep consolation from the generous, reverent, and loving attention continually paid to the sites by those who live in much closer proximity to them.

Mustafa Kemal, a general in the First World War but better known as "Ataturk" once he became president of postwar Turkey, famously said in 1934 to the first wave of New Zealanders, Australians, and Englishmen visiting the Gallipoli battlefield where so many of their countrymen lay buried from the protracted campaign of 1915 that the foreign dead "have become our sons as well."[28] The US government does not encourage the foreign hosts of our overseas cemeteries to consider our dead as their own, but ample evidence exists that many abroad do feel a particularly strong attachment to the ABMC sites and the soldiers who rest in them. The French "cemetery associate" at the Somme American Cemetery, for example, is from the third successive generation of her family to work at the site, and she speaks with justifiable pride of the work her grandfather did in helping to establish the cemetery over eighty years ago and what other relatives have given to the site since then.[29] A Dutch guide at the Netherlands American Cemetery once claimed that "the people in this region actually consider themselves *to be* American!"[30] Every one of the 8,301 graves at the latter site has been "adopted" by local residents. Such a commitment, often passed down through multiple generations of the same family, entails regular visits to the grave in question and periodic decorations of it with flowers.[31]

General Pershing foresaw that this sort of bond would develop between the American dead and the local inhabitants near the burial sites. On Memorial Day 1919, before giving an address at the large American cemetery then taking shape on the old Meuse-Argonne battlefield, Pershing noted in his diary that he had thanked the French civilians on hand "for their sympathy and their offer to do all in their power to care for the graves of our American soldiers."[32] Eight years later, addressing American Legionnaires in France on the tenth anniversary of the US entry into the

Great War, the then-ABMC chairman said at the Suresnes cemetery outside Paris: "No soldier could ask for a sweeter resting place than on the field of glory where he fell. . . . The land he died to save vies with the one which gave him birth in paying tribute to his memory, and the kindly hands which so often come to spread flowers upon his earthly coverlet express in their gentle task a personal affection."[33] In words such as these, Pershing captured sentiments that have endured from that day to this.

Because ABMC sites are sometimes more numerous than American diplomatic outposts, most notably in France, and because host nationals visit them in such large numbers, commission personnel are likely to be the only "official" face of the United States many overseas nationals ever see. In October 2010, the superintendent of the Saint Mihiel American Cemetery was asked whether he understood himself to be an "ambassador" for his country. Without hesitation he pointed to the more than four thousand gravesites arrayed outside his window and said: "*They're* the ambassadors, not me."[34] This called to mind something another superintendent had said years earlier to a group visiting the Normandy cemetery—that the dead buried there were "still serving their country." A similar observation about the likely impact of such large concentrations of American dead permanently resting in overseas sites appeared in a *New York Times* editorial as early as December 1919.[35]

Both the living and the dead associated with each cemetery, therefore, represent in powerful and lasting ways the essence of our national values—most specifically, the causes and principles for which Americans have been willing to fight and die far from home. There is good reason to believe, as a result, that the sites generate broadly positive feeling abroad toward our country. As General Andrew J. Adams, soon to become the commission's third secretary, said about the ABMC's work during congressional testimony in March 1968: "I know of no program or activity which promotes more sympathy, understanding and friendship for the United States among people of the countries where the memorials are located."[36] General Mark Clark made the same point during a 1980 meeting of the commission that he chaired at a notably dark moment of the Cold War: "During these times of one international crisis after another, one thought keeps running through my mind about this Commission and its responsibility, and that is that there is no US activity abroad which generates more good will for our country, and what we believe in, than the ABMC system of cemeteries and memorials."[37] Even with the Cold War over, the American personnel serving at ABMC sites deserve to be numbered among the most important representatives of the American people on several foreign continents.

To remember and honor the service of American soldiers across the seas most effectively, what they actually did must be preserved and represented as accurately and faithfully as possible. Inevitably, therefore, the ABMC's mission has always embraced education. Since 2007, especially, when the commission dedicated its first "interpretive center" at the Normandy cemetery, the ABMC has given education an increasingly high profile within its overall operation. While the action of American military units has been amply chronicled over the years, efforts continue daily at all the cemeteries to compile information about the individuals who rest in the sites in hopes of bringing their stories to life. The "cemetery associate" at Brookwood affirmed in 2011, for instance, that it was the staff's ambition someday to have compiled personal profiles on every one of the 468 soldiers buried there.[38] The cemetery associate at the Flanders Field cemetery, Chris Sims, has compiled into a book accounts of the lives of every one of the 368 interred there. A guided tour of the Normandy cemetery, moreover, routinely includes individual stories about the men and women resting beneath the headstones that have been gathered from official records as well as family sources and are being augmented every day.

Informing visitors about what actually happened on overseas battlefields, in any case, has been a priority for the commission since its inception. With only a few exceptions, ABMC cemeteries, monuments, and memorials are situated exactly where the most important American combats occurred. As will be shown in the next chapter, the American Battle Monuments Commission grew out of an earlier agency, the Battle Monuments Board of the War Department, whose principal purpose was to mark permanently the World War I battlefields in Europe with commemorative plaques. All of the ABMC memorials, from the outset, have been bedecked with maps and inscriptions designed to convey to the visiting public important facts about the American war effort in the surrounding area. In recent years the agency has chosen the words "Competence, Courage, Sacrifice" to characterize the service of all those whom it honors and commemorates. Whatever the expanded program of interpretive centers might yield in terms of additional facilities and more knowledge about individual soldiers lying in the cemeteries, its origins are clearly to be seen across the entire history of the ABMC.[39]

This book proposes to treat the history of the American Battle Monuments Commission in narrative form. Somewhat surprisingly, no one has produced such an account before now. Much like the American public that seems to know little of the commission's existence and work, historians have not paid a great deal of attention to the agency's past. The memoir of General Thomas North, who served as ABMC secretary for more than two decades following the Second World War, probably comes closest to a complete account of the commission's work—and North shared in a great deal of it even before he became secretary. But that memoir is unpublished, contains numerous small errors of detail, and is notably light on the first phase of the commission's history.[40] Lisa Budreau's thorough study of America's efforts between 1919 and 1933 to commemorate its soldiers and its mission in the Great War pays substantial attention to the ABMC and has been immensely useful to my own work. Her principal intent, however, was something other than a complete history of the commission, even though she comes close to providing one for its first ten years.[41] In the same vein, Steven Trout's work on American remembrance of the First World War during the interwar period contains interesting and important information on the ABMC, including a wonderfully rich prologue on Dwight D. Eisenhower's service to the commission during the 1920s.[42] But, like Budreau, Professor Trout's broader focus was elsewhere. G. Kurt Piehler's 1995 book on American remembrance[43] and John W. Graham's more recent work on the Gold Star Mother pilgrimages[44] shed valuable light on the commission's work as well, but in connection with other objectives. These works and more, especially those on the subject of historical remembrance in connection with the two World Wars, have greatly facilitated my own study by so fully elucidating the broader context for what, in my case, will be a narrower agency history.[45]

It comes as a further surprise that the biographical literature bearing upon the ABMC story is so notably thin. As previously noted, neither the Pershing nor the Marshall biographies, although numerous, pay much attention to either man's service to the commission. Published studies of the lives and careers of other ABMC chairmen, most notably World War II generals Devers and Clark, are much rarer, and those that do exist pay almost no attention to the ABMC service of either man. In the case of one of the most recent Devers biographies, much of the scant detail about the general's ABMC chairmanship is wrong.[46] The only biographies offering substantial perspectives on the contributions of other men who have served the commission in major roles are those of Dwight D. Eisenhower.[47]

As a result of these limitations in the published literature about the ABMC, the principal sources for this book have been archival. Hundreds of cartons of commission records are in the National Archives at College Park, Maryland. They contain, most importantly, minutes of commission meetings, reports submitted by the overseas personnel to the Washington office, reports on the construction and maintenance of the ABMC sites around the world, and sheaves of correspondence of commission personnel, often with veterans and relatives of those buried in the overseas cemeteries. The European office houses many boxes of archival material dating from the earliest years of the commission, but these holdings are in such disorder that they have not figured largely in this study. Individual cemeteries keep archival materials as well, but these collections are quite spotty and there is little system to what they contain. With the exception of the more bountiful holdings at the Normandy site, the materials at the cemeteries themselves have not contributed substantially to this study.[48] Records of the National Commission of Fine Arts, finally, have furnished particularly valuable information.[49] This latter body still oversees the design of any new construction at ABMC sites.

The personal papers of the first two chairmen and other assorted individuals who gave important service to the commission have been exceptionally rich sources, none more so than the Pershing Papers in the Library of Congress. The general's "official" correspondence wound up in the ABMC Records in the National Archives, while "personal" materials were catalogued with his private papers in the Library of Congress. The latter collection contains copies of many of Pershing's speeches on important ceremonial occasions, as well as invaluable letters to and from T. Bentley Mott, his West Point classmate, pertaining to the latter's highly unusual mission to German-dominated Europe between 1942 and 1944 to find out how the American memorials were faring in enemy-occupied territory. The Marshall Papers (at the Marshall Library in Lexington, Virginia) have served in similarly important ways to supplement material in the ABMC Records Group.

Among the most fervent hopes for this book, finally, is that it will not only record, but also disseminate the principal elements of the nearly one hundred-year-long history of the ABMC and help explain why this agency is such an important instrument of the American people and their government. The book will recount the history of a federal agency, but it will also tell the story of how the overseas memorials came to be, and of how generations of US government employees of numerous nationalities working on several continents have carried out the commission's assigned tasks of remembrance and preservation. By far the most rewarding and inspirational sources have been the ABMC personnel, past and present, with whom I have had the privilege of conversing during more than three decades of travel to the sites and the years of work spent on this project. These officials are living fonts of memory and always willing to share what they know. Not only can the commission personnel explain interesting and important facts about their sites, but they have all had countless interactions with veterans and relatives of those who have worn the uniform and, in many cases, rest in the cemeteries. From such personal encounters, and visits to almost all of the ABMC sites, has come a profound sense of how these cemeteries and monuments, and those who serve there, continually bear both silent and spoken witness to the "competence, courage, and sacrifice" of the American soldier.

1

Remembrance Begins, 1919–1923

From the End of the Great War to the Creation of the American Battle Monuments Commission

The establishment of the American Battle Monuments Commission (ABMC) in March 1923 was a direct result of the First World War and the national desire permanently to commemorate what the country's soldiers had done. But the American people did not wait for the birth of this new federal agency to start their journey down the path of remembrance. By the time Congress created the commission, important decisions had already been made regarding final interment of the seventy-five thousand military dead from the war. The Graves Registration Service (GRS) of the US Army had selected sites and begun construction of all eight permanent American cemeteries in Europe. Over forty-five thousand bodies had been shipped home for burial at the request of their families. From May 1919 onward, Memorial Day observances at the European cemeteries became important and well-attended annual rituals for Americans posted overseas and officials and ordinary citizens of the host countries, as well as occasions for reaffirming the friendship between the United States and its wartime partners. Private individuals and associations, several states, and the War Department, moreover, had already erected, or made plans to erect, monuments and battlefield markers to commemorate the wartime deeds of the American armed forces.

Many of the foregoing developments had prefigured the work of the

American Battle Monuments Commission. By 1923, for example, the GRS was well along with the work of getting the bodies of the war dead to their final resting places on both sides of the Atlantic. The National Commission of Fine Arts (CFA), thirteen years the ABMC's senior, had laid out a basic plan for the eight permanent American cemeteries in Europe that had won the personal approval of the president of the United States. The Battle Monuments Board (BMB) of the War Department, a committee of five army officers created in June 1921, had spent nearly two years formulating plans and policies for the marking of European battlefields where soldiers of the American Expeditionary Forces (AEF) had seen particularly important action. When the BMB dissolved in the summer of 1923, it was widely assumed throughout the government that the newly established ABMC would simply execute the program that the earlier panel had outlined. Still, the new agency would have much to do and much opportunity to chart its own course. Indeed, Congress's decision to organize the ABMC in the fifth year after the war affirmed that any program of creating and maintaining memorials abroad would require the direction and coordination of a more broadly representative body than either the War Department or the army could ever be, with expertise more suitable to the wide range of tasks at hand.

The war that the United States fought in 1917 and 1918 was unlike any other in the nation's experience before that time. In less than twenty months as a formal belligerent, the country sent more than 2 million soldiers three thousand miles to the European combat zone. In roughly seven months of significant fighting on the Western Front, more than seventy-five thousand Americans had died.[1] The country had never before participated in a military effort of such immensity and cost so far from home. Nor had it ever faced the challenge of what to do with so many dead at such remote distance, or how to memorialize the efforts and achievements of such a large armed force that had waged war in foreign lands.

Permanently burying the American dead was among the most immediate priorities of the government once the test of arms had ended. At the time of the November 1918 armistice, fatalities from General Pershing's forces were scattered among thousands of locations in multiple countries. Fifteen thousand of the dead lay in "isolated" graves, likely to be found anywhere from remote forests to village churchyards and even the gardens of private homes. No fewer than two thousand "temporary" cemeteries contained the rest—six, ten, forty, or a hundred or more at a time.[2]

The last time the United States had fought a war overseas—against Spain in 1898—all of the 5,931 bodies of soldiers who had died abroad came home, at public expense. Government officials and the American public alike expected the lost from the European war all to return home as well. Indeed, in early September 1918, more than two months before the guns went silent, Secretary of War Newton Baker promised as much in an announcement that appeared in the national press.[3] When Baker affirmed that the US government would bring all of the American dead back from Europe once the war ended, however, he knew neither what the final number would be nor when the war would end.

Once the fighting did stop, it became evident all too quickly that the secretary's public declaration was more easily spoken than fulfilled. In the words of the GRS historian, "the unexpectedly large number of casualties, and possible changes in the opinions of the people made a reconsideration of the whole matter essential."[4] As the final American death toll revealed itself more clearly with the armistice in place, anxiety built within the government over the high cost of repatriating all of the American dead as well as the sheer logistical complexities involved. Although Secretary Baker never reneged on his September 1918 pledge, he and his department soon decided that before a soldier's body would be shipped home at government expense, the family would have to request it.[5]

In March 1919, consequently, the War Department mailed 74,770 ballots to the next-of-kin of the soldier dead that gave to each family the right to decide whether the body of its loved one would remain in an American cemetery abroad, or be returned to the family.[6] In the case of a married soldier, the widow made this decision; if the dead soldier was unmarried, the father decided, or if he was dead, the mother. If the soldier's widow was remarried, his parents filled out the ballot.[7] Once the authorized person registered the decision about final disposition of the remains, the government considered it to be irrevocable.

Entrusting the selection of final resting place to the families of the soldier dead had at least two advantages: it allowed thousands of Americans an individual choice regarding where their dead loved ones would rest, and it relieved the government of the expensive prospect of repatriating all of the bodies. A less foreseeable consequence of this approach was a spontaneous public debate over the decision that the bereaved families should make.

Soon after the War Department began contacting the families, rival pressure groups formed in an effort to steer the thousands of individual choices one way or the other. The Bring Home the Soldier Dead League advocated leaving none of the American fatalities on European soil, while the Field of Honor Association promoted the idea that the dead should remain where they had fallen in cemeteries built and maintained by the US government.[8] Prominent public figures, such as former president William Howard Taft, labor leader Samuel Gompers, industrialist Cornelius Vanderbilt, and AEF chaplain Charles Brent, helped to form the latter of the two groups in January 1920. The other side had put together its organization a few months earlier and garnered support mostly from family members of the war dead.[9]

Despite the obvious delicacy of the decision facing thousands of bereaved families, the argument in the public square featured surprisingly indelicate charges. The Bring Home the Soldier Dead League openly suspicioned, for example, that the French government and people preferred that the American dead should remain where they had fallen out of a crass desire to reap financial reward from the visitor and tourist traffic that would surely stream to any overseas burial sites. Harsher cynics professed to be "unimpressed" by the array of promises coming from France that any American dead left there would be well cared for and revered by the local population. The other side charged that the funeral directors' lobby in the United States was chiefly responsible for pressure to repatriate the remains, out of fear for all the business they would lose if the dead were left buried where they fell.[10]

The Field of Honor Association openly appealed to the families of the dead to make one more sacrifice for the country by deciding to leave their loved ones in Europe permanently.[11] Former president Theodore Roosevelt quickly became a compelling example of this point of view. Roosevelt's young son Quentin had perished in aerial combat over the Aisne-Marne region of France in July 1918. When the army, at its first opportunity, offered to exhume and repatriate the dead flyer's body, the retired chief executive had declined, citing the family's strong preference "that Quentin shall continue to lie on the spot where he fell in battle, and where the foemen buried him."[12] Roosevelt reiterated his family's choice of a final resting place for their son in a November 1918 letter later released to the public: "We feel that where the tree falls there let it lie."[13]

When General Pershing weighed into the debate, he echoed the recently deceased ex-president (Roosevelt died on January 6, 1919). In an August 1919 cable from France to the War Department that appeared in the *New York Times,* the AEF commander observed: "I believe that, could these soldiers speak for themselves, they would wish to be left undisturbed where, with their comrades, they fought the last fight." Looking more to the future, Pershing continued: "The graves of our soldiers constitute, if they are allowed to remain, a perpetual reminder to our Allies of the liberty and ideals upon which the greatness of America rests."[14] A few months later, in an editorial, the same newspaper cited the views of one of Pershing's divisional commanders, General John F. O'Ryan, that as long as American graves remain in France, "their occupants would continue in no small measure to do what they were doing—what they gladly, proudly, and gloriously did—when they gave their lives: they would still be serving their country."[15]

At least one other high-ranking representative of the army privately saw the issue in the same way. Major H. R. Lemly, officer-in-charge of Arlington National Cemetery and prominently placed within the Cemeterial Division of the Quartermaster Corps, wrote the chairman of the Fine Arts Commission in May 1919 lamenting the secretary of war's handling of the final interment of the American dead because it allowed for the possibility that great numbers of them would be repatriated. If the high cost of bringing bodies home—which Lemly correctly reckoned would be $30 million dollars well before the actual number to be returned was known from the polling of families—could be applied to burying our soldiers overseas, "the finest military cemeteries in the world" could be created in Europe. More importantly, the major wrote, those sites would be "a perpetual reminder to the nation of the American soldier and of the decisive part taken by the United States in the World War." To repatriate remains, by contrast, would mean that "the bodies will be scattered all over the country" and the effect of concentrating them in designated sites of remembrance would be lost. Lemly was so sure of this last point, moreover, that he concluded: "The matter does not even admit of discussion."[16] What is so striking about the language of the early advocates of leaving the American dead in the foreign ground upon which they had fallen is how accurately it foresaw what the overseas burial grounds would indeed become. It should be further clarified that Lemly's criticism of the secretary of war's willingness to assume the one-time expense of repatriating large numbers of remains was not an argument that leaving the soldier dead in Europe would be less financially burdensome on the government, because in the long run, given the annual cost of maintaining the memorial sites, this could never be the case. The major simply meant that, if applied to the construction of overseas cemeteries, the $30 million needed to ship bodies home could build wonderfully beautiful American burial grounds. As will be shown later, the ABMC spent almost $2.4 million, and the GRS spent $2.6 million, on the construction of eight permanent cemeteries for the portion of the American war dead whose families chose to have them remain in Europe.

Certain actions by the French government in the months following the armistice offered support to proponents of keeping the dead on the European side of the Atlantic by threatening substantial delays to any repatriation of American remains. In February 1919, the Minister of the Interior in the cabinet of Premier Georges Clemenceau decreed that none of the bodies then buried in France could be exhumed and transported out of the country. At the same time, a bill designed to effect the same restriction for a period of three years was presented to the national parliament.[17] The French decree did not prohibit the transfer of bodies from temporary burial sites to larger collection cemeteries inside the country, for this action would quicken the restoration of local farming in the old battle zones. But Clemenceau and his ministers wished to avoid the strain that movement of tens of thousands of bodies out of the country would impose on the badly wounded transportation infrastructure of France. Doubts also abounded within the French public and leadership alike over the health risks from retrieving so many decomposing corpses into the open air. The Paris government, furthermore, had already decided to prohibit the immediate return of dead French soldiers to their own families and understandably feared resentment from its bereaved populace if it looked like Americans were getting preferential treatment in this regard.[18]

Henry White, one of the five commissioners who accompanied President Wilson to the Paris Peace Conference, wrote in July 1919 that he strongly supported what the French had done. It made sense on sanitary grounds and also strengthened the rationale for concentrating the American dead in European cemeteries of our own making. White was already familiar with the Suresnes cemetery in the Paris suburbs and opined that others like it would "ere long be . . . beautiful" and ultimately become "place[s] of pilgrimage for our country."[19] Major Lemly actually viewed the French restrictions as a good reason for the War Department to change its policy on repatriation and announce that no American bodies would ever be returned home.[20]

For their part, the French attempted to take some of the sting out of their government's actions with offers to facilitate American efforts to secure ground for permanent cemeteries. On Memorial Day 1919, an occasion that produced substantial public displays of French reverence for the American dead, Secretary Baker released to the press correspondence between General Pershing and Marshal Henri-Philippe Pétain, commander of the French army at the end of the war. Pétain had written to Pershing that "France would be happy and proud to retain the bodies of the American victims who have fallen upon her soil," and promised to help the United States establish permanent cemeteries on the battlefields of the war. The AEF commander had replied that "I would be exceedingly happy to avail myself of the courteous offer of your assistance," but told Pétain that the determination of family preferences in such matters had only just begun and presumably would not be abandoned.[21] Indeed, no matter how generous Pétain's overture to Pershing may have been, it did not deter the War Department from its policy of letting the bereaved families choose what the government should do with the remains of their dead loved ones.

The State Department, moreover, kept up steady pressure on the French to relax their restrictions on the removal of bodies. In March 1920, a new ministry under Alexandre Millerand agreed to the formation of a commission of three American and seven French officials to resolve the matter. After two weeks of deliberations, under the chairmanship of Minister of Pensions André Maginot, the commission agreed to allow the Americans to remove bodies from the wartime zone of operations beginning September 15, 1920, effectively cutting in half the proposed length of the original prohibition. In the end, the French yielded to the argument that the Americans sought potentially to remove a very small portion of the millions of soldiers then buried in France and that families in the United States were suffering undue emotional distress over the prospect of protracted delays in the desired repatriation of their loved ones.[22]

While Americans continued to debate with themselves over where the dead should rest, and with the French over the freedom to act on their decisions, ballots from the affected families streamed into the War Department. A substantial majority had registered their choices within the first twelve months of the canvas. From the outset, most of the surviving relatives asked the government to bring the remains of their loved ones home. By the time the balloting ended in 1921, 61 percent had so chosen. That meant 46,352 bodies were to be sent back to the United States or to some other destination requested by the family, while 29,265 bodies would remain in Europe.[23]

Once the families had exercised the option the War Department had given them, and the French government had green-lighted removal of the American remains, getting all of the bodies to their final resting place could carry forward in earnest. Shipments of remains occurred at a brisk pace during the final quarter of 1920, and by year's end the GRS had sent 11,534 bodies back to the United States. Another 31,945 followed in 1921, and the final 2,109 went home in 1922. The remaining 764 bodies were sent to destinations other than the American homeland.[24]

Collecting the American bodies from temporary and isolated tombs for shipment home or for permanent burial in Europe was time consuming and emotionally wrenching. This process was directed by agencies other than the American Battle Monuments Commission. Several thousand army troops, many of them African Americans, worked for the Graves Registration Service to accomplish the task of exhuming the bodies, often reburying them for a time in larger collection cemeteries before moving them to where they would finally rest. The countless hours of grim toil necessary to complete this work were one thing; the staggering quantities of material and resources required were another. Thousands of metal caskets had to be shipped to Europe. Hundreds of trucks and rail cars had to be secured for the transport of the bodies. Legions of clerks were put to work establishing and documenting the identity, organizing the numerous movements, and pinpointing the final destination of each body. In time-honored military fashion, procedures were devised to regulate the process at every stage. By far the most demanding thing about this work, however, was that it required veritable armies of human beings to dig up, handle, transport, and often reinter only to dig up again the remains, in various states of decomposition and disfigurement, of other human beings. Historians have begun to recount this story with complete candor and appropriate sympathy only in the past couple of decades.[25]

US policy on the disposition of its war dead contrasted sharply with that of Great Britain, which permitted no repatriation of remains. With more than ten times the total number of war dead as the Americans, and with all of them to be buried overseas, therefore, the British created a network of cemeteries along the old Western Front that dwarfed that of their Yankee cousins. Some of these sites contain as few as a couple dozen interments, for the British were especially keen to bury their dead as close as possible to where they had fallen in battle. The Americans learned a great deal from the work of Sir Fabian Ware and his Imperial War Graves Commission (now the Commonwealth War Graves Commission), but, as will be shown in the next chapter, never sought merely to copy it.[26]

The War Department took charge of the permanent burial of the approximately thirty thousand doughboys remaining in Europe, just as it supervised the repatriation of the American dead. The agency decided that the United States would maintain "comparatively few cemeteries" abroad, but generally with higher numbers in them than the British sites. As the GRS's *History of the American Graves Registration Service* observed, "the great distances involved and the large force necessary for upkeep" made it "impossible" for the Americans to copy the British model. With the placement of their permanent sites, the Americans sought to accomplish two purposes: to have their cemeteries on ground that was significant to the course of the war and the actions of their own troops and, where possible, to place the burial grounds in the "most advantageous and ideal situations" for people who wished to visit them.[27]

Locations for the permanent cemeteries were confirmed during 1920 and 1921 as the War Department determined more clearly the number of burials that would be necessary. By the end of 1920, the agency had chosen five sites: Suresnes, Romagne (in the Meuse-Argonne region), Belleau Wood (in the Aisne-Marne), Bony (in the Somme), and Brookwood (near London).[28] In August 1921, when it was more completely known how many graves would be required, three more locations were added: Fère-en-Tardenois (Oise-Aisne), Thiaucourt (Saint-Mihiel), and Waregem (Flanders Field).[29] These final additions also ensured that there would be a permanent cemetery on each of the most prominent American battlefields of the Great War.

Rarely was it possible, however, to satisfy the dual ambitions of locating the sites on militarily significant ground that was also easily accessible to would-be visitors. Suresnes cemetery, for example, fronted a major thoroughfare and enjoyed a panoramic view of Paris a few miles off in the distance.[30] Brookwood cemetery, similarly, was within easy reach of London and found itself in the midst of a larger, long-established, and well-known complex of civilian and military graveyards.[31] While each of these sites was convenient to visitors to both national capitals, neither was on ground that had figured in the war's combats. The overwhelming majority of the American dead remaining in Europe were destined for cemeteries on the actual battlefields. In every case, these sites were harder to get to and often inconspicuous to travelers on the main highways. Nevertheless, the GRS offered compelling justifications, always in terms of how the ground in question had figured in the military action, for each of these more remote sites.

The cemetery at Romagne, on the western end of what Pershing's soldiers knew as the heights of Cunel, occupied ground "where the American troops met with most stubborn resistance" during the all-important Meuse-Argonne battle. It would contain dead from just about every division in the AEF as testimony to the immensity of the war's climactic campaign.[32] The Aisne-Marne cemetery was situated at the edge of Belleau Wood, "where soldiers and marines made common history, to the glory of American ideals and traditions."[33] Acreage at the edge of the village of Bony was selected for the Somme cemetery, at a place of "aggressive and desperate fighting" along the old Hindenburg Line, where American troops had fought "shoulder to shoulder" with their British partners in the final stages of the war.[34]

Each of the three cemeteries added to the group of permanent sites in August 1921 similarly highlighted important American combats. The Oise-Aisne site, near Fère-en-Tardenois, occupied ground that figured decisively in the Allied counteroffensive of July and August 1918 that pushed the Germans back beyond the Vesle River, resulting in "one of the most complete and significant victories of the war."[35] Thiaucourt, near the southeastern base of the strategically sensitive Saint-Mihiel salient, where the American First Army fought its initial battle, was selected to host a cemetery because it was "on the battle line and constantly under fire," and was liberated by American troops at great cost to the enemy.[36] The Waregem site, finally, would commemorate "the spirited advance made by the two American Divisions [37th and 91st] sent in October, 1918, to assist the 6th French Army in Belgium."[37]

In the midst of the War Department's determination of where the permanent cemeteries would be located, Secretary Baker appealed to the Fine Arts Commission for its help with the design of the sites. Established by Congress in 1910, this seven-member board was responsible for supervising the artistic quality of any monuments erected under the authority of the United States. As of 1915, and for the next twenty-two years, its chairman was Charles Moore.[38] An art historian and prominent city planner, Moore had helped found the CFA five years earlier. Although not a professional artist himself, he served on the commission with three architects, one landscape architect, a painter, and a sculptor.[39] When Congress created the American Battle Monuments Commission in 1923, the founding statute required that the two commissions collaborate on the design of all of the country's overseas war memorials. Meanwhile, before the new agency appeared, the Fine Arts Commission would play a critical role in planning for the burial grounds overseas.

To equip them for their role in the creation of the cemeteries, Secretary Baker decided that Chairman Moore and some of his colleagues should make an inspection visit to Europe. The secretary communicated this desire to the commission through Colonel Charles Pierce, head of the Graves Registration Service, at the CFA meeting of September 20, 1920. Upon their return from such a trip, the commissioners were told, they should "make definite recommendations as to the action to be taken for their [the cemeteries'] development."[40] At its October 9 meeting the commission learned that Baker had approved funding for Moore and three others to make the journey as soon as topographic maps of the proposed sites requested from France could reach Washington.[41]

The Fine Arts Commission delegation—Moore and co-members William M. Kendall (an architect) and James L. Greenleaf (a landscape architect)—made the European inspection during the spring of 1921. Major George Gibbs, another landscape architect, was detailed by the quartermaster general to the project at Moore's explicit request and traveled with the three CFA commissioners.[42] The quartet sailed from New York on March 5 and disembarked at Antwerp, one of the principal bases established by the GRS for its ongoing program of repatriating remains. The chairman and his colleagues actually departed Washington, D.C., on March 4, Inauguration Day for the new president, Warren G. Harding. Moore recalled that he was careful to make a courtesy call to the incoming secretary of war, John Weeks, before proceeding with his trip, and that Weeks promised his full support to the mission. The three Fine Arts Commission members sailed home two months later from England. Gibbs stayed an extra month in Europe to refine the group's plans for their eventual presentation to the War Department and President Harding. While in Europe, the CFA representatives also spent a lot of time with

Colonels Pierce and Harry Rethers, the two highest-ranking officers in the GRS.[43] Until the newly appointed members of the American Battle Monuments Commission visited the European cemeteries and battlefields on a similar inspection three years later, this 1921 tour represented the most thorough and ambitious trip of its kind.

The War Department had already established important guidelines for the permanent cemeteries by the time Chairman Moore and his colleagues left the United States. Special (in other words, privately funded) monuments would not be permitted on any of the cemetery grounds. No distinction of rank was to be made in arranging the graves; officers and enlisted men would rest side by side. All the headstones were to be uniform and contain the same information about every buried soldier. At the time of the Moore delegation's trip, finally, it was not anticipated that chapels would be built inside each cemetery; rather, existing chapels in adjacent villages were expected to serve whatever need might arise for religious space.[44] Moore actually wrote years later that he wanted the cemeteries themselves to be "places to which one may go with a sentiment of respect and peace, as into a church or a sacred place."[45]

While at sea on the front end of their trip, Moore and his colleagues agreed on a "fundamental plan" for the artistic layout of each cemetery. The burial grounds would be arranged in blocks. Small, uniform headstones would mark the graves, with "ample space of green grass" between them. Spacious grassy areas would surround the cemetery buildings as well, with "wide spreading trees indigenous to both America and France" equally plentiful.[46] As the commissioners visited each site, moreover, they addressed such issues as how to create suitable approaches from each of the nearby towns; how to design attractive layouts for walkways, roads, planting spaces, monuments, and outbuildings; and how to provide for the ongoing maintenance of each site by well-qualified caretakers sheltered in appropriate quarters on the cemetery grounds.[47]

While in the French capital during the second week of their trip, the Americans met with War Minister Louis Barthou, who gave to their mission his "unhesitating blessing." Moore recalled that Barthou assured his guests that "the land of France . . . was at our disposal" for cemetery sites, "subject, of course, to payment of its individual owners."[48] After he had seen all of the sites, and witnessed the ongoing work of the Graves Registration Service in recouping bodies and interring them in their final resting places, Moore had high praise for the manner in which the army laborers performed their difficult tasks. "The painstaking care in handling, the reverent attention given to each body, the orderliness of the work and the carefulness shown with the records," he wrote, "were reassurance to the parents and wives who gave so utterly to their country."[49]

After two months on the ground, the visiting inspection team finished its work. When Colonel Rethers was asked to review their proposals before the group's departure from London, he reacted supportively, but worried that the scope envisioned for the cemeteries might be too elaborate and expensive for the War Department.[50] Final judgment on the ideas of the Moore delegation, in any event, would await fuller review by higher authorities in Washington. Upon his arrival in New York in mid-May, Moore told the *New York Times* that "no detail would be omitted to make the overseas cemeteries a credit to the American nation," and no parent "need ever feel that the graves were not being cared for properly."[51]

The chairman personally delivered the recommendations of his commission to the president of the United States on August 22, 1921. The report he shared with Harding contemplated permanent American cemeteries at Suresnes, Romagne, Belleau, Bony, Brookwood, and Waregem (Belgium), and held out the likelihood of more. It also contained numerous findings on the current condition of the burial grounds and proposals for the further development of them. Harding listened "with manifest interest" to his presentation of the commission's plans, Moore later recorded, and did his own "patient examination" of the drawings of how the cemeteries were to be improved from their current state. When the president finished his review of the accompanying documents, he declared his approval of the commission's plans and his commitment to see them funded.[52] This unequivocal White House support was sufficient to overcome initial objections by Budget Director Charles Dawes that the vision of Moore and his colleagues for the cemeteries would cost the government too much money.[53]

The CFA chairman met with the president four months later to seek Harding's approval of a detailed appropriation for the next fiscal year to begin implementation of the Fine Arts Commission's plans for the permanent cemeteries. Moore was especially anxious to secure this first installment of funding (approximately $850,000) because it would include the amount necessary to obtain additional acreage around the sites to make them, in his view, sufficiently spacious. Even though the appropriation request Moore took to the White House at the end of 1921 bore the approval of the quartermaster general, the secretary of war, and the army chief of staff (General Pershing), the chairman complained publicly that "a few officers" were still trying to "cut and slash" the plans to save money.[54] In defense of his funding request, Moore insisted that "every foot of land" to be acquired for the burial grounds had the object of securing "natural and obvious boundaries or to prevent the domination of the American cemeteries" by neighboring structures of any kind.[55]

Once again, the president was won over to the CFA chairman's program. After approving the requested appropriation, Harding asked Moore to deliver the following statement for him to reporters at the White House gate: "I [the president] am entirely in sympathy in doing for those men who lie in France the same as for the men who have come here; that those cemeteries in France should be treated with the utmost reverence and respect, just as we do the cemeteries here."[56] With the chief executive solidly on board, Congress passed a joint resolution early in 1922 authorizing the secretary of war to spend a sum not to exceed $856,680 "for purchase of such real estate as is necessary to establish suitable burial places in Europe for American military dead, and for suitable and necessary improvements thereon."[57] Before the year was out, the desired ground at all eight sites was in hand and the envisioned improvements were under way.

The United States acquired the land for its European cemeteries in two different manners. On several occasions, use of the ground for permanent burial of American soldiers was simply granted, free of charge, by the host government. Shortly after the war ended, for example, the French government donated the entire 130 acres required for the large American cemetery at Romagne, as well as most of the ground for the Suresnes cemetery.[58] The Belgian government did likewise in 1922 for the Flanders Field cemetery.

As War Minister Louis Barthou had signaled to the Moore delegation in March 1921, however, the French government required payment from the US government for the hitherto privately owned land on which the additional cemeteries would be built. Under the terms of a bilateral agreement signed on July 27, 1922, the French volunteered to acquire legal title to the desired sites for the Somme, Oise-Aisne, Saint-Mihiel, and Aisne-Marne cemeteries on condition that the Americans reimburse them for the costs of purchasing the land from private owners. Once the Americans had covered the purchase price, the French government would cede to them "free and perpetual use of the grounds so acquired" as war cemeteries and forever exempt those sites from any duties or taxes. In the event that the US government ever chose to close down its permanent cemeteries, Article III of the agreement required that "the grounds thus evacuated shall be sold by the French Government, and the net proceeds of such sales be paid by the French Government to the Government of the United States."[59]

Whether the Americans acquired their cemetery grounds by purchase or by gift, possession and control were ceded to them for as long as their war dead stay buried there. Under the 1922 agreement, American authorities remained free to administer said grounds without interference from the host government. All told, the United States reimbursed the French almost $27,000 for the more than 110 acres purchased for five of its six permanent cemeteries.[60]

For the sole American cemetery in Belgium, the GRS selected ground contested by the 91st Division in late October and early November 1918. The Belgian government procured this land without charge to the Americans and continues to hold title to it. In an accord signed on October 26, 1922, the Belgians ceded exclusive use and control of the site to the United States so long as it remains a military cemetery.[61]

To obtain the ground for the Brookwood cemetery, the American authorities paid the privately owned London Necropolis and Mausoleum Company, under another 1922 agreement, "consideration" in the amount of 5,500 British pounds ($20,267) for the formal grant of a 4.36-acre parcel. The Americans possess exclusive rights to erect monuments, control the layout, and preserve the site, so long as it remains a national cemetery. Since the improvements undertaken by the Graves Registration Service on the recommendation of the Moore commission, as well as the permanent concentration of burials, were accomplished at Brookwood by June 1924, this cemetery claims to be the first of the permanent American overseas burial sites to have been completed.[62]

In their finished form, the eight American cemeteries vary considerably in size. Brookwood and Flanders Field each contain less than five hundred graves. Suresnes and Bony have 1,541 and 1,844 burials, respectively. The Aisne-Marne cemetery contains 2,289 graves. The number of burials at Romagne, by contrast, exceeds 14,000, almost half the total number of the American dead that remained in Europe from the Great War. The last three cemeteries to be made permanent—Oise-Aisne (6,012 burials), Saint-Mihiel (4,153 burials), and Flanders Field (368 burials)—

afforded the GRS an increment of 10,533 graves beyond the capacity of the five sites initially selected.

It did not take long for the American cemeteries to become prominent focal points of remembrance. As early as the first Memorial Day after the war, and well before the dead to remain in Europe were permanently sorted from those to be repatriated, important commemorative ceremonies took place at these sites. Not surprisingly, the cemetery nearest Paris, in the suburb of Suresnes, hosted some of the grandest of these commemorative events. On May 30, 1919, President Woodrow Wilson, who had been in the French capital since the previous January at the head of the American delegation to the peace conference, made the short trip to deliver the dedicatory address at the unfinished cemetery. On the same date, General Pershing did similar honors 150 miles to the east, at Romagne.

Wilson's appearance at Suresnes drew a large crowd that included what would become over the years, although on a smaller scale, a predictable assortment of personnel from the resident American, British, and French diplomatic and military communities. Marshal Ferdinand Foch, the closest the victorious wartime partners ever had to a unified field commander, was among those present.[63] Despite having spent nearly five months in Europe by Memorial Day, the president was accustomed to visiting neither the battlegrounds nor the burial grounds of the war. General Pershing, Premier Clemenceau, and Britain's Prime Minister David Lloyd George had urged him repeatedly to make such visits, but the American leader had stubbornly refused almost every such entreaty. It is likely that Wilson's visit to Suresnes marked only the second time he had seen an American war cemetery in France.[64]

One intimate who was with him on May 30 described Wilson as "preoccupied and nervous" on the drive to the ceremony.[65] The president used the occasion to do what countless Memorial Day speakers at these shrines have done every year since: pay solemn tribute to the dead soldiers and the cause to which they had given themselves, and render homage to the historically close relationship between the United States and the host country. With the looming prospect of thousands of American dead resting permanently on French soil, Wilson clearly perceived that the friendship with our oldest ally stood to become stronger than ever. In this spirit, he spoke with striking tenderness about the cemetery and the French people who were already showing great reverence for the American dead.

The men resting on the Suresnes hillside, Wilson observed, "though buried in a foreign [land], are not buried in an alien soil. They are at home, sleeping with the spirits of those who thought the same thoughts and entertained the same aspirations." The president also had reassuring words for the American mothers who would forever be an ocean removed from their beloved sons. "The noble women of Suresnes," he said, "have given evidence of the loving sense with which they received these dead as their own. . . . They have cared for their graves, they have made it their interest, their loving interest, to see that there was no hour of neglect, and that constantly through all the months that have gone by the mothers at home should know that there were mothers here who remembered and honored their dead."[66]

At the conclusion of his remarks, as he was laying a wreath on an American soldier's grave, a French woman approached Wilson with flowers of her own and asked if she could add them to the grave. The president nodded his assent, and the woman laid her floral tribute alongside his. According to one account, the usually "stern and hard" Marshal Foch, at Wilson's side and clutching his arm throughout the moment, "turned away with tears in his eyes."[67]

On the same day, General Pershing spoke at the Romagne site destined to become the largest permanent American cemetery in Europe.[68] Then a collection point for those recently exhumed from temporary and isolated graves in the Meuse-Argonne region, this cemetery was situated right in the middle of the 1918 battlefield. The Meuse-Argonne offensive had commenced forty-seven days before the armistice and continued up to the moment on November 11 when the guns stopped firing. Well over one hundred thousand of Pershing's troops were casualties in the engagement that still stands as the bloodiest battle in American history.[69]

Unlike at Suresnes, where no combat had occurred, Pershing's audience on that first postwar Memorial Day stood amid the ubiquitous scars of a momentous struggle. As the American commander's own diary recounted: "The entire scene about the cemetery brought to one very sharply the tremendous damage and loss which has been caused by this war."[70] In his Memorial Day address, Pershing expressed sadness for the soldiers of the Meuse-Argonne whose graves surrounded him. "We weep today over their graves because they are our flesh and blood," he said. But, characteristically, the AEF commander also expressed pride "that they so nobly died" and observed that the cemetery would always be a "sacred plot . . . consecrated as a shrine where future generations of men who love liberty may come to do homage." Although he would come back to the battle sites yearly for the next two decades to honor his dead comrades, Pershing bid farewell to them with words that also evoked fond images of France: "Here, under the clear skies, on the green hillsides and amid the flowering fields of France, in the quiet hush of peace, we leave you forever in God's keeping."[71]

What happened on Memorial Day 1919 at the two most prominent overseas American cemeteries established a model for subsequent years right down to the present. Memorial Day a year later, as the GRS's *History of the American Graves Registration Service* recounted, "was fittingly observed in every European country where our soldier dead were laid to rest." Even without the president of the United States and his top commander presiding at such ceremonies in 1920, "all possible honor was rendered to our men who had met the Great Adventure."[72] Wider sponsorship and promotion of the 1920 events enhanced their scope. The GRS teamed up with the newly established American Overseas Memorial Day Association, the American Legion, and countless anonymous individuals who were tending to the still widely scattered burial plots to decorate the graves and conduct the ceremonies that year. The *Washington Post* claimed that 497 separate ceremonies took place.[73]

French officials and ordinary citizens alike played key parts in these early postwar Memorial Days. The *New York Times* headlined in May 1920 that "All France Unites in Paying Honor to American Dead."[74] Remarks by Marshal Pétain highlighted that year's ceremony at Suresnes for a reported crowd of ten thousand. Echoing the sentiments expressed a year earlier by President Wilson and General Pershing, the Frenchman said: "Those families who weep for their dead will find consolation in the thought that their loved ones sacrificed their lives in the cause of and on the soil of a land towards which their hearts were traditionally turned—in and for a nation which aided in the foundation of your Republic and which the sons of America have learned to look upon almost as their native land. . . . They are not resting as strangers in a strange land, these soldiers of liberty. . . . These tombs will be forever watched over with the same pious care as that which our country gives her own children."[75]

On Memorial Day 1921, similar scenes unfolded. With the process of repatriation of the dead in full swing, both of the principal speakers at Suresnes, Marshal Pétain and the American ambassador Hugh Wallace, expressed regret that most of the American fatalities would soon be gone from the soil in which they had lain since their deaths. "Could I have my way," the ambassador bluntly asserted, "these graves would never be disturbed."[76] Pétain claimed that he and his countrymen "regret it infinitely" that so many of the American dead were leaving their graves in France. Of those permanently remaining, the marshal said: "They are the basis of an eternal friendship."[77]

The journey home for the repatriated bodies occasioned equally poignant tributes to the American dead. Most remains traveled to their port of embarkation by truck or train. During the spring and summer of 1921, however, the Meuse River and canal network furnished one of the main routes to the port of Antwerp, departure point for the Atlantic crossing. Organized and spontaneous displays of respect and affection occurred all along the way. As the GRS's *History of the American Graves Registration Service* noted: "Had those heroic soldiers come from their own firesides, the sturdy people of the Meuse and Ardennes could have paid no greater respect nor shown more gracious sympathy than they did in their devoted demonstrations along the route."[78] One of those who spoke on behalf of an entire Belgian village that turned out to see the convoys go by said of the Americans: "You gave us food, you gave us clothes, when we were in want of all. But that is not enough. When you saw that victory and freedom were at stake, you gave us your sons."[79] If this small sampling of what Europeans said and felt toward the American dead seems overly anecdotal, it should not be discounted. Words and sentiments like these are still expressed by the host peoples at ceremonies of remembrance held every year at the ABMC sites.

It should be recalled that the foregoing developments—determining on which side of the Atlantic the individual soldier dead would permanently rest; location, acquisition, and design of the American cemeteries; and the establishment of the overseas burial grounds as focal points of annual commemorative ceremonies—all preceded the establishment of the American Battle Monuments Commission. With regard to the cemeteries, the ABMC would be called upon to beautify already established sites, a task it would undertake to impressive effect as the 1920s progressed. After considerable discussion with the War Department, construction of the federally funded war monuments did become the sole preserve of the new commission.

Even before determining that there would be permanent American burial grounds abroad, the War Department envisioned erecting monuments on the European battlefields to mark and explain the accomplishments of our soldiers. Although final interment of the dead and the creation of the eight overseas cemeteries quickly took priority over this second important commemorative project, General Pershing seemed anxious to get the monuments program under way at the earliest possible moment. In June 1919, while he was still in France supervising the demobilization of his forces and the retention of a portion of them for occupation duty in Germany, the AEF commander cabled to Washington that he had ordered the preparation of "a list of selected sites suitable for monuments to commemorate the work of Combat divisions." He did so in the belief that Congress would be anxious to appropriate money for the acquisition of such ground and the construction of memorials on the European battlefields, and in the hope that the War Department would be ready with a program as soon as that moment arrived.[80]

The country's most famous living soldier made two additional recommendations that presaged the future work and scope of authority of the yet-to-be-established American Battle Monuments Commission. One was that at each location marked for an American memorial, a relief map should be prepared to depict the topographical context of the military action to be commemorated. The second was that a committee composed of artists and representatives from the War and State Departments should be set up to ensure that all monuments, whether privately or publicly funded, were "artistically acceptable" and unobjectionable on diplomatic grounds.[81] It is instructive that General Pershing was so insistent about the need for the American government to establish some mechanism to regulate commemorative structures on the European battlefields. Aware of what had happened at Civil War sites, the AEF commander clearly sensed that private individuals or groups would be in such a hurry to place monuments in the old combat zone that, in the absence of a designated regulatory body, they might behave irresponsibly.

As it happened, Pershing's fears about the behavior of private actors proved better founded than his expectation that official Washington would act quickly to take control of the erection of monuments. Prior to their return home, veterans of some units did hastily place markers and makeshift monuments where they had fought. These markers were often installed without securing the permission of private landowners or lacked either artistic appeal or the strength to last for long. Such conduct, needless to say, earned the Americans no goodwill from the host nationals.

Inaccurate historical information on some of the monuments, moreover, caused contention among veterans and upset among army officials back home. Yet, the War Department was stubbornly slow to act on Pershing's advice and assume supervision of all commemorative activity.

Pershing renewed his recommendation that the national government should take full and direct control of the raising of overseas monuments in January 1920 when he learned of a dispute between two army divisions over an inscription on one of their monuments. The response of the secretary of war was to request that his counterpart at the State Department engage the French and Belgian governments in conversation about how they would like to see the Americans erect battlefield monuments. But this initiative utterly failed to address the total absence of official supervision of the design, construction, or placement of monuments.[82]

What finally jarred the federal bureaucracy out of its lethargy was a request from a veterans' group for information on how to erect a monument in France that no American official could answer. In February 1921, Lieutenant H. N. Gilbert, chairman of the 30th US Infantry (3rd Division) Marne Memorial Association, wrote to the Paris embassy with a long list of questions relating to how his group should pursue its desire to erect a memorial near the village of Crezancy.[83] As the unit's only surviving officer, Gilbert planned to go to France himself to arrange for and supervise construction. Before doing so, the lieutenant wanted the US ambassador to tell him about French policy on such matters. Did the French desire American memorials in their country? Would land for his regimental monument be given free of charge? How might such a free grant of land be arranged? What procedures were in place for the perpetual care of memorials once they were built? Might necessary building materials or parts for the monument be permitted to enter France duty free from the United States?[84]

Surely no one could fault Lieutenant Gilbert for the nature or the particulars of his inquiry. Ambassador Wallace, however, had no answers to give him because no such conversations had taken place with the French, nor had anyone in Washington formulated relevant policies. When he was forwarded Gilbert's letter, Colonel T. Bentley Mott, the US military attaché in Paris, strongly advised that the War Department pursue such talks with the French and develop its own guidelines for overseas monuments. If these actions were taken, "battle monument associations, whenever formed, can be told exactly what conditions must be fulfilled by them, and under what conditions the French Government permits the monuments to be erected." Without such determinations, Mott concluded, Americans would continue to present their individual cases to the Paris embassy with no chance of being told accurately or authoritatively what to do.[85]

As it circulated within the War Department, Lieutenant Gilbert's inquiry ultimately found its way to the War Plans Division. In May 1921, this group formulated a remarkably comprehensive series of policy recommendations: (1) The War Department should undertake the marking of European battlefields and not leave the task to private individuals; (2) relief maps should constitute the markers and, if practicable, the metal for them should come from captured German and Austrian guns; (3) the War Department should control the "design, construction, and location" of the battlefield markers; (4) the general plan for the American program should be submitted to the French, Belgian, and Italian governments with a request for their approval and assistance, especially with acquisition of land for the markers; and (5) a board of officers should be appointed to prepare "detailed plans and estimates," draft necessary legislation, and generally speak for the War Department and to the War Department about any issues relating to the monument program.[86] The outlines of the future activity and authority of the American Battle Monuments Commission are plainly visible in this important memorandum, although for most of the next two years the focus of the discussion of war memorials abroad remained in the War Department.

The most immediate result of the War Plans Division's memorandum was the creation a month later of the Battle Monuments Board (BMB). The original orders to this group were "to prepare a detailed plan for marking American battlefields in Europe, and to supervise the execution of the plan after its approval by the Secretary of War." Beyond this, the War Department leadership envisioned that the new board would wield the broad authority over the building of *all* overseas monuments urged by two years' worth of advice from General Pershing, and indirectly by the correspondence spawned by Lieutenant Gilbert. The memorandum from the War Plans Division had explicitly affirmed that the "erection of separate monuments by or on behalf of American troop units should be subject to control by the War Department with respect to design, construction, and location." A subsequent directive from the adjutant general's office, moreover, had instructed the members of the new board to "make your recommendation in each case" as to the acceptability of proposals from such groups "to set up separate monuments."[87]

Regardless of the degree to which the Battle Monuments Board ultimately succeeded or failed to live up to the hopes of those who created it, this panel of officers constituted the first working group within the national government to focus its sustained attention on the monument-building effort. Five army officers comprised this board, one each from the Infantry, the Corps of Engineers, the General Staff, the Adjutant General's Department, and the Judge Advocate General's Department.[88] Colonel John McAuley Palmer, who enjoyed particularly close ties with Pershing, chaired it. Promoted to brigadier general in 1922 while serving as aide-de-camp to the army chief of staff and as chairman of the Battle Monuments Board, Palmer was described by Lisa Budreau as Pershing's "'scholarly' general."[89] In 1942, the general of the armies himself rated his gifted subordinate as "one of the best staff officers ever produced by our Army."[90] Palmer presided over twelve of the fourteen BMB meetings between September 1921 and March 1923. He also wrote the board's final report in August 1923, which contained numerous recommendations to the newly established American Battle Monuments Commission.

The mandates given to the Battle Monuments Board to design a program for national monuments abroad and to serve as a clearing house for all such proposals from public and private entities seemed a firm step toward vesting control over this element of the American commemorative effort in the federal government. Strangely enough, however, the Battle Monuments Board never embraced the second of these responsibilities, leaving the placement of private monuments to continue in an unregulated state. The BMB did outline an extensive and detailed program to mark the American battlefields in Europe, although this eventually died on the drawing boards. In short, the panel never came close to fulfilling all the mandates originally envisioned for it. Less than a year after beginning their own work, in fact, the five officers recommended that Congress replace them with a newly constituted commission.

From its first meeting, the Battle Monuments Board set out to establish certain guidelines for the federally funded overseas memorials, many of which endured beyond the BMB's extinction. The monuments erected under its authority, for example, were to honor the service of soldiers and tell their story to tourists. The workmanship in the monuments was to be "of [the] highest standard." Several different "classes" of monument should be erected, from "large" edifices on each of the greatest of the American battlefields, such as the Meuse-Argonne and Saint-Mihiel, to smaller, plainer monuments at other significant places where Pershing's doughboys had fought. The thrust of the BMB's initial decisions was to reject showiness and boastfulness about the United States' effort in the war, but to insist on excellence in the quality of the overseas monuments. "Monuments must properly represent the United States—be perfect in all respects," Palmer and his colleagues declared.[91]

Between the first and second board meetings, Colonel Palmer and Colonel Spaulding visited the nearby Antietam battlefield looking for ideas about how to design American monuments in Europe. The two officers professed to be unfavorably impressed by the quality of the bronze work on the Antietam monuments, and resolved to seek higher standards for the European markers.[92] At its second meeting, the panel further determined that the nation's coat of arms and the words "United States of America" should appear on every monument it created, and that "in general, no units lower than a division" should be specifically commemorated. It also resolved to share news of its activity periodically with the press and to collect data for an article in a major magazine, such as *National Geographic,* to generate public interest in its work.[93]

In November 1921, the Palmer board turned its attention to the knottier question of what to do about monuments already erected by American units, and policies to regulate the future construction of such commemorative edifices. Remembering that concern about such private activity had been central to the creation of the Battle Monuments Board, the officers adopted at their third meeting standards for identifying "unsuitable" monuments and a procedure for negotiating their removal. In cases where the flawed markers could not be removed, the BMB resolved to place monuments of their own in close proximity in order to overcome the effect of bad designs or erroneous information.[94] Visible in these decisions was the board's desire to hold all monuments of American origin to certain standards of accuracy and attractiveness, but also an implicit acknowledgment that the US government lacked the unilateral authority to remove undesirable pieces from foreign soil. The latter concession was among the earliest indications that the BMB was not likely to wield the fullest degree of control over American monuments abroad envisioned by those who created it. Later actions would confirm the board's unwillingness to rule on the acceptability of monuments proposed by outside groups before they were built.

Major Xenophon H. Price, executive officer to the Battle Monuments

Board, had carefully explored how the panel might play the role of regulatory body for the building of monuments by different organizations in a memorandum prepared prior to the November 1921 meeting. At the direction of Colonel Palmer, who was anxious to get "a definite decision" out of the board at the upcoming meeting, Price framed rationales for the whole spectrum of possible approaches—from authorizing no monuments beyond those that were part of its own project, to imposing no limitations at all upon what private parties could do. One of the strongest arguments Price posed for stricter control by the BMB was that it would prevent minor wartime actions of American troops from receiving exaggerated importance on some overdone monument. The weightiest argument for a more liberal policy was the danger that the War Department might offend veterans' groups or other private organizations by denying them the freedom to memorialize their own activities.[95]

Consideration of a more assertive role for the War Department board in the regulation of battlefield monuments became sidelined, however, when the panel began planning for its own eclipse by a new, more inclusive and permanent commission. At the meeting of December 7, 1921, with all five members present, the principal item of business was discussion of a new agency "to supervise the plans and construction of the monuments for marking the battlefields of Europe."[96] With decisions on the extent of its own authority unresolved, and much work still left to do on its own program of monument placement and construction, the Battle Monuments Board was preparing to go out of business.

Upon reflection, this is not altogether surprising. The five officers had pursued their plans for government-built monuments far enough to know that their program would ultimately find expression in legislative proposals. Inevitably, Congress would require some agency to oversee the project and would expect this supervisory agency to be more broadly representative of official Washington and the country than any five army officers or even the War Department could be. Indeed, the BMB formally recommended on December 7 that the new commission should be composed of the secretary of war, the general of the armies, one US senator, one member of the House of Representatives, one representative from the American Legion, one representative from the Fine Arts Commission, and one army officer detailed by the secretary of war to serve as secretary to the commission.[97] As if to confirm the limited scope and duration of their own authority, Palmer and his fellow officers explicitly declared at this same meeting that it was not their responsibility to rule on the historical accuracy of any overseas monuments already in existence.[98]

Once it had resolved to hand over its own duties to a new commission, the BMB proceeded to formulate detailed designs for a network of overseas monuments. By mid-January 1922, the Palmer panel had formally ratified a four-page proposal, entitled "Plans of the Battle Monuments Board," which its successors could presumably implement with congressional approval. Although the ABMC ultimately passed over the BMB's recommendations for a very different plan of its own, the BMB's proposal represented the first organized script from any US government agency for a program of monuments on the European battlefields.

The "Plans of the Battle Monuments Board" identified four categories of monuments and markers to be built abroad as a record in bronze and stone of the US Army's actions and accomplishments in the combats of the Great War. The "basis of the project" was to be approximately seventy-five "Relief Map Monuments," designed to depict the battle sites from vantage points that combined "prominence with accessibility." These monuments were supposed "to show operations of American divisions at all places where ground was either lost or gained." "Outline Sketch Map Monuments," tentatively fifty in number, were "to show front lines along which American troops trained or occupied sectors." While similar to the first category of marker, these would be smaller and would not depict rises and dips in the terrain. At least one of this second category of monument was to be erected for each American division and for each time it occupied a portion of the front line. An unspecified number of "Special Monuments" were intended to mark additional places of importance, such as where the first doughboy was killed, wounded, and taken prisoner on the Western Front, or where individual units most prominently distinguished themselves in action. The plans also called for bronze tablets to be affixed to certain buildings that served as headquarters for important components of the AEF, such as the General Headquarters in Paris and Chaumont, the Service of Supply in Tours, and the First Army at Souilly. The January 1922 summary further envisioned that "index maps" to the smaller markers in the most important areas of operation would be positioned at particularly accessible points to make clear to visitors the full extent of what there was to see in any given area. It was understood that these rudimentary visitor centers would be "either in or very close to our permanent cemeter[ies]." Preparation of appropriate pamphlets was foreseen as well, along with "the complete photographing of all our battlefields in Europe."⁹⁹

In short, the Battle Monuments Board fully appreciated the importance of an organized and centrally supervised program of preservation and commemoration on the overseas battlefields. As the BMB wrapped up its own work, it sought to fashion a network of monuments and information centers that would "make easy a study of operations on the ground and permit visitors to locate without any trouble the exact points most interesting to them." It is noteworthy that the Palmer group also sought at least some degree of integration of its own sites with the American cemeteries. It understood, finally, that this work of remembrance should be undertaken by the national government in order to treat all operations "in the order of their importance," to ensure the accuracy of the historical markers, and to acquire the sites and provide for their upkeep properly. "The markings should be done as soon as possible," the BMB proposal concluded, to obviate the need for private entities to proceed with their own monuments.¹⁰⁰

The most important decision taken at any of the BMB's final few meetings came on March 27, 1922, when the four officers present rejected a proposal to create a marker for the "Lost Battalion," a detachment of the 77th Division that had attained considerable renown during fighting in the Meuse-Argonne in October 1918. A two-fold concern had motivated this action. First, the board sought to be consistent with earlier assertions that the government should only memorialize actions of division-size units or greater. Economy was the second consideration: the more numerous the markers, the greater the burden on the federal taxpayer. Lest the BMB appear to be too parsimonious and unsympathetic to the desire to commemorate some of the most famous actions of the war, however, the officers proposed that "smaller units should be encouraged in every way possible to mark with their own funds actions of importance to them."¹⁰¹ With the encouragement it gave to "smaller units" to create battle markers with their own funds, in any case, the Battle Monuments Board contradicted its own expressed goal that the government's program should be so complete as to eliminate the need for other groups to construct monuments. More effective direction of the federal effort to construct a comprehensive collection of overseas battlefield monuments clearly would have to await the launching of a new commission.

A legislative package containing the proposals of the BMB for an overseas monuments program and a new commission to create it progressed from the War Department to Capitol Hill in late February 1922. Of the two major components of the bill, officially labeled H.R. 10801, Congress concerned itself primarily with the creation of what came to be called the "American Battle Monuments Commission." Cover letters from President Harding, Budget Director Charles G. Dawes, and Secretary of War John Weeks urged approval of the War Department bill.[102] The legislation was referred to the House Committee on Foreign Affairs on March 6, and Chairman Stephen G. Porter of Pennsylvania held the first hearing on the measure nine days later.[103]

As it happened, H.R. 10801 was not the only plan before the Congress in 1922 for a federal commemorative project and a new commission to supervise it. Two months earlier, Representative James W. Husted of New York had introduced H.R. 9634, whose unique feature was the creation of an American Memorial Highway Commission to mark and preserve French and Belgian highways over which American troops had "marched to victory."[104] At the request of the secretary of war, Chairman Porter had deferred action on the Husted bill until the BMB could finalize the War Department's proposal and get it to Capitol Hill. As it began hearings, the House committee considered both bills simultaneously. By the time of the final round of hearings at the end of 1922, however, the War Department's measure had completely eclipsed the competing project.[105]

What the two bills had in common were provisions authorizing the nation's chief executive to appoint a commission to design and supervise the nation's overseas commemorative program. The Husted bill called for a panel "not to exceed thirteen members" and stipulated that the secretary of state and the US ambassadors to France and Belgium all serve on it. The measure's principal object, after all, was to enlist French and Belgian support for the creation of the aforementioned memorial highway network. Unlike the War Department's bill, H.R. 9634 did not make specific provision for a large assortment of federal monuments on foreign soil. Nor did it carry a large price tag, since it proposed essentially to incorporate already existing French and Belgian highways into its commemorative plan. The American Memorial Highway Commission, moreover, was to be merely "the channel of communication" through which American citizens or associations desiring to erect war memorials in France or Belgium were to work with the appropriate authorities in those countries, not necessarily an agency with the power to screen proposals from outside groups to create monuments.[106]

By contrast, H.R. 10801 provided for an eight-member panel and explicitly vested it with the authority to carry out the battlefield marking project already detailed by the Battle Monuments Board. The War Department's bill also empowered its commission to regulate similar projects by all non-federal actors and agents. H.R. 10801 stopped short of giving its commission explicit power to veto undesirable non-federal monuments, but it did require such potential builders to guarantee to the new body that their edifices would be "maintained and kept up in the same manner as the memorials erected by this commission."[107]

In sum, a congressman supporting H.R. 9634 favored a less expensive project whose centerpiece was a memorial highway network requiring close cooperation with the French and Belgian governments to create and maintain it. One who preferred H.R. 10801 wished to see the United States build scores of metal and stone markers of its own design on the sites where its soldiers had recently fought a European war.[108] However Congress decided between these two bills, the national government was going to have a new agency to effectuate and maintain its program of overseas memorials.

The War Department's proposal monopolized endorsements from inside the federal government. Budget Director Dawes and Secretary Weeks both emphasized, in their initial rationales for H.R. 10801, the urgent need for "central supervision" of the nation's commemorative effort. Monuments already in place, most of which had been erected by American soldiers before their repatriation, were "mainly of temporary construction and with little architectural beauty." Both officials claimed that in no recorded case had proper arrangements been made with private European landowners for placement of the monuments. Worse still, the historical accuracy of such markers was often "doubtful." The bulk of them came from five or six divisions, in fact, leaving the false impression that these units had done most of the AEF's fighting.[109] Secretary Weeks urged quick passage of his department's bill in order to prevent further embarrassment from the erection of even more structures by the long list of "States, societies, and individuals" lining up to do so. With H.R. 10801 as law and a new commission in place to see that its objectives were fulfilled, he insisted, the AEF's accomplishments would be accurately, fairly, and permanently enshrined. The European host countries, American tourists, veterans, and students would all benefit from this. Weeks was especially enthusiastic that the proposed array of monuments stretching from the North Sea to Switzerland "will be very beneficial in tightening the bond of friendship between the United States and France."[110]

The secretary of war maintained that the composition of the new oversight commission deserved especially careful consideration. Its size should be small, he wrote, "so as not to be unwieldy." But the members "should be representative of the country at large, holders of responsible positions, and preferably men interested in questions concerning war memorials in Europe." Weeks justified the spot on the commission recommended for the secretary of war "because a large part of the preparatory work and actual construction work can be most properly handled with means available in the War Department." The additional requirement that an army officer serve as secretary of the commission was desirable to Weeks because of the capacity of such an individual to master and expedite "all phases" of the work of the new agency.[111]

In the initial hearings, however, the House committee heard solely from proponents of the Husted bill. No representative of the Battle Monuments Board or its parent department testified. This was because Chairman Porter, who personally favored H.R. 10801, sensed hostility on the part of other committee members and the public toward anything coming out of the War Department at that time. The issue driving such widespread antipathy toward the military establishment was the Harding administration's determination to keep veterans' bonuses small, in the interest of reducing pressure on the federal budget. Porter suspended action on both legislative proposals after the March 20 hearing for what turned out to be eight months. Lisa Budreau has claimed that, but for the chairman's astute intervention, the Husted bill "would surely have defeated the War Department's proposal" and become law.[112]

When Porter's committee again took up consideration of the two bills, H.R. 10801 monopolized their attention. At Porter's encouragement, the War Department had built a solid basis of public support for its own bill during the intervening months, principally through appeals to veterans' organizations in the states.[113] John McAuley Palmer, soon to become a brigadier general, was the lead witness for H.R. 10801 when it came before the House committee on November 28, 1922. To build his case for the necessity of a new commission to supervise the erection of *all* American monuments in Europe, the BMB's chairman recounted at length the 1921 imbroglio involving Lieutenant Gilbert, the 30th Infantry Association, and Colonel T. Bentley Mott. As an example to be avoided,

Palmer also made extensive reference to the disorderliness that attended the marking of the Gettysburg battlefield for decades after that battle because of the absence of active federal supervision. In short, Palmer's explanation and defense of the War Department/BMB bill was forceful, succinct, and authoritative. At one point during his dialogue with Porter's committee, a member invited the BMB chairman to comment on H.R. 9634, but Palmer claimed that he was unfamiliar with the rival bill and refused to be drawn into a discussion of it.[114]

Before concluding its hearings, the House committee heard testimony in support of H.R. 10801 from such witnesses as Major Xenophon H. Price (secretary to the Battle Monuments Board), and Fred and Josephine Bentley of Chicago, prominent Gold Star parents. Written endorsements of the bill had also come from a host of organizations, including the American Legion, the Veterans of Foreign Wars, and the Reserve Officers Association, as well as the Fine Arts Commission.[115] The long interruption Stephen Porter had imposed between the initial and closing round of congressional hearings on the establishment of a new commemorative commission had plainly worked in favor of the War Department's bill.

At a four-hour meeting on January 29, 1923, in executive session but with Major Price also in attendance, Porter's committee prepared its final version of the measure and then passed it without opposition. The full House unanimously approved the committee's text, now H.R. 14087, on February 19, and the Senate followed suit on March 2. Two days later President Harding signed into law the bill creating the American Battle Monuments Commission.[116]

The law of March 4, 1923, contained almost nothing from the Husted bill and differed in one substantial respect from H.R. 10801. Whereas the original version drafted by the Battle Monuments Board had specified who was to serve on the new commission, the final bill gave to the president of the United States virtually complete freedom to choose the designated number of members. Only the requirement that the secretary be a regular army officer was retained from the original proposal. In the new law, however, the secretary was to be, in effect, a nonvoting eighth member of the commission, while H.R. 10801 had called for him to be one of the core seven.[117] Other important provisions of the ABMC's founding statute stipulated that all members of the commission were to serve without compensation at the pleasure of the president; that the commission had complete discretion over the erecting and siting of overseas memorials, provided all proposals for the design and material for them gained the approval of the National Commission of Fine Arts as well; that the commission could request that the president detail personnel from any government department, the army, navy, or marine corps to assist in its work; and that the president should "make the necessary arrangements with the proper authorities of the countries concerned to enable the commission to carry out the purposes of this Act."[118] Section 2 of the law further charged the ABMC to assemble an "historical photographic record" of American combat sites in Europe and file it, when completed, with the records of the War Department.[119]

Significant authority over the erection of memorials by groups or individuals other than the national government also came with the new law. Section 8 directed and empowered the commission "to cooperate with American citizens, States, municipalities, or associations desiring to erect war memorials in Europe *in such manner as may be determined by the commission*" (italics by the author). If somewhat vague, this language quickly came to be interpreted by the ABMC as full authorization to approve or veto proposals of such non-federal entities to build memorials. The law gave the commission similar authority over the actions of other agencies of the national government.[120]

Rather than mandate implementation of the battle marking program passed on to the ABMC by the Battle Monuments Board, the March 1923 statute directed the ABMC simply to "prepare plans and estimates for the erection of suitable memorials to mark and commemorate the services of the American forces in Europe and erect memorials therein *at such places as the commission shall determine*" (italics by the author). It was understood that such plans could include architectural designs and artistic works for the already existing GRS cemeteries.[121] After taking into account all the provisions of the statute, one newspaper judged that the founding of the ABMC was "the first business-like attempt of Congress to make provision for building suitable monuments where American soldiers fought in the World War."[122]

With its own authority and function plainly superseded by the enactment of H.R. 14087, the Battle Monuments Board quietly dissolved. In his final report to the secretary of war, General Palmer nevertheless noted the "efficient and economical way" in which the BMB's proposed commemorative project would serve the nation. He speculated that the ABMC, of its own volition, would "without doubt" adopt it.[123] Palmer also commended the sizeable body of historical research his group had produced, "which had mainly to do with the accurate locating of front lines occupied by American troops in Europe," and was now available to the new commission.[124]

At its final meeting, five days after H.R. 14087 passed, the BMB also declared itself on the key question of who should serve on the new commission. "The importance of this commission cannot be too highly emphasized," the group asserted. "It is obvious that the success or failure of this commission will depend upon its personnel."[125] The BMB's general recommendations were that the ABMC members should be "prominent men" and "completely representative" of American society. That the secretary of war should have a seat on the new board was "of the greatest importance" because of the key role his department's personnel had already played in preparations for the marking of battlefields, and because he had ongoing access to funds, facilities, and expertise that could advance the commission's work. General Palmer's group also recommended the appointment of General Pershing by virtue of his service as AEF commander, and because his "knowledge of operations and conditions abroad will be indispensable to the work of the commission." One senator and one member of the House of Representatives were proposed as members to "represent the people at large in the country," and for the legislative support they could provide in furtherance of the commission's work. Stephen Porter, who had shepherded the ABMC's enabling law through its first stages of approval on Capitol Hill, was the BMB's choice from the House because he was "greatly interested in this work and familiar with the problems involved." Major Price was proposed as secretary in view of the "very creditable manner" with which he had performed in the same capacity with the Battle Monuments Board.[126] After reviewing the report from General Palmer, it is worth noting, General Pershing wrote that the document "has my entire approval."[127]

President Harding, of course, possessed sole authority to appoint the commission, and he did so in June. While this study has not determined whether the chief executive ever saw the parting counsel of the Battle Monuments Board or Pershing's accompanying endorsement, Harding followed portions of it. The general of the armies, one senator, one congressman, a representative from the American Legion, and Major Price as secretary all secured presidential appointments. Neither the secretary of war nor Representative Porter, however, made it onto the commission.

The president departed from the BMB's specific recommendation with the remaining three appointments as well.

The secretary of war received formal notice of President Harding's selections on June 21, 1923.[128] General Pershing topped the list. He was the only active military officer with a vote on the commission and, as a Missouri native, one of only two of the seven members who was not from the East Coast.[129] The other Midwesterner, and the only one with no military service at all, was Josephine L. Cody Bentley, a Gold Star Mother from Chicago.[130] The US senator on the commission was Republican David Aiken Reed, of Pennsylvania. Reed had seen wartime service in France with the 79th Division and was credited with having played an important part in moving the ABMC's founding statute through the Senate.[131] The commissioner appointed from the House of Representatives was John Boynton Philip Clayton Hill, a Republican from Maryland, who had also seen wartime service in France, with the 29th Division.[132] Thomas W. Miller, the youngest appointee, had served with the 79th Division in France, where he received a Purple Heart and a special citation from General Pershing for "especially meritorious and conspicuous service" in the Meuse-Argonne campaign. Prior to his enlistment in the army in 1917, Miller had served as Delaware's secretary of state and a member of Congress.[133] D. John Markey, from Maryland, was a Spanish-American War veteran and won a Distinguished Service Medal while an officer with the 29th Division in France in 1918. He had testified on H.R. 10801 to Porter's committee in November 1922 as chairman of the Military Affairs Committee of the American Legion.[134] Robert G. Woodside, a Pittsburgh attorney, had won the Distinguished Service Cross as a captain with the 3rd Division in France in July 1918. He did lengthy service with the Pennsylvania National Guard as well, and had also been one of the earliest commanders-in-chief of the Veterans of Foreign Wars.[135]

The military establishment and General Palmer in particular, according to Lisa Budreau, reacted warily toward the heavily civilian make-up of the commission. The House committee's final meeting on the War Department bill in January 1923 had been "bitterly contested," principally over the question of who would actually compose the commission.[136] General Palmer claimed that leaving the president complete discretion to appoint the membership had been necessary to overcome lingering congressional animosity on other counts toward the War Department.[137] What the original seven commissioners made of their service, in any event, would be the ultimate measure of their effectiveness and worthiness, and the vindication or condemnation of Harding's choices.

If the president's appointees did not completely conform to the guidance given by the Battle Monuments Board and the secretary of war, they did not diverge from it by a very wide margin. Both of the major national veterans organizations had prominent members on the commission. All five civilian males, moreover, had done military service in France during the 1917–18 war, and three had come home with decorations. The legislative branch had its representatives, too, albeit exclusively from one side of the aisle, and the commission's lone female had a son buried in one of the eight permanent cemeteries soon to come under ABMC's control. General Pershing and Major Price, both career soldiers, occupied the highest executive positions within the new agency. Civilians did indeed hold the majority of seats on the commission, but the collective experiences and personal perspectives the six of them brought to their ABMC work—military service in wartime, civic involvement ranging from elective office to voluntary associations, and in at least one case the sacrifice of a son to the national cause in the Great War—were far from ordinary.

For General Pershing to serve as the commission's first chairman guaranteed an elevated standing to the new agency. The six other members chose him unanimously as permanent chairman at their first gathering in September 1923. Four meetings of the group passed before the chairman found it possible to attend his first one. But from April 1924 onward, the soon-to-be-retired general chaired thirty-four of the forty-one commission meetings prior to the outbreak of World War II.[138] For the last quarter-century of Pershing's life, in fact, the bulk of his official energies and efforts went into the work of the new agency.

Pershing's enduring bond with the men of the AEF had been sealed during the bloody fighting of the war's final months. His service as victorious field commander, general of the armies, and army chief of staff argued powerfully enough for his appointment to the new commission. Since the war, an additional element of his service to the nation argued equally strongly that he was right for this role. Even before his triumphant return home from France in September 1919, Pershing had become a highly visible and forceful figure in the developing national pursuit of remembrance. A collection of high-profile personal appearances after the fighting stopped—first in Europe, and ultimately on both sides of the Atlantic—uniquely positioned the general to symbolize and speak for the

American soldier and the cause for which he had fought in the Great War. It is not too much to say that, for most of the three decades between the armistice of 1918 and his death in 1948, John J. Pershing was unofficially, but undeniably, the "chief of national remembrance."

Participation in an impressive array of ceremonies in Europe marking the end of the war launched Pershing into this special role. His speech at the sprawling Meuse-Argonne cemetery on the first postwar Memorial Day, as we have already seen, had sounded a number of the chords the general would routinely strike during a generation of oratorical tributes to his soldiers and their service. Pershing was present on many additional occasions meant to honor him, his country, and the American soldiers who had helped to win the recent struggle of nations. In June 1919, for example, he traveled to England to receive an honorary degree from Oxford University and was back in London a month later to participate in the British capital's great victory parade. On June 28 he attended the formal signing of the Treaty of Versailles, and on the 4th of July he reviewed thousands of French and American troops in the Place de la Concorde with the leaders of the French government. Ten days later, the general paraded down the Champs-Élysées in the impressive Bastille Day victory celebration.[139]

Upon his return to the United States, Pershing was given a hero's welcome with parades through New York City and Washington, D.C. On September 18, he addressed a joint session of Congress. News of his extraordinary elevation to the rank of general of the armies had reached him in the mid-Atlantic on September 5, and Congress supplemented that honor with a joint resolution of thanks to him personally, and to "the officers and men of the American Expeditionary Forces," that was read just before he gave his address in the House chamber. Beginning in December 1919, a three-month inspection trip took the general to every region of the country and enabled tens of thousands more of his countrymen to see and hear him.[140]

Throughout the early 1920s, before Pershing assumed the leadership of the ABMC, the general spoke on many patriotic occasions—Memorial Days, Flag Days, and Armistice Days most notably—and appeared at the most important ceremonies held to honor soldiers who had fought under his command or as wartime comrades. In 1921, for example, he spoke in July at Hoboken, New Jersey, as a shipment of more than seven thousand repatriated American dead arrived from Europe.[141] In October, President Harding sent him abroad to confer Medals of Honor upon the Unknown

Soldiers of both France and England.[142] In November, upon his return to the United States, he traveled to Kansas City in the company of Marshal Foch to participate in the ground-breaking for the Liberty Memorial (now the site of the National World War I Museum), and back to Washington, D.C., for the interment of the American Unknown Soldier on the third anniversary of the armistice.[143]

Pershing's public oratory was always unstinting in its praise of the American soldiers and the country that had produced them, their wartime partners, and the righteous cause for which they had fought and prevailed. He never shrank, moreover, from advocating the uniqueness of the bond between the United States and France. While Americans and British, Belgians, Italians, and French together valued and fought for the same ideals and possessed "a thousand ties of sentiment and affection," the general declared that "our deepest and most enduring bond comes from the soil of France, where our own dead sleep forever beside their French brothers in arms."[144] In John J. Pershing's hands, the American Battle Monuments Commission and the sites it created would bear especially powerful witness to the courage, decency, and sacrifice of the nation's soldiers in the Great War and become enduring symbols of and venues for the continual expression of the friendship between the United States and its oldest ally.

Bolstered by a 1923 statute that gave it broad authority, led by a man with a uniquely profound connection to the soldiers who, in his view, had won a great victory for a noble cause, and animated by a strong desire to portray and preserve the memory of that victory in shrines that would outlast time itself, the American Battle Monuments Commission began its work. The next decade and a half would see the fulfillment of the new agency's original mission of beautifying the permanent cemeteries and erecting a network of monuments along the battle lines where American soldiers had seen important action. General Pershing averaged more than a third of each year between 1924 and 1939 in Europe closely supervising the execution of the ABMC's memorial program. Chairing meetings and directing the business of the commission occupied substantial amounts of the general's time when he was in the United States as well. An array of important decisions, challenges, frustrations, and sometimes bitter arguments also attended those years when the first generation of overseas American monuments and cemeteries made their way from meeting dockets and drawing boards to permanent reality in flora and stone.

2

The New Commission Goes to Work, 1923–1938

Organizing and Implementing the Nation's Overseas Commemorative Program

During its first decade and a half, the American Battle Monuments Commission established itself as two entities: a panel with seven voting members (plus a nonvoting secretary) appointed by the president of the United States, and a larger agency staffed by employees on two continents whose job it was to execute the directives of the governing committee. The commission opened offices in Washington and Paris during its first year. It convened formally forty-five times between September 1923 and November 1938, with General of the Armies John J. Pershing in the chair on thirty-four of those occasions. Out of these meetings came the design and direction of the national government's overseas commemorative program.

The principal legacy of the commission's first fifteen years are the steps it took to beautify the eight permanent cemeteries in France, England, and Belgium, and the eleven monuments and two commemorative plaques it erected in France, Belgium, and Gibraltar (a colonial dependency of England). The present chapter will show, however, that the ABMC did far more during the first phase of its history than build monuments and cemetery chapels. In fulfillment of their 1923 legislative mandate, General Pershing and his fellow commissioners formulated policies to bring under control what had hitherto been the unregulated proliferation of private and non-federal American war memorials on foreign soil. Numerous decisions were made either to grant or deny permission to outside groups seeking to build their own commemorative structures abroad. The commission also articulated an administrative structure for itself and defined a working relationship with other federal agencies—most notably the Commission of Fine Arts (CFA)—whose authority overlapped its own. The ABMC determined that chapels would be built and Latin crosses or Stars of David made of Italian marble would adorn the graves of each soldier buried in the permanent American cemeteries. The commission created its own Historical Section, moreover, to clarify and record as accurately as possible the actions of American forces in France and Belgium. A photographic archive of the combat sites was also compiled, along with two different guidebooks to the World War I battlefields published in 1927 and 1938. When sold and disseminated among the American public, these publications confirmed the young agency in an educational mission that continues to this day. Finally, the work of the commission took its own members to Europe on multiple occasions for inspection visits and important ceremonial occasions. General Pershing alone made no fewer than fifteen such trips between 1924 and 1939.

The commission's first annual report, issued in November 1924, highlighted four principal objectives for the new agency: "to commemorate by suitable memorials and markers the services of the American Forces in Europe"; "to secure supervision over the locations, designs, materials and inscriptions of memorials that might be erected abroad by Americans"; to provide for the maintenance of any memorials it decided to build; and, finally, "to complete the historical photographic record of the war."[1] Important early actions positioned the agency to fulfill these responsibilities.

At its first meeting, the group voted to notify a large collection of officials and organizations—governors of states and territories, for example, and a host of veterans' organizations—of its existence, its statutory mandates, and its desire to know of any plans that the notified parties might have "for the erection of monuments or memorials abroad."[2] At the second meeting two weeks later, the commission instructed its secretary, Major Xenophon H. Price, to request that the secretary of war refer to the ABMC any and all plans his department might have for monuments and/or buildings to be erected within the eight permanent American cemeteries in Europe.[3] At their third meeting, the commissioners formally asked the secretary of state to notify the American ambassadors in France, Belgium, and Italy of the existence and authority of the ABMC and to give it clearance to communicate directly with this trio of overseas officials regarding plans for American memorials in their host countries.[4] A prompt response from Secretary of State Charles Evans Hughes confirmed his willingness to recognize the commission's authority over "all matters pertaining to war memorials and monuments in Europe."[5] By the end of the next year, the French and Belgian governments had pledged not to allow any American organization or agency to build a war monument on their territory that had not been approved by the ABMC.[6] Plainly, throughout this initial wave of communications and directives, the commission confirmed its intention to become the authorizing agency for the creation of all American war memorials in Europe that no earlier entity had been.

One of the most important federal agencies with which the ABMC shared authority was the Commission of Fine Arts. Members of this body, as recounted in the previous chapter, had conducted a high-profile inspection visit to the overseas cemeteries at the request of the secretary of war in 1921. The whole commission, furthermore, had been collaborating with the Graves Registration Service on the design of these memorial sites for more than two years. The ABMC, consequently, voted at its first meeting to invite the Fine Arts chairman, Charles Moore, to appear at its next gathering.[7] This consultation afforded Moore an important opportunity to brief the new board on where things stood on the ground in Europe, and also to begin establishing a common understanding of how the two agencies could most profitably work together.

Not known for mincing words, Moore was in bold character when he met with the Battle Monuments commissioners in October 1923. He reported that numerous American monuments already dotted the overseas landscape, and that "a great many" of them were "bad."[8] None of the states or divisional units that had put up these monuments had applied for permission to do so from his agency, and this impeded the nation's ability "to do the very best it can." The best would never result, Moore said, from an uncontrolled environment that permitted people to "rush in and do something [with a war memorial]" that poorly served the country. The Fine Arts chairman urged the ABMC to read its statutory mandate broadly and wield boldly the power to approve or disapprove plans for "any monument or memorial that represents the United States" abroad.[9]

Moore also made clear his strong commitment to making the American cemeteries as prominent, and as beautiful, as possible. He frequently referred to how the British were organizing their cemeteries. Acknowledging that there would be differences in design between the two nations' overseas burial grounds, he expressed concern that the many hundreds of British sites, compared to our eight, threatened to overwhelm the collective impact of the American memorials. "If our part in the war is going to become apparent at all in France," the feisty guest asserted, "we must do something more than make these cemeteries simply white spots on the side of the hills." Enlarging the American sites with more adjacent land, putting walls around them, making suitable entry gates, planting beautiful trees and other flora, and installing well-designed permanent headstones were important ideas Moore proposed to make the cemeteries stand out.[10]

The guest advocate also had plenty to say about what would quickly become a contentious issue: the shape of the headstones marking each American grave. As of October 1923, the wooden crosses used in the temporary cemeteries still adorned the American graves, and Congress had thus far appropriated no money for permanent headstones. Moore envisioned that the markers in the European cemeteries would eventually resemble the square, squat model found in Arlington National Cemetery. Indeed, the current secretary of war had formally approved this design for the overseas sites in April 1922, on the recommendation of the CFA.[11] Moore was aware, at the same time, that General Pershing favored stone crosses, but he abruptly dismissed the feasibility of this idea. "The British wanted a cross, too," he noted. "Everybody wants the cross, but you can't have the cross in marble. It breaks. It is too fragile—that is all."[12]

As it turned out, the preference of the ABMC chairman for crosses was not so easily overcome, especially once the general's fellow commissioners also embraced it. For the moment, in any case, the Fine Arts chairman's initial encounter with the new commission passed most amicably. When Senator Reed, presiding officer at the October 2 meeting, concluded that the discussion had "pretty well outlined the manner in which these two commissions can work in entire harmony," Moore readily agreed. As far as the latter could see, there would not be "the slightest bit of friction at all" between the two commissions.[13] Reed's summation encapsulated how the two bodies ought to share their responsibilities. The ABMC, he said, would supply "the initiative" for the building and beautification of overseas memorials, and the CFA would supply "the helpfulness and the guidance, as far as the aesthetic side of it goes."[14]

A month later, the commission approved "in principle" the plan that had originated with the Battle Monuments Board to mark the American battlefields in Europe. Toward the fulfillment of that project, Secretary Price was authorized to seek the new agency's first formal appropriations from Congress. Along with these actions, the commissioners decided that "in order to properly perform their duties" they would need to travel, as a group, to Europe for a firsthand inspection of the cemeteries as well as some of the sites envisioned for battlefield markers.[15] This move marked an important moment in the ABMC's effort to develop its own comprehensive commemorative program.

In January 1924, the commission took steps to establish a more permanent base of operations in the Old World. Army lieutenant Thomas North, of the field artillery, was approved as an "assistant" detailed to the commission to take charge of photographing the American battlefields in Europe. North, who went on to serve the ABMC through the next five decades, was also directed to establish an office for the agency in Paris and do "other necessary work" across the Atlantic. He sailed for Europe in early April, accompanied by a photographer detailed to the commission by the secretary of war to take the authorized pictures of the American battlefields. On June 1, North opened the ABMC's first Paris office on the Rue de Tilsitt. The full commission sailed from New York on June 14, minus Secretary Price, who had traveled earlier to assist North with advance preparations.[16] The stated purpose of the expedition was "to make a study and investigation of the American battlefields and cemeteries in Europe."[17]

Before actually seeing the European burial grounds, the ABMC commissioners had resolved on two separate occasions to retain headstones in the shape of Jewish and Christian symbols in the American cemeteries.[18] These decisions were at odds with the longstanding preferences of the War Department and the Fine Arts Commission. Indeed, two successive secretaries of war dating from 1920 had already approved a design for the grave markers modeled on that of the national cemeteries in the United States.

In the intra-governmental contest of wills that followed, the older agencies had had a significant head start in developing their case. Four years before the ABMC was created, the CFA and the War Department had collaborated with architect Charles A. Platt to design a permanent headstone for the overseas cemeteries that was to be made of American white marble, rise sixteen inches above the ground, and contain no reference to the religion of the interred soldier. Charles Moore's vision of a permanent cemetery abroad has been described as that of a "little Arlington," with gravestones to match.[19] The influence of Charles Pierce, the original head of the GRS, also weighed heavily upon this initial design. Pierce had recommended to the quartermaster general as early as July 1919 that the temporary wooden crosses then marking American graves not be made permanent. Jews were already demanding a different marker for the graves of their co-religionists, and Pierce did not want to see such diversity disrupt what he termed "the desirable harmony which should characterize national cemeteries." By the end of 1920, the Arlington-style model had won the approval of Secretary Baker and a subcommittee within the War Department that included representatives of the Catholic community, the American Legion, the US Marine Corps, the CFA, the American Institute of Architects, and the AEF chaplaincy.[20]

Two years later, and still prior to the creation of the ABMC, the headstone model was enlarged to rise twenty-four inches above the ground and also widened to make it more durable and allow more space for inscriptions, including sufficient room to offer the families of the dead the opportunity to add personalized messages of sixty letters or less on the back of the marker. The appropriate emblem of religious faith for each of the dead, either a Latin cross or a Star of David, was to appear at the top of the headstone, but not constitute the entire shape of the marker.[21] When Secretary Weeks approved this updated design in April 1922, its proponents considered the matter settled—and so it was until the ABMC came to life in the following year.

The Fine Arts Commission remained staunchly wedded to the established design. As already noted, Chairman Moore had argued to the ABMC in October 1923 that crosses could neither make sufficiently durable headstones nor provide an adequate surface for inscriptions. Moore further believed that the smaller stone, closer to the ground, would enhance "the perspective of green grass" he wanted to dominate the overseas cemeteries. The Fine Arts chairman insisted that cemeteries filled with taller headstones in the shape of one or the other of the religious symbols would create a less attractive "perspective of stone." He reiterated to Secretary Price in January 1924 that the Fine Arts Commission "would regret" any change to the already agreed upon shape of the headstone.[22]

Moore's arguments fell upon deaf ears at the ABMC, whose members judged that the objections against promoting an alternative model at such a late stage were "not insurmountable."[23] Senator Reed was especially impressed with the beauty that crosses would bring to the cemeteries, and he found a clever way to mock the design endorsed by the Fine Arts Commission. "Imagine [John] McCrae's poem rewritten like this," he told his fellow commissioners: "'In Flanders Fields the poppies grow [sic] Between the—squat little headstones—row on row.'"[24]

General Pershing, although yet to attend his first ABMC meeting, signaled his support for the group's stance from Paris. "The white cross," he wrote, "has become to my mind such an important feature in marking the graves of our Dead that I think it should be retained if at all possible."[25] Pershing's personal view had been influenced by extensive correspondence he had received in earlier years from "prominent men" and survivors of AEF troops buried in France. Many of the latter group claimed that they had been persuaded to leave their loved ones permanently buried overseas because they were "impressed by the effect of the crosses" and "very loathe to see the graves of their sons or husbands marked by some other form of monument."[26] Pershing's desire to make the crosses permanent apparently solidified by the end of 1921, but he did not openly advocate it within official circles until the ABMC embraced the same view.[27]

Important national organizations also registered their support for the position that the ABMC chose to champion. The executive committee of the American Legion, in a formal resolution passed on January 15, 1924, endorsed crosses as headstones because they had come to represent for the entire nation, and especially those who had lost loved ones in the war, "an impressive emblem of sacrifice for country and humanity."[28] The Gold Star Fathers Association had passed a similar resolution in November 1923 and made an even more forceful case for embracing the religious symbol as a model for the permanent headstones. "This is a Christian Nation," the association declared, "and the meaning of these fields of crosses, when properly understood, should be broad and high enough for everyone and offensive to none."[29]

Congressional control over funding for the permanent markers meant that final say in the matter resided on Capitol Hill. The two elected lawmakers serving on the ABMC, Congressman Hill and Senator Reed, were entrusted with making the commission's case there. In April 1924, with General Pershing chairing a meeting for the first time, Hill was able to tell his colleagues that he and Senator Reed had secured a provision in the relevant appropriation requiring "that the headstones furnished hereunder shall be of such design and material as may be agreed upon by the Secretary of War and the American Battle Monuments Commission."[30]

The adoption of such language in the funding authorization for the cemetery markers had significant implications. By the end of 1924, Secretary Weeks had yielded to the preference of the ABMC on the shape of the headstones.[31] His successor, Dwight Filley Davis, gave final approval to the more detailed design of the crosses and Stars of David the following year.[32] In persuading Congress to vest the power to determine both "design and material" for the headstones in the Pershing board and the secretary of war, Hill and Reed had also managed to exclude the CFA from any role in the definitive settlement of this debate. The language of the 1924 appropriation had effectively trumped Section 3 of the ABMC's founding statute requiring "That before any design or material is accepted by the [Battle Monuments] commission, the same shall be approved by the National Commission of Fine Arts."[33] When the CFA later tried to involve itself in the selection of the material for the headstones, Secretary Price reminded his counterpart at the other commission that, because of the "special legislation" governing this matter, neither its views nor its approval would be required.[34]

No doubt savoring the outcome in their first interagency test of strength, the seven commissioners and James Mangum, who had been appointed chief clerk in the Washington office six months earlier, kept their June sailing date for Europe. The group was on European soil in an official capacity from June 21 until July 23, 1924, when some returned to New York from France on the *George Washington*.[35] General Pershing chaired a trio of meetings during the journey, although much of the business pertained to mundane administrative details about travel reimbursements. At the last formal gathering before heading home, the commissioners shared their impressions from the multitude of sites visited. Sadly, the minutes recorded nothing of the substance of these discussions.[36]

Congressman Hill and Commissioner Markey, accompanied by Mangum, spent five additional days in Italy in search of suitable sites for American monuments there. The trip took them to Venice and Rome and enabled them to traverse areas in the northeast of the country where American troops had seen action in the final weeks of the war. Premier Benito Mussolini gave the American delegation a brief audience in the late afternoon of July 19. Earlier in the day, the Americans had placed a wreath at the tomb of the Italian Unknown Soldier and met with the general in charge of the country's war cemeteries.[37]

While the full commission was in England, Belgium, and France, its activities adhered to a similar pattern. The commissioners always paid tribute to the host country's war dead in a public ceremony. In Belgium and France, they dined with the respective heads of state and government. In England, they conferred at length with Sir Fabian Ware, chief of the Imperial War Graves Commission, whose experience in the design and construction of overseas military cemeteries was without equal.[38] They visited all of the major American battlefields and paid homage at numerous French ones as well. Finally, and perhaps most importantly, they inspected the permanent American cemeteries, all but two of the future sites of US monuments on French soil, a number of French burial sites, and monuments raised by Missouri, Tennessee, and numerous divisions of the American army.[39]

The trip yielded countless impressions and informed much of the commission's upcoming action. The group declared itself "impressed" at the quality of care given to the American cemeteries, but still acknowledged "many things which are not as they should be."[40] The burial sites were generally devoid of architecture and art. The only buildings in them were caretakers' houses and structures to lodge guests. Gateways, flagpoles, and other decorations were merely "passable" in their current state. The commissioners could not escape the impression "that the work [in the cemeteries] has been done with a minimum expenditure of funds." Compared to the British sites, "where everything is of the best," the appearance of the American burial grounds definitely needed improvement.[41]

Toward this end, the commission unanimously recommended in November 1924 that a chapel "of nonsectarian character should be erected in each of the cemeteries." Such buildings would "add a religious touch" to the burial grounds, provide places to which visitors could repair for meditation and prayer, and attract attention away from the plainer buildings that were currently dominating the architecture of the sites. The chapels would "serve also as some slight testimonial of the Nation's debt to the men who are buried there."[42] The commissioners further authorized permanent stone walls to sharpen the outer borders of the cemeteries, paved roads, and paths to improve their infrastructure, and more trees and shrubs to enhance their beauty. Finally, General Pershing and his colleagues observed that each cemetery should contain some sort of memorial to those listed as missing in action in each battle region. Separate monuments within the grounds might be appropriate for these soldiers, the commissioners reasoned, or possibly some remembrance of them could be "worked into the design of the chapels."[43]

The commission members were particularly impressed by what they saw in the British cemeteries, and by what they learned from representatives of the Imperial War Graves Commission.[44] Although the Americans never sought to make their commemorative sites mere replicas of those of their overseas cousins, they took special note of "certain general principles" in the design of the British cemeteries. One was that the engineering work should be planned and executed with the "idea of permanence in mind." Another was "to make the graves themselves the most striking feature in the cemetery and the one to which the attention is irresistibly attracted." The latter principle laid much emphasis on the headstone, a matter with which the American commissioners were already thoroughly engaged. The ABMC commissioners also noted that the British were installing road signs throughout France and Belgium to catch the eye of passing motorists and direct them easily to the sites.[45]

By the time the Americans came to England in 1924, the Imperial War Graves Commission had established the principal elements of its own model for the British war cemeteries. Each of the burial grounds was built around a "stone of remembrance" and a "cross of sacrifice" whose size and design were the same in every site. The headstones were of uniform shape and uniform material. Only the personalized inscriptions contributed by the families of the dead and the biographical information about each soldier varied from marker to marker. No private memorials were to be permitted in the British cemeteries, and no distinction of social or military rank was to determine how the graves were arranged.[46]

Another important opportunity the 1924 tour had afforded to ABMC members was the inspection of nearly seventy existing American memorials in Europe. While several of these were judged to be "attractive" or "entirely suitable," many more were not. The commission determined that three of the five monuments to the 1st Division were not even on ground liberated by that unit.[47]

Like the old Battle Monuments Board, however, the commission sensed that it lacked the legal authority to remove monuments already placed. Nonetheless, its European inspection tour stiffened the group's determination to control the creation by Americans of any new commemorative structures overseas. Before they left Paris to come home, members told the press that American monuments abroad should be confined to those approved by the government. The existing example to be avoided, they agreed, was Gettysburg, whose battlefield was covered with monuments and markers of all shapes and sizes honoring subjects ranging from individuals, to units great and small, to the fighting men of whole states. The ABMC, by contrast, wanted the American monuments to memorialize the dead, not to glorify "individual divisions or commands."[48]

In keeping with these publicly declared intentions, the commissioners enacted a comprehensive set of "Regulations Governing the Erection of World War Memorials in Europe by Americans" at their first meeting after returning home. Two principles dominated this policy statement: that no American memorial would be erected to any unit smaller than a division and, "as a general rule, monuments should be erected to organizations rather than to troops from a particular locality of the United States."[49] A four-step procedure was prescribed for any group or individual seeking to create a memorial, beginning with approval by the ABMC and the CFA of the "general idea" of the project, and ending with approval of the proposed site by the host government and securing of the ground.[50] Failure to receive clearance at any of these stages meant that the monument could not legitimately be built. It is easy to see in these regulations how, at last, officials of the national government proposed to prevent other Americans from erecting monuments overseas whose designs were undesirable, that the host governments did not want, or on ground for which legal title had never been secured.

If the commissioners, a full year into their collective endeavor, were still a long way from making any "dirt fly" on the old European battlefields, their inspection trip definitely inspired them to organize more effectively to pursue their mission. In November 1924, three members appointed by Pershing at the ninth meeting to serve as a "Committee on Memorials" produced a lengthy report after studying "the whole question of American memorials in Europe."[51] Among the seventeen individual resolutions ratified by the commission was a recommitment to build a chapel in each of the eight permanent cemeteries. The panel also ordained that the complete monument program should consist of "important structures" on the major Meuse-Argonne, Saint-Mihiel, and Aisne-Marne battlefields; "historical monuments of modest design" at thirteen additional locations (some of which were later eliminated from the plan); and a monument to the Services of Supply at Tours, France. Bronze tablets, finally, were to mark the locations of General Headquarters at Chaumont, and First and Second Army Headquarters, respectively, at Souilly and Toul.[52]

Before the tenth meeting was over, the commission had addressed additional issues regarding the beautification of the cemeteries. The Committee on Memorials was directed to implement the ABMC's decisions regarding permanent headstones. A further set of regulations established that no variation among the headstones would be permitted in any of the burial grounds, and that no memorial monument or building would be placed in any of them without the formal approval of the ABMC.[53] The latter provision was a way for the commission to protect its own design for the improvement of a particular site against any disruptive action by the GRS, which was still completing the permanent burials and was responsible for the maintenance of the graves areas.

The first application of the commission's supervisory procedures came two months after their adoption. General William G. Price, president of the Pennsylvania Battle Monuments Commission, appeared before the panel seeking approval of its own monument-building program in France and Belgium.[54] General Price was a much-decorated officer from the 28th Division who had also played an important role in organizing the American Legion in Paris in 1919. By his side in November 1924 was Dr. Paul Philippe Cret, a Philadelphia architect retained by the state commission. A native Frenchman who had taught at the University of Pennsylvania since 1903, Dr. Cret was appointed as the ABMC's consulting architect in September 1925, with the strong endorsement of the Fine Arts Commission, and continued in that role until his death in 1945.[55]

General Price and his architect won the approval they were seeking for designs and sites at three locations (Varennes, Nantillois, and Fismes) in France and one (Audenarde) in Belgium.[56] Once all of the necessary clearances were obtained, the three Pennsylvania monuments proposed for French sites were built within the next three years. The Audenarde site was eventually ceded to the ABMC for one of its own monuments after the Pennsylvanians abandoned their own plans there. One might conclude that giving permission to Pennsylvania to erect a series of memorials to its own soldiers contradicted the commission's own "Regulations" adopted two meetings earlier that seemed to rule out monuments to "troops from a particular locality." It will be noted, however, that the ABMC had embraced this policy only "as a general rule," and in this instance simply chose to ignore it. Pennsylvania was a populous state that had contributed large numbers of troops to the national war effort; its own battle monuments commission was two years older than the ABMC and had carefully developed its plans; and the spokesmen the Keystone State sent to Washington to plead its case plainly impressed the Pershing board.

When the commission convened in March 1925, it turned its attention to naval memorials. The ABMC had considered how best to commemorate the wartime service of US naval personnel, especially those who had died, at its third meeting in November 1923. Senator Reed told his fellow commissioners on that occasion that 467 sailors had been killed in action during the 1917–18 war, another 843 had died of wounds, and 5,334 had succumbed to illness. Some of these men were to be buried in the permanent American cemeteries abroad. Since all of the military experience on the commission was with the army, the ABMC voted to ask the secretary of the navy directly for his suggestions.[57]

Commissioners Markey and Miller, along with Secretary Price, had immediately constituted a "Committee on Naval Memorials" and collaborated during ensuing months with a comparable group appointed by the secretary of the navy. The full commission soon resolved to build "large memorial monuments" at Southampton and Brest to commemorate naval action in British and European waters; to place a reference on the Meuse-Argonne monument to the fact that naval guns had assisted in the American attack there; to change the proposed US Army monument in Rome to a US Army and Navy memorial; and to build "small memorial monuments" at Corfu (Greece), Ponta Delgada (Azores), and Gibraltar. An appropriation of $300,000 for these projects was incorporated into the commission's request for Fiscal Year 1926.[58]

By early 1925, the commission was plainly beginning to get up to speed with its own monuments program. Congressman Hill reported at the March meeting that Congress had agreed to the commission's proposal for $1.8 million for FY 1926 to fund the three large army monuments already proposed and smaller ones at twelve additional sites. An extra $1.2 million was appropriated for "the erection of chapels, walls, and other permanent improvements" in the eight cemeteries. Armed with the promise of this appropriation, the commissioners directed Dr. Cret to visit every place selected for an ABMC memorial during the coming summer and to formulate recommendations as to the best locations and most appropriate character and design for each structure.[59]

Exactly half of the total appropriation of $3 million was directed to the army monuments, with more than half of that portion designated for the structures to be built on the three greatest American battlefields. Each of the twelve "historical monuments" envisioned for the wartime combat zone across Belgium and northeastern France was budgeted at $30,000. The memorial to the Services of Supply at Tours was to cost $150,000. The other structure of intermediate size, a monument in Nancy to commemorate the province of Lorraine as the hub of American activity along the Western Front, was budgeted at $130,000. The five naval memorials were to receive a total of $275,000—the two large edifices at Southampton and Brest costing $100,000 each and the three smaller sites at Corfu, Ponta Delgado, and Gibraltar running $25,000 apiece.[60]

Quietly abandoned in the foregoing activity was the commission's earlier stated intention of implementing the Battle Monuments Board's proposal for marking the European battlefields. The 1924 trip to Europe convinced the Pershing board that the BMB's program was not worth undertaking after all. The ABMC's commitment to the plan of the Palmer group had always been "tentative," a later report claimed, and was only used in earlier years as a basis for securing appropriations from Congress. While the BMB project had once "appealed very greatly to the members of the Commission," it was now to be eclipsed. It had called for monuments that were too numerous, too small to be easily seen, too difficult to access, and too hard to maintain. The battlefields to be marked, moreover, had "practically disappeared" by 1925, and the once fought-over ground had returned to cultivation or been reincorporated into villages.[61] Although this decision produced some dismay on Capitol Hill,[62] the ABMC members left no doubt about their intention to pursue a new scheme unbridled by earlier commitments.

Standards for determining the most suitable locations for the commission's own monuments were ratified in May 1925. Memorial edifices were to be placed on ground where American forces had actually fought in the late war. They were to be readily accessible to the visiting public. They should be prominent enough to be "visible across country" to those inclined to visit them. And they should have "a commanding view over the region covered by the [military] operation"—or, failing that, should mark "the place where the outstanding feature of the operation took place."[63] It should be noted that no such formal guidelines were ever established for siting the cemetery chapels. With the range of possibilities narrowed to the space within the cemetery confines, it was left to the consulting architect to make these determinations on his own, subject always to the commissioners' final approval.

Pershing's absence on a diplomatic mission during the latter half of 1925 caused impatience on the commission, but did not markedly slow its work.[64] Based on a detailed report from Dr. Cret on his summer inspection trip, the commission approved sites and tentative funding in November for all eight of the cemetery chapels. The initial projection was that these structures could be built for $1 million. The most expensive of the chapels ($320,000) was to be at Romagne; the least expensive ($50,000) at Waregem.[65] At their fifteenth meeting, the commissioners designated architects for each of the chapels and proposed monuments. The agency had initially considered putting designs for each memorial site out for bids, but ultimately concluded that the rules of the American Institute of Architects for such competitions were too burdensome. In the end, the architects "assigned" to each project by the ABMC were to receive a $250 fee for submitting two designs for each site. If the commissioners judged neither to be satisfactory, the group considered itself under no further obligation to the architect. When a design was accepted, however, the architect was formally engaged for the project in question.[66]

In the midst of the first stage of selection for monument sites and designs, the panel also resolved important details regarding the cemetery headstones. An inscription for the markers of unknown burials was adopted at the May 1925 meeting and read as follows: "Here rests in honored glory an American soldier known but to God."[67] A new secretary of war, Dwight Filley Davis, gave his official approval to this wording at the same time he approved the final design for the shape of the headstones during a courtesy call the commissioners paid to him in early November.[68] Criticism from the *New York Sun*, however, prompted Secretary Davis a month later to request that the commission change the word "but" in the inscription for the unknowns to "only." Pershing's agency stood its ground, however, and Davis did not pursue the matter any further.[69] Secretary Price later recounted that the editor of the *Standard Dictionary* had prompted this brief controversy by advising the newspaper that, although "but" was perfectly grammatical, "only" was a better word because it could mean only one thing. As far as Price was concerned, after six months of working on language for the inscription and entertaining several different alternatives, the current version said exactly what the commission desired.[70]

The choice of material for the headstones sparked a far greater controversy. In its earliest discussion of this matter, the commission had shown a clear preference for white headstones. Senator Reed had seen fit to name marble explicitly in the motion (already noted) from November 1924. But six months later the commissioners had accepted another motion made by Reed at Dr. Cret's behest naming French white stone as a second possibility.[71] American granite also entered the discussion with strong backing from its own trade association, several other organized groups, and at least one commissioner—Mrs. Bentley.[72]

By invitation of the ABMC, the president and secretary of the American Granite Association, a number of granite dealers from different parts of the United States, and a congressman from the granite-producing state of Massachusetts appeared at the November 16, 1925, meeting to advocate their product for the overseas grave markers. Discussion focused on the durability of granite as compared with other stones. The commissioners were also interested to hear about cost and how the material could be transported to the European sites. At least one article in the press foresaw that the high cost of the American stone might prove "a very serious objection" to its employment in the overseas cemeteries. The encounter between the commission and the lobbying group adjourned on the understanding that the association would prepare a written brief on the advantages of their material for the ABMC to consider at its next meeting.[73]

By two meetings later, the commission had received the promised follow-up letter and discussed it, as well as communications from the Gold Star Fathers Association and the Service Star Legion, all promoting granite for the headstones. Thus, when the War Department solicited bids, producers of all three types of stone under consideration—marble (both Italian and American), French white stone, and American granite—entered the fray.[74] When it convened in June 1926, the commission reviewed the bids for each one, and also heard renewed pleas from representatives of the American Granite Association. At the end of this meeting, the ABMC recommended to the secretary of war that *either* Italian (Carrara) marble *or* French white stone should be used.[75] These two materials happened to be bid at the lowest cost: $14.50 per cross and $15.50 per star in the case of Italian marble, and $19.00 and $22.00, respectively, in the case of the French product. American marble was more than twice as expensive as the Italian. The bids for New Hampshire and Vermont granite were highest of all, at $78.00 (cross)/$84.00 (star) and $115.00 (cross)/$129.00 (star), respectively.[76]

The commissioners justified their final choice on multiple grounds.

Either the Italian or French stone would give "a superior result as far as beauty is concerned," and at a cost that is "very much less" than any of the American contestants. Being European materials, moreover, it would be easier and cheaper to procure and ship them to the American cemeteries. Finally, each of these choices would "fulfill all necessary requirements of durability."[77] The secretary of war approved the ABMC's recommendation on July 14, but declined to make a final selection between the two materials until the commission could counsel him further after inspecting full-sized models of the headstones in both stones.[78]

The secretary of war's action did not halt the discussion; indeed, agitation for American granite continued for several more months. Secretary Price had earlier shown concern about the potential power of the granite lobby. "If it [the pressure for granite] develops in considerable strength," he had written Thomas North in Paris at the end of June, "it will work havoc with all of our plans."[79] But the granite backers were stubbornly persistent because, to them, there was simply no denying that their stone was the most durable. If the principal question for the ABMC was whether the nation's overseas war memorials should be "temporary" or "ever-lasting," and the obvious answer was the latter, they reasoned that granite headstones *had* to be the choice. Proponents of this viewpoint conceded that granite was a more expensive material to purchase, but argued that it would save the government money in the long run. Marble headstones, they said, would likely have to be replaced multiple times during the expected life span of granite markers. One analysis from the Granite Association boldly declared that "the total cost of maintaining granite monuments over a reasonable period of time is frequently as much as fifty percent less than the cost of maintaining monuments of any other material over the same period of time."[80]

The commission had also heard from André Ventre, architect-in-chief of the French government, on this increasingly nettlesome question. Ventre's knowledge of his own country's climate, and his experience with the maintenance of historical monuments all over France, persuaded him to urge the Americans not to select any kind of marble for their headstones. "Marble, regardless of what quarry it comes from, will not resist the vigorous climate of the north and east of France," he said. "It tarnishes, scales and corrodes no matter what its hardness is. One cannot imagine employing marble for a work that should last centuries." Acknowledging that granite was "not white enough to stand out on the grass," the Frenchman recommended "the usual white French building stone" as the best choice. "Examples of the resisting power of this stone are the carvings on Notre Dame cathedral," he observed proudly, "which are intact after a thousand years."[81]

Secretary Price, based on his own study of the matter, told the commission that granite would not necessarily be the "most economical in the end because it lasts longer." Given the price differential between it and marble, which the ABMC Secretary reckoned conservatively at a multiple of three, the US government would incur comparable cost for each of the two if marble headstones had to be replaced every twelve or thirteen years. But Price figured a more likely life span for marble to be fifty years, which decisively refuted the Granite Association's claim that its stone would be cheaper in the long run. He also believed that the French stone "would be the most suitable and economical," but declined to make that a final recommendation until all bids could be fully evaluated.[82]

As it happened, the contract went to the producers of Carrara marble, but not before General Pershing had signaled his fascination with the properties of yet another contender—Numidian, or North African, marble. Just days before ending his 1926 European inspection tour, the general had seen a sample of this stone in the office of the Graves Registration Service in Paris and become infatuated with its beauty and its superior durability over other kinds of marble. Pershing immediately complained to Secretary Price that the War Department had failed to investigate this substance and secure bids for it from the outset. He further directed Price to represent to the other commissioners that this material was the chairman's preference, and to request their opinion on it as a final selection for the headstones.[83]

Nothing about this last-minute attempt to reopen the discussion pleased Price, who had written ten days earlier of his intention to recommend that the commission accept the Carrara bid and was soon to be on the receiving end of the secretary of war's frustration with foot-dragging at the ABMC. The major was particularly upset with General Pershing for leading the last-minute charge for Numidian marble.[84] The other members of the commission, in any case, never changed their earlier recommendation to the secretary of war, and Davis's decision in favor of Italian marble just days before the ABMC meeting of October 7 finally settled the matter.

Carrara marble came out the choice for three reasons: its cost, its availability, and its beauty. Secretary Price had noted as an argument for the Italian stone in an earlier memo that the secretary of war would be obliged by law to accept the lowest bid on any material that was deemed suitable for the purpose at hand.[85] But the key determinant all along, from the ABMC's standpoint, seemed to be the color of the Carrara stone. That quality overrode concerns about durability, as Price later explained, and made it the choice that promised best "to retain, in so far as possible, the effect of the present existing [temporary] white headstones." None of the other materials in contention for the contract "answered the requirements of the commission as to whiteness."[86] The final decision did not spare the ABMC members, with General Pershing in the chair, one more encounter with advocates for American granite. After listening for over an hour to more arguments for the homeland's product at the October 7 meeting, however, the chairman calmly declared that as far as he and his fellow commissioners were concerned, the matter was closed.[87]

Early in 1928, the commission addressed two final matters pertaining to what was to go on the cemetery headstones. Information about the buried soldier on the front of each marker was to include name, rank, unit, date of death, and the state of residence at the time of his entry into the military. The War Department had used this format on the temporary markers and carried it over to the permanent ones. At the ABMC's twenty-seventh meeting, the commissioners voted to recommend to the secretary of war that "Killed in Action" or "Died of Wounds" also appear, as applicable, on each headstone, along with any military decoration the deceased may have received.[88] The first recommendation was never implemented, however, and the only decorations typically noted on the permanent markers are the Medal of Honor (the complete inscriptions for such recipients are engraved in gold), the Distinguished Service Cross, the Distinguished Service Medal, and the French Croix de Guerre.

At the same meeting, the ABMC unanimously approved a recommendation from the quartermaster general of the army that relatives of deceased soldiers be allowed to place "a quotation or term of endearment," not to exceed sixty letters, on the *back* of the headstones.[89] This offer to surviving loved ones had been talked of since the first efforts by the War Department to design a model for the American headstones. Thomas North recounted that the inspiration for this practice came from the British, who solicited such brief passages from the families of their war dead and engraved them on the front lower portion of the headstones.[90] To this day, anyone walking among the graves in a British cemetery from either of the two world wars cannot fail to be moved by the power of these intimate verses, which appear on almost all of the headstones of the known burials.

When this opportunity was extended to the nearly thirty thousand American families with dead in an overseas cemetery, however, it bore little fruit. Only nineteen headstones had such passages inscribed on their backs.[91] Some of these are verses of Holy Scripture; others come from English literature, or were composed by the families themselves. But most responses submitted by American families were so pedestrian—for example, "Killed in Action"—that they were deemed unworthy of display.[92] The offer was not even made to survivors of the World War II dead resting in ABMC sites. It is almost certain that the average visitor to our country's World War I cemeteries in Europe will never notice any of these rare inscriptions.

Final determination of which monuments the ABMC would actually build was reached after General Pershing returned from South America. A discussion "at great length" of the entire project of seventeen army and five navy structures yielded a decision at the October 18, 1926, meeting to reduce the proposed number to "a minimum consistent with complete commemoration."[93] This rather vague standard resulted from an increasingly pressing fear that the United States might wind up with too many war monuments in Europe.

While a number of sites for ABMC monuments had already been selected by this time, other prospective venues were proving problematic. The search for a suitable location for a naval monument in either London or on the southern coast of England bogged down because so many other memorials were already in place from earlier wars, or planned in commemoration of the 1914–18 conflict.[94] In Italy, the problem was political: the Mussolini government showed little enthusiasm for an American monument in Rome and was not cooperating with the ABMC's efforts to secure a site there. At its twentieth meeting, the commission voted to postpone indefinitely its consideration of a memorial in the Italian capital.[95] Although interest in both of these projects persisted, the commissioners voted in October 1930 definitively to drop the English site as part of a thinning of the naval memorials from five to two.[96] Prospective designs for a Rome monument were reviewed at a 1928 commission meeting, after the State Department had urged reinstatement of that project the previous year,[97] but there is no evidence that the commission ever considered the idea further.

The American monument-building program encountered its own unique hindrances in France. Action on an American monument in Nancy, for example, fell victim to local bitterness over Washington's determination to collect debts from its wartime partner. ABMC officials had selected the site for such a memorial, but in May 1926 the Nancy city council rejected the commission's plans. One councilman, referencing a recent bilateral agreement that still required the French to make debt payments to the United States, called the Americans "pitiless creditors" who would "burden us down to our grandchildren." The local authorities were willing to allow the ABMC a site at another location that would have obliged the builders to demolish an existing fountain.[98] But Secretary Price saw that offer merely as a way for the Nancy council to shift an unwanted expense of their own to the Americans.[99] General Pershing and his fellow commissioners soon decided to drop the project.[100] Early in 1927, Price instructed Thomas North to communicate this decision to the mayor of Nancy, but he was careful to advise his subordinate across the Atlantic to express regret when he did so, and to give as the reason simply "that we are reducing the number of monuments."[101]

The elimination of the Nancy site reflected the commission's emerging consensus that earlier proposals for the monuments it intended to build had been too ambitious. In March 1926, General Pershing and his fellow commissioners had considered the question of "limiting or prohibiting entirely" the monuments they would permit other Americans to build in Europe. Still sensitive to the large number of non-federal structures in place from the years before the commission had assumed the authority to control such activity, the members even began to go public with their concerns about a potential overabundance of US monuments in foreign lands. Pershing observed that "the bounds of good taste" might be exceeded if the ABMC did not tighten the guidelines for acceptable structures—both its own and those of other entities. As a later press release from the agency put it, the fact that our country had only fought during the final stages of the Great War and had fewer troops and lighter losses than the major European powers in the fray seemed to argue for a more modest complement of national monuments.[102]

In response to this concern, the commission resolved to permit construction of only those memorials from outside entities that would be "useful" in the neighborhoods of the local inhabitants. Bridges, commemorative fountains, public buildings, or other community improvements were judged suitable under this criterion.¹⁰³ In addition to the rationale already explained for its tighter standards, the ABMC strongly encouraged its countrymen to show their "gratitude and love for our soldiers" by constructing more memorials *inside* the United States. Most importantly, this would obviate the need for long-distance maintenance, which too often went neglected. "Many of those [overseas monuments] now erected give the impression that the people who put them up have forgotten their existence," the commission declared. The years since the war had shown that proper upkeep of such edifices was "almost impossible . . . except through Government agencies."¹⁰⁴

The commission's choices for its own commemorative program came to reflect the publicly articulated concerns. At the twenty-third meeting in February 1927, with all members plus Dr. Cret in attendance, a final list was approved of just eight locations for monuments in France—Montfaucon, Montsec (Saint-Mihiel), Château-Thierry, Blanc Mont (Champagne), Bony (Somme), Cantigny, Tours (Services of Supply), and Brest (naval)—and two for commemorative tablets (Chaumont and Souilly).¹⁰⁵ In addition to the London/Southampton, Rome, and Nancy sites where monuments would never be built, six more locations in France were eliminated at this meeting.¹⁰⁶ By the end of 1930, the commission had reduced the original proposal for five naval monuments to two—Brest and Gibraltar.¹⁰⁷ With two Belgian sites (Audenarde and Kemmel) confirmed in the meantime for smaller edifices, the final roster of ABMC memorials to be constructed, after roughly seven years of study and deliberation, totaled eight cemetery chapels, eleven monuments, and two plaques.

As it narrowed and finalized its own program, the agency's more explicit standards for monuments it would allow other entities to build were repeatedly tested. An entreaty from the state of Ohio in October 1926 prompted a fuller clarification of what was "useful" and "not useful." Within the former category, the commission replied, could be a fountain, provided that proper maintenance and a permanent water supply were assured, and that the structure was "located where it will be used." Similarly, a clock tower would qualify, "provided it is equipped with a clock and proper maintenance is assured." Finally, the reconstruction of a church was deemed "useful," along with suitable commemorative tablets on or inside the structure to identify the sponsoring agency. Explicitly ruled out were such merely ornamental devices as memorial crosses placed near churches and benches in parks.¹⁰⁸ Petitioning groups could find that even these clarifications might be subjectively applied. A request by the 37th Division Battle Monuments Commission (of Ohio) for ABMC permission to erect a clock tower in the "new" Montfaucon (the "old" village had become the property of the French government in its completely ruined state) was refused in March 1927 on the grounds that the proposed structure was so large that it was "more monumental than useful in character."[109]

During the first fifteen years of the ABMC's history, representatives of associations seeking to build monuments in Europe appeared before the commission on more than a dozen occasions. The agency also entertained numerous written requests for such clearance. Rejections or deferrals far outnumbered outright approvals. Rejection was invariably the response to requests by private citizens to place statues in the cemeteries, or to any petition for a monument from a unit smaller than a division. Designs deemed not to be "useful" to the host inhabitants were sure to bring disapproval as well. A number of proposals for monuments to individual divisions were deferred until the ABMC could determine how it might incorporate the honoring of specific units into its own commemorative program.

The Pennsylvania Battle Monuments Commission possessed the best record of securing ABMC approval for structures it wanted to build. State associations from Ohio and Massachusetts received approval for a portion of their monuments programs. The Virginia Battle Monuments Commission, by contrast, won no support from the ABMC in 1927 for its somewhat belated desire to place tablets commemorating the state's war dead on structures it intended to help certain French villages erect in honor of their own local dead. The Virginians were told simply that their idea was "not in harmony with the policy of the Commission concerning useful memorials and could not be approved."[110]

One of the most controversial turndowns by the ABMC involved a request from the 316th Regiment of the 79th Division (ironically, a Pennsylvania unit) to build a monument on the Borne de Cornouiller, known to the Americans as "Cornwilly Hill." This spot was on the east bank of the Meuse river north of Verdun and was captured four days before the armistice after bloody and extended fighting. On the recommendation of its own Historical Section, the commission denied permission for the monument in March 1925. The ABMC's judgment was that the service of this unit was not "of a more distinguished character" than other regiments of the 79th Division or in comparison with "the average American regiment that served on the battlefields of France."[111]

Eight months later, the commission learned that the 316th was proceeding with construction of the monument anyway. In a cleverly deceptive move, agents of the regiment had persuaded the mayor of Verdun to facilitate a contract between them and a local charity whereby, in exchange for a substantial donation from the regimental association, the local French agency would actually build the monument and circumvent the ABMC's authority. As Thomas North later reported, the prefect of the Meuse had also denied permission for this monument.[112] Remarkably, the project was going forward in defiance of the agencies of two national governments.

Major Dwight D. Eisenhower came upon the completed monument in 1929 while doing research for the revised ABMC battlefield guide. When Ike's report found its way to General Pershing, the AEF commander's instinctual response was to ask local French authorities to demolish the offending structure. When they refused to do so, Pershing appealed directly to Prime Minister André Tardieu, who was sympathetic and actually helped foster the eventual compromise settlement. For their part, the sponsors of the monument sought the protection of President Herbert Hoover, although he declined to get involved. Most hurtful of all had to be when the general of the armies came under a barrage of criticism in the Pennsylvania press from his wartime comrades-in-arms. Only in August 1931 was a resolution reached whereby the monument was legalized. At Pershing's insistence, however, the inscription on it was changed to commemorate the service of *all* the American troops who had fought in that region.[113]

For whatever heat this particular dispute generated, it illuminated a great deal about how the ABMC understood and sought to wield its authority over the entirety of American overseas monument building. It also revealed how veterans' groups sometimes found the commission's decisions unjustly restrictive of their desire to commemorate their own wartime actions. In leaving this incident, it is worth noting further that the edifice Pershing tried so forcefully to eliminate remains the only American monument from the 1914–18 conflict to be situated east of the Meuse River, in a region where the AEF had seen significant combat during the war's final battle.[114]

Another Pennsylvania regiment, the 315th, found a somewhat different way to circumvent the ABMC's authority. During the summer of 1930, commission personnel discovered a plaque on a building in Nantillois (Meuse-Argonne) that read, "Erected in Memory of the Glorious Dead of the 315th Infantry U.S.A." Veterans of that unit had funded construction of the building and given it to the village for use as a "community house," but had not sought the permission of the ABMC for the commemorative plaque.[115]

When General Pershing reported this development to the full commission in October 1930, he noted that the sponsors from the 315th had expressed regret that they had unintentionally violated ABMC policy and offered to abide by whatever decision the agency might make regarding their memorial. The general also observed that the residents of Nantillois "greatly desired" the building, and that it served "a very useful purpose." In view of these considerations, the commission ratified Pershing's recommendation to approve the building, while requiring again that the memorial plaque be changed to honor the men from all American units who had died in that region.[116]

The subsequent history of the 315th's commemorative building in Nantillois illustrates the central problem with privately erected monuments. Over the years, funds for upkeep dwindled. By the aftermath of World War II the building had become, in North's words, "dilapidated and filthy" and, more importantly, an embarrassment that local inhabitants inevitably associated with the United States.[117] As one of the prefects of the Meuse, Charles Magny, had observed to North during the 1920s: "We Frenchmen cannot be expected to differentiate—Pennsylvania, Ohio, 28th Division, American Battle Monuments Commission, all are Americans to us. Their monuments are American monuments."[118] ABMC personnel have been particularly sensitive to this reality since the beginning of the agency.

The experiences of the 315th and 316th Regiments revealed that the ABMC's control over the erection of war memorials by Americans was not airtight. By contrast, the unsuccessful effort of the 93rd Division to gain authorization for a monument to three of its regiments composed of African American troops—the 369th, 371st, and 372nd—did not expose any flexibility in the commission's authority. Veterans from this division pursued their campaign for a commemorative structure chiefly in the Congress of the United States because one of their wartime officers was Representative Hamilton Fish of New York. As spokesman for the effort to gain ABMC approval for this monument, Fish was not easily deterred—although, in the end, neither he nor other members of his unit were able to overturn the commission's judgment against their proposed monument.[119]

The 93rd's project originated in the mid-1920s as a bill in the House of Representatives. Congressman Fish, while aware of the ABMC's policy that American monuments were not to commemorate units smaller than a division, believed that an exception should be made in this case because of the unique racial composition of the three regiments in question, and also because of their outstanding combat record and the unusually heavy 40 percent casualty rate they suffered.[120] ABMC commissioner Thomas Miller testified before the House Foreign Affairs Committee early in 1925 while the bill was undergoing hearings. Miller's recommendation to the commission was that the units should receive "appropriate commemoration by tablets or otherwise" on monuments already approved for construction by the ABMC, but that the African American regiments should not have a memorial all to themselves.[121]

Congressman Fish was not willing to accept this rebuff without a fight. Pressure for a dedicated monument to the 93rd Division continued on Capitol Hill and led to a spirited debate within the House Foreign Affairs Committee in March 1926. Senator Reed testified on the ABMC's behalf on that occasion and swapped particularly harsh rhetoric with the New York lawmaker during three days of hearings. Before the verbal fury ended, Fish had warned that the ABMC ought to "be very careful that there should be no reasonable ground for them [the African American veterans] to think that they were discriminated against." Reed had retorted that he saw no reason "why we should treat those people better than we treat whites."[122] The House committee ultimately yielded to the commission's judgment and accepted that Fish's division would be mentioned on the national monument closest to where it had seen action.[123]

In short, by the end of its first seven years, the ABMC had definitively determined the monuments it would build, ruled on structures it would either allow or forbid other American entities to build, and made plans for the beautification of the eight permanent cemeteries. Actual construction had been rather slow to begin, however, and the commission had heard some criticism over the slow pace of its work.[124] The commission's policies and the decisions made to implement them, moreover, had not met with universal approbation, often because they had denied to those wishing to commemorate individual combat achievements the freedom to do so. Nonetheless, by the time the agency had dedicated all of its own structures, it expressed confidence that the memorial program it had undertaken and overseen on the nation's behalf "adequately commemorates all units of the American forces in Europe during the World War."[125]

Not counting its own eleven creations, the ABMC's 1938 inventory of all overseas monuments to American soldiers of the Great War numbered ninety-one altogether. Seventy-seven of these had been put up before the commission was in a position to approve or disapprove them. Sixty-one honored the first five divisions of the American army. Six more honored additional divisions—the 26th, 28th, 30th, 80th, and two to Ohio's 37th. Almost all of these commemorative sites were fashioned in stone; however, one was an ornamental wrought iron railing on a bridge, one was a stained glass window, and three were tablets. The more limited number of structures dating from after the time that the commission was in full operation confirms the degree to which General Pershing and his fellow commissioners had exercised their authority to impose limits on the proliferation of overseas American monuments.

To authenticate the location of its own monuments, the inscriptions on them, and its evaluation of the requests of other entities to build commemorative structures abroad, the commission had set up a Historical Section during its first full year. President Coolidge was asked in February 1924 to detail three officers—two from the army and one from the marine corps—to the ABMC to conduct this work. The principal endeavor of this trio was to establish "the battle lines of all American units for each day during their service at the front in Europe."[126] Upon the initial collection and collation of records from the War Department pertaining to the positioning and operation of numerous army divisions, the commission's research team dispatched letters to "all officers down through company commanders and to certain enlisted men" seeking their input to verify or correct what was already on file. The succession of officers assigned to the ABMC's Historical Section ultimately produced maps and wrote narrative summaries for eighty different operations involving dozens of units. The voluminous correspondence generated by this project fills more than a hundred cartons in the National Archives and, as the commission's 1925 annual report noted, "resulted in an immense amount of valuable historical information which it would be impossible to obtain after the present generation."[127]

The work of the Historical Section on the Great War continued through the 1930s and well into World War II. The ABMC researchers also collaborated closely with their counterparts at the Historical Section of the Army War College, with both groups liberally exchanging data that they had independently compiled.[128] Secretary Price later noted that the process of establishing the accuracy of the maps and the narrative summaries that accompanied them, especially in view of the numerous conflicting opinions that came with the huge volume of firsthand testimonies, could never be considered "as definitely terminated."[129] The totality of the Historical Section's work supported the 1944 publication by the Government Printing Office of a twenty-eight-volume collection entitled *Summary of Operations in the World War*.[130] Much of the material collected also found its way into the commission's two guidebooks for the European battlefields, published in 1927 and 1938.

That there ever was an ABMC battlefield guidebook is inextricably connected to the national commemoration of the tenth anniversary of US entry into the Great War and the large pilgrimage to the European combat zone organized that year by the American Legion. In December 1926, looking toward the latter event, General Pershing directed the Historical Section to prepare such a publication in time for the Legion's "Second AEF" convention the following September in Paris.[131] Thomas North recalled that during their 1924 overseas inspection tour the ABMC commissioners had noted that "no suitable guidebook to the American battlefields existed." The directional aids to the wartime combat zones that did exist, according to North, were by European authors who generally disregarded the American perspective on the war and provided incorrect information on our battle sites when they did mention them.[132]

The Historical Section was certainly experienced enough by early 1927 to tackle such a challenge. But additional staffing was urgently needed. In January, General Pershing appointed the aforementioned Major Eisenhower, age thirty-six, to the Historical Section essentially to direct the production of the guidebook. As one scholar has noted, "Only [Secretary] Price himself . . . would exercise greater authority over the project."[133] Ike and his colleagues managed to have the finished work to the printer in time for an August release to the public, and the run of twenty thousand copies was quickly bought up—most of it, no doubt, by eager Legionnaires bound for their imminent Paris reunion.[134]

Well-received as the first ABMC guidebook was, it soon became apparent that it contained numerous errors and merited redoing. Eisenhower and most of his staff had put the book together in the commission's Washington office, even though the subject matter was thousands of miles away. As Professor Trout reports, much of the data on French roads and topography of the battle sites had been collected earlier, and some of it was transmitted inaccurately across the ocean.[135]

When Eisenhower finished his assignment in August 1927, he left the ABMC for a year at the Army War College, armed with a glowing letter of recommendation from General Pershing.[136] In June 1928, however, the ABMC chairman made clear that he wanted Ike back to spearhead the production from the Paris office of an expanded and revised guidebook. The middle-aged major agreed to rejoin the commission and sailed for France with his wife and son that summer on what turned out to be a seventeen-month term of service.[137] While the new guidebook did not appear in print until the spring of 1939, Eisenhower contributed a number of the expanded sections on battles and operations that had been treated more tersely in the earlier edition, initiated the preparation of several new sections Pershing wanted, and wrote many of the captions for the hundreds of photographs contained in the later edition. When his colleagues at the Historical Section honored him with a farewell party in October 1929, they awarded him "the immortal title of GUIDEBOOK IKE."[138] Thomas North writes especially favorably about Eisenhower's service in Paris. "We were all impressed by his outstanding talents, but also won by his simplicity, modesty, and generosity of spirit." Ike's younger Paris colleague added, "His departure in the fall of 1929 was a blow to the pleasant camerarderie [sic] of the office."[139] Trout believes that Eisenhower's experience with the ABMC, especially the time he spent exploring and studying the World War I battlefields, played no small part in the major's formation as the future Supreme Commander of the next Allied force called upon to fight and win a European war.[140]

In the meantime, the "Second AEF" convention drew great numbers of American veterans to the French capital to mark the tenth anniversary of the original doughboys' arrival to wage war. General Pershing, who had returned to the United States in mid-June from his 1927 inspection tour of the overseas memorial sites, sailed again from New York on September 10 in the vanguard of a veritable fleet of twenty-seven ships carrying 18,224 fellow pilgrims.[141] Once in Paris, the Americans paraded down the Champs-Élysées to the enthusiastic welcome of 2 million spectators,[142] feted themselves at dinners attended by Prime Minister Raymond Poincaré, President Gaston Doumergue, and Marshal Foch, and made visits to the numerous villages where they had billeted as soldiers and to the permanent cemeteries on the old battlefields. Upon his return home in early November, Pershing declared the Legion pilgrimage "a great success," observing that the reception by the French had been "very cordial" and that the positive effect on bilateral relations "should be permanent."[143] In advance of the event, the old AEF commander had told reporters that the convention would be "a great pilgrimage of good-will," and that it was "prompted by motives to re-establish the intimate friendly relations [between France and the United States] that existed during the war."[144]

Several years later, a very different collection of "pilgrims"—the Gold Star Mothers and widows—would begin to leave the United States by the thousands for the sites of memory along the old Western Front. In an action without precedent or repeat, Congress voted $5.3 million in February 1930 to support government-sponsored and -hosted trips to the American cemeteries in Europe for women whose sons or husbands (if they had not remarried) were buried there. These pilgrimages took place during each of the next four years, with the last group returning to the United States in August 1933. A total of 6,654 women, some of whose husbands accompanied them at their own expense, availed themselves of the government's offer to visit the graves of their loved ones.[145]

While the eventual destination of each group of "pilgrims" was one of the eight ABMC cemeteries, the Pershing commission had little to do with the administration of this program. Rather, the army's Quartermaster Corps planned, arranged, and conducted the trips, right down to the smallest details. Because the actual burial grounds were still under the control of the Graves Registration Service, moreover, the army directed the construction of temporary buildings to serve as "hostess houses" at the four largest cemeteries (Meuse-Argonne, Oise-Aisne, Saint-Mihiel, and Aisne-Marne), with rest areas, seating space for group luncheons, and expanded medical services also provided.[146]

The Gold Star Mother pilgrimages coincided with the peak period of construction of the ABMC monuments and chapels, and with the final stages of beautification of the cemeteries. In all four years of the pilgrimages, they took place between May and August/September and always included several days in Paris or London before journeying to the cemeteries. Government officials not only accompanied the travelers but greeted them when they assembled at their East Coast departure point and when they arrived at their European destination. General Pershing, whose inspection trips to the ABMC sites overlapped with the pilgrimages in each of their four years, often spoke to the mothers and widows in France. The remarks he made to the first group of African American pilgrims upon their arrival in Paris in June 1931 were no doubt typical of what he said on all such occasions: he was glad they had come; he knew that sad times awaited them when they finally beheld the grave of their loved one; and they would realize "when they looked out over the white crosses of the cemeteries where their sons and husbands lie, that the sacrifice was not in vain, and that their memories would be tenderly cherished down through the years."[147]

Putting in place an administrative structure, devising policies, and creating permanent sites designed to foster an appropriate and orderly cherishing of memories of the dead soldiers from the Great War was indeed the business of the American Battle Monuments Commission from its inception. The events and achievements explained in this chapter constitute a large part of that story. Even before they were finished, the overseas American cemeteries and monuments had assumed a prominent place in the nation's organized effort to honor and remember the exertions and sacrifices the war had exacted.

But there remains to recount the conceptualization and construction of the sites themselves, as well as to describe the physical design, placement, and appearance of the memorials. General Pershing, Secretary Price, the six other commissioners, Consulting Architect Paul Cret and many others recruited from the American artistic community, Thomas North, and civilian and military personnel of all ranks on the ground in Europe played their respective parts in directing and accomplishing this vital component of the ABMC's work. The next chapter will endeavor to bring to fuller light this part of the commission's history.

3

Building the American Memorials in Europe, 1925–1933

The siting, design, and construction of the ABMC memorials—eight cemetery chapels and eleven monuments—spanned the years between 1925 and 1933. As already recounted, it took the commission until February 1927, and nearly two dozen meetings, to agree on the definitive list of monuments it would erect. But the last stages of the selection process had mostly involved the elimination of projects proposed earlier; thus, many of the eleven sites had already been chosen and, in some cases, acquired before the commission finalized its list. The completion of the Montfaucon monument in 1933 ended the construction phase for the nineteen memorial structures. A major article in *National Geographic Magazine* in January 1934, authored by General Pershing, confirmed to the American public the realization of the ABMC's original project.[1] As chapter 4 will recount, finally, the dedication of each chapel and monument in 1937 formally concluded the first creative portion of the commission's history, exactly twenty years after the United States entered World War I.

During its first two years, the Pershing board had met a dozen times and made important progress toward establishing its commemorative program. It had organized offices in Washington, D.C., and Paris, visited the European battlefields where its activities would focus, and formulated standards for its own memorials and those that other entities might seek to build abroad. The appointment of Paul Cret as consulting architect, which Secretary Xenophon H. Price later described as "one of its earliest and most fortunate acts," equipped the commission to proceed in earnest with its artistic endeavor.[2]

Dr. Cret, as noted in the previous chapter, had first crossed paths with the ABMC in November 1924 during an appearance on behalf of the Pennsylvania Battle Monuments Commission, a board that was two years older than its national counterpart and would take only three years to complete its own much smaller monument program in France. Cret had already established a national reputation as the designer of well-known public buildings, among them the Pan American Union and Folger Shakespeare Library in the nation's capital, the Detroit Institute of Art, and the main building on the campus of the University of Texas. He was a logical choice to take charge of the design of memorials for his adopted state. In January 1925, CFA chairman Charles Moore ventured to recommend the French-born Philadelphian to Senator Reed for the position of Supervisor of Designs and Construction for the national program.[3] Two months later, after the ABMC engaged Dr. Cret to inspect potential monument sites during the coming summer, Secretary Price informed the Fine Arts chairman that the native Frenchman would be asked to accept a more permanent position "if his work during the summer is satisfactory."[4]

In September 1925, upon completion of the summer travels, Cret signed a contract with the commission to serve as their consulting architect. Major Price described his duties as follows: "Dr. Cret will supervise the preparation of preliminary plans and designs for all memorials, buildings and tablets of the commission's projects, and carry on all negotiations with respect thereto until such plans and designs are approved by this Commission and the National Commission of Fine Arts."[5] When the ABMC formalized its relationship with this accomplished artist, it gained access to a wealth of advice on design issues and someone who could serve as an indispensable intermediary between architects and army officers cast in the role of debating artistic points from radically different perspectives and banks of experience.

Robert Woodside, acting chairman while General Pershing was in South America, claimed in the 1925 annual report that the commission planned to complete its entire program by the tenth anniversary of the armistice (November 11, 1928).[6] This timetable proved wildly optimistic. Indeed, very little dirt was turned over by the time Woodside's original target date had come and gone. Before 1925 was over, the commission had approved individual sites recommended by Dr. Cret for the eight chapels, although every one of these approvals was subject to General Pershing's review upon his return from his diplomatic mission.[7] While the selection of architects for each of these structures followed quickly, designing and definitively siting all eight chapels was not accomplished until early in 1928. In the case of the monuments, the preliminaries before construction could begin took much longer because of the necessity for the commission to acquire the land from private or public owners.

Seven architects were chosen for the eight chapels, with Ralph Adams Cram being assigned both the Aisne-Marne and Oise-Aisne structures. Seven additional architects were chosen to design the monuments. Several of them received multiple projects within the overall ABMC program, topped by Dr. Cret, who was assigned the chapel at Flanders Field, the monuments at Château-Thierry and Bellicourt, the cemetery headstones, and the commemorative plaques at Chaumont and Souilly.[8] Secretary Price observed years after the ABMC chapels and monuments were built that the designers had been chosen "with great care," purposely included older as well as younger men, and embraced "a number of the most prominent architects practicing in the United States at that time." The quality of their finished products, he concluded, testified "to the genius of the American architects."[9]

The seven chapel architects, or their firms, all worked out of East Coast cities—one from Boston (Cram and Ferguson), two from Philadelphia (Paul Cret and George Howe), and four from New York City (Thomas Harlan Ellett, Charles A. Platt, Egerton Swartwout, and the firm of York and Sawyer).[10] The structures they designed for the ABMC are centrally positioned in each of the cemeteries. At Flanders Field, the 368 graves literally surround the chapel. In each of the other seven cases, there are no graves behind the chapel; rather, the headstones are arrayed much as the players of an orchestra might arrange themselves in front of their conductor. Upon entering through the front gates of the Saint-Mihiel and Oise-Aisne cemeteries, which occupy flat to gently sloping land, the visitor sees the chapel one hundred to two hundred yards distant across a wide, partly grassy and partly paved divide separating multiple grave plots. At the Meuse-Argonne, Aisne-Marne, and Suresnes sites, where the landscape slopes more sharply, the chapel is on the highest ground within the cemetery, with the graves arrayed in equal portions on either side of the upwardly inclined approaches to it. At Brookwood, the chapel is similarly centered within the cemetery along the rear perimeter of the graves area, although it is not on markedly raised ground. Only at the Somme cemetery is the chapel at the lowest elevation within the site, centered along the walled southeastern perimeter, with the 1,844 graves arrayed before it on rising ground.

The central placement of the chapel in each cemetery reflected the commission's belief not only in the importance of each of these structures as places of prayer, but in the beautifying effect they would have on the eight sites. During his first year as consulting architect, Paul Cret told Ralph Adams Cram that "the Chapel is more the crowning feature of the Cemetery." It did not need to be a large structure, Cret added, because it was not going to host services. The number of visitors to any of the cemeteries at any given moment was likely to be small, he believed, because of their location remote from large population centers—"with the exception of the one near Paris." In addition to furnishing religious space to visitors, many of whom would be mourners, the chapels were to afford room for inscriptions and the naming on walls or special plaques of those who had perished in local fighting with no known graves.[11]

A few months into 1927, the commission had approved designs for all eight chapels.[12] Two additional decisions were made by unanimous vote. "As the United States is a Christian nation," the commissioners declared, "the interiors of these chapels should be Christian in character." Secondly, they resolved that "the interiors of these chapels should be made as beautiful as they can be made." If additional funds were necessary to achieve the desired levels of beauty, they should be acquired and applied to the effort.[13]

Not surprisingly, the commission's employment of the "Christian" character of the United States as a rationale for the artistic content of the chapels raised concerns that Americans of the Jewish faith might feel slighted. At its March 1927 meeting, the commission agreed that the Star of David should appear in the interiors of the chapels, "provided its use as compared to that of the cross has about the same relative importance as the number of star headstones in the cemetery bears to the number of cross headstones."[14] H. L. Glucksman, executive director of the Jewish Welfare Board, appeared at the next meeting four months later to express the views of his organization "concerning the question of the religious character of the chapels." The minutes from that meeting record nothing of the exchange between Glucksman and the commissioners.[15] Given the vague nature of the standard formulated at the earlier meeting, it would be equally impossible to establish with much certainty how faithfully the designs of each chapel have adhered to the stated ratio of Christian and

Jewish content. In each one of the ABMC chapels to this day, in any case, stone tablets imprinted with Jewish stars and the first ten Roman numerals to signify the Ten Commandments bear witness to the Jewish contribution to our nation's religious tradition and to the service of Jewish soldiers in the two world wars.

When the commission assigned an explicitly Christian character to the chapels, it did not alter the concept initially formulated by Dr. Cret for how these structures were to be used. As construction of the chapels neared completion early in the 1930s, the commissioners ruled on whether they could be used by local congregations for regular religious services. General Pershing and his colleagues decided that, "for many reasons," such use would be "inappropriate," and ordered that similar requests in the future should be denied as well.[16] That policy still holds.

Upon General Pershing's return from his 1927 European inspection tour, a serious debate over where to situate the chapel in the Aisne-Marne cemetery developed within the commission, but mostly between the chairman and the chief architect of the project, Ralph Cram. During the several months necessary to resolve this matter, much came clear about the commission's thinking, especially that of its leader, regarding the place of the chapels in the larger design of the cemeteries, and also the relationship among the individual cemeteries within the full ABMC program. The depth of Pershing's involvement in the determination of artistic details in this instance, and in numerous others in months to come, confirms that the general of the armies was no mere bystander, or nominal leader, in the commission's business; rather, he had to be satisfied with the memorials down to the last element of appearance or positioning, or they did not get built.

The location of the Aisne-Marne cemetery posed unique challenges for the placement of the chapel. This burial site was designed in the shape of a "T," with its top edge flush against the base of a hill that rises into the famed Belleau Wood, scene of the bloody struggle waged mostly by US Marines in June 1918. The cross bar of the T is where the 2,289 graves are arranged in two symmetrical plots that arc gently back toward the base of the hill. The stem of the T is partly a grassy mall that bisects the burial plots, and also a much longer pathway extending to and from the village of Belleau. The two main cemetery buildings flank the paved entranceway just before the grassy area takes over. Crowning the T, on the highest spot in the cemetery, is the chapel.[17]

To emphasize its commanding position within the grounds, and in keeping with directions from the Fine Arts Commission, the chapel was designed as a tower. Charles Moore told Secretary Price that his commission had two preferences for this building: that it not be a structure "of the ecclesiastical type of architecture," and that it occupy a spot on the "military crest" of the hill that marked the beginning of Belleau Wood.[18] Ralph Cram dutifully produced a design and a "footprint" for the chapel that conformed to these directives.[19] Here matters rested until General Pershing came home with other ideas.

Pershing opened the commission's twenty-sixth meeting, an all-day affair in mid-November 1927, with an enumeration of his concerns about the design of several of the memorials prompted by his recent visit to the sites. In the case of the Aisne-Marne chapel, the general observed that the current plan for the structure was too imposing for the top of the hill at the edge of Belleau Wood. Either the chapel would have to be smaller, or it should be moved farther down the hill. It should not be allowed to "overshadow the cemetery," in any case, nor should its dimensions be out of harmony with "the relative importance of the cemetery."[20]

The latter reference exposes one of the most interesting and important elements of Pershing's overall conceptualization of the ABMC's memorial program. In the general's mind, the magnitude—whether actual size, or the less tangible quality of grandeur—of each cemetery or monument was supposed to correlate with the importance of the fighting in the area of the particular site. The AEF commander believed his three greatest battles to have been, in order of importance, Meuse-Argonne, Saint-Mihiel, and Aisne-Marne. The ABMC's longstanding decision to locate its three most significant monuments in this trio of regions reflected his judgment and wishes. The general also insisted that the commemorative structures in each area conform to his ranking of their importance. In other words, the grandest of the war monuments should be in the Meuse-Argonne, the second grandest should memorialize the fighting at Saint-Mihiel, and the third grandest should be somewhere in the Aisne-Marne. Even though the chapel to be erected at the edge of Belleau Wood was in the Aisne-Marne cemetery, Pershing did not believe that the *size* of that cemetery, relative to all of the others, merited a structure as "imposing" as the one Ralph Cram and his associates had designed.

Over the objections of Chester N. Godfrey, a representative of Cram's firm who addressed the November 18 meeting, the commissioners concluded that the chapel ought to be reduced in size if it were to remain at the crest of the hill. They also proposed to consider a new design suitable for a structure placed farther down the hill.[21] A vigorous effort ensued at the Cram and Ferguson office in Boston to comply with the ABMC's new directives. A week after the meeting, Godfrey outlined three new "schemes" for the commission's consideration. One retained the original design of the chapel, but at a position halfway down the hill. Godfrey noted that this option would address an additional concern of Pershing's: that at the top of the hill the structure would simply be inaccessible to many visitors. A second scheme included a slightly modified design for the chapel that better suited it for positioning partway down the hill. The third scheme featured an entirely new design.[22]

Secretary Price, working out of the Paris office at the time so that he could supervise construction details more closely, lent his support to the original chapel design and took an altogether different viewpoint from Pershing's regarding what he termed "the principle of relative values." In one of his periodic communications with the chairman, he sought to assuage the latter's concern that the Belleau chapel, as originally designed, conferred a higher rank upon that cemetery than it merited, especially in relation to its much larger neighbor a dozen miles away at Fère-en-Tardenois. Even if the chapel at the Aisne-Marne site seemed more impressive than its nearby counterpart, Price wrote, the *overall* impression created by the latter burial ground would always be more powerful simply because of the significantly greater number of graves it contained. "No feature at Belleau will ever equal the beauty of the large field of crosses at Fère-en-Tardenois," the secretary insisted.[23]

Price offered a second rationale for the suitability of the Belleau chapel's design. Unlike the ABMC commissioners, who usually visited all the sites during their European trips, few ordinary visitors would do likewise. As a result, the secretary reasoned, "there will be very little comparison between the cemeteries" performed in the average instance. "Most people" would visit "a particular cemetery," and in all likelihood that would be Belleau. If more people saw the chapel there than anywhere else, that was all the more reason why it "must make a favorable impression." The original design did so, in Price's estimation, but the new ones under consideration did not. "The old design might be placed further down the slope if considered essential, but it ought not to be replaced by another one."[24]

Price's arguments eventually prevailed, but it took an impassioned personal plea from Ralph Cram to General Pershing to settle the increasingly troublesome disagreement. Cram wrote the ABMC chairman from France, where he had also gone at the end of 1927 looking to resolve a number of design matters that had arisen in connection with both chapels entrusted to his firm. The architect described himself as "not only gravely concerned but deeply distressed" over the design issues regarding the Belleau Wood memorial. Cram was wholly supportive of Pershing's idea that the chapel should be moved off the top of the hill and affirmed, in fact, that that had *always* been his preference. But, he made clear his strong desire to preserve the original design for the building and challenged the general's contention that, if unaltered, it would give "a predominating importance to the cemetery at Belleau Wood."[25]

That site, Cram claimed, was already the most visited of all the American cemeteries and was bound to remain so. "It strikes the keynote, in a way, of the whole series," he said, while insisting "that the design and dimensions [of the cemetery chapel] are . . . consistent with the whole composition [of the memorial program]." Cram boldly suggested that Pershing "may perhaps have failed in a measure to visualize the ultimate effect" of the chapel as the architect conceived it. "The original scheme is right in design, dimensions, and scale," he wrote, imploring the general to yield to the shared professional judgment of Paul Cret, the CFA, and himself in favor of the original design.[26]

Cram's approach broke the impasse. The commission met next in early January, at which time the chairman read aloud the architect's letter in its entirety. Pershing and his colleagues were persuaded to retain the original design for the chapel, although the floor of the structure was to be repositioned about halfway down the hill.[27] Pershing and Cram met face to face at the Aisne-Marne cemetery early in the spring, weeks after the chairman had written the architect thanking him for his "most interesting and helpful letter" and expressing pleasure at the "very happy solution of the question."[28]

During the summer of 1928, another controversy developed when the chairman formed the opinion that the altars in both chapels Ralph Cram was designing were too "Catholic." Captain Harris Jones, of the Corps of Engineers, told Secretary Price that the original design for the altar in the Aisne-Marne chapel "does not conform to the commission's non-sectarian policy, as it would unquestionably give the average American Protestant the definite idea of a Roman Catholic altar." He wrote in the same vein about the centerpiece of the Oise-Aisne chapel, calling it "beautiful," but adding that it "would certainly offend a great many people." Pershing had echoed the same sentiments in a letter of his own to the architect.[29] As a result, the altars were redesigned. Dr. Cret later informed the chairman that the refashioned spaces "are not open to criticisms on the ground of ritualistic sculptural decoration as were the first ones."[30]

All of the foregoing is meant to suggest the scope of artistic issues that had to be managed in the course of creating the individual ABMC memorials. Concerns similar to those involving the Belleau chapel arose at Bony and Romagne. In the former case, the principal question was where to place the building. The chapel was originally intended for a central position at the lower end of the "long axis" of the site—namely, at the bottom edge of the sloping ground in which the remains of 1,844 soldiers were buried in four rectangular blocs. After his own visit in 1927, the chairman recommended to the commission that the chapel be repositioned at the end of the "short axis" of the cemetery, halfway up the slope along the outer perimeter of the site, meaning that a visitor could enter the graves area through the main gate and proceed on a straight line across the grave blocs, past the centrally located flagpole, directly to the chapel.[31]

When the commissioners agreed to this revised plan, architect George Howe asked for more time to study the matter.[32] Two meetings later, in February 1928, and freshly returned from his own visit to the site, Howe persuaded the commission (by a 4–2 vote, with Pershing abstaining) to keep the Bony chapel at the end of the cemetery's "long axis" after all. At that same meeting Howe also won unanimous approval for the design of the chapel, after he had reviewed it in light of his recent inspection of the site.[33]

Pershing's concern about the chapel at Romagne was that it was too high and too broad—in other words, "too large for its surroundings." At its especially eventful twenty-sixth meeting, the commission discussed this issue but resolved to make no specific recommendations until the chairman could confer with the architect.[34] What Pershing learned from his subsequent encounter with Louis Ayres, of the firm of York and Sawyer, was that the desired reduction of the height of the central building and the length of the loggias extending laterally from the chapel had already been made. When the general reported this to the commission at its January 1928 meeting, the members approved the revised dimensions and the project went forward.[35]

The exterior designs of the eight chapels present a variety of shapes and sizes. In magnitude, the different structures generally correlate with the size of the burial grounds over which they preside. The largest chapel is in the Meuse-Argonne cemetery; the smallest is in the Flanders Field site. At Oise-Aisne and Saint-Mihiel, the second- and third-largest cemeteries, the chapels are centrally placed at the outermost (from the entrance gates) edges of the sites, and are connected to museum buildings by a semicircular colonnade (in the former case) and a circular peristyle (in the latter case). The chapel at Aisne-Marne, as already indicated, is in the shape of a tower. At Suresnes, the current chapel complex is enlarged by covered loggias extending laterally to memorial rooms devoted to each of the two world wars. (Suresnes is the only one of the original eight ABMC cemeteries with interments from both conflicts.) Before the loggias were added after 1945, the boundaries of the chapel were tightly framed by the width of the wrought iron entry gate at the bottom of the slope occupied by the burial grounds. The Brookwood and Somme chapels rise above basically square footprints in their respective locations.

The chapel interiors are unabashedly religious in their content. Each has an altar as its centerpiece—at Oise-Aisne there is actually a second one outdoors at the center of the peristyle—and Latin crosses occupy prominent places as well. At Bony, the cross in crystal glass on the rear facade of the chapel also opens into the building just above the altar and arguably stands out more than any other single feature of the structure. The cross at Meuse-Argonne is suspended above the altar, with a bank of eleven national flags beneath it. At Aisne-Marne, Oise-Aisne, and Suresnes, smaller versions of the cross stand on the altar.[36]

Additional religious symbols and inscriptions are commonplace. In the center of the altar at Bony, for instance, is embossed a wreath of grapevines encircling the symbol that, to the ancient Greeks, meant "the anointed one" (Christ).[37] Three stained glass windows above and to the left and right of the Aisne-Marne altar depict Saint Louis (one of the medieval Crusaders), Saint Michael triumphing over evil, and Saint Denis (one of the patron saints of France).[38] On the face of the interior altar at Oise-Aisne, in a circle between two marble panels, is "the carved figure of a pelican feeding her young, symbolic of Christ feeding the masses."[39] The religious inscriptions that refer to the dead are meant to console the living: "Peaceful they rest in glory" (Aisne-Marne); "I give to them eternal life and they shall never perish" (Suresnes); "With God is their reward" (Oise-

Aisne); and from the book of Hosea, "I will ransom them from the power of the grave, I will redeem them from death" (Flanders Field).[40]

Stained glass and/or mosaics adorn almost all of the chapels. "The principal decorative feature" inside the Suresnes chapel is a mosaic depicting the Angel of Victory "bearing a palm branch to the graves of the Fallen."[41] At Flanders Field, the ceiling in the small chapel is done in mosaic, and at Saint-Mihiel mosaic shields displaying the national colors of France and the United States are on the walls at both ends of the chapel.[42] Aisne-Marne boasts the largest number of stained glass windows (five). In addition to the three already mentioned, two on either side of the alcove contain the coats of arms of the United States and six of its partners during the Great War, as well as the insignia of I and II Corps and the nine divisions that fought in that region.[43] Two large windows on the eastern and western walls of the Meuse-Argonne chapel similarly honor the numerous American divisions that saw action in that great battle.[44] Insignia of the major units that participated in the First World War are also portrayed in stained glass windows on either side of the altar at the Somme cemetery.[45]

In keeping with one of the earliest purposes conceived for the chapels, panels remember the missing by listing their names and the same additional information inscribed on the marble headstones of the known dead: rank, unit, state of residence at the time of entering the service, and presumed date of death. At Brookwood (563), Aisne-Marne (1,060), Somme (333), and Oise-Aisne (241), the names are engraved into the interior stone walls of the chapels. The forty-one Flanders Field missing are engraved on panels of rose marble framed in bronze on the side walls of the chapel interior.[46] At Suresnes, four bronze panels inside the chapel contain the names of 974 Americans who were lost or buried at sea during the Great War.[47] The black marble tablets listing the 284 missing at Saint-Mihiel are mounted on the wall of the museum, with the names and other information in bronze.[48] At Meuse-Argonne, the 954 names of the missing are engraved on stone tablets in the two sheltered, but otherwise outdoor loggias. A separate panel there is devoted to those who perished without a trace during the ill-fated and little-remembered American expedition to northern Russia between 1918 and 1921.[49]

Typical inscriptions honoring the missing read: "The names here recorded are those of American soldiers who fought in this region and whose earthly resting place is known only to God" (Meuse-Argonne), or

"The names recorded on these walls are those of American soldiers who fought in this region and who sleep in unknown graves" (Oise-Aisne).[50] In areas where individual remains have been found and subsequently identified, rosettes appear by the engraved names. Such discoveries are neither systematically pursued nor specifically foreseeable, but they will undoubtedly continue to happen as the years wear on. When they occur, the next-of-kin are given the same options for burial that families were given at the end of both world wars.

Many inscriptions reveal that the cemeteries and chapels are meant not just to honor and remember the dead, but also to express the nation's gratitude for their sacrifice. Typical of passages found in the World War I chapels are these: "This memorial has been erected by the United States of America as a sacred rendezvous of a grateful people with its immortal dead" (Suresnes and Meuse-Argonne); "This chapel has been erected by the United States of America in memory of her soldiers who fought and died in Belgium during the world war. These graves are the permanent and visible symbol of the heroic devotion with which they gave their lives to the common cause of humanity" (Flanders Field); and "This chapel has been erected by the United States of America in grateful remembrance of her sons who died during the world war" (roughly word for word the same at the Somme, Oise-Aisne, and Saint-Mihiel cemeteries).[51]

Chapel artwork leaves no doubt that these edifices are also integral parts of military memorials. In addition to the adornments of a religious character and the emblems of nations and individual military units, there are innumerable carvings of soldierly articles and men in arms. At Oise-Aisne, for example, a soldier is carved above each of the outer two (of four) piers of the peristyle. Scattered about other surfaces of that structure are carvings of entrenching tools, a field telephone set, a rifle and bayonet, a gas mask, and numerous other articles that would have been familiar to any combatant.[52] The exterior of the Aisne-Marne chapel exhibits a similarly diverse array of military implements, many of which are intended to honor specific services, such as infantry, artillery, tank corps, aviation, engineers, and medical.[53]

Unlike the memorial/chapel complexes in the ABMC's World War II cemeteries, none of the World War I chapels display battle maps. Only at Saint-Mihiel and Oise-Aisne, where "museum" buildings adjoined the chapels by colonnade or peristyle and could house such exhibits, are battle maps to be found inside cemetery grounds.[54] This would not have been an issue at Suresnes or Brookwood because neither of those cemeteries lay within a battle zone. Visitors to the Meuse-Argonne, Aisne-Marne, Somme, or Flanders Field burial sites who wish to trace the combats that claimed the lives of the soldiers in the cemeteries are obliged to do so with displays on the nearby monuments—Montfaucon, Château-Thierry, Bellicourt and Cantigny, and Audenarde and Kemmel, respectively.

While most of the artwork in the World War I cemeteries is in or around the chapels, other parts of these sites, such as the entrance gates, exhibit prominent artistic touches as well. Visitors to the Somme memorial enter the graves area through an ornamental, grilled gate of bronze.[55] The Meuse-Argonne cemetery, traversed by a French departmental highway, has pillared stone entrances at its eastern and western ends. Statues of an American eagle and a Gallic rooster (*Coq Gaulois*) facing each other top the two pavilions at the western gateway.[56] The entrance to the American section of the Brookwood site is marked by two large stone urns "decorated with bald eagles with their wings outstretched," and "resting on a shield . . . evocative of the Great Seal of the United States."[57] Aisne-Marne, Saint-Mihiel, Flanders Field, Suresnes, and Oise-Aisne all have especially prominent entrances dominated in each case by stone pillars and iron gates.

Walls standing several feet high and containing decorative stonework add to the beauty of many of the cemeteries, most notably Meuse-Argonne, which is surrounded by an impressive stone barrier more than a mile and a half long. But the full commission rarely quibbled about walls, for their chief purpose was simply to set the cemeteries off from their surroundings. At some sites, metal fencing or hedges serve this purpose. Early on, the commissioners decided that General Pershing alone should resolve questions about the height and other details pertaining to walls.[58] Later, the commission asked the architects of the eight cemetery chapels to make sure that gateways and walls did not disrupt artistic harmony throughout the sites and to submit their findings directly to the chairman and the consulting architect, with Pershing fully authorized to resolve any problems.[59]

No American cemetery from the First World War is as full of individual works of art as Saint-Mihiel. In addition to what has already been mentioned, this site contains a large sculpture at the center of the memorial peristyle meant to represent an ancient funeral vase; another ornamental urn at the center of an overlook behind the memorial complex that faces toward the Montsec monument twelve miles to the southwest; a sundial, in the form of an eagle at rest, in the midst of floral gardens at the center of the four burial plots, with the motto of the American Battle Monuments Commission engraved upon its base—"Time will not dim the glory of their deeds"; and a statue along the northern perimeter containing the sculpture of a young American officer in field uniform standing against the backdrop of a sixteen-foot-high cross. This piece, whose inscription reads, *"Il dort, loin des siens, dans la douce terre de France"* ("He sleeps, far from his own, in the sweet soil of France"),[60] is the only work of privately donated art in any of the American cemeteries. The story of how it came to be there deserves recounting.

Walker Blaine Beale, an army lieutenant from Maine serving with the 78th Division, died from combat wounds on September 18, 1918, six days into the Saint-Mihiel campaign. His family chose to have him interred in the American cemetery there. Years later, the soldier's mother, Harriet Blaine Beale, independently commissioned the well-known American sculptor Paul Manship to create a statue to be placed in the cemetery to honor all the soldier dead resting there.[61] Neither her son's name nor her own appeared anywhere on the statue.

Manship completed the statue in 1928, and Mrs. Beale acted immediately to have it placed in the cemetery. Secretary Price later speculated that the small monument had cost its sponsor $40,000 and that, absent any intervention by the commission, it would have been placed in the cemetery, with or without formal approval, sometime in early July. Thomas Harlan Ellett, architect of the cemetery chapel, had already written approvingly of this placement of the statue some months earlier.[62]

The commission learned of Mrs. Beale's action in time for its twenty-ninth meeting. After "very thoroughly" considering the proposed gift, and in keeping with its already established policy of declining private gifts for display in the cemeteries, the panel rejected it.[63] General Pershing evidently did not realize for some time that Harriet Blaine Beale was the daughter of James G. Blaine, secretary of state to Presidents James Garfield and Chester Arthur, a former US senator from Maine, the Republican presidential nominee in 1884, and someone whom he admired. It is not known exactly when the general made this connection. When he did, however, the idea of placing the Manship statue in the Saint-Mihiel cemetery gained new life.

Secretary Price informed the commission in August 1930 that the chairman had been reviewing the matter "over a considerable period of time" and concluded that the gift of the statue should be accepted after all. As Price put it, "It will not only be a distinct addition to the cemetery but its acceptance will clear up a difficult situation." Still sensitive to the idea that the commission was violating one of its strictest precedents in accepting privately donated artwork, the secretary rationalized that "such a fine work by an outstanding sculptor which will harmonize so well with the other features of a cemetery" would likely never be offered again. There was no inconsistency between this action and the commission's refusal of another statue offered years earlier, Price continued, because the two works "are not in the same class as works of art." Dr. Cret, finally, had added his endorsement of the idea of placing the statue in the cemetery to that of architect Ellett expressed earlier.[64]

The commission minutes contain no mention of this action, suggesting that the agency's two top officers wanted no official record of it.[65] Price and Pershing apparently remained nervous for a long time about the departure from precedent that they had quietly engineered. Early in 1935, the ABMC secretary wrote the chairman that he had received "several inquiries lately" about the soldier monument at Saint-Mihiel. The most serious had come by phone from the quartermaster general's office. Price advised his superior that Mrs. Beale should be contacted, "as it is very probable she has been talking." He further counseled Pershing that "if this rumor [about the statue] has spread to any great extent, the Commission will have to remove the monument and replace it by an urn or other decorative feature."[66]

Starkly revealed within this tale is that the actions of the ABMC's original leadership were not always devoid of personal politics, and that the chairman and the secretary did not want it found out that they had operated on a double standard in the case of the Beale statue. Neither the article Pershing wrote in 1934 for *National Geographic* nor the current edition of the ABMC's informational pamphlet says anything about how this beautiful piece of art became part of the Saint-Mihiel cemetery. Whatever preferential treatment or chicanery may have put it there, in any case, cannot diminish the degree to which the statue has enhanced the beauty of the site and offered a fitting tribute to the continuing reverence of the French people for the American dead that rest forever in their "sweet soil."

One final element relating to the ABMC's beautification of the cemeteries remains to be considered—namely, the arrangement of the graves.

All five of the permanent cemeteries located on French battlefields of the Great War originated prior to the armistice as temporary burial grounds under the authority of the US Army's Graves Registration Service. When the War Department determined which sites would become permanent, work got under way to fashion the cemeteries in accordance with plans developed by the Fine Arts Commission during its own European inspection tour in 1921. Arrangement of the graves equidistant from each other, and in perfectly ordered rows, was a major part of this original blueprint. Because the repatriation of those dead whose families wanted them home coincided with this remaking of the eight burial grounds into permanent sites, the final alignment and filling in of the rows of graves could proceed in tandem. As remains were exhumed for shipment home, emptied graves could be reoccupied with bodies whose families had chosen for them to rest in Europe. While this often meant that certain of the dead needed to be exhumed and reinterred yet another time, it was necessary to produce the flawless organization of the bodies and headstones envisioned by the CFA, and which has been such an impressive feature of the American cemeteries to this day.[67]

Veterans of the 27th Division blocked efforts to realign graves at the Somme and Oise-Aisne cemeteries, however, because they objected to the movement of their dead comrades simply to improve the appearance of the permanent sites. These protests found a sympathetic ear with Assistant Secretary of War J. Mayhew Wainwright, a former officer in the division. Wainwright convened an ad hoc panel of himself, General Pershing (then army chief of staff), and the quartermaster general in 1922 that heard testimony from the objectors and decided that no more already-buried bodies would be moved within those two cemeteries. Any irregularities in the alignment of graves would simply have to be tolerated.[68]

When the ABMC inherited this situation, Secretary Price left little doubt regarding his own views on the matter. "The graves in all cemeteries, with the exception of certain sections in the Oise-Aisne and Somme, have been arranged so that the markers are equidistant apart and in rows spaced at regular intervals," he wrote in the 1925 annual report. "This regularity is very effective and adds greatly to the appearance of the cemetery. Where not regularly arranged, the effect is disturbing." Having earlier described the general condition of all the cemeteries as "satisfactory," Price clearly saw the irregularities of the graves at two of the sites as part of the "much still to be done."[69]

But the secretary's printed comments on this matter prompted a stiff rebuke from Senator Reed. "I am not sure that this irregularity seriously diminishes the beauty of the cemeteries," the latter wrote in September 1925. "I believe that both at Bony and Seringes [Oise-Aisne] it is possible to have cemeteries altogether beautiful without re-arranging these graves." The senator further objected to the disturbance of any of the graves, especially in the pursuit of purely aesthetic concerns, and told Price: "I think it is a shocking thing to be digging up the bodies of soldiers who were buried seven years ago simply in order that their headstones may be more regularly aligned."[70]

As time passed and nothing was done to eliminate the irregularities, expressions of criticism directed at the commission grew more frequent. Robert Woodside, reporting on the inspection visit he had done with fellow commissioner D. John Markey in the summer of 1926, declared that the appearance of the Oise-Aisne cemetery was "entirely spoiled" as a result of the uneven graves. He also urged that irregularly aligned interments at the Somme site "should be rearranged," and observed disapprovingly that pursuing other elements of the beautification of that cemetery was being hindered by the requirement that the graves "remain undisturbed."[71] More ordinary visitors who encountered the irregular patterns in the graves similarly objected.[72] These complaints eventually persuaded General Pershing that something needed to be done. Price informed Lieutenant North in September 1926 that the chairman "seems to feel that it was a mistake not to have arranged all graves in regular order in the first place."[73]

Accordingly, the commission voted in October 1926 to recommend that the secretary of war order the rearrangement of graves.[74] Because the Graves Registration Service would actually perform the necessary physical labor, the desired directive had to come from the War Department—and Secretary Davis complied. The decision to complete the rearrangement of the graves at the affected cemeteries happened to coincide with the final selection of Carrara marble to be the material for the permanent headstones. Once the way was cleared for the graves in all of the cemeteries to be aligned and spaced in the same manner, the permanent headstones could be so placed during the months that followed.[75]

No sooner was the ABMC's beautification of the cemeteries completed than a veterans' group sought to retrieve a body for burial in the United States. In June 1934, an Ohio chapter of 42nd Division veterans petitioned for the removal of the remains of Dyer J. Bird from plot H of the Meuse-Argonne cemetery. Private Bird was the first of that famous unit to be killed in the Great War, and the chapter that bore his name in Marion, Ohio, wanted his body to rest in a newly designed "Veterans block" of the local cemetery. The local chaplain claimed that with the interment of Bird's body there, the Marion site could serve as a "national monument to the Rainbow Division."[76]

Despite sympathy for the request expressed by then Army Chief of Staff General Douglas MacArthur, a veteran of the division,[77] the ABMC ultimately rejected it. Important national organizations lined up against the petition from the outset. The president of the Gold Star Mothers Association, Mathilda Burling, and the national commander of the American Legion, E. A. Hayes, declared themselves firmly against the Ohio group's request. "If a pole [sic] of all Gold Star Mothers were taken," Burling wrote to the secretary of war, "I feel that they would emphatically protest the removal of a single body or the disturbance of the beauty and peace of any cemetery overseas."[78] The American Legion commander echoed the belief that "there should be no desecration of their graves," and also noted that since those resting in the overseas cemeteries were there "by the consent of their nearest of kin," no outside authority should be allowed to move them.[79] At its May 1935 meeting, after hearing in person from Rainbow Division veterans, the Pershing board decided once and for all that "no removal of any body from any of these cemeteries should be permitted under any conditions whatever."[80]

The creation of the national monuments overseas entailed its own challenges. According to Thomas North, the commission's decision to build the monuments at locations separate from the cemeteries "conformed to the practice of the epoch." The British, French, and Belgians had all made the same decision.[81] Proceeding in this manner meant that the Americans would have to acquire eleven additional parcels of land and set up the same number of independent construction sites and design processes. New treaties with the host countries were also necessary to facilitate the acquisition of land for the monuments and to establish the terms for its use by the US government. To this end, diplomatic agreements were signed with France and Belgium, respectively, in August and October 1929 that sold to the host governments for a single unit of their currency the monument sites the Americans had privately purchased, then ceded them back to the United States for perpetual use as war memorials free of rent or taxation. Exceptions to this arrangement could come when a host government chose to cede land for an American memorial from its own public domain free of any charge.[82]

Eight of the eleven monuments were located where Americans had actually fought during the closing months of the war. The Meuse-Argonne monument crowns the heights of Montfaucon, won by Pershing's doughboys on September 27, 1918, the second day of the battle, and rests amid the ruins of a completely destroyed village by the same name. In similar fashion, the Saint-Mihiel monument occupies the summit of the *butte de Montsec*, a commanding point on the battlefield where American soldiers won their first major success as an independent fighting force earlier in the war's final September. The third of the three "large" ABMC monuments overlooks the Marne River outside Château-Thierry from Hill 204, a hotly contested point in the early days of American participation in the Aisne-Marne battle of late spring and early summer 1918. In keeping with guidelines laid out by the commission in 1925 for the siting of its own monuments, each one of this trio of edifices can be seen for miles in a manner that is bound to attract notice and, it is also to be hoped, visitors.

The five smaller battlefield monuments, while less prominent in size and location, nonetheless occupy sites of considerable importance to the story of the nation's involvement in the Great War. The Cantigny monument sits in the center square of the French village taken by the 1st Division in May 1918 in the first successful offensive action by American troops. In the Somme sector, the monument at Bellicourt straddles a tunnel for the Saint Quentin canal that was part of the Hindenburg Line defenses pierced by American troops fighting under British command in the early autumn of 1918. At Sommepy, a small, castle-like tower sits amid German trenches and dugouts atop Blanc Mont, taken by Pershing's troops during the final battle of Champagne five weeks before the armistice. In Belgium, the smallest of the ABMC's battlefield monuments occupy sites at Kemmel and Audenarde, where Americans fought, respectively, under British and Belgian command during the decisive Allied advance of the war's final weeks.

Of the nine army monuments, the only one not on a battle site commemorates the Services of Supply headquartered in Tours. The remaining two components of the ABMC project for the Great War are naval monuments—a tower built into the ramparts defending Brest, primary port of entry for the AEF in western France, and an archway in the network of steps connecting the upper and lower parts of Gibraltar meant to honor the achievements of the US Navy in the Mediterranean and its unique comradeship with its British counterpart.

The commission agreed to ten of these eleven sites at a trio of meetings during the final two months of 1925. Dr. Cret and Secretary Price had returned from their summer inspection tour with recommendations for the siting of each of the monuments proposed at that time. The commissioners actually approved a total of fifteen placements (even though a third of that number would never be built) before the year was out. In view of General Pershing's absence in South America, these approvals were understood to be provisional until he could review and ratify them.[83] As it happened, the location of the Sommepy monument had to await the chairman's on-the-ground inspection during the summer of 1926, and the definitive siting of the Montfaucon monument in 1928 was also made subject to Pershing's judgment alone after protracted difficulties with the French over a variety of issues.[84] The location of the Audenarde memorial, originally agreed on at the fifteenth ABMC meeting in November 1925, was changed to its present spot in October 1926 after the commission voted to take over the site vacated when the Pennsylvania commission decided to abandon its own plans for a commemorative structure there.[85] The Gibraltar memorial, finally, was not sited or designed until the end of 1929.[86]

In November 1925 the commissioners had named fourteen different architects or architectural firms for what was then twenty-seven design projects, eight of which were the cemetery chapels and nineteen of which were monuments, including all but one (Gibraltar) of the eleven ultimately built. All of the ABMC's architects had their offices in Boston, New York, Philadelphia, or Chicago. New Yorker John Russell Pope secured the largest of the monument projects at Montfaucon. In this first round of assignments, Dr. Cret took on the designs for Aisne-Marne and two smaller sites, but he ultimately accepted the Bellicourt and Gibraltar projects after the monuments at Juvigny and south of Soissons originally given to him were abandoned. Egerton Swartwout of New York, initially assigned the chapel at Brookwood cemetery and the monument (never built) in London, took over the Montsec project after Cass Gilbert, the first choice of the commission, declined it.[87] Arthur Loomis Harmon of New York completed the monuments at Tours, Cantigny, and Sommepy, although Philadelphian Harry Sternfeld had been the original choice for the latter assignment. The Philadelphia firm of Mellor, Meigs, and Howe undertook the Kemmel project, and Sternfeld did the one at Audenarde. After the death of Chicagoan Howard Van Doren Shaw in 1926, surviving members of his firm took on the design and completion of the Brest monument.[88]

Lieutenant Thomas North, working out of the commission's Paris office, was authorized to secure the land for each of the monument sites.[89] He claimed in his memoir that, in general, "the French and Belgian people and officials with whom we dealt were both sympathetic and fair," and that "difficulties were by far the exception."[90] But certain parcels were particularly hard to obtain from their private owners, sometimes because of greed, sometimes because of the need to gain the approval of scores of different owners of the desired site, and sometimes because political issues intruded upon the transactions.

The clearest case of greed involved the procurement of the site for the Kemmel monument, often referred to as the Ypres monument because the more famous of the two towns is only six miles away. North later described this edifice as "a minor monument along a main highway." The local burgomaster demanded such a high price for the desired plot that the ABMC officer refused to pay it. "Fortuitously," North later recounted, "a far preferable site" in a neighboring town (Vierstraat) was offered as a gift by its local authorities, and the monument was ultimately placed there.[91]

Acquisition of the sites for large monuments at Château-Thierry and Saint-Mihiel was complicated by the size of the needed parcels, the staggering number of owners due to the repeated subdivision of holdings, and the blurring of property lines with the passage of years. The former of the American structures required twenty-seven acres, and the latter forty-two acres plus the trace for a winding approach road to the three hundred-foot-high summit of Montsec. North reckoned that the Château-Thierry site was composed of 575 different parcels, while the Saint-Mihiel site included 1,000 separate lots. Assuming all of the owners could even be identified, they also had to be located, contacted, and brought to agree on a reasonable price for their holdings. The Paris office employed local notaries to assist in contacting the owners and bringing them to terms, but the process in these two cases was especially onerous.[92]

Once they had agreed to sell to the Americans, the local owners were so slow about signing over deeds for the Montsec site that construction of the approach road and monument itself was held up even after contracts had been let. Impatient to get to work, one of the contractors, with North's permission, paid a local official to pass through the streets of villages with a bugler and drummer to announce that, the next day, the Americans would furnish transportation to nearby Commercy, where the landowners could register the required signatures. Wine was to be provided along the way to sign the deeds over to the Americans. According to North's account, the French owners complied "without exception," and the way was cleared for the commission to take possession of the land.[93]

Political controversies during the mid-1920s held up the ABMC's acquisition of its desired monument site at Tours. The city council, dominated by leftists ("quite pink" was North's characterization), initially blocked the project. When the American officer pressed to know why, a local professor also active in politics told him that the "grasping, cold-blooded attitude" of the United States toward repayment of war debts "had forfeited the sympathy of the middle classes," and "the bloodthirsty treatment of the innocent Sacco and Vanzetti" had "alienated . . . the working classes."[94] Not to be deterred, North lobbied local newspaper editors and appeared personally before the executive committee of the city council. The American officer persuaded the skeptical Tours politicians to change their stance on the grounds that the proposed monument would bring tourists, especially veterans, from the United States to their city, would create jobs for the area's construction workers, and would pay tribute to the excellent relationship between local citizens and the thousands of Americans who served there during the war. He also pointed out that the monument had "nothing whatsoever to do with the Sacco-Vanzetti trials, and very little [to do] with war debts." A promise by the Americans that the monument would recall only the logistics of the war, not the actual fighting, also smoothed the final approval of the project.[95]

If it was sometimes a challenge to obtain monument sites, on at least one occasion a large tract of historically important French land came unsolicited into the commission's possession.[96] As 1931 came to an end, ownership of the entirety of Belleau Wood passed to the ABMC from a private association that had purchased it a decade earlier but could not keep itself adequately funded. On the heels of an impressive ceremony in 1923 that transferred ownership across the Atlantic, interest among tourists in Belleau Wood had declined into the middle of the decade. Whereas Charles Moore reported in 1923 that twenty-five thousand people had visited the site the previous year, the superintendent of the neighboring Aisne-Marne cemetery, Adolph Kaess, reckoned that roughly half that number had come in 1925.[97]

The first approach from the association leadership about a possible ABMC takeover of Belleau Wood came in the spring of 1926. General Pershing replied to Elizabeth Van Rensselaer Frazer that his agency, then in the midst of acquiring sites for its own monuments, was reluctant to assume control of any more property.[98] Three years later, General James Harbord, the new president of the Memorial Association, inquired anew of General Pershing about the ABMC's willingness to take possession of Belleau Wood. The commission refused to make a decision, however, until a "thorough study" could be made.[99] There matters stood into the first months of the new decade until the persistent effects of the economic downturn pushed the private group to the brink of insolvency. On March 10, 1931, General Harbord formally petitioned the ABMC to purchase Belleau Wood for one dollar.[100] As if the dire condition of the association needed additional confirmation, a *Washington Post* story six weeks later foretold the closure of the hallowed site on June 30, 1931, due to lack of funding.[101]

General Pershing polled his fellow commissioners in March 1931 and discovered almost unequivocal support for the acquisition of this "sacred spot."[102] Secretary Price later reminded the chairman that the ABMC should not acquire title to the land until it was unencumbered by outstanding obligations.[103] Once this condition was satisfied by the defunct association, Belleau Wood finally became the property of the American Battle Monuments Commission on November 30, 1931.[104]

It could be said that the two hundred-acre tract amounts to a twelfth monument site acquired by the ABMC after the First World War to honor the outstanding service of American soldiers. Since 1955, a monument to the 4th Marine Brigade, "a black granite stele to which has been affixed a life-size bronze relief . . . of a Marine attacking with rifle and bayonet," has occupied a clearing in the center of Belleau Wood.[105] The inspiration for that commemorative structure came from a 1953 visit by the commandant of the marine corps, who "noted with deep concern" that no mention of the unit of June 1918 fame was to be found anywhere in the Aisne-Marne cemetery, the chapel, or the Wood itself.[106] A formal request by the marine corps to erect such a monument was approved by the ABMC in March 1954, and the finished work was dedicated on November 18,

1955.[107] It is significant that the idea for such a memorial edifice had not originated earlier, but worth recalling that the Pershing-era commission held firm to its rule that the ABMC would not approve monuments that honored units smaller than a division.

The commission approved designs for the first generation of its own monuments between its twentieth meeting (October 1926) and its thirty-first meeting (December 1929). The erratic path toward a definitive design for the Montsec monument reveals a great deal about how the ABMC and CFA worked together in such matters, and about how the architects sought to bring to fruition the agencies' vision for a national program of commemorative structures. Egerton Swartwout submitted three different designs for the edifice atop Montsec in a five-page memorandum prepared for the commission's last meeting of 1926. "Design A" called for a circular colonnade in classical form seventy-five feet high from ground to top. "Design B" offered a similarly classical model for a rectangular structure resting on an elevated platform and ringed by columns twenty-four feet high supporting a thick roof reminiscent of the Lincoln Memorial. "Design C" proposed a simple shaft seventy feet high.[108]

The architect's recommendation to the ABMC was "Design B," and the ABMC initially agreed with the architect's advice.[109] Within two weeks, the Fine Arts Commission had reviewed the same three designs and registered its vote for "Design A," citing its belief that "a circular colonnade is best adapted to the topography [of Montsec]."[110] Upon hearing this news, the architect wrote Secretary Price that he would be glad "to build the round scheme," but "extremely sorry" if he could not build the rectangular one. Swartwout also opined that the CFA might have arrived at its recommendation in undue haste, a suspicion Price, who had attended the Fine Arts meeting on January 8, later echoed.[111]

At the ABMC secretary's request, Swartwout patiently prepared a new and expanded defense of his and the Pershing commission's preference for the rectangular structure. His overall desire was "to submit to your Board something that would fit the site and be appropriate; not too elaborate or grandiose; something that could be built within the appropriation, and also something that would be original and different from any memorial that has been erected." He made clear that his designs were the product of firsthand inspection of the site, viewing it from every perspective, and careful study "off and on for a year and a half" of maps and photographs of the "detailed contours" of where the monument was to rest.[112]

At Secretary Price's request, the Fine Arts Commission agreed to reconsider its own recommendation. In February 1927, Chairman Moore and a number of his fellow commissioners came to New York City to confer with Swartwout. The architect presented his case for the rectangular design so effectively that he later wrote Price: "I am inclined to think from what Mr. Moore and the others said, that they will agree with us . . . [and] co-operate in every way with your Commission."[113] A letter from Chairman Moore to the ABMC secretary confirmed Swartwout's impression that the CFA would indeed reverse its position on the two schemes, clearing the way for the realization of the rectangular design.[114]

When General Pershing revisited Montsec later in the year with "Design B" in his mind, he came away with doubts. The chairman feared that the scale of this proposal was too small to give the desired impression of grandeur when seen from a far distance, and not large enough to merit its place as the second-most-important commemorative structure (to Montfaucon) in the overall scheme. During the closing weeks of 1927, Swartwout met General Pershing in the latter's Washington office. The chairman placed scale models of the three "large" ABMC monuments side by side in order to demonstrate to the architect his sense that the twice-approved design for Montsec was too small. Swartwout afterward conceded to Pershing that "in seeing the models in close proximity there was no question that the scale of the original seemed nearly half the scale of Montfaucon and Château Thierry."[115]

The architect immediately set out to produce a new design modeled on the circular shape of the original "Design A." The height of the columns was raised from twenty-four feet (in "Design B") to forty-two feet. Instead of the statue originally envisioned for the center of the rectangular colonnade of "Design B," the new concept called for a relief map of the Saint-Mihiel battlefield as the centerpiece, thus opening up the high space within the colonnade and creating a more impressive effect when viewed from the surrounding plain. Even though Swartwout understood that no observer would ever be able to compare all three of the commission's large monuments by seeing them together in the same space, he could not deny the epiphany he had had when viewing the trio of models in Pershing's office. "I feel sure that it would be a mistake to adhere to the original scheme," he later told the general, and he proceeded most agreeably with the modified design.[116]

Both commissions ratified the revised plan for the monument in January 1928.[117] The Fine Arts commissioners' new verdict could not have been difficult for them, for as Swartwout had reminded General Pershing, the newly proposed concept was "very similar to but an improvement on the original scheme they all preferred."[118] When the final design found its way to a completed structure four years later, Secretary Price was especially effusive in his praise of it. "The monument is one of the most impressive that I have ever seen," he wrote Pershing. "It is a great success and is worthy of all care and money spent on it."[119]

Initial concerns about the size of the Aisne-Marne monument were more easily dispelled. Dr. Cret designed this structure in the form of a rectangular double colonnade, with a massive American eagle on its east facade (looking toward the Marne River valley) and "heroic size figures [clasping hands] representative of France and the United States and the longstanding unity and friendship between the two nations" on its west face.[120] The architect's preliminary design won the commission's unanimous approval on October 9, 1926.[121] Within three days the design was forwarded to the Fine Arts Commission and quickly approved there.[122]

Early in December, however, General Pershing expressed concern that the original scale of Cret's concept threatened to be more impressive than the column planned for the Meuse-Argonne sector. After the ABMC ratified a scaled-down version of Cret's design on December 21, Price was obliged to go back to the CFA to ask anew for its approval.[123] But the latter panel balked at diminishing Cret's original design. In the words of Chairman Moore, he and his colleagues "regard it as a mistake to reduce the size of the monument, which is none too large to be effective in the landscape."[124] In the end, a design that sized the structure between Cret's original scale and the ABMC's reduced version won approval.[125] But, once again, Pershing had demonstrated that no monument would be built until he was satisfied with the details of its design.

One of the most important decisions about an inscription for any ABMC monument was made for the one at Château-Thierry. Under the sculpted eagle on the east facade, at eye level for visitors, is a map designed by Dr. Cret depicting the position of US forces in the Aisne-Marne region on July 18, 1918, when the first of the major Allied counteroffensives began, and also showing the ground gained thereafter. This map and the orientation table directly across the stone platform on which the monument rests comprise the most significant portion of the educational content built into this structure. Between the base of the eagle and the top of the map is space for an inscription. The architect's initial suggestion was for the following wording: "Time passes but deeds endure."[126] Six months later, Secretary Price informed Dr. Cret that the inscription would read: "Time will not dim the glory of their deeds."[127] General Pershing is commonly acknowledged as the author of this revised version.

The submission of bids for the Aisne-Marne monument caused the ABMC leadership concern that significant cost overruns would be necessary to build the desired structure. In June 1928, Secretary Price informed General Pershing that the lowest bidder on the proposed edifice had exceeded by $80,000 the allotted amount of $230,000. The worried subordinate attributed the high price to general increases in the cost of construction in France during the three years since the original budgetary grant from Congress. As he was loathe to recommend scrapping Dr. Cret's design for the monument, however, Price told the chairman that the commission would simply have to take the federal budget director and key congressmen "into its confidence" in hopes of securing the needed augmentation of funds.[128]

General Pershing concurred in this analysis and requested that Price formulate an estimate of the necessary funding increases for him to take personally to the budget director (Herbert Mayhew Lord). The chairman imagined that a total supplement of $500,000 might be required to cover the totality of overruns at monument sites, especially when the higher costs of "walls, landscape gardening, . . . and interiors" (presumably of the cemetery chapels) were taken into account. "I do not anticipate any difficulty in having the authorization increased by this amount," Pershing observed, "or more if we need it." The most important consideration always had to be the standard for the material and workmanship that went into the overseas monuments. "Regardless of cost we *must* not think of lowering the quality of the material for these memorials," Pershing continued, "which we hope are to stand for the rest of time. I wish especially that the foundation should be like the very Rock of Ages."[129]

As could have been anticipated from the extent of the chairman's involvement in the details of design for other monuments in the ABMC project, Pershing took an especially strong interest in what happened at Montfaucon. The monument there required the largest single share of the commission's resources, the leadership's energy, and also time to build. From approval of the architect's initial design, through selection and acquisition of the site, construction of the monument, fashioning the artwork on it, to the engraving of inscriptions took almost seven years. Along the way, a daunting array of difficulties had to be overcome.

The commission awarded the design for its most prominent monument to one of the most renowned American architects of his generation, New Yorker John Russell Pope. As testimony to his professional standing, Pope had served on the Fine Arts Commission from 1912 to 1922. His two most famous creations—the National Archives building and the Jefferson Memorial in Washington, D.C.—actually came after his ABMC work was finished. But the Montfaucon edifice originated during an undeniably high stage of Pope's repute. This did not mean, however, that the architect had much awareness of the work that had been entrusted to the Pershing commission. Five months after he had been selected for the Montfaucon assignment, Paul Cret saw the need to instruct him on the fundamentals of the overseas memorial project, including some surprisingly suggestive counsel about the kind of monument that would best suit the Meuse-Argonne site.

The consulting architect revealed much about his own understanding of the purpose and significance of the ABMC's monuments in one of his early letters to Pope. The edifice Pope was engaged to design, Cret wrote, should be "purely a decorative monument with, of course, a dignified character." Above all, it should be "suitable for the site." There would be inscriptions on it that would be agreed upon later. Battle maps would also be part of the site, "for the tourists," but they need not figure in the basic design of the monument. Because the structure was to be sited amid the preserved ruins of a village, there would be little opportunity for landscaping. The monument would rest upon a terrace, but not occupy a very great area. To Cret, this meant that it "will probably be fairly high." Given all of the foregoing, the consulting architect conceded that his new partner in the memorial project might well settle upon a tall shaft as the most suitable design, but insisted that he was not suggesting this "unless you feel it is the proper thing to do." Dr. Cret's summary advice: "Do something beautiful." "This is the most important monument erected by the Commission," Pope was told, "and for this very reason it has been entrusted to you."[130]

Pope submitted a white Doric column topped by a statue representing "liberty" as his design, and the commission approved it during its final meeting of 1926. The Fine Arts Commission did likewise in early January.[131] Within a year's time, however, and after revisiting the site, General

Pershing proposed that the monument, most particularly the statue atop it, should be turned from facing west to facing south, the direction from which his doughboys had come in September 1918 on the way to taking Montfaucon hill.[132] Concern also arose among the ABMC commissioners that the scale model of Pope's column, when considered alongside similar models of the Montsec and Aisne-Marne structures, "did not take its rightful place as the most imposing memorial." To ensure that the monument conveyed the message that it stood on the AEF's greatest battlefield, the suggestion was made to increase its height by twenty feet.[133]

In the wake of these proposed changes, Otto Eggers, Pope's representative before the commission, promised to assess the feasibility of turning the monument, but admitted that the topography of the existing site on the western slope of the hill might rule out the change. He was also skeptical of adding twenty more feet to the column, noting that Doric shafts "have a limit as to their proper height." Eggers did suggest, however, that there was another site more suitable to accommodating these changes on the southern edge of the ruins of the village church, more toward the center of the hill and at a point where the ground sloped more steeply.[134] After Pope's office had worked out the desired changes, and the CFA ratified them, the ABMC voted to authorize its chairman "to select such site on Montfaucon as he thought best and to give final approval to such site as he might select."[135] With Pershing's blessing, the monument stands today on the alternate location originally envisioned by Otto Eggers.

Acquisition of the monument site from the French government brought its own complexities. Lieutenant North first inquired about placing an American monument on the crest of the war-torn hill in October 1925.[136] But it was June 1927 before the French government gave the ABMC permission to build there, and August 1938, a year after the finished edifice was dedicated, before all remaining issues regarding the terms by which the Americans would possess the site were definitively settled.

The most difficult problem stemmed from the fact that the desired site was a war ruin. Authorities in Paris had already set aside Montfaucon "to perpetuate for all time an object-lesson of the devastation of the war." They feared that a major construction project would spoil that effect.[137] With broken stones, standing remnants of walls and foundations from the devastated village, and irregular ground from the heavy shelling present at the site, moreover, there were also liability concerns about possible accidents that might befall visitors. As if such plainly visible issues were not enough to frustrate the American interest in obtaining the site, the bad feeling between Washington and Paris during the mid-1920s over payment of war debts left French authorities ill disposed to do favors for any agency of the US government.[138]

The prefect of the Meuse endorsed the idea of an American monument on Montfaucon by the end of 1926. This important local official even assured Lieutenant North that he would veto any effort by the French to build a memorial on the same site.[139] Clearance from Paris was still slow to come. Secretary Price put John Russell Pope on notice in February 1927 that if a deal could not be reached to place the structure he had designed on Montfaucon, the monument "will be erected at some similar site in the vicinity, and the same specifications and working drawings will apply to the new site."[140]

A month later, General Pershing, accompanied by Dr. Cret, made his first trip of the new year to the French capital in hopes of concluding an agreement on "this question and those related to other monuments."[141] The decree authorizing the construction of the monument "on the territory of the commune of Montfaucon" was issued on June 17.[142] But it took more than a decade longer to resolve all the details of how the Americans would actually possess the land, and to determine that the US government, not the French, would assume full responsibility for preservation of the war ruins and any accident liability on the site.[143]

As construction progressed, new issues came to the fore. General Pershing's first look at a model of the statue that was to surmount the monument proved especially unsettling. The Fine Arts Commission had approved the design for the figure representing "liberty" on February 12, 1931, one day after Major Price had sent them photographs of the sketch model made by sculptor A. A. Weinman of New York.[144] It is unclear why the ABMC chairman did not react to depictions of the proposed statue for more than a hundred days thereafter. But when he finally did, nearly two months into his annual European inspection tour, Pershing telegraphed his strenuous disapproval.

Weinman's initial conception of the sculpture atop the Doric column had the figure's head bent downward and tilted slightly to the right, with its right index finger in contact with its right temple, as if it were in deep thought or reflection.[145] Pershing took the pose to suggest that the statue meant to convey sadness over the losses of the bloody Meuse-Argonne battle. He wired Price in the most urgent terms: "It [the figure] should not represent grief or similar emotion but should symbolize either an ideal for which the soldiers fought such as liberty or the results attained victory or something typical of the American Army during the World War." The general further instructed his subordinate to give this matter "immediate continuous personal attention from now on" and to notify him "at once" if the sculptor was not deemed competent to complete the project satisfactorily.[146]

The chairman's cable was forwarded to John Russell Pope in London. Pope confessed that the model of the statue conformed to a design he had personally suggested to Weinman. The architect believed that a form reminiscent of Rodin's *Penseur* ("Thinker") would convey the desired impression of "power, justice, and liberty." Pope conceded, however, that the statue should be modified "if the figure carries the impression of grief or similar emotion."[147]

Secretary Price's prescription for the way to address Pershing's concern was to get Dr. Cret more involved. The characteristic competence and forbearance of the consulting architect indeed played no small part in resolving this particular problem. Cret quickly saw that "a change in the arm of the figure [atop the monument]" would alter the appearance from "an expression of grief" to one of "achievement." He assured Secretary Price that Pope and Weinman would start at once on a new model, and suggested that Pershing plan on visiting the sculptor's studio upon his return from European travels at the end of the summer.[148]

Pope soon confirmed that Weinman had produced a "modified model for the Montfaucon figure" that eliminated "the quality objected to."[149] Cret echoed this assessment after visiting Weinman's studio and inspecting the new model firsthand. The statue was now to face straightaway to the south, as if gazing into the infinity of space and time, with head upright and right hand extended skyward as it clutched "the laurel of victory." The consulting architect reported that there was "a decision and alertness in the movement of the figure, which was lacking in the original model," and assured Price that "it has my unqualified approval."[150] Within a week, Charles Moore had brought members of the Fine Arts Commission to Weinman's studio and endorsed the new model.[151]

All that remained was for Pershing to signal his concurrence, which he did by the end of August based principally on Dr. Cret's recommendation.[152] Once back from Europe in early October, the general confirmed that he was "much pleased with the new figure" after seeing six photographs of it and after a firsthand inspection of models in Weinman's New York studio.[153] The chairman's insistence that the accomplishments of his troops be commemorated in the manner he judged most fitting had prevailed yet again.

When the statue was mounted on the monument a year later, a new problem surfaced. The body was positioned such that it faced twenty-five degrees to the west of straight south.[154] Secretary Price, increasingly impatient to see the monument finished, responded to this latest setback with rebukes aimed at both the sculptor and the project's architect. Price was especially irritated that instructions from Pope's office had not clearly communicated to the workers at the site how the statue was supposed to face. While assuring himself that the statue could be repositioned "without too much trouble," Pershing's subordinate did not avoid undiplomatic language. "The whole affair seems quite ridiculous," Price observed. "An experienced architect, a sculptor of reputation, a highly-paid local representative and an extensive Commission organization in Paris and yet no instructions were given as to the facing of the statue."[155] Nor was sculptor Weinman completely immune from the secretary's ire. At the end of a seven-page summation addressed to him, Price observed that "turning a 45 ton statue, 160 feet in the air" had not been easy after all, but had been accomplished.[156] Pope's final return salvo expressed regret, but steadfastly refused to accept responsibility for the error and made clear his own irritation with Price's criticism.[157]

Another round of contentiousness between the ABMC secretary and the architect developed over the placement of inscriptions on the Montfaucon monument. One of the rationales commonly used by the commission when it refused to permit petitioning groups to construct monuments commemorating individual American divisions was that the *national* program would make its own provision for such remembrance in detail. Indeed, the other seven battlefield monuments the agency built on the old Western Front together made specific mention by name of the two American armies, two corps, two engineer battalions, one French corps, and at least nineteen US divisions.[158] For reasons that are not entirely clear, however, the Doric column and its approaches were designed and almost completely constructed before anyone had decided definitively upon the content and placement of the inscriptions.[159] When the commission's Historical Section began producing content for the inscriptions, Secretary Price approached John Russell Pope for his counsel on how best to incorporate the engravings into the facing of the monument, and the architect was not at all inclined to be helpful. The "inscriptions now proposed should have been a part of the original program and then properly provided for," Pope complained. The architect also declared the location for the bulk of the inscriptions along the base plinths of the monument to be "most unsuitable" and "damaging to the [architectural] design."[160]

Price continued for the next couple of months to consult with Pope over the placement of the inscriptions, but the secretary's insistence that they be engraved at the base of the monument completely alienated the testy architect. Dr. Cret was similarly unable to bring Pope to support the views of the commission leadership on this matter.[161] The secretary ultimately recommended that the commission should work out a solution itself, with only Dr. Cret's involvement.[162] Three months later the Pershing board voted to do just that.[163] As Price had put the matter to the chairman a few days before the commission meeting: "The situation is approaching absurdity with the monument finished and not a single inscription in shape to be carved."[164]

Within a few weeks of the full commission's intervention, Price reported from Paris that carving was under way for the inscriptions, and he predicted that they would look "exceptionally well." The secretary concluded that the final touches on the monument would make the whole structure "very impressive." He added, with evident satisfaction: "Recently we have been overrun there with visitors."[165]

The inscriptions whose placement caused John Russell Pope so much distress were the most elaborate and extensive of any of the World War I memorials built by the ABMC. Twenty-three individual divisions, and the most important locations where each one had seen action, found mention along the base of the monument. Five French units that fought alongside the Americans and two US divisions held in reserve are also commemorated there. A description nearly three hundred words long of the American operations in the Meuse-Argonne sector greets visitors inside the vestibule at the bottom of the stairs that ascend to the top of the column. A lengthy personal tribute from General Pershing to his troops is also mounted on one of the vestibule walls. Finally, on the northeast wall of the vestibule is a map of the region that depicts in detail the positions and paths of advance of each of the American divisions in the great battle.[166]

When Secretary Price recounted and critiqued the construction process for the ABMC memorials (cemetery chapels and monuments) in his

1938 report, he did not mention cantankerous American architects as one of the chief challenges that had to be overcome. Rather, he cited as major obstacles along the way the "differences in language and customs"; the scarcity of American personnel who were both competent to supervise construction work and fluent in French; the fact that French and Belgian contractors were not bonded; habitual collusion in bidding, especially among Parisian contractors; and generally lower construction standards than in the United States. Even though all of these difficulties were present throughout the seven years it took to complete the commission's building program, Price took heart that "the results obtained are considered equal to that of similar work in the United States, and the project was completed without a single case of dishonesty or financial irregularity among the personnel of the Commission's organization." By the time of Price's "Final Report," the ABMC had "no outstanding financial disputes with any of the contractors who worked on its construction project in Europe," and all payments it had made to overseas and American suppliers had passed muster with the comptroller general.[167]

General Pershing's 1934 article in *National Geographic* magazine introduced the nation's newly built overseas memorials to the American people. At the conclusion of that abundantly illustrated and exceptionally comprehensive piece, the AEF commander expressed to the mothers and other relatives of the soldier dead, especially, but to "every American citizen" as well, an enduring commitment: "that the United States Government has kept and will continue to maintain its trust in perpetuating the memory of the bravery and sacrifices of our World War heroes. 'Time will not dim the glory of their deeds.'"[168] At the first meeting of the commission since the completion of construction, and mere days before the general's article appeared, expressions of "great satisfaction" came from Commissioners Hill and Markey, who had just returned from viewing the new memorials. The chairman expressed to that same meeting his own "satisfaction with the manner in which it [the overseas work] has been done."[169]

Almost four more years passed before each of the memorial sites was dedicated. Those long-awaited occasions would afford the commission an even grander stage on which to showcase its collection of commemorative structures. The fulfillment of the ABMC's original mandate would also bring to the fore hard questions about the agency's future.

4

The Completion of the ABMC's Original Mission and Looking toward an Uncertain Future, 1937–1938

By the middle of the 1930s, construction of the European cemeteries and monuments was all but finished, and the American Battle Monuments Commission stood on the verge of fulfilling its original mandate to create sites commemorating the nation's service and sacrifices in the First World War. Significant tasks remained unfinished. None of the new memorials had been formally dedicated. The new guidebook, in preparation since the previous decade, was still not ready to go to press. Secretary Xenophon Price knew also that he would have to prepare a final report for the president of the United States. This task stood to be more onerous because only three annual reports had ever been compiled, with the most recent of them coming in 1926.

But the creation of overseas memorials had always been the chief reason for the existence of the commission, and as construction crews departed the completed sites, speculation inevitably arose about the agency's future. The ABMC leadership sensed most keenly at this time that the commission's days might be numbered. Once the agency accomplished what it was created to do, there would be little reason for it to continue to exist. Reports in the press made it appear that the completion of the European sites would not only mean the end of the commission,[1] but also the definitive retirement from public service of John J. Pershing. The aging general of the armies fueled such speculation about himself when he told an interviewer in July 1937 that the dedication of the ABMC memorials "will complete my work."[2] As the 1930s progressed, Pershing seemed convinced that the same would be true for the small agency he had led from the start.

All of the ABMC memorials were dedicated between May and October 1937. Price drafted the commission's final report and left his post as secretary in January 1938. The updated and revised guidebook at last found its way into print in April 1939. In the aftermath of President Roosevelt's first reelection, however, a new threat to the longevity of the commission materialized when the White House set out to streamline the national administration by merging smaller agencies like the ABMC into larger departments. In the event that fulfillment of its original mandate was not sufficient cause for disbanding the commission, Congress and the president seemed poised to take away its independence in the name of bureaucratic efficiency.

Yet, none of the developments that presaged the demise of the commission as an autonomous agency brought about either its extinction or its absorption into some larger government department. Instead, the dedication of the nineteen overseas sites proved to be the most important moment for the ABMC since its creation. Its place at the very center of the national commemoration of the twentieth anniversary of American entry into the Great War garnered extensive press coverage that highlighted the importance of the commission's work as never before. A Congress increasingly suspicious of President Roosevelt's motives and ambitions, moreover, frustrated the bulk of his plan for restructuring the federal government and rescued the ABMC from the administrative chopping block. And finally, General Pershing would overcome a near-fatal bout of illness in early 1938 and continue for another ten years as the ABMC chairman. The extremely high personal standing that the venerable old soldier enjoyed with his countrymen and with his commander in chief may actually have been the commission's ultimate salvation, about the same time as a new European war was breaking out with its own uncertain prospects for the involvement of the United States and for the security of the nation's brand new collection of overseas war memorials.

The formal dedication of the ABMC sites, in the twentieth year after the United States had entered the Great War and in the fifteenth year after the agency's founding, was a major step toward completion of the commission's work. Apart from their actual design and construction, the official inauguration of the cemetery chapels and battle monuments was the largest of all the agency's undertakings before World War II necessitated a new round of construction. General Pershing gave dedicatory addresses at the two most important memorials—the cemetery at Romagne, largest of all the burial sites, and the monument at Montfaucon that commemorated the bloodiest of America's battles. Sixteen Americans delivered dedicatory addresses at the other European memorials, and dozens of other speakers from the United States and the host countries, including two heads of state, made remarks as each one of the commemorative sites officially began its service.[3]

Thoughts of the dedication ceremonies naturally arose as the construction of the American memorials neared completion. The first year that the ABMC targeted for these events was 1931. Fifteen such ceremonies between May and September of that year were proposed in the early planning. Dedications of the cemetery chapel at Thiaucourt and the monuments at Brest and Tours were to be delayed the longest because those structures were taking longer to complete. Secretary Price's operating assumption was that all the memorials would be finished by May 1, 1932. He explicitly endorsed the idea that there should be no dedication until construction of the monument in question was completed.[4]

At its December 1930 meeting, the commission considered a report compiled by a special subcommittee appointed by General Pershing a month earlier. The commissioners had already abandoned the idea of dedicating any memorial in 1931 and resolved to hold all of the inaugural ceremonies in the summer of 1932. Important guiding principles for the future ceremonies were also adopted at this meeting: a dedication ceremony should be held at each site; the relative importance attached to each individual ceremony should accord with the overall importance of the memorial "in the Commission's project"; formal dedications should occur only after the monument was completed; the ceremonies "should be planned by the Commission in a modest manner"; at least one member of the commission should attend each ceremony; total speech-making should be "limited to as near twenty minutes as possible"; and arrangements should be made for Catholics, Protestants, and Jews "to have religious representation at the ceremonies in the cemeteries."[5]

Events would soon prove that the December 1930 meeting had settled very little. By the end of 1931, a full-blown debate had broken out within the ABMC leadership regarding how the dedications should be conducted. In October of that year, Major Price fired the first shot from Paris when he submitted a comprehensive report to General Pershing that contained an elaborately detailed schedule for twenty dedication ceremonies between July 18 and August 14, 1932. This plan even included ceremonies at Chaumont and Souilly, where simple commemorative tablets were to be dedicated. Price's proposal also had all seven commissioners attending all twenty ceremonies. A twenty-first event to dedicate the Gibraltar memorial was to be held "about August 20" in the presence of those commissioners who chose to travel to that more remote location. Price noted that all of the memorials "will be in good shape in time for the dedications," though not necessarily finished. Still, the secretary assured the chairman that his proposed schedule was "workable" and he recommended that it be adopted.[6]

After reviewing Price's report, James E. Mangum in the Washington office prepared a very different memorandum of his own. Mangum was not sanguine about the prospect of organizing a ceremony at each of the twenty-one memorials. "The dignity of each ceremony must be in keeping with the dignity of the United States," he wrote. "It is believed that it would be better to have no ceremony at all at a particular place than to have one which is not commensurate with the dignity of the country and occasion." Mangum emphatically concluded that it would be "*impossible* to formulate *any* plan that is both *appropriate* and *practicable*" (his emphasis) to meet this standard twenty-one times over. He recommended to General Pershing that the commission plan for "one important ceremony at one place," accompanied by "the simplest sort of ceremony at each of the memorials," instead of overtaxing itself with a substantial ceremony at every site. "The Government's fundamental purpose in erecting memorials in Europe was to commemorate all services of all American forces in Europe during the World War," Mangum continued. "The fact that separate memorials were erected is only a detail in achieving the fundamental purpose; and the different memorials, therefore, are component parts of one unified whole rather than separate and independent things." Mindful of the Depression, moreover, the Washington officer predicted that people at home would object to sending such "a large amount of money out of the United States at a time when there is so much need in America."[7]

Mangum's memo appeared to win over General Pershing and Senator Reed. Both commissioners made clear at the next meeting that they doubted the wisdom or propriety of holding ceremonies at each memorial site. The chairman observed that dedications "strung out" over a long period of time and numerous sites "might create a bad impression in Europe as well as in America." Consolidating the dedications, he argued, "would create a better impression and save time and money."[8] Reed echoed this view, adding that "if too many dedications were held the ceremonies would become perfunctory and lose their zest." The commission adopted the senator's motion that only five ceremonies be held—at Brest, Chateau-Thierry, Montfaucon, Waregem, and Brookwood—between July 14 and 31, 1932.[9] But the issue was far from settled.

At the end of November 1931, still anticipating that dedications would take place in the following year, the chairman wrote to Price in search of the "least objectionable" way of proceeding. Acknowledging that "any plan that can be formulated" was bound to evoke some valid protest, Pershing reiterated that he was "inclined to prefer one impressive ceremony in each country . . . (with possibly two in France), and to make the programs at the other monuments as simple as possible and probably simultaneous." He further urged Price to renew his study of the matter in light of the "tentative" action the commission had taken at its most recent meeting.[10]

Price responded from Paris with crystal clarity. As stubbornly as Mangum had asserted the impossibility of conducting satisfactory dedications at each site, the commission secretary insisted that *"there must be a dedication for each memorial"* (his emphasis). Leaving aside the importance of the size of the ceremony, or who might attend it from the United States, Price repeated that a ceremony at each site was *"essential."* This was so, especially, for the benefit of people in the host countries. "All of the local people expect it [a ceremony at each memorial] and they will not understand if it is omitted. Each community has been looking forward to such an event all the while the memorial in their vicinity has been worked on. For anyone who knows conditions over here," the secretary concluded, "this statement is not open to argument."[11]

The argument rested, at least for the time being, on this transatlantic standoff. If the expectations of the "local people" argued most forcefully for ceremonies at each site, as Price maintained, the state of host country politics, as well as those at home, had to be considered as well. On the last day of 1931, General Pershing recommended to the commission that there be no dedications in 1932. "To hold the elaborate ceremonies and incur the large expenditures contemplated during the period of severe depression," he wrote, "would undoubtedly arouse criticism among our people as well as among the people of France and England."[12] The chairman's recommendation won the approval of every commission member and bought time for all concerned to agree on how to proceed.[13]

As it happened, the postponement approved for 1932 lasted five years. The full commission held no meeting during that year. At the thirty-fifth meeting, in May 1933, there was no discussion of dedications.[14] When Pershing observed to Reed that the situation in the new year (1933) looked "even less favorable" than 1932, the senator replied, "I feel very strongly that the present crisis in the National finances makes it distinctly improper that we should attempt to have any dedication ceremonies in France during this year."[15] At the December 1933 meeting the commissioners voted unanimously to hold no dedications in the following year.[16] The new year passed, as had 1932, without a meeting of the full commission. In May 1935, with General Pershing presiding at the thirty-seventh meeting, dedications were discussed, but "it was decided that no action on this subject should be taken at the present time."[17] For seventeen months thereafter, the full commission did not meet.

It is clear, in any case, that Pershing made a decision during his 1936 European inspection trip that planning should begin anew for the dedications. In late July of that year, US Army captain Mark Boatner, officer-in-charge of the Paris bureau, began preparing memoranda at Pershing's request on the understanding that there would be ceremonies in 1937.[18] The formal inauguration of the principal Canadian monument, on Vimy Ridge, played an important role in returning the dedications to the front of General Pershing's mind. The grand ceremony held on July 26, 1936, had brought the prime minister and sixty-three hundred Canadian veterans to Europe. Substantial complimentary entertainment and accommodation for the North American visitors came from both the French and British governments. The goodwill surrounding this event had even moved Adolf Hitler, just days before the Olympic Games opened in Berlin, to invite fifty of the Canadians to Germany and entertain them "rather elaborately."[19]

Captain Boatner had attended the Vimy Ridge event and observed what he believed the Canadians had done well and poorly. The Paris bureau chief formulated his thoughts and recommendations for Pershing during the coming weeks regarding how the Americans ought to proceed with their own plans. The ABMC leadership even consulted with Cana-

The Completion of the ABMC's Original Mission   123

dian authorities to learn from their experience. A lively correspondence took place between the commission's Washington office and officials in Ottawa during the second half of 1936. The Americans were especially eager to hear from their northern neighbors on such matters as how many personnel were needed to plan dedication ceremonies, what kind of formal receptions should accompany them, and how the events should be budgeted and funded.[20]

The thirty-eighth meeting of the commission on November 16, 1936, held less than three weeks after General Pershing returned from his European inspection tour of that year, concentrated almost solely on the dedications. The general expressed "his gratification at the manner in which the memorial project had been completed," and he put to the commission the idea that the memorials should be formally inaugurated in 1937. After considering the question "at length," the commission decided unanimously to hold the dedication ceremonies in July 1937, subject to the approval of President Roosevelt and Congress. Moreover, the commissioners finally accepted Secretary Price's long-held view that each of the monuments and chapels erected by the ABMC should have its own ceremony.[21]

A number of factors made 1937 a suitable year for the dedications. Construction of the memorials was not only completed, as Pershing had noted, but the landscaping and horticultural work at the various sites was also advancing nicely. Shortly before the commission held its thirty-eighth meeting, Franklin Roosevelt had been resoundingly reelected, which seemed to diminish earlier skittishness about spending a sizeable sum of money on overseas ceremonies. Franco-American ill will over issues of international finance also had abated, as had (for the moment, at least) the pace of aggression on the part of the Fascist dictators in Europe. Perhaps most importantly, 1937 would mark the twentieth anniversary of America's entry into the Great War. The commission could anticipate, therefore, that large numbers of veterans from the United States would once again be in Europe, as they had been in 1927, and available to attend the numerous ceremonies.

Once the commission committed definitively to 1937 for the dedications, it still had to determine and secure the necessary funding, organize and schedule the ceremonies, and establish protocols for the selection and invitation of special guests. Secretary Price was entrusted with preparing a cost estimate, and in early January 1937 he advised Pershing that $200,000 should be sought from Congress.[22] The commission also decided in November 1936 that "the principal ceremony" should be at Montfaucon, site of the grandest monument on the greatest American battlefield of the war. Price also proposed that the six chapels in France should be dedicated on Memorial Day 1937, while the remaining two chapels and thirteen monuments and tablets should be dedicated during the second half of July.[23] Some commissioners had already advocated July 4 as the best day for the Montfaucon ceremony, but the full body ultimately decided to allow the chairman to set the dates.[24] With regard to the special guests, the commission conceded that the president and Congress would wish to designate their own representatives to the ceremonies, but agreed that "prominent members" of the host governments and "certain local dignitaries" would need to be invited as well. The consensus at the November 1936 meeting, reversing an earlier decision of the commission, was that separate invitations to the nearest relatives of those buried overseas would not be sent.[25] A great many of them, after all, had recently come to the sites at government expense on Gold Star pilgrimages.

As Pershing moved to his Arizona retreat for the winter and Secretary Price finished a stint at the Army War College, the bulk of the responsibility for planning the dedications fell upon Captain Boatner. Among the Paris officer's initial concerns were that ample funding be secured, with suitably flexible authority for spending it; that the Montfaucon site be adequately prepared to accommodate the large numbers expected to attend its ceremony; and that the occasions be scheduled at times that would allow for maximum participation by American veterans, but also when sufficient ship transportation would be available to bring the anticipated thousands across the Atlantic. Boatner cited as a desirable model for the ABMC dedications the precedents associated with the Gold Star Mother pilgrimages. Money had been spent then "for an extraordinary variety of purposes," he recalled, "and no exception was taken on any item by the Comptroller." His fears that the Montfaucon site might prove inadequate for a crowd "like the one at Vimy" led him to contemplate an alternative plan to hold the most important dedication on the grounds of the more spacious cemetery at Romagne. Boatner also prepared Pershing for the likelihood that the American Legion would pressure the chairman to move the dedications to October in order to coincide with the organization's planned pilgrimage to France and allow for the availability of more steamship transportation than during the busy summer season.[26]

Pershing's response to Boatner's preliminary assessment came from

Tucson the day after the New Year. The chairman was mute on the matter of funding—that had been left to Secretary Price to work out with the Budget Bureau and Congress. Despite Boatner's worries about the physical suitability of Montfaucon for the grandest of the ceremonies, the general insisted that the "big show" must be held there, and that the most distinguished collection of dignitaries from France and the United States would assemble there "much as was done at Vimy." The chairman held fast also to the proposed scheduling, arguing that an autumn date would mean "less agreeable" weather and fewer American tourists. Pershing directed Boatner, finally, to prepare a full outline of the Paris office's plans for the dedications in time for the next meeting of the commission in April, and to arrange for the cemetery chapels built by the ABMC to be dedicated on Memorial Day. Acknowledging that the latter proposal had been Colonel Price's for some time, the general at last conceded that "there is something in the idea."[27]

Captain Boatner responded to Pershing's January directive with a twenty-seven-page memorandum, accompanied by a six-page cover letter, containing precise plans for the dedication of all eight cemetery chapels on Memorial Day and all the monuments (except Gibraltar) in mid-July between the American and French national holidays. The proposed schedule for the monuments was to commence at Montfaucon on the 4th of July and end in Paris with an American wreath-laying on Bastille Day (July 14) at the tomb of the French Unknown Soldier beneath the Arc de Triomphe. Such a conclusion, Boatner observed, "would in effect be paying honor to the French war dead as the final gesture and would be a graceful way of concluding our activities." He further recommended that no effort be made to coordinate the dedications with the American Legion pilgrimage, a position that Pershing had already appeared to embrace.[28]

A month later, Captain Boatner was obliged to inform his general that Marshal Pétain, France's most revered living soldier, had vetoed the idea of ending the American dedications at the Arc de Triomphe on Bastille Day. Pétain told Boatner that July 14 was simply "not an appropriate date" for the kind of gesture the American had initially envisioned.[29] Pershing's eventual decision to dedicate most of the monuments in August rendered this issue moot.

At the thirty-ninth meeting, on April 14, the commission formalized the decision to dedicate all six cemetery chapels in France on Memorial Day. Since this action allowed only six weeks' lead time for preparation, the panel deferred the chapel dedications at Brookwood and Flanders Field until the larger program later in the summer.[30] At the fortieth meeting a week later, the commissioners authorized General Pershing to "arrange the dates and other details incident to the dedications" of all the remaining ABMC sites, with the understanding that the inauguration of the Château-Thierry monument would be deferred until early October to coincide with the veterans' pilgrimage to France. The chairman immediately announced that the principal ceremony at Montfaucon would take place on Sunday, August 1, "unless some unforeseen development should make it impracticable to hold the ceremony at that time." It was also decided that all commission members would attend that ceremony, and that at least one member should be present, "if practicable," for each of the others.[31] Pershing explained a few days later to the acting director of the Bureau of the Budget, in the course of giving him formal notice of the commission's intention to seek a special appropriation of $200,000 for these events, that he had recently conferred with President Roosevelt and that the chief executive shared the commission's commitment to carry out the dedications in 1937.[32]

As it happened, Congress did not approve the budget supplement in time for it to cover any of the dedications on Memorial Day. Consequently, those ceremonies, while never designed to be on par with the one at Montfaucon, did not involve large official delegations from the United States. Rather, they adhered to the more typical, already established Memorial Day format, with a mix of dignitaries participating from the French political and military ranks as well as from the American diplomatic and veterans communities residing overseas. Representatives of the Paris chapters of the American Legion and Veterans of Foreign Wars presided over four of the six events, while members of the American Overseas Memorial Day Association officiated at the other two.

General Pershing, who had spoken at the first Memorial Day observance at the Romagne cemetery, returned eighteen years later to dedicate the chapel that the ABMC had erected along the southern heights of the expansive site. The AEF commander had sailed for Europe on April 28, a week after the second commission meeting that month. On his way to France he had stopped in England to serve as the official military representative of the United States at the coronation of King George VI.[33] He would remain abroad until a month after all the dedications were completed, almost two hundred days, his third-longest stay on the continent as the ABMC chairman. The principal speakers at the other five chapel dedications were the US ambassador to France, William Bullitt, and Édouard Daladier, vice premier (under Léon Blum) of the French government, at Suresnes; General Adelbert de Chambrun, a descendant of Lafayette, at Aisne-Marne; US Consul General Addison M. Southard at Oise-Aisne; Alvin Mansfield Owsley, US ambassador to the Irish Free State (and a wartime veteran of the 36th Division), at Saint-Mihiel; and at the Somme, Florence Becker, president general of the Daughters of the American Revolution, who became the first woman to give such an address at an American cemetery.[34]

Like all other Memorial Day commemorations since 1918, those dedicating the American cemeteries in France did honor to the soldiers who had fought and died in the Great War. "In the fullness of youth, our heroic dead were the very flower of young American manhood," Pershing said at Romagne. "Proud of their country and its traditions they knew no fear but had faith in the righteousness of their cause."[35] In the same spirit at Suresnes, Daladier, who as prime minister sixteen months later would sign the infamous Munich Pact with Adolf Hitler, addressed "the faithful and grateful salute of France to the memory of the valiant sons of America who lie asleep forever in our soil."[36] Mrs. Becker's praise was even more effusive for the troops and the ideals for which they had fought. The soldiers of Pershing's army, she said, were "our representatives." Seeking no reward for themselves, they "were the embodiment of nobility—animated emblems of the Republic's genius—seeking neither fame nor renown—but only their country's justification and to uphold its honestly acquired rights."[37]

The speakers paid tribute with comparable emotion to Franco-American friendship. Pershing observed that the presence of so many French veterans at the Romagne ceremony confirmed that "the passage of years has strengthened the ties of friendship so firmly welded when American and French soldiers fought shoulder to shoulder through those terrible years of war."[38] Ambassador Owsley told his audience that "we have in America a deep and abiding sentiment for France," and acknowledged that he was touched "at the evidence of good will and friendship you show me as the representative of the American nation." Of the soldiers lying in the cemetery before him, Owsley said: "Sleeping where they fell, here let them lie. Soldiers of America, we would exalt you above all earthly things. Favorites of the Mother Country, we commit you forever into the care and tender solicitude of your comrades and friends from France."[39]

The most urgent keynote in all the May 30 speeches, however, was the desire for peace. "As we stand today among these white crosses," Pershing remarked, "we can but believe that if the millions of World War dead could speak again, both friend and foe with one accord would cry aloud for peace."[40] Owsley identified "the preservation of Peace" as the "common concern today" of both France and the United States.[41] Ambassador Bullitt claimed that the desire to achieve peace had brought American troops to France in 1917 and 1918 "from every state in our Union and from every walk of life." With evident sadness, however, he acknowledged that the soldiers who had died in battle, while now "discharged" from the ongoing fight for peace, had not won that battle, nor had the survivors either. The ambassador concluded "that Peace is to be won not by war, but by reason; not by shells but by thought; not by bombs but by friendship; not by fanatic creeds but by the old principles of Christianity."[42]

The dedication of the American monuments and the two remaining cemetery chapels came later. On June 8, Pershing wrote Ambassador Bullitt that "the only [ceremony] that need interest us at this time is the monument at Montfaucon." The centrality of that structure in the upcoming spate of dedications reflected the general's enduring sense of the importance of the Meuse-Argonne battle to the American effort in the late war. In Pershing's view, the August 1 ceremony was meant not only to commemorate the efforts of the soldiers in that great combat, but also "the friendly spirit of comradeship and the cooperation between the French and American armies and peoples during the World War." Montfaucon, moreover, would be the only site whose dedication French president Albert Lebrun was expected to attend. "All other ceremonies of dedication to be held after August 1 will be secondary and local," Pershing observed, except for the one at Château-Thierry in October that would coincide with the American Legion pilgrimage.[43]

Back in Washington, the commission held its final meeting on June 9 before commencing its own travels to Europe. The official delegation from the United States was to include, in addition to all seven members of the commission, the present secretary of state (or his alternate); those who had served as secretary of war and secretary of the navy during the world war; the senior officer in command of naval forces in Europe during the war; the heads of the American Legion, Veterans of Foreign Wars, Disabled American Veterans, and the American War Mothers (all organizations incorporated by Congress); chaplains from the Protestant, Catholic, and Jewish faiths, with one each from the American Legion and V.F.W. to be nominated by their respective organizations; and, finally, two dozen members of Congress. The commission also stipulated how much of the $200,000 special appropriation would be devoted to ten different categories of expenditure. The largest budget lines were travel expenses from the United States, the physical installations necessary for all the ceremony sites, and the compilation of an audio-visual record of the dedications.[44]

The funding proposal worked its way through Congress during the month of June with the full support of the White House. In his letter accompanying the budget request, President Roosevelt called the ABMC sites "America's tangible symbols abroad of the gratitude which we bear to those who served and died in the World War." That they should be dedicated with appropriate ceremonies, the president asserted, was "eminently fitting." While acknowledging that these events had been postponed "because of one circumstance or another, from year to year," the president confirmed that he had conferred with Pershing and "fully agreed with his view" that the dedications "should no longer be delayed." The commander in chief urged Congress to make the requested grant "at the earliest practicable date."[45]

That date turned out to be June 28, when both chambers approved the relevant joint resolution less than five weeks before the Montfaucon ceremony was scheduled to take place. Action in the House of Representatives had reduced the appropriation to $175,000 by cutting the congressional delegation to three members from each chamber.[46] In any case, this sum proved more than sufficient. James Mangum reported in March 1940 that the commission eventually returned almost half of the budgeted money to the Treasury.[47]

Recruitment of the official delegation from the United States began as soon as the funding request passed out of the House committee. Designated members received a telegram of invitation from General Pershing as well as a follow-up letter from Secretary Price informing them that space on the SS *Manhattan*'s July 14 sailing from New York was being held for them and that $1,000 had been appropriated for each delegate's travel expenses. All the individual had to do was to accept or decline the invitation.[48] The Speaker of the House chose two veterans of the world war—J. Walter Lambeth of North Carolina and Lister Hill of Alabama—and a member of the Foreign Affairs Committee, Charles Eaton of New Jersey, for the delegation.[49] The president pro tempore of the Senate selected Ryan

Duffy of Wisconsin, Ernest W. Gibson of Vermont, and Richard Russell of Georgia, but the senators did not arrive in Paris until several days into the succession of monument dedications because they were obliged to stay in Washington until the final resolution of President Roosevelt's scheme to pack the Supreme Court. Ambassador Bullitt and General Pershing hosted a dinner in Paris on August 4, at which the recently arrived senators were introduced.[50]

Even without the three American senators, the ceremony at Montfaucon on Sunday, August 1, was the grandest of all the dedications. Accounts indicate that more than three thousand invited French and American guests were on hand, and an equivalent number of local residents. All Americans living in Paris were invited to the ceremony as guests of the American Battle Monuments Commission, and five special trains carried nearly fifteen hundred of them to Verdun and Sainte-Menehould to meet shuttle buses that drove them the rest of the way to the more remote monument site. Traveling by this route took the attendees within sight of the Chateau-Thierry (Aisne-Marne) monument and Belleau Wood, and also through the heart of the Argonne forest. Meals were served, at the commission's expense, on both sides of the mid-afternoon ceremony. President Lebrun traveled first to Romagne, where General Pershing and Ambassador Bullitt met him, and placed a bronze palm on the altar of the chapel there. (This palm is now mounted on a wall inside the recently expanded visitor center at the Meuse-Argonne cemetery.) The presidential party then proceeded, with the two high-ranking Americans, to Montfaucon.[51]

The ceremony itself lasted ninety minutes and was broadcast throughout Europe and coast-to-coast within the United States by both the National Broadcasting Company and the Columbia Broadcasting System. Ambassador Bullitt served as master of ceremonies and gave the first address. Speeches by the elected deputy from the Department of the Meuse, the national commander of the American Legion, Harry Colmery, General Pershing, Marshal Pétain, President Roosevelt (broadcast from the United States), and President Lebrun followed. The prime minister of France, Camille Chautemps, and the foreign minister, Yvon Delbos, were also present but did not speak.[52]

The crowd saved its loudest ovations for the two greatest soldiers present, Pershing and Pétain. With Foch, Haig, Joffre, and so many of the other important generals from the Great War already deceased, the appearance of the commanders of both the AEF and the French army from the final stages of the late war made the event at Montfaucon an especially "high moment."[53] One of the most dazzling elements of the ceremony came an hour into it, with Roosevelt's five-minute address live by radio from the presidential yacht at Quantico, Virginia. The account of one attendee reported that, immediately upon the conclusion of Ambassador Bullitt's introduction, "almost like a miracle, the voice of Mr. Roosevelt issued clearly and distinctly from the loud speaker."[54]

Although the sheer drama of the August 1 event was unrivaled, what the speakers said conformed quite closely to the pattern of the Memorial Day dedications. Three French newspaper headlines nicely captured the thrust of the speeches: "A Moving Display of Franco-American Friendship," "Franco-American Brotherhood of Arms Celebrated at Montfaucon," and "Mr. Roosevelt and Monsieur Lebrun Unite Their Voices in a Common Appeal for Peace."[55] Plainly, the difficulties of the current international situation overshadowed the moment. The year of the dedications held no European crisis to rival the Italo-Ethiopian War of 1935–36, the remilitarization of the Rhineland of 1936, or Hitler's moves against Austria and Czechoslovakia in 1938. But throughout 1937 the Fascist dictators of Germany and Italy openly flaunted international agreements by assisting the forces of Francisco Franco in their effort to destroy the democratically elected government of Spain. The Japanese, moreover, were waging a brutal war of conquest in China. If Europe was not yet on the brink of war, neither was it courting perfect harmony, and the conflict in Asia was an especially stark reminder that the Great War had not ended all violence among nations.

In light of such dark realities, General Pershing's remarks were particularly compelling. "If amidst the difficult problems that confront all nations today, there exists a profound aversion to all violent solutions," he said, "it is because so many millions of men are alive who know the horrors of war. The last conflict profited no one and left so many problems unsettled." The old soldier decried that the peace was so ill-assured, that the build-up of weapons continued at "ruinous cost," and that "distrust and hatred still reign." If no remedy could be found for "the folly of our times," he speculated, a new war would mean "the end of western civilization."[56]

The two heads of state focused more on the historic friendship between France and the United States, and the desire of both nations to live in a peaceful world. Neither country sought conquests, said Roosevelt. Rather, "both desire to live in peace with all nations." With his closing salute to the French Republic, Roosevelt praised a friendship "as old as the American nation itself."[57]

While Lebrun echoed the sentiments of his transatlantic counterpart, he paid special tribute to the "disinterested gesture of the young men who crossed the Ocean to bring us their help and their support." Without doubt, Lebrun declared, the Americans who had come to Europe twenty years earlier remembered that the French had helped their forefathers at Yorktown. But, there was more behind their commitment to fight. "They [the Americans] sensed deep within them that the essential principles on which all free civilization is founded were menaced. They came to defend [those ideals]." At least one newspaper account reported that Lebrun received more applause than Roosevelt at the end of his remarks because more of his audience could understand French than English.[58]

Amid the impressive oratory of that memorable day, the most visible centerpiece of the program was the newly erected monument itself. Harry Colmery seemed most struck by the permanence of the monument; he referred to "this majestic column of granite" that symbolized "the eternal affection of the American veterans for their brothers in the brave Allied armies." Pershing said that the column "testifies one more time to the bonds that have united France and our country for nearly two centuries." When the ABMC chairman had finished his dedicatory address, and during what one account described as "a hushed silence," the young daughter of wealthy financier and Pershing intimate Bernard Baruch threw a switch releasing a huge American flag on its slow ascent toward the observation platform at the foot of the statue atop the 175-foot column. The honor of delivering the final words of the program that day was given to President Lebrun: "One last time I bow before this memorial, raised on a little strip of French land, now become American. Across the centuries our people will guard it with pious memory."[59]

The momentous gathering at Montfaucon drew attention to an additional fact: the widespread wartime devastation in the Meuse region, from which a significant but incomplete recovery was proceeding. Ten of the more than eighty French departments had experienced particularly heavy damage between 1914 and 1918. The Department of the Meuse had hosted some of the bloodiest and most protracted fighting on the Western Front, including the huge battles of Verdun (in 1916) and the Meuse-Argonne. The monument dedicated on August 1 occupied the top of a prominent hill on which had stood a village that the war completely destroyed. Naomi Lisle recalled the message on signs that greeted the thousands of guests for the 1937 ceremony reminding them that "the hill is still in its wartime state and that they should exercise great care in walking among the ruins."[60]

The National Geographic Society in Washington, D.C., was particularly interested in the ongoing effort to rebuild the devastated areas. In a news bulletin it issued about the dedication of the ABMC monument, entitled "Montfaucon, Where Peaceful Farms Have Replaced Grim Battlefields," the society gave a generally upbeat assessment for its American audience of how the area had come back since the armistice. "Although parts of the Argonne forest still lie shattered and wasted, and, in sections of the Meuse valley, chalky subsoil thrown to the surface has made farming unprofitable, much reconstruction has taken place."[61] While much rebuilding had undeniably occurred, the sadder reality was that the population of the Meuse department in 1937 was barely 80 percent of what it had been before the war, and it similarly lagged the other war-torn areas of France in several other categories of recovery.[62] Indeed, to this day, the region shows persistent signs of economic and demographic stagnation.

Ten more dedications—the two remaining cemetery chapels at Flanders Field and Brookwood, and monuments at Montsec, Sommepy, Bellicourt, Brest, Tours, Cantigny, Kemmel, and Audenarde—took place during the first half of August 1937. The timetable of all the ceremonies had been arranged to make possible the presence of the entire official delegation at each one. Master of ceremony and principal speaking duties after Montfaucon rotated through the delegation. With the exception of General Pershing and Senator Reed, the latter of whom did not travel to Europe, each ABMC member presided over at least one ceremony. Vice Chairman Woodside gave the dedicatory address at Brookwood on August 15. Similarly, eight of the members of the larger delegation were tapped for principal addresses, and all got to make remarks at least once.

The two remaining dedications of ABMC sites—the monuments at Gibraltar and at Château-Thierry—had to await October. More by coincidence than design, they took place on consecutive days. The remoteness of the memorial at Gibraltar, combined with complications stemming from the Spanish Civil War, caused the commission to turn over that dedication entirely to the Navy Department and the State Department. The date eventually chosen for the event, October 6, coincided with the presence of a squadron of US ships in the western Mediterranean. Rear Admiral A. P. Fairfield, whose flagship, the USS *Raleigh,* led the American flotilla into the British outpost, delivered the dedication address. Consul Herbert O. Wilson presided over the ceremony. No ABMC personnel were present.[63]

The October 7 ceremony at Château-Thierry was the last of the ABMC dedications. As already noted, this program had been delayed until the second American Legion pilgrimage could arrive in France. Ten years earlier, the Legionnaires had recrossed the Atlantic twenty thousand strong on the tenth anniversary of America's entry into the world war. In 1937 the traveling veterans numbered little more than five thousand, but they enjoyed bountiful hospitality from the host government. For the six days that they were in France, the fifty-two hundred Americans received their lodging and meals at the expense of 40 million Frenchmen. The Legionnaires were grandly feted on several occasions, most notably at an October 5 luncheon in the spacious courtyard of the Hotel des Invalides in the presence of Marshal Pétain. Two days later, they traveled with General Pershing in a convoy of buses and automobiles forty miles to Château-Thierry for the dedication of the Aisne-Marne monument. The ABMC chairman chose as principal speaker at that event General James Harbord, commander of the brigade of US Marines that had won immortal renown in the fighting in nearby Belleau Wood in June 1918.[64] Harry Colmery also spoke on October 7 and reminded his audience that the 8,301 Americans buried in two ABMC cemeteries (Aisne-Marne and Oise-Aisne) within fifteen miles of the monument were "a permanent reminder of the last grim twilight of the War and the final victory." Of the dead soldiers, Colmery concluded: "Their task is done. Ours remains before us."[65]

Indeed, the dedications had been as much about the present and future as they had been about the past. Even though far from home, they had been solemn acts of national remembrance. They had also occasioned strong affirmations of present intentions and inspiring expressions of future commitments. The American memorials were meant, after all, to symbolize the strength and permanence not only of the nation's resolve to honor the soldiers of the Great War, but of its devotion to the ideals for which the men had fought. The enshrinement of past deeds in marble and granite, it was hoped, would forever remind new generations of their responsibility to defend what others had died for. The speeches in May, August, and October 1937 powerfully conveyed all these sentiments to the thousands at the sites who had heard them, and to the larger audience connected to the events through the extensive media coverage.

In addition to the live radio broadcasts of the August 1 event by CBS and NBC, print media in the United States also paid considerable attention to the dedications. The *New York Times* reported at length on the Memorial Day ceremonies at the six cemeteries in France and began running articles on the August ceremonies as early as the 4th of July.[66] Both the departure from the United States and the arrival in Europe of the official delegation were noted later in that month, and full texts of Pershing's, Pétain's, and Roosevelt's speeches at Montfaucon ran on page 3 of the paper's August 2 edition.[67] *Time* magazine ran a substantial piece on the dedications and the work of the ABMC in its August 9 edition.[68]

General Pershing's role in the commission's achievements received particularly favorable and extensive coverage; indeed, the *Times* had sub-headlined its August 1 article on the Montfaucon ceremony "A Triumph for Pershing."[69] A day later, the paper editorialized: "The American Battle Monuments Commission, under the chairmanship of General Pershing, has performed a most gracious national service in providing permanent memorials for both the dead and the living who alike offered their all: chapels, monuments, enduring bronzes. Together with the cemeteries they are our 'cloud of witnesses' in France—witnesses of our lasting remembrance of those who perished there, giving them assurance of 'praise that grows not old'—but witnesses, too, of our permanent possession of these (to us) most precious acres in France, where our dead lie."[70] Along with praise of Pershing came speculation about his retirement.[71]

The end of what was arguably ABMC's most eventful year to date, in any case, begged the most important, existential question: Would the commission survive the successful fulfillment of the work it was created to do? As far back as November 1931, the agency had adopted a tentative policy aimed at providing for the permanent maintenance of its memorials after its probable disbanding. The formal motion adopted at the thirty-fourth meeting recommended that once the monuments and chapels were built and dedicated, the seven commissioners would resign. Care of the American memorials in England, France, and Belgium would then be entrusted to the respective American ambassadors in those countries, operating through their military attachés. Such a transfer of authority, finally, was to be done on the proviso that diplomatic agreements would be secured with the appropriate host governments to prevent the future erection of any additional American war monuments—private or public—on their soil.[72]

A year later, Secretary Price, who had not been present at the November 1931 meeting, made his own recommendations to General Pershing. The commission should notify the president that it intended to disband on December 31, 1933, by which time all of the memorial sites would be finished. Major administrative details to be addressed in the interim, according to the secretary, included final reports, reassignment of commission personnel, ensuring adequate maintenance of the ABMC sites, and securing necessary legislation to preserve controls against "the erection of nonuseful American memorials in France."[73]

A couple of developments overturned these early plans for the commission's termination. Construction of the memorials, first of all, took longer than the secretary had anticipated. If delay in finishing the monuments were reason for postponing the dedications, it was also reason for pushing back final determination of the future of the commission. Early in 1934, more importantly, Pershing secured President Roosevelt's agreement to issue an executive order that turned over to the ABMC "all functions of administration pertaining to national cemeteries and memorials located in Europe now vested in or exercised by the War Department."[74] On the first day of the new year, administrative authority over those cemeteries and memorials was supposed to pass to a new bureau within the War Department called the "American War Memorials in Europe." Under circumstances that have been described as "mysterious," Roosevelt intervened to short circuit these plans. The new Executive Order 6614 that he issued entrusted the completed memorials solely to the ABMC and effectively terminated the work of the Graves Registration Service in Europe as well.[75] Even with the new lease on life it received from this presidential action, however, later events would prove that the Pershing board's standing as an independent body was still not guaranteed.

What brought the future of the commission most urgently to the fore a few years later was the Roosevelt administration's desire to reorganize the executive branch of the federal government. The president presented to Congress a five-point plan to accomplish this at the beginning of 1937. Huge Democratic majorities in both houses resulting from the 1936 election seemed to preordain that the bill would become law. The provision that most jeopardized the ABMC empowered the president to create two new cabinet bureaus (for a total of twelve) and then bring "every executive agency" under the direct control of one of the dozen expanded departments.[76] In the name of streamlining the government, small agencies such as the ABMC were targeted to lose their independence and come under the authority of one of the larger units of administration.

If this were to be its ultimate fate, Pershing and Price set out to influence the choice of the commission's future home. The secretary assessed the situation for Pershing in a memorandum that greeted the chairman upon his return from the European dedications in November. "The reorganization bill now before Congress," Price wrote, will give the president "the power to consolidate activities and departments of the Government as he desires. . . . In view of the circumstances, it seems to me that the commission should within the next few weeks decide concerning its future status." Price was especially determined to prevent the ABMC's absorption into the Interior Department, an eventuality that seemed likely and which he believed would displease a majority of the commissioners.[77]

General Pershing responded with a letter to Secretary of War Harry Woodring in early January 1938 expressing his "personal opinion" that "the duties of the American Battle Monuments Commission should at some time in the future be transferred to the War Department and that the commission as at present constituted should cease to exist." Such a transfer, which presupposed enactment of the president's bill, should not take place before the commission had completed its work on the battlefield guidebook, Pershing observed. He explained further that the commissioners would discuss the agency's fate at their next meeting "in the spring," after which he would feel empowered to make "concrete recommendations" to the president.[78]

Secretary Woodring replied within two weeks to Pershing's letter and told him that the War Department agreed with his (Pershing's) views. He promised that "the necessary action will be taken by the War Department at the proper time to carry out your wishes."[79] The president wrote the ABMC chairman the same day. After expressing his gratitude for the work done by the commission, "and for its desire to cooperate in Governmental reorganization," Roosevelt indicated that "before taking any action on this matter," he would await receipt of the recommendation to which Pershing had referred that presumably would come out of the commission's next meeting.[80]

Two developments altered the trajectory of events. One came a month after the correspondence just recounted. It involved Pershing's health. The general had experienced at least one serious bout of illness in England on his way to the earliest ABMC dedications. By the beginning of 1938, however, he was wintering and relaxing in Tucson, with the stress of extended European travels and engagements behind him. Nevertheless, toward the end of February the elderly chairman was hospitalized after being stricken with severe chest pains. He passed in and out of coma and, in the words of one of his biographers, suffered from uremic poisoning "of considerable magnitude." On February 27 his condition seemed so hopeless that the army was asked to send a funeral train, along with Pershing's best uniform, to Arizona. But two days later, as if by some miracle, he rallied and began a steady recovery. By the end of April he was in New York City for his son's wedding, and in August he was well enough to make his annual trip to Europe.[81] What the illness and other distractions in Pershing's life meant, in any case, was that the commission did not hold its anticipated meeting in the spring and, therefore, did not make any follow-up recommendation to the president at that time regarding its own fate.

The other development pertained to politics and, given the balance of power on Capitol Hill, was much harder to imagine than a crisis in the aged general's health. Despite the large numerical advantages enjoyed by the president's party in the Congress, Roosevelt's reorganization bill failed in the House of Representatives on April 8, 1938. While a revised version of the bill did pass a new Congress in 1939, the latter measure did not contain the same mandate to reassign all the smaller executive agencies to one of twelve enlarged cabinet departments.[82] Provisions in the new measure that still allowed the president to streamline the executive branch held out danger to the independence of the ABMC that would persist into the following year. As it turned out, the commission dodged this threat with its standing intact. When Pershing finally convened the group in November 1938, in what turned out to be the last meeting for seven years and the last Pershing would ever chair, neither fears of government reorganization nor the question of the commission's future even came up.[83]

The key to the commission's near-term survival, finally, may have been altogether serendipitous. Apparently unbeknownst to Pershing or his closest subordinates, President Roosevelt told reporters in October 1939 that he would make no move to alter the ABMC's status so long as the general remained alive.[84] Although Roosevelt's senior by more than two decades, Pershing managed to outlive the younger chief executive by three years.

In January 1938, a month before Pershing took ill and mere days before his own retirement from ABMC service, Secretary Price completed a draft of what was supposed to be the commission's final report to the president.[85] On the general's orders, the report was filed after Pershing had seen it. There is no evidence that the blank spaces Price had left in it were later filled in, or that the report ever found its way to the White House.[86] The document, in any event, contains a wealth of information about the entirety of the first generation of the commission's work.

Price's account pronounced especially favorable judgment on the 1937 dedications. "Held under almost perfect weather conditions," it noted, "the ceremonies were in every way a credit to the United States and had a very fine effect upon international understanding and friendship." As he concluded the document, moreover, the outgoing secretary expressed the commission's gratitude to all the agencies of government, both American and European, that had supported and facilitated its work. The four presidents of the United States during the ABMC's lifetime, as well as the Congress, were cited together for "the sympathetic understanding which they have always had of the Commission's work and problems and for their unwavering support which has made the accomplishments of the Commission possible."[87]

One of the most conspicuous blank spaces in the report had to do with the future of the commission. Plainly, Price expected a meeting later in 1938 to produce the anticipated final recommendation to the president on what should be done with the agency. The other blanks had mostly to do with the final accounting of commission expenditures, which presumably would have to await, at the very least, the formal close-out of the current fiscal year. Even with the incomplete financial data, the secretary was able to document that the ABMC had spent approximately $2,360,000 on beautifying the eight cemeteries, and an additional $2,050,000 on the eleven monuments and two commemorative tablets, for a total of $4.4 million on the complete building program. The most costly cemetery construction had been at Romagne ($657,000); the least costly at Flanders Field ($68,000). The most expensive monument had been Montfaucon ($655,000); the least expensive had been Kemmel ($16,500). The two commemorative plaques at Souilly and Chaumont had totaled a modest $3,000. On top of the foregoing amounts, by Price's calculation the Graves Registration Service had spent $2.6 million on construction and maintenance of the cemetery burial grounds before surrendering complete authority over the sites to the ABMC in 1934.[88]

At five minutes to midnight on January 30, 1938, Colonel Price closed out his service as the first secretary of the American Battle Monuments Commission with a most cordial letter to General Pershing. Not lost on Price was the fact that the two men had been together as chairman and secretary since the commission's beginning. "I would like as my last official act," he wrote, "to express my appreciation for the many kindnesses which you have done for me and the many pleasant memories which I have of our long association together." While reaffirming his eagerness to get back to "normal Army work," Price assured the chairman: "My work with the Commission has always been intensely interesting to me, and I will miss it very much as well as my personal relations with you."[89]

The nearly fifteen years that Xenophon Price served as the ABMC's first secretary proved to be the centerpiece of a notably distinguished army career for the Saginaw, Michigan, native. Price had graduated from West Point seventh in his class (of 450) in 1914 and been commissioned into the Corps of Engineers. He had spent a year as an aide to President Wilson before sailing to Europe with the AEF in 1917. Price earned a master's degree in civil engineering from the Massachusetts Institute of Technology in 1921, the year before he was assigned to the Battle Monuments Board. When he became ABMC secretary in 1923, he was thirty years old. Price's obituary credited him with composing the inscription on the Tomb of the Unknown Soldier, which became the inscription on the headstones of the unknown dead in the overseas cemeteries as well. Price's guiding hand upon the commission's construction program and the preparation of both editions of the battlefield guidebook was arguably indispensable. He also served as a staff officer in Europe between 1942 and 1945 and witnessed the Normandy landings. As will be noted in the next chapter, his position with the advancing American army throughout the summer of 1944 enabled Price to inspect many of the memorials built under his supervision as their locations were liberated from German control. By the time he died in 1979, at the age of eighty-six, Price had been awarded the Distinguished Service Medal with oak leaf cluster, the Legion of Merit, the Bronze Star, and the French Legion of Honor.[90]

Work on the new guidebook was still under way when the first commission secretary finished his long tenure. Revision of this publication had been a major project of the ABMC Historical Section and senior staff almost since the moment the first version had appeared in 1927. No one seemed to anticipate that the guidebook revision would take as long as it did. Indeed, the secretary's correspondence throughout the 1930s is filled with expressions of frustration at how slowly the new publication was coming along. However, in May 1937 Price told the chairman that once the general's comments on the completed manuscript text were received, it would take only two to four months to have the book published.⁹¹ Five months later, with the dedications completed and the secretary back in Washington, the colonel told his superior that he was "devoting my time almost exclusively to the Guide Book" and hoped soon to have his work done on the final proofs. Final approval of the finished manuscript, however, would rest with Pershing. If the general were back in the States before November 15 and could sign off on the finished text by then, Price told him, the book could see the light of day by the time the secretary left his post.⁹²

No matter how much the outgoing secretary may have consoled himself with such an optimistic thought, there would still be no guidebook in print before April 1939. The health problems and travel commitments that distracted Pershing across the whole of 1938 kept pushing back publication. It must be said, in any case, that the finished product, entitled *American Armies and Battlefields in Europe,* remains a fitting capstone to the first generation of the commission's work. It is as much a history of the American army in the Great War, and of the ABMC's effort to commemorate the soldiers' actions, as it is a manual for visiting the overseas battle and memorial sites. An almost giddy Price wrote Pershing upon receiving his first copy of it: "I am as happy as can be that the guide book is out and I treat it like a child with his first toy. Every page and every paragraph brings back some memory."⁹³ Captain William Bessell wrote the chairman ten days later from Paris to report that another of the early readers had received his copy with the same childlike enthusiasm. In the latter case, it was the duke of Windsor, who had received from Superintendent Walter Shield a complimentary copy of the book during his and the duchess's visit to the Romagne cemetery. The former king, Shield told Bessell, "was like a child with a new toy" as he paged through it.⁹⁴ For anyone who likes maps, photographs, expert commentary, and other historical treasures, the book is still bound to evoke similar responses.

By the time *American Armies and Battlefields in Europe* was finally published, the extraordinary events of 1937 and 1938 had passed. The dedications were over; the final report was buried in a file; Secretary Price had moved on; General Pershing had survived his brush with death; and the commission's future as an independent agency, if not completely assured, seemed safe enough for the body to cease planning for its own demise. The abundant publicity about the dedications, and the impressive guidebook, moreover, stood as a rich, authoritative, and public record of the ABMC's first generation of endeavor and achievement. When General Pershing departed for what turned out to be his last visit to Europe in June 1939, he could do so with the satisfaction that his small agency had accomplished its principal mission, and still had a mission going forward.

Harsh European realities, however, soon stalked the newly built, newly dedicated American memorials. Pershing's prediction in 1937 that the dedications "will complete my work" was not fulfilled. When the chairman embarked on his final Atlantic crossing, he actually set sail into the final stages of the old world's "gathering storm." Several months before, in March and April 1939, respectively, Hitler had helped himself to the last territorial conquests he would garner without shooting—the rump Czechoslovak state and Memel (from Lithuania). By the time summer was over, and mere weeks after Pershing had returned to the United States, Germany attacked Poland and the European war began. When France and the Low Countries became an active theater of combat in May 1940, the ABMC sites wound up in the middle of the fight. If this war would not find the elderly general of the armies once more in command of millions of soldiers in the field, it still had an important role for him. From a continent away, he would lead a complex effort to see his cherished memorials and the personnel entrusted with caring for them safely through Europe's next self-made catastrophe.

Six original ABMC commissioners at Bentley grave, Oise-Aisne cemetery, 1924. (Courtesy of the ABMC)

General Pershing at Bentley grave, 1924. (Courtesy of the ABMC)

General Marshall at Suresnes dedication, September 1952. (Courtesy of the ABMC)

General Devers (center) chairing an ABMC meeting in 1963. (Courtesy of the ABMC)

Mrs. Bentley at her son's grave, Oise-Aisne cemetery, 1924. (Courtesy of the ABMC)

Paul Cody Bentley's permanent headstone, Oise-Aisne cemetery. (Author's photograph)

Marble quarry in Carrara, Italy. (Courtesy of Rebekah Dell)

Colonel Xenophon H. Price, ABMC secretary, 1923–38. (Courtesy of the ABMC)

General Thomas North, ABMC secretary, 1946–68. (Courtesy of the ABMC)

General Andrew J. Adams, ABMC secretary, 1968–92. (Courtesy of the ABMC)

Montfaucon monument. (Author's photograph)

Montsec monument. (Author's photograph)

Montsec monument from a distance. (Author's photograph)

Aisne-Marne monument, Château-Thierry. (Author's photograph)

Bellicourt monument. (Author's photograph)

Cantigny monument. (Author's photograph)

Sommepy monument. (Author's photograph)

Monument to the Services of Supply, Tours. (Author's photograph)

Chapel and graves, Somme cemetery. (Author's photograph)

Chapel and graves, Brookwood cemetery. (Author's photograph)

Chapel interior, Somme cemetery. (Author's photograph)

Chapel and graves, Aisne-Marne cemetery. (Author's photograph)

Meuse-Argonne cemetery. (Author's photograph)

Chapel, Meuse-Argonne cemetery. (Author's photograph)

Chapel interior, Meuse-Argonne cemetery. (Author's photograph)

Memorial palm given by France's President Albert Lebrun in 1937, visitor center, Meuse-Argonne cemetery. (Author's photograph)

Grave of Medal of Honor recipient Freddie Stowers, Meuse-Argonne cemetery. (Author's photograph)

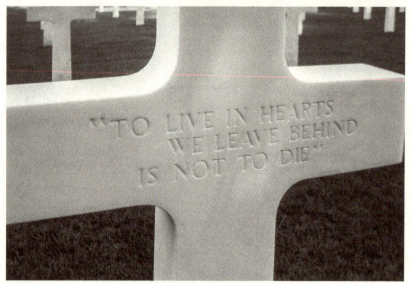

Family's inscription on the back of a headstone, Aisne-Marne cemetery. (Author's photograph)

Eagle sculpture at Saint-Mihiel cemetery, with motto "Time Will Not Dim the Glory of Their Deeds." (Author's photograph)

Doughboy statue donated by Harriet Blaine Beale, Saint-Mihiel cemetery. (Author's photograph)

Normandy memorial and reflecting pool. (Author's photograph)

Top of Normandy memorial, "Spirit of American Youth Rising from the Waves" statue. (Courtesy of John Quint III)

Peggy Harris (on left) at Normandy cemetery Memorial Day ceremony, 2011. (Author's photograph)

Netherlands cemetery chapel, with Memorial Day wreaths, 2017. (Courtesy of John Quint III)

Memorial Day wreath from King Willem-Alexander, Netherlands cemetery, 2017. (Courtesy of John Quint III)

Netherlands cemetery Wall of the Missing, Memorial Day, 2017. (Courtesy of John Quint III)

Graves at the Netherlands cemetery. (Courtesy of John Quint III)

Memorial at Henri-Chapelle cemetery. (Courtesy of John Quint III)

"Guardian Angel" sculpture, Henri-Chapelle cemetery. (Courtesy of John Quint III)

"American Eagle," chapel sculpture, Ardennes cemetery. (Author's photograph)

Chapel and graves, Brittany cemetery. (Author's photograph)

"Youth Triumphing over Evil," chapel sculpture, Brittany cemetery. (Author's photograph)

Utah Beach monument. (Courtesy of John Quint III)

Chapel and graves, Épinal cemetery. (Author's photograph)

Jewish commemorative tablet, Cambridge cemetery. (Author's photograph)

"Brothers-in-Arms" statue, Sicily-Rome cemetery. (Author's photograph)

> 7th July 1960
>
> They met death, that we should be granted life anew.
>
> Standing at their graves, as our thoughts turn to them in reverence and gratitude, we may be assured, they are not here, but let us know that they always abide with us.
>
> While young, they have preceded us on the path of life.

Letter of Dedication from Queen Juliana of the Netherlands, American cemetery, July 1960. (Author's photograph)

Grave of Medal of Honor recipient Theodore Roosevelt Jr., Normandy cemetery, Memorial Day, 2011. (Author's photograph)

Marine monument, Belleau Wood. (Author's photograph)

5

The American Battle Monuments Commission and World War II, 1939–1945

When war broke upon Europe in September 1939, the American Battle Monuments Commission was responsible for the maintenance and preservation of seven cemeteries and eleven monuments on the continent, and a lone cemetery in England. Having been deliberately sited in most cases on the battlefields of the First World War (of the eight cemeteries, for example, only Brookwood and Suresnes were not in combat zones of the Great War), these memorials would soon be in the region of violence of a second great European and global conflict. Not only American burial grounds, chapels, and monuments would be at risk in this new round of fighting, but the commission's personnel as well. Twenty-four of the ABMC employees serving in Europe by 1939 were American, and they had roughly three dozen dependents.[1] Many more employees were Europeans, a number of whom had signed on with the commission's work from the very beginning of the postwar construction effort that had produced the nation's overseas cemeteries and memorials.

During the months that followed the first shots in Poland, the impact of war waxed and waned in the areas distant from the actual fighting. But the well-being of ABMC sites and personnel remained a constant concern of American officials on both sides of the Atlantic. The period of "Phony War" (from September 1939 to May 1940) in the west occasioned certain inconveniences to the agency's employees and their families in Europe and prompted preliminary conversations about providing for these individuals if a more serious emergency were to develop. When

Hitler's legions did attack and overrun France and the Low Countries following May 10, 1940, ABMC sites found themselves in an active war zone and American personnel were forced temporarily to leave their posts for safety in southwestern France. By the end of July 1940, however, the cemeteries and monuments were reoccupied by their American staff and it appeared that, even with the sovereignty of France and Belgium at an end, the representatives of a neutral America might find a way to pursue their mission under the newly established German control. But life in the occupied regions that were home to the American memorials had become so challenging and threatening by the spring of 1941 that ABMC chairman and General of the Armies John J. Pershing, in close consultation with the State Department, ordered that all American employees of the commission, with their dependents, be repatriated from France and Belgium. The memorials of the past war would be entrusted to the care of personnel from the host countries and left to their fate. Another round of combat passed through the neighborhoods of many of the cemeteries and monuments with the liberation of western Europe three years later. Remarkably, the nearly six years of violence and four years of German occupation took, with one notable exception, a very small toll on the ABMC sites and left little restoration to be done. They would be easily enough returned to their pre–World War II condition, just as the task of creating permanent resting places on the war-torn continent for the new generation of American dead was beginning.

ABMC officials could not help but notice the increasing fragility of the European peace as 1938 gave way to 1939. In September 1938, only a last-minute trip to Munich by British and French leaders, and hefty concessions to Hitler once they got there, had averted war. Less than six months later, in violation of the Munich Pact, German troops entered Prague and occupied what was left of a sovereign Czechoslovakia. Communications between the commission's Washington and Paris offices reflected the heightened anxiety stemming from these developments. Two weeks after the Prague incursion, for example, Captain William W. Bessell, the officer-in-charge of the European office, remarked in a letter to General Pershing that "rumors were flying almost as fast in this building as they did last September." Bessell further noted that Ambassador William Bullitt had held a staff meeting recently at which the top diplomat was "extremely pessimistic" and predicted that there would be a war "this spring."[2]

As it happened, Bessell and Captain Kenner Hertford, the administrative officer and second in command at the European office, had already taken the lead at Ambassador Bullitt's request in crafting plans to be put into effect at the Paris compound in the event of war. Bessell noted that it was "rather gratifying to realize that the two plans for emergency measures in the embassy were prepared by commission personnel who have no official connection with the embassy other than to work here."[3] The officer-in-charge had also laid out specific "Emergency Measures" for the ABMC field personnel to follow in a confidential memorandum dated March 20, 1939 (five days after the Germans marched into Prague). The crux of this design called for all ABMC employees of American nationality, in the event of war, to remain at their posts until otherwise directed by the Paris office or "competent local civil or military authorities." Bessell's instructions further stipulated that cemetery superintendents should make no effort "to prevent the departure for either military or personal reasons of any non-American employee." In the event of an order to evacuate, the superintendents were told to shut off and drain all water systems, shut off electrical systems, close and lock all doors, and post a notice at all facilities for which they were responsible that read as follows: "This monument and the land surrounding it are the property of the Government of the United States of America and it is requested that they be respected as such." Before leaving their posts, finally, superintendents were "to advise the nearest civil or military authorities of their departure" and make no further attempt "to remove any government property or records" from their sites.[4]

Pershing came to Europe himself in June 1939 on his annual inspection tour of ABMC sites. The *New York Times* reported on June 7 that the general, then in his seventy-ninth year, had stood the sea voyage well. Bessell wrote James Mangum (in Washington) two days later that the chairman "seemed in good health, although he requires the occasional attention of his doctors."[5] The general's arrival in France coincided with Captain Bessell's departure. At the beginning of July, as the outgoing Paris officer and his family prepared to leave the capital, Pershing watched as Marshal Henri-Philippe Pétain presented Bessell with the Legion of Honor award for his service in the ABMC's European office.[6] On August 2, Captain Charles G. Holle became the new officer-in-charge in Paris. Eight days after that, the chairman boarded the SS *Manhattan* for New York.[7] The venerable old soldier had crossed and recrossed the Atlantic dozens of times since 1917 when he had come to the land of Lafayette to take up his duties as AEF commander. When he embarked on his August 1939 sailing, Pershing saw Europe for the last time. He arrived home a mere two weeks before Germany's invasion of Poland launched the troubled continent into its new nightmare.

As neutrals in the conflict, and with almost all of the initial violence concentrated in eastern Europe, ABMC personnel of American nationality expected to maintain a certain distance from the war that would likely be denied to Frenchmen, Belgians, or Englishmen. But it was a long-held belief throughout Europe that any war would mean the decimation of urban populations by indiscriminate bombing from the air. In early October, therefore, the European office relocated to Dreux, a medium-sized provincial city about fifty miles west of Paris, in the hope that ABMC employees could be insulated from aerial threats to the French capital. Holle and the staff began operating out of this new office on October 9.[8]

By all indications, the work of the commission continued fairly normally from Dreux. Holle reported on December 1, 1939, for example, that all ABMC sites had been inspected during the month of November and that Armistice Day commemorations had been held at six of the cemeteries.[9] The ceremony at Romagne, the largest of the American burial sites, was especially elaborate. There, the French Army staged a full-scale "parade under arms" in the presence of General Alphonse Georges, the second highest ranking officer in the French military hierarchy.[10] As it happened, this would be the last such commemoration in France for at least five years.

Among the changes the war brought was that ABMC personnel were now required to secure special authorization from the host government to travel from Paris into the "Zone of the Armies" northeast of the capital, where many of the American cemeteries and monuments were located. "We have had no trouble obtaining the necessary papers in traveling on the roads," the officer wrote Pershing in mid-October, "except of course the frequent stops to exhibit our authorities for traveling." Holle also told the chairman that the French Army had placed a four-man guard on Montsec, still a natural point of considerable military value, but had assured him that "they would take all measures necessary to prevent accidental damage to the monument and surroundings."[11]

Holle's heightened concern was not limited to the ABMC monuments, but included agency personnel and their families as well. His anxiety was greatest, not surprisingly, for his own wife and twin ten-year-old sons. Even though there had been virtually no fighting on French soil by the end of the war's first month, Holle wrote Mangum requesting authorization to lay plans for the evacuation of his dependents and those of Captain Hertford "so that we can take immediate action if it should become expedient or necessary."[12] Six weeks later, the captain wrote Mangum again and rehearsed at much greater length his concerns for all the American employees of the ABMC. Just because more than two months of the "Phony War" had produced few outright dangers and minimal inconveniences to commission personnel and their families was no cause to believe things might not suddenly change for the worse. "The possible circumstances envisaged are, among others, the development of economic conditions making continued residence of families in France inadvisable, or military operations causing the actual evacuation of our cemeteries."[13]

But the American bureaucracy furnished no answers to the Paris officer's numerous hypotheticals. Nor, for the time being, was serious thought given to planning for the evacuation of commission personnel from their overseas posts. Even after France's outright defeat in June 1940, the hope in Washington was that, with the fighting all but officially over on the Western Front and America still neutral, conditions in France and Belgium would stabilize favorably enough for Americans to take up anew the work of maintaining the memorial sites.[14]

Captain Holle had not waited for this turn of events, however, in the case of his own family. One month before the German invasion of France and the Low Countries, the Paris officer cabled Washington that he was sending his wife and sons home "because of developments and increasing difficulties in living conditions."[15] Coming two days after the war had expanded to Norway and Denmark, it is hard to resist the conclusion that this specific turn of events prompted the Holles' decision. Indeed, when the captain later explained his action more fully to General Pershing, he cited "the spread of the war" and "the difficulties of living here . . . and the possibility that later on it might be more difficult to get them home" as the factors that had persuaded him and his wife to take this step when they did. In addition, he noted that supplies of food and coal were growing tighter in Paris, as was the availability of transportation to other parts of France and beyond.[16] In sum, Holle's reasons for sending his family home mirrored the concerns he had expressed on behalf of all ABMC personnel and their families as early as the previous November.

The decision the army captain made for his family—and the request he made for the ABMC to fund their transfer home—touched off a classic bureaucratic tussle in Washington. When the Paris officer asked the commission to pay for the repatriation of his family, the Washington office was at pains to impress upon him that it simply had no funds to pay for the move. Ultimately, the War Department agreed to reimburse Holle for these travel expenses. For the immediate term, other ABMC officers and their dependents stayed at their European posts.[17]

The hot war that Holle's wife and children managed to avoid by their timely return home burst in full fury upon ABMC sites and personnel alike on Friday, May 10. The operations the Germans launched that day would carry them, within six weeks, to a complete subjugation of France, Belgium, the Netherlands, and Luxembourg, and leave only Churchill's Britain in a posture of active hostility against them.[18] Several cemetery superintendents would later report on German military activity in their vicinities. Adolph Kaess, the superintendent at Romagne, noted that a number of German planes had flown "back and forth" over his site as early as May 9, and that shortly after midnight on May 10 "we heard a heavy rumbling over our house which lasted for hours." Later that same morning Kaess reported heavy bombing within six kilometers of the cemetery, and by midday bombs were falling two kilometers in back of the site. By Sunday, May 12, the passage of bombers over the cemetery and the French anti-aircraft fire had become so intense that fragments of steel showered the grounds and narrowly missed Mrs. Kaess as she ventured out to feed the fish in the basin down the slope from the superintendent's quarters. Two days later, Kaess decided to evacuate himself and fifteen others—a mix of American and French employees and their dependents. The superintendent was careful to note that upon leaving the cemetery he had followed all steps "as prescribed in Office Order No. 15, dated March 20, 1939."[19]

The situation was similar elsewhere. Orlando Overstake, superintendent at Bony, reported that the German bombing of targets near his location in the rear of the forward French positions in Belgium had increased in intensity and proximity from May 12 onward. He evacuated his cemetery on the morning of May 17.[20] Overstake's counterpart at Thiaucourt, George C. Gorham, reported only sporadic bombing in the region until May 16, when the cemetery's host village was heavily attacked and at least four bombs fell within 250 yards of the burial grounds. After a night in which more than forty villagers, including the mayor, slept in the cemetery office and chapel basement, Gorham evacuated early on the morning of May 17.[21] It took the danger a bit longer to find its way farther west to the Oise-Aisne cemetery, but Superintendent John J. Dillon reported German planes directly over the site on May 16, and added that fifteen parachutists had landed nearby the next day. He evacuated at 2:30 that afternoon as French farmers pursued the skyborne invaders, and he carefully noted that he, too, had followed all the procedures stipulated in the March 1939 memorandum.[22]

On May 18, orders came from Holle to evacuate personnel from Belleau and Château-Thierry, two of the ABMC sites closest to Paris. The officer-in-charge could report that by late afternoon of that day "the entire contingent of our evacuated American personnel and their families [had] arrived in Dreux."[23] The next day, almost all of these personnel headed south to ride out the rest of the battle of France in the vicinity of Bordeaux, comfortably removed from the actual fighting. Holle held back some of the men to serve as truck drivers, but noted that the rest "could serve no useful purpose at Dreux" and needed to move to a safer location. The captain also predicted that the first temporary location of the ABMC's European office would likely become an enticing target for German bombers because a new military airfield was just now being established in the vicinity.[24]

The accounts of the American evacuees on their way to Dreux provide a vivid picture of the chaos and peril that befell France in the early days of the May 1940 fighting. Highways throughout the eastern and northeastern parts of the country became quickly clogged with civilian refugee traffic trying to move away from the violence, and French military traffic moving both toward and away from it. Holle wrote General Pershing on May 23 that "the refugee situation and the congestion on the roads are almost indescribable. . . . Military motor convoys going in both directions and refugee vehicles (automobiles and horse carts) become almost inextricably intermingled."[25] The evacuation parties from the American cemeteries invariably got caught up in this disorder. Superintendent Kaess, for example, had a collision with an army truck that disabled his car while traveling in blackout conditions shortly before midnight on May 14. He was three hours into his journey, but barely twenty kilometers from Romagne.[26] The Overstakes got mired in a makeshift convoy of refugees and French troops outside of Péronne on May 17, and as the procession ground to a halt six German planes appeared overhead and started bombing and strafing. Overstake and his family took cover in a ditch, but his car was hit several times by bullets, and other cars in the front and rear of his were set on fire.[27] Throughout these often perilous journeys, the good fortune of the ABMC evacuees held, and all managed to escape the zone of combat with little more than a few bumps and bruises.

As for the cemeteries and monuments, not until the fighting ended could Holle and the ABMC personnel assess and report any damage. Undeniably the Americans had left to their respective fates almost all of their burial grounds and shrines to the memory of the soldiers of the Great War. Of the eight cemeteries, only Brookwood remained in the care of an American superintendent two weeks into the German offensive. Holle's report of May 22 noted that the cemeteries at Thiaucourt, Belleau, and Bony had been left in the charge of their senior French employees, but speculated that since the latter site had already come under German occupation the employee had probably departed. In the case of Thiaucourt and Belleau, the French caretakers could only be expected to remain on site and in communication with the European office "if conditions permit." When the two American administrators at the Suresnes cemetery were given leave to evacuate with their families to southern France, charge of the site was given to an "old and extremely reliable French employee" from Romagne, and the European office was still close enough to exercise direct supervision. There was no contact for the moment with Flanders Field, however, and the Meuse-Argonne and Oise-Aisne cemeteries had been completely emptied of all personnel. A similar variety of situations prevailed at the monument sites.[28]

Holle made no attempt to conceal the emotional toll of what had just happened. He wrote to Pershing two weeks into the German onslaught: "I fully realized all the adverse aspects and effects of what might be bluntly called deserting our cemeteries, particularly to the relatives of the men buried there, and therefore was reluctant to withdraw our personnel until forced to. On the other hand I could see no justification for jeopardizing the safety of our employees and their families by keeping them too long in situations in which they could accomplish absolutely nothing." Some consolation could be taken, however, from the fact that the Germans did not seem to be targeting the American sites. "Apparently," Holle observed to his boss, "the German aviators knew of the locations of our cemeteries and, so far as I know, no cemetery was actually a target."[29] Little more than incidental harm came to the cemeteries and monuments during the first battle for France, but this fact could not be known for many weeks.[30]

With his field personnel mostly gone from their posts, Captain Holle tried to keep the work of the European office going as long as he could from Dreux. But as the military campaign moved inexorably toward its conclusion, the danger moved closer and closer to the ABMC's temporary European headquarters. The initial trajectory of the German Army through France was that of a left-handed "sickle cut" moving out from the eastern bank of the Meuse River in and around Sedan and aimed at Abbeville, near where the Somme empties into the English Channel. The path of this march had carried Wehrmacht troops right through the vicinity of the Romagne and Bony cemeteries during the first ten days of the campaign. Between May 20 and the beginning of June, the bulk of the fighting concentrated on the channel ports, culminating at Dunkirk. By the time that harbor city fell on June 4, the Germans had already begun to drive south toward Paris, and after three more weeks they had overrun the entire northern half of the country. The capital was declared an "open city" and occupied on June 14, and the French submitted to Hitler's armistice terms on June 22. One of the most important provisions of this cease-fire was the division of the country into occupied and unoccupied zones. German military authority would prevail in the former, and that of a reorganized French government under Marshal Pétain, with its "capital" at Vichy, in the latter. All of the American cemeteries and monuments in France were situated in the occupied zone.

As the Germans bore down on Paris and its environs, Captain Holle monitored the situation every day with the military attaché at the embassy. On Sunday, June 9, he and Hertford concluded that they ought to evacuate Dreux in two days' time. The information available to the two officers then indicated "that there was no immediate danger—at least not for three or four days." The presumed respite would allow the opportunity for an orderly departure of the remaining ABMC personnel from both Paris and Dreux and the packing and removal of office files and records.[31]

While trucks were being loaded on June 10, however, German dive bombers struck at Dreux and bombs fell "in the immediate vicinity of the office." Holle recounted that "railroad, bus, telephone, electricity and water service was . . . completely interrupted," and "it was impossible to communicate with Paris." The evacuation convoy left Dreux a day ahead of schedule and, as a result, many household and personal possessions of the departing personnel had to be abandoned.[32] The ABMC evacuees eventually settled in Gujan-Mestras, a coastal town of about ten thousand people twenty miles southwest of Bordeaux. Holle had already secured office space there, close enough that the American consul in Bordeaux would be available for communication and other kinds of support.[33]

During much of the six weeks spent at Gujan-Mestras, Holle and Hertford kept busy organizing the use of available vehicles and drivers for follow-up evacuations of American personnel and equipment hitherto scattered about northern France, and transmitting important communications. A mix of ABMC and embassy personnel had taken refuge together, and some of the latter contingent soon began to leave France by way of Spain and Portugal. Hostile military action stopped on June 25, in accordance with the terms of the Franco-German armistice. The two captains and Superintendent Kaess attended the "minute of silence" ceremony held that morning by the monument to the dead of the 1914–18 war in Gujan-Mestras. Holle suspended all official activities that day because the French government had set aside the time for national mourning.[34] The next day, the officer was already anxious to inspect the ABMC cemeteries and monuments "preparatory to the return of our personnel as soon as possible."[35]

A request from Acting Ambassador Anthony Biddle to collect some of his belongings left near Tours afforded Captain Holle an opportunity to see firsthand if he could move about on French highways now that the fighting had ceased. He encountered no difficulties during his two-day foray in late June, which also allowed him to see that the ABMC monument in Tours had suffered only slight damage from shell fragments. On June 30, Holle recorded: "Awaiting further developments, stabilization of occupation of area by the Germans and establishment of rules and regulations for circulation and movement on roads."[36] Whatever decrees the Germans might issue would plainly affect what the commission's chief field officer saw as his next move: the return of the evacuated ABMC personnel to their normal postings.

During the first few days of July, a collection of personnel assigned to the ABMC and the military attaché's office actually prepared to return to Paris. Cars and trucks were packed and made ready for a July 4 departure from Gujan-Mestras. But when Holle started out on his own journey a day ahead of the larger group, he learned from French authorities on the road to Limoges that the Germans had closed the border between the occupied and unoccupied zones, that two hundred thousand automobiles were backed up along the route he intended to take, and that he would be marooned in Limoges indefinitely if he tried to pass through there. Without any means of communicating this news to the convoy intending to leave the next day, the officer and two colleagues traveling with him returned to their starting point to hold the others in place until the entire route back to Paris could be explored.[37]

Captain Holle and his companions left again the next day (July 4) by a different route on what turned out to be a twelve-day inspection tour of all seven ABMC cemeteries in France and Belgium and nine of the eleven monument sites. Upon his return to Gujan-Mestras on July 16, Holle organized fifteen vehicles for the departure three days later of all fifty-nine ABMC employees and dependents who had evacuated their posts weeks earlier. By sundown on July 19, most of this group had returned to occupied Paris, while one truckload of personnel and baggage had peeled off in Tours for the direct run to Thiaucourt. By the end of the month, all of the ABMC sites were once again under direct American supervision.[38]

What the leadership of the European office learned from the inspection tour, and what the returning personnel would discover days later, was that the majority of the buildings on the ABMC sites had been entered and ransacked in their absence, but that the burial grounds and monuments had come through the military onslaught with little damage.[39] The havoc wreaked upon the temporary commission headquarters at Dreux was especially striking. "Every file cabinet and every trunk and box containing personal property had been opened," Holle reported, "and the contents not only scattered all over the premises but . . . carried from house to house [within the ABMC complex]." The officer marveled at the intentionality of the vandalism because it "was perfectly evident that the office building was that of an American Government agency."[40] At Belleau, Fère, and Waregem, the quarters and outbuildings had been badly vandalized. Although the residences of both the superintendent and assistant superintendent were found to be "in disorder" at Romagne, a German officer had left a notice to his troops cautioning against doing any damage. Twenty-five German officers and men signed the visitors' register there between June 18 and July 1.[41]

The worst damage to the memorials themselves had occurred at Belleau and Romagne. At the former, Holle reported that "about 100 headstones" (of the 2,289 in the cemetery) had been damaged, windows in numerous structures had been shot out or smashed in, and the exterior of the chapel had been chipped "in a number of places by shell and bomb fragments."⁴² There was further evidence that machine gun emplacements had been set up in the cemetery and that troops had actually occupied the cemetery grounds. At Romagne, about fifty headstones near the chapel had been damaged by shellfire, the western entrance to the cemetery had suffered bomb damage, the cemetery wall at the eastern entrance had been partially dismantled, and one panel of the door to the chapel "had been hacked out" by a sharp instrument to allow seeing into the building but not entering it.⁴³ Not one of the monuments was seriously damaged, although the Germans had placed an observation post on top of the Château-Thierry monument and thoroughly ransacked the basement storage areas of that large structure. Two French soldiers and one German had also been buried on the monument grounds.⁴⁴

Two Belgian employees at Flanders Field reported the most dishonorable incident of German vandalism during the initial blitzkrieg. On May 23, they claimed, as invading troops entered Waregem and the cemetery, one of the soldiers took down the American flag, tore it up, and carried it away. Of all the ways in which the Germans had disturbed the peace of the ABMC sites, this was the one that brought forth a formal diplomatic protest from the Americans. When Holle arrived at the site on July 12 and heard this story, he could at least take some comfort that Superintendent William Moses, from whom nothing had been heard since the mid-May evacuations, was on duty in the office to welcome him.⁴⁵

The captain's travels also provided a rare opportunity to survey physical damage to the French hinterlands from the recent fighting. On his way back through Paris, eager to get some word to General Pershing of what he had seen, Holle dashed off a four-page letter to the chairman on July 14. After describing in sparser detail the widespread destruction he had seen and the damage to ABMC sites, he concluded: "Considering the general destruction over the entire northern France, I believe we are very fortunate to have suffered such slight damage to our memorials." He went on to tell Pershing that he had also passed "a number of French, German, and British World War cemeteries on our trip and saw no evidence of deliberate damage or vandalism."⁴⁶

In early August, once the superintendents had all returned to their sites, Holle and Hertford, now both promoted to the rank of major, made another inspection tour. This time they wanted to confirm that American personnel "had been satisfactorily re-installed," to arrange for repairs and make sure that proper maintenance was resumed, and to see that personnel were paid. The German takeover of France and Belgium had completely disrupted banking, and Holle had had to deliver compensation in cash for the weeks of fighting to all the ABMC personnel he could find at the sites during his July trip.[47]

Setting out again on such a lengthy circuit through occupied territory posed a new set of difficulties, two of which were that the Germans had prohibited travel across the Somme and also across the Belgian border. After attempting fruitlessly for several days to secure permission from the German authorities in Paris to make the trip, the two majors simply started out on August 7. Not surprisingly, they were stopped at the Somme crossing nearest Bony and barred from proceeding without the necessary authorization that they should have gotten in Paris. Holle was carrying papers in German that he had prepared and signed himself and decorated with a red seal, and which identified him and Hertford as employees of the US government and described their errand, but these did not pass muster with the first Germans they encountered. They were luckier at a small provincial outpost whose guards permitted the Americans to proceed after all. As Holle observed to Pershing, who must have smiled at the pluck and daring of his men, "the substance of this story is that the Germans are still not very well organized for handling the traffic, in general seem to have instructions to be accommodating to Americans, and the ordinary soldier and non-commissioned officer can be impressed with official looking documents." Major Holle also reported to the chairman on his August trip in a manner designed to stir the aged commander to reflect critically upon the latest fight between France and Germany.[48]

In the course of his remarkably thorough August inspection tour, the resourceful major observed the condition of dozens of American World War I memorials erected by agencies other than the ABMC. Most of them had come through the fighting without significant damage. The 3rd Division monument at Château-Thierry, however, had been "badly damaged"; the ornamental wrought iron honoring the 5th Division on the bridge at Dun-sur-Meuse had been destroyed; and the commemorative bridge to the 28th Division erected by the Commonwealth of Pennsylvania at Fismes had been likewise destroyed. Damage to bridges—commemorative or otherwise—is understandable due to their nature as military targets. By contrast, the majestic Pennsylvania monument in Varennes, which had been designed by the commission's chief architect, Paul Cret, was found to be in "good condition."⁴⁹ In September, Holle reported on eight more monuments he had been able to see, all of which had survived, and by November he had checked out twenty-five more and found virtually no damage of consequence.⁵⁰

By the end of November, Holle recounted the repair of damage to the cemeteries and monuments of the ABMC that had been done to date. "I think we have accomplished about all that will be practicable for the present and, for that matter, for some time to come," he told the chairman. Headstones needing replacement at Belleau had been engraved and were ready to be put in place. Broken windows from the Belleau chapel were in the process of being repaired (some of the more seriously damaged ones had to be taken to Paris to be worked on by more skilled craftsmen), and Holle expected that work to be completely finished early in December. In October the door to the Sommepy monument had been taken to Paris for skilled repair. It also would be ready for reinstallation in early December. Fixing the damaged door to the Montfaucon monument, replacing damaged stones in the outer steps to it, and replacing the damaged headstones at the Romagne cemetery could only be done when skilled craftsmen were once again available. The fact that these latter two sites remained in a restricted military zone and "our personnel" could not visit them made it "impracticable to make any other repairs," Holle wrote, "and it appears that it will be a long time before further work can be initiated."⁵¹

Since October the head of the Paris office had, in fact, been complaining of increasingly tight travel restrictions. By that time the Germans had taken on a more severe attitude of noncooperation toward the American officials still in Paris. Under the terms of the June armistice, the historic French capital was in the zone occupied and administered by the German military and was no longer the official capital at all. Ambassador Bullitt had departed in June and his replacement was destined to reside in Vichy. According to a memorandum Bullitt wrote in November 1940, President Roosevelt told the outgoing ambassador that he had sent General Edwin "Pa" Watson to offer the ambassadorial post in France to Pershing, but that the latter had declined it.⁵² As the Germans saw it, in any case, the United States had no reason to retain diplomatic personnel in Paris. The occupying authorities, consequently, were growing more and more reluctant to accord them and ABMC personnel any special status. Holle was particularly upset that he could no longer travel to all of the French and Belgian memorials. Hitherto, he had simply struck out on such trips with his own homemade credentials and relied on his capacity to persuade guards at checkpoints along the way to honor them. Now, the rump American embassy in Paris was advising him not to do that, fearing that if he did make it to such places as Waregem, where he had not been allowed to go since early August, the Germans would not permit him to return to Paris.[53]

In a carefully prepared memorandum dated October 5, Major Holle formally requested permission of the German authorities in Paris for him and three of his assistants to visit American cemeteries and monuments in the restricted travel areas of Belgium and northeastern France. After naming all the ABMC sites in both the restricted and nonrestricted areas, the officer explained the necessity of regular monthly visits, "oftener if circumstances demand," for what he described as "the purposes of administration, supervision, inspection, payment of personnel, etc."[54] After ten days, the German reply was that the permission he had requested "cannot be granted at the present time." Rather, Holle was told that "the military cemeteries and monuments in that zone are under the protection of German troops." Any damage sustained at the sites "as a result of military action" would be restored, the Germans claimed, and their army graves officer stood ready to carry out any desire the Americans might express to him, including delivering salary payments to ABMC personnel.[55] The latter offer was declined, and the frustrated and disappointed major told commission headquarters that he would "pay and supervise by mail" the otherwise inaccessible sites.[56]

As 1940 wound down, tighter restrictions on travel were not the only evidence that the German occupation had become more onerous. Gasoline was so scarce that grass in the cemeteries was being cut with scythes and hand lawnmowers.[57] "The local press," Holle observed in late November, "is entirely German controlled." Communication between the occupied and unoccupied zones of France was "still entirely suspended." While there were indications at last that the French people were beginning to stir from the lethargy of humiliation they had been in since June to a posture of more active resistance toward their enemy, this otherwise encouraging development (to an American, at least) had a downside: the Germans were taking on an increasingly threatening retaliatory posture toward ordinary civilians. When a field telephone line was cut near Belleau in October, for example, the Germans selected local citizens at random and imprisoned them without trial as hostages. Several of the French employees at Aisne-

Marne cemetery had been apprehended and held in this incident. With all of this in mind by late November, Holle decided to raise with the chairman the prospect of the complete evacuation of American employees.[58]

Assuring Pershing that his highest-ranking officer in Europe did not want to appear "alarmist," Holle exposed his growing fears for the ABMC's American employees. His clearest worry was that these people would be trapped and at the mercy of the Germans if formal hostilities were to break out between the United States and Hitler's Reich. Because the commission's employees were almost all stationed at "isolated locations" with which it was already difficult to communicate, Holle surmised that, in the event of war, it would take at least a week to collect all of his personnel in Paris. More ominously, when the major had observed to Maynard Barnes, chargé d'affaires in the rump American embassy, that commission personnel should enjoy special status if Germany became formally our enemy, the career diplomat had countered that he did not see any difference between ABMC employees and any other American citizens. This disturbing utterance moved Holle to ask Pershing to take up "the situation of our Service" with the State Department in Washington and ensure that any move to evacuate diplomatic staff "would definitely include our personnel."[59]

Even more chilling was Holle's awareness that the Imperial War Graves Commission (the British counterpart to ABMC) had failed to make adequate provision for the evacuation of its staff members from their postings in France and Belgium prior to the outbreak of serious fighting there earlier in 1940. "As a result," he informed Pershing, "their employees had to shift for themselves." He shared with the general reports that some of the British personnel had been picked up by the Germans and sent to concentration camps. Without knowing all the details of the plight of these unfortunates, Holle reasoned to his superior: "There is no indication that our employees would be treated any differently if the United States became involved in the war."[60] In fact, 206 of the 540 British field personnel caught up in the German blitzkrieg failed to escape the war zone. Most of these were eventually interned by the Germans, and more than a dozen did not survive the war.[61]

If Major Holle rightly feared that a similar fate awaited his own colleagues if his superiors did not act wisely, he nevertheless concluded his November report to General Pershing on a more reassuring note. Even with a number of the cemeteries and monuments off limits to visits from

Paris, the major observed that "so far no unsolvable problems have arisen." While the travel restrictions posed an obstacle to the smooth running of his office and to the complete fulfillment of his responsibilities, he resolved that "we must continue to get along as best we can."[62] Still, in raising the prospect of another evacuation, Holle had confronted Pershing with an option the chairman was not yet ready to exercise. As it happened, the more junior officer's tour of duty with the commission in Europe ended before the issue came up again. Officers-in-charge at the Paris office typically served between one and two years in that post, and Holle was ordered to quit the French capital "on or about December 26, 1940," make his way to Washington, and report on arrival to the acting secretary of the commission "for such duty as may be assigned."[63]

Colonel T. Bentley Mott assumed his duties at the head of the European office a week into 1941. Born in 1865 and a classmate of Pershing at West Point, Mott had played a prominent role on the general's staff during World War I and spent a number of years as the military attaché at the Paris embassy. He had retired to live in France with his French wife during the 1930s, and was thus close at hand and already a Pershing friend and confidante when Major Holle needed to be replaced. As it turned out, the service Mott would give to the commission in 1941 was only the first of several remarkable stints he would contribute as the chief representative of the ABMC in Europe through the war years and into the immediate postwar period.[64]

Mott's appointment coincided with the first clear indications from the State Department that the days in Europe of the American employees attached to the commission might be numbered. Acting on a recommendation from the embassy at Vichy that the ABMC staff should be "drastically reduced" and that "serious consideration" should be given to "withdrawing the American field personnel with a view to repatriating them," Assistant Secretary of State Breckenridge Long wrote to Pershing in mid-January to know the general's views. Maynard Barnes had reported from Paris to his superiors some days earlier that it was becoming "increasingly difficult" to get food in the former capital and that he had closed the old embassy commissary. Barnes had also expressed the belief that the ABMC staff attached to the Paris office should at least be halved.[65]

Pershing, who was wintering in San Antonio, took two months to respond to this approach from the State Department. In mid-March, before answering Long's letter, the chairman wired Mangum seeking both his and the recently repatriated Holle's analysis of what was really behind the State Department's desire to have the ABMC reduce its American personnel in Europe. Was it concern over food shortages, the general wondered? Or was it worry over the possibility that war might suddenly break out between the United States and Germany? If the former prospect, Pershing opined that food could be shipped to embattled ABMC staff from the United States. If the latter prospect, he observed, "that would seem rather remote according to our best information." Whatever was driving State Department concerns, the chairman made no effort to conceal his reluctance to repatriate any portion of the ABMC contingent. "In my opinion, we need the service of all the employees we have," Pershing declared to the commission's acting secretary. He still sought Mangum's and Major Holle's assessment as to whether the number of American employees abroad could be reduced "without material detriment to our obligations of proper maintenance and repair."[66]

Both officers were skeptical of the soundness of any advice coming from Maynard Barnes. While Holle and Mangum differed in their assessments of the imminence of war with Germany and the urgency of repatriating the ABMC staff, however, they both advised Pershing that preparations for the latter eventuality should begin right away. These included getting passports in order, seeking out the necessary funds for repatriation, and setting up a plan to transfer responsibility for caretaking of the American sites to some French bureau. The general was also encouraged to involve the Washington office in clarifying the eligibility of transferred ABMC personnel to hold civil service jobs once they returned to the United States and canvassing the availability of replacement jobs of all sorts for the returning Americans.[67]

Pershing's answer to the State Department in late March was that the ABMC would neither withdraw nor diminish its European staff at this time. In his communication to Secretary Cordell Hull, the general laid bare his own understanding of the unique mission entrusted to the agency and its overseas employees. "The Commission's duties, particularly with respect to the cemeteries, constitute a responsibility of great trust and honor, and I feel it incumbent upon us to continue to carry out these duties under the direct supervision of our established organization unless circumstances of a most compelling nature should make this impracticable." Pershing conceded that he was "not unmindful" that current conditions in France posed "a number of inconveniences and hardships to our personnel." But none of these yet argued in favor of adopting the recommendations of the State Department's Paris office that people should be brought home. It was Pershing's belief, in fact, that "most, if not all, of these [ABMC] employees would prefer to remain at their posts of duty." Almost all of the two dozen men in question were AEF veterans who had remained in France "continuously since the War," their former commander noted. Most of them had French wives and were raising families in France; consequently, they would experience "serious personal and family problems" if they were required to go to the United States. Pershing admitted, furthermore, that the commission had nothing for these folks to do in America, and that the need for them to find new employment would require "extensive readjustments." In closing, he assured Hull that he would defer to the State Department's recommendations "if you should determine at any time that the best interests of the United States as a whole would be served by withdrawing our American personnel from Europe, or that the personal safety or freedom of our American officers or employees require their removal from a danger zone." But, in the general's mind, such a point had not yet arrived.[68]

Under-Secretary of State Sumner Welles replied four days later to Pershing's letter and told the chairman that the department had sent copies of it to the embassies in Vichy and Berlin. The explicit objective in so doing was to enlist those outposts in helping ABMC personnel get their passports in order, but Welles also promised his agency's assistance in a more thoroughgoing way as well.[69] As April came and went, Pershing's concern shifted to getting assurances from Secretary Hull that ABMC personnel would enjoy equal standing with other government employees when it came to gaining access to food shipments from the United States and securing exit visas from the Germans. Hull offered such assurances on April 28 once he received confirmation of them from his staff in Paris.[70]

The very next day, however, Colonel Mott wired Pershing through the embassy at Vichy a new recommendation with which, he said, Maynard Barnes was in "full accord." ABMC employees in the field should be brought immediately to Paris, with per diem and funds provided for their maintenance and travel. Mott cited the existence of a "state of emergency" stemming from the potential difficulties that could attend the necessity of evacuating American employees of the government from occupied France. Those difficulties had to do with travel inside and outside of France.[71] The realities were much the same as Major Holle had reported six months earlier. The Romagne, Thiaucourt, and Bony cemeteries, and the nearby monuments, were in essentially a "no travel" zone. Flanders Field cemetery and the Audenarde and Kemmel monuments were on the other side of a closed frontier as well. The only way to traverse these boundaries was to secure special permission from the Germans, which never came easily or quickly, if it came at all. The obvious fear was that if the personnel in these isolated posts were not collected in Paris while Germany and the United States remained at peace, it might not be possible to evacuate them at all in the event of war. As May dawned, moreover, events signaled all too clearly that hostilities were expanding and intensifying, and that relations between Berlin and Washington were likely to deteriorate. Most ominously for the Americans, Congress had passed the Lend-Lease Act in March. Its open-ended provision of aid to Britain and any other countries that would stand against Hitler gave the lie to American neutrality and promised to embroil the United States more deeply in the conflict.[72]

Pershing agreed without evident hesitation to Mott's (and Barnes's) recommendation that the commission's American field personnel should be collected in Paris. On May 5, the general cabled orders to the European office that all American employees and their families be brought from their postings throughout France and Belgium to the Paris area. A mere four days later, however, Cordell Hull advised the general that the commission should undertake the full repatriation of its American personnel "as soon as possible." The secretary of state explained to Pershing that he made this recommendation "in view of the present international situation, of the growing disruption of transportation and communication facilities in France, and of the unpredictability of future developments." Recalling Pershing's March 24 letter, Hull paid due homage to the commission's unique responsibility and informed the general that his department had held off coming to this sterner counsel out of deference to that. But repatriation "has now become imperative," the secretary asserted, and he expected Pershing to agree. Even to start the process of collecting ABMC personnel immediately would not spare the "tedious and prolonged formalities" that the Germans would throw in the way. As if to break down any remaining shred of resistance the old soldier might offer to this bitter step, Hull concluded succinctly: "Your men do not have diplomatic status."[73]

The ABMC chairman did not resist this counsel. On May 13, Pershing directed that all of his American personnel on the European continent return, with their families, to the United States. In that same directive he ordered that a formal request be made of General Pierre Vincensini, now a senior official in the Vichy French cabinet of Marshal Pétain and formerly head of the ministry responsible for war cemeteries, "to take over and administer all our establishments in France."[74]

The actual evacuation of the roughly sixty American personnel and their dependents took more than two months to complete. In view of the budgetary constraints upon the ABMC, the State Department authorized travel expenses for wives and minor children of the commission's civilian employees from its own funds.[75] The route home went from Paris to the Spanish border at Hendaye, then on to Lisbon for sea passage to New York. It was necessary to secure multiple clearances from the Germans—inter-zonal passes to reach Paris, and special visas to exit France—and these were often slow in coming. The first American evacuees, mostly embassy personnel, did not reach Lisbon until June 13. By the end of the month, a large collection of ABMC personnel had set sail from the Portuguese capital. The final group, which included Colonel Mott and his wife, Superintendents Kaess (Meuse-Argonne), Moses (Flanders Field), and Overstake (Somme), and assistants from Meuse-Argonne and Aisne-Marne, left Lisbon on July 26 and arrived in New York on August 1. Mott later reported that the Germans had repeatedly gone back and forth with his group over permission to leave France and detained them three days at Hendaye. The journey to Lisbon, he observed, had been "exhausting" and "a very wearing process upon the nervous system of everybody."[76]

The non-American employees of the commission, of course, had stayed behind and were expected to continue with their duties. Mott had left 1.2 million francs in an account with the French Post Office from which General Vincensini was authorized to draw their salaries.[77] A similar arrangement was made through the Belgian Ministry of the Interior for the maintenance of the cemetery and monuments in that country.[78] By this means was provision made for the preservation of the ABMC sites while the Americans were gone.

The commission's archives contain a thick packet of reports on the condition and upkeep of the sites made quarterly, beginning October 1, 1941, by Pierre Rod, the designated chief of repair and maintenance for the American cemeteries under the authority of General Vincensini. These reports meticulously recorded monthly payments made to salaried employees, maintenance work done, and costs incurred. The documents were routinely forwarded to Washington, at first by the US embassy at Vichy, and later by the Swiss through the American Legation in Bern.[79] Pershing assumed that there would be some slippage in the quality of care and maintenance during the time that American supervision was absent. As the chairman wrote to Secretary of the Treasury Henry Morgenthau early in 1942, in the course of discussing a requested appropriation of $30,000 for upkeep of the overseas sites during Fiscal Year 1943: "I have no intention of trying to maintain our establishments on even the limited scale prevailing up to last August; on the contrary, I expect to spend only such amounts as are required to keep them from undue deterioration, so that when normal times return, large sums will not be necessary to restore them to satisfactory condition."[80]

One of the earliest "casualties" of the outbreak of fighting in western Europe, and the subsequent occupation of France and Belgium, was the Memorial Day observances at the American cemeteries. Because of the timing and nature of German military operations in 1940, only the Brookwood cemetery was able to hold its scheduled ceremony that year. Superintendent John T. Ryan reported that seven hundred people, including representatives from the American Overseas Memorial Day Association, the Imperial War Graves Commission, the American embassy, and the British and American Legion posts in London, attended the June 2 commemoration.[81] (Two days later, Operation Dynamo, the evacuation of the Dunkirk beaches, concluded its rescue of almost 350,000 British and French soldiers over a nine-day period.)

In 1941, according to sketchy newspaper reports filed through Vichy, American participation in Memorial Day observances in occupied France was largely limited to Paris. After a short service at the American Cathedral on May 30, Colonel Mott led roughly twenty of his countrymen to Suresnes cemetery, where they decorated a number of graves. French villagers conducted similarly simple ceremonies at burial grounds outside of the capital, for many of the American officials had evacuated those outposts days earlier. "Flowers and green leaves were placed on the graves," the *New York Times* reported, and the American flag was flown over all six cemeteries in France.[82]

Brookwood hosted the only overseas Memorial Day observance in 1941 that resembled those of more ordinary times. Superintendent Ryan reported that eight hundred people attended this June 1 service. The presence of such figures as Clementine Churchill, wife of the prime minister, and Major-General Sir Fabian Ware, the venerable founder and head of the Imperial War Graves Commission, suggested that the occasion was, in fact, far from ordinary. Coming three weeks before Germany's attack on the Soviet Union, at a time when Britain was standing virtually alone in the actual combat with the Axis powers, it is hard to escape the conclusion that the British made use of the Brookwood commemoration to express their fervent hope that the United States might be persuaded formally to enter the conflict. As the attendees gathered at the cemetery's stone of remembrance, Reverend Marcus A. Spencer, minister of Saint John's Presbyterian Church in Kensington, London, led them in a prayer replete with language from Lincoln's Gettysburg Address that left its ultimate purpose patently clear: "We pray Thee that as America has been led by Thee to aid without stint from afar, she may now hold back no longer. May she take that further step of complete brotherhood of aim and of arms, of risk and of sacrifice. So may we as a nation pledge the last full measure of devotion that the cause of freedom shall not perish from the earth."[83]

Memorial Day observances were not the only regular activity of the ABMC that was suspended during the war. Throughout the entirety of the conflict, the seven-member American Battle Monuments Commission did not meet. The forty-fifth meeting of the commission in November 1938, the last one before the war began, had concentrated largely on the trivial business of the distribution to interested groups of moving pictures from the 1937 dedications and the disposition of relics from Belleau Wood.[84] Chairman Pershing occasionally sent memoranda during the war to commission members to update them on important developments. But, as the chairman wrote Mangum in March 1941, just weeks before he ordered the evacuation of American personnel from France and Belgium, there seemed little for the oversight body to do but "await the end of the War in Europe."[85]

If Pershing seemed content not to have the full body convene during the war years, Franklin Roosevelt was nonetheless committed to maintaining its full complement. In June 1941, when one of the original seven commissioners (General J. B. P. Clayton Hill) died, the nation's chief executive quickly appointed a replacement.[86] Thus, when peace was restored in 1945, the full roster of commission members was ready to take up the next round of commemorative work.

The latter story awaits us in the next chapter. For now, what of the work of ABMC personnel after the American employees returned home, and what of the fate of the cemeteries and memorials? The former officer-in-charge of the commission's Paris bureau, Colonel T. Bentley Mott, was destined for, by far, the most interesting wartime experiences. Pershing's West Point classmate had gained promotion to brigadier general upon his return to the United States and was later appointed as a special disbursing officer for the ABMC. Notwithstanding his harrowing journey out of France, Mott was back in his adopted second country before a year had passed on a mission authorized by the ABMC chairman and approved by the State Department. General Pershing described the official purpose of Mott's return to France in 1942 as "to make payments in connection with the maintenance of the commission's establishments" in occupied Europe, to gather information about the condition of the sites, and to monitor how the arrangement with General Vincensini was working.[87] Although the United States was at war with Germany by then, diplomatic relations remained intact with the Vichy French government, and this gave Mott his entrée onto the war-torn European continent. As will be shown below, however, the amazing odyssey that would keep the elderly agent of the commission in Europe until the spring of 1944 was actually spawned of a complex mix of personal—his own, and General Pershing's—and official concerns.

When (then) Colonel Mott and his wife arrived in the United States with the last of the ABMC evacuees in early August 1941, they immediately sought to unwind from their taxing travels. But after two weeks of a quiet retreat in suburban Philadelphia, the devoted subordinate wrote his high-ranking friend expressing a desire to return to France. Mott confided to Pershing that his wife had cancer, that she wanted to live out her days in her native land, and that he wanted to be with her. Had it not been for his sense of obligation "to finish properly the job you had confided to me and come home with all our [ABMC] people," Mott explained, the couple would never have left France four weeks earlier.[88]

By early November 1941 Pershing had agreed to have the Motts return to Europe on ABMC business once Georgette had had surgery and regained sufficient strength to withstand the trip. Within a month, however, it became clear that the sick woman was not strong enough to undergo the anticipated operation.[89] To complicate things still further, Germany declared war on the United States on December 11. General Mott conceded to Pershing the day after this momentous development that the plan to send him and Georgette back to France was likely "in the soup," while noting that they would still do the trip if it were to prove possible.⁹⁰ On January 3, 1942, Mott wrote Pershing again, this time from the commission's headquarters in Washington. He was more convinced than ever that his going to France on ABMC business would be "very useful indeed," and he did not believe it would be that hard to get there.⁹¹ His wife's health had improved enough for her to travel, and she was prepared to forego the earlier planned surgery. Diplomatic relations with the Vichy French regime remained intact, moreover, and Pershing still seemed willing to send them. As it turned out, with the United States and Germany formally at war, the greatest new difficulty to be overcome was procuring transportation across the Atlantic on a neutral vessel. The Motts finally sailed from New York on May 7 aboard SS *Drottningholm* of the Swedish-American Line and arrived in Lisbon nine days later.⁹²

During the months of waiting for the elderly couple to secure transatlantic passage, General Pershing had come up with a third matter for them to address in Europe: the personal affairs of the older general's longtime lady friend Micheline Resco. Like Georgette Mott, Micheline was French. Pershing had met her in 1917 and, despite being more than thirty-five years her senior, had discreetly maintained a romance with her that he renewed during each of his numerous visits to France to pay homage to his dead soldiers and tend to ABMC business. The general had gotten Micheline to safety in Washington, D.C., amid the tumultuous events of May and June 1940, with the help of thousands of dollars of his own money and the intervention of well-placed US diplomatic personnel on both sides of the Atlantic. But she still had family and property in France. Once there himself, General Mott would be able to assess how both were doing and, if need be, provide assistance.⁹³

Upon their arrival in Lisbon in May 1942, it took the Motts another month to get to Vichy. In his first communication with Pershing from the French capital shortly after his arrival, Mott described the warm greeting he had received from Henri-Philippe Pétain during a chance encounter with the elderly *Maréchal* on the street.⁹⁴ Plainly the abiding respect and affection that had developed between Mott and Pétain, and Pershing and Pétain, as they had worked closely together during the decisive moments of World War I would pay significant dividends for Mott throughout his delicate mission.

In addition to a rich sampling of his initial impressions of the alternate French capital, Mott's first letter to Pershing from Vichy contained encouraging news about the ABMC sites and their continuing preservation. He told the chairman, for example, that he had already held a preliminary conversation with a representative of General Vincensini and hoped to meet the French general himself in early July.[95] According to Mott, the representative told him "that as far as he knows nothing has happened to our cemeteries or monuments—everything [is] as it was a year ago." The American envoy also reported that he had worked out a way with his French contact to settle all of the commission's financial obligations through the end of the current fiscal year. More good news came with Mott's explanation that he had, "by good luck," run into an old French employee of the American embassy in Paris who personally knew members of the ABMC staff still working at Suresnes, where Mott had created a makeshift office for the rump Paris staff before he and the other Americans had departed France in July 1941. Through her, Mott was able to communicate information to the three European employees there regarding what the chairman wanted them to do and what he wanted to know back from them. He observed enthusiastically to Pershing that "I am really more in contact with them [the ABMC personnel] and the cemeteries than I could have hoped for." Mott expected, furthermore, to meet with Pierre Rod in Vichy before the month was out to receive a firsthand report on the condition of the sites.[96] Once this latter meeting took place, Mott informed his superior in Washington: "Everything is going along all right and I think you were right to send me here. It was useful, even necessary, for Battle Monuments business."[97]

Sadly, Mott's situation in Vichy never looked as good as it did in the first few weeks. As the summer wore on, he grew increasingly preoccupied with his wife's declining health. In mid-August, the American emissary wrote ominously about his wife's condition and raised the possibility that the couple would leave Vichy to seek better care for her in Switzerland.[98] In mid-September, Mott updated the ABMC chairman on each of the three major matters that had brought him back to France. Georgette's condition had deteriorated to a point where, in view of the scarcity of good doctors and hospital facilities in Vichy, he decided to move her to Lausanne. Aware that he would likely be away from France for some time, Mott reassured his old classmate about ABMC concerns: "My Battle Monuments business is all in order and I have been able to communicate with the Paris office. There is nothing I have not already reported. I can, therefore, with your consent quite readily remain a while in Lauzanne [sic]." Finally, the loyal subordinate asked the chairman to "give our regards to Micheline" and tell her that "I have done what she asked and as far as I can learn her affairs are all in order."⁹⁹

The Motts took up residence in the Riviera resort of Cannes on October 8. Plans changed because Georgette was judged too weak for a long car trip to Switzerland, but not for a shorter journey by direct train to the Mediterranean coast. The move away from Vichy was especially fortuitous on political grounds, for exactly one month later, in response to the Allied invasion of French North Africa, the Germans erased the old demarcation line and occupied the hitherto unoccupied zone. But Cannes was located in the small section of prewar France that Hitler had designated for occupation by the Italians. For the moment, then, the couple was within the jurisdiction of a less threatening enemy and not likely to be menaced. Mott told Pershing much later that the Italians were, in fact, "most courteous." A letter from Pétain, in which the marshal undertook personal responsibility for the Motts' conduct, surely helped their standing with their newest wartime hosts.¹⁰⁰

Georgette Mott died in Cannes on January 26, 1943, fulfilling her wish that her life would end in her native country. Her husband chose to remain in the Riviera refuge. Less than eight months later, in mid-September, he was arrested by the Gestapo. A succession of intervening events had stripped away the American's security. The overthrow of Mussolini in July had led to Italy's formal surrender to the Allies on September 3, which had prompted Germany's occupation of mainland Italy and the southeastern section of France hitherto controlled by the fickle ally. The Germans had nothing against General Mott, a later report said, but quickly judged his presence in Cannes "undesirable."¹⁰¹

From October 1942 to September 1943, the entirety of Mott's stay in Cannes, Pershing heard virtually no news from him. When initially taken into German custody, Mott was assured that his new hosts only wanted to ask him a few questions. As he later told Pershing, however, "from that moment I did not again see my quarters in Cannes—and they never did ask me any questions." He was taken ultimately to a camp for interned Britons and Americans in Vittel (about 150 miles southeast of Paris) and, while there, was denied permission to communicate with the Swiss consulate or anyone else. "I was not treated harshly," he wrote later, "but I was a prisoner." After a month he was sent to Paris, where the German embassy eventually arranged for his exchange and return to the

United States in March 1944. During the wait for his journey home, Mott enjoyed several months of supervised freedom in Paris and the opportunity for direct contact with the commission's Suresnes office and with the French officials who were overseeing maintenance of the American cemeteries and monuments.[102] There is not a lot of additional detail or elaboration in the available documentation about Mott's experiences between his arrest in September 1943 and his repatriation six months later. The very idea, in any case, that a seventy-eight-year-old American general was enjoying even a shred of liberty in the heart of German-occupied Paris mere months before the Normandy landings is but one of the elements that makes the story of Mott's second European mission for the American Battle Monuments Commission so thoroughly engrossing and utterly improbable.

Once back on American soil, Mott was able more thoroughly to update the Washington office on just less than three years of upkeep and supervision of the ABMC sites by the French caretakers. Upon his earlier return home in August 1941, the elderly officer had reported "no fresh injuries to any of the cemeteries or monuments" since Major Holle's reports from the summer of 1940—except for the thorough destruction of the memorial at Brest caused by bomb damage from January 1941 and more deliberate dynamiting by the Germans in July of the same year.[103] In May 1944, Pershing's erstwhile envoy was able to sum up "that practically nothing of any unusual character due to the war has happened since I made my report . . . in August 1941."[104]

In his final report, Mott recalled the standards for wartime maintenance that Pershing had laid down—"namely, that any injury occurring through action of the weather, or from accidental or constructional causes, must be repaired; no degradations must be allowed to develop so as to make their repair later on more expensive; but money must not be spent on mere beautification; wise and economical upkeep alone is expected"—and confirmed that they had been upheld. Even with the monetary restrictions in place with the Americans gone, Mott noted that "the cemeteries have uniformly presented a pleasing appearance—grass cut and shrubberies cared for." He claimed, moreover, to be "reliably informed" that "there is not one sign of neglect in any of them." Rod's reports would show that the masonry in the various structures of the sites, woodwork, and tombstones had all been regularly inspected and "kept in a good state of preservation." Mott concluded that this favorable state of affairs was "due to the work of the permanent caretakers on monthly salaries, generally men of long service with us," and that it required "almost no extra expense" to attain. He further informed Pershing that French officials had been carefully keeping records of American aviators who had died and been buried in France, such that it would not be difficult to locate and identify their bodies after the war. Twenty-five of the fifty-three dead Americans were already resting in Clichy cemetery north of Paris, Mott reported, and the graves were properly marked with wooden crosses and surrounded with flowering plants and shrubs. "My belief is," he concluded, "that these attentions are due to the kindness of [the] French inhabitants."[105]

The report from Pershing's longtime associate also chronicled how the United States was able to keep funds for the maintenance of ABMC sites flowing to the responsible French agency. As already noted, Mott had left 1.2 million francs in an account for General Vincensini before leaving France in July 1941. This filled out the appropriation for the fiscal year ending June 30, 1942. When he returned to France in June 1942, Mott deposited the FY 1943 appropriation ($30,000, which exchanged into 1.5 million francs) in the same account for the *Secrétariat des Anciens Combattants*. When this sum ran out on June 30, 1943, and it was not possible for Washington to communicate with Mott, the French Treasury advanced its own money to the Secrétariat to keep up the salaries of ABMC employees. In January 1944, once the American officer had made it to Paris from the Gestapo camp and restored contact with his own government, the $30,000 for FY 1944 was transferred to him through the Swiss embassy in Berlin and the Swiss consul in Paris. Mott deposited this money with the French Treasury for the ABMC account, thus retiring the debt incurred since the previous June and covering the ongoing expenses down to June 30, 1944. After that date, Mott told Pershing, the French would still be willing to "pay our bills and charge to our account," but Paris was seeking some formal assurance that any money advanced to the ABMC would be repaid after the close of hostilities.[106] Little could Mott know that, almost a month to the day after he had sent this report to his wartime chief, the Allies would land on the beaches of Normandy and the war in western Europe would enter its final phase.

This next round of combat inevitably meant that the ABMC sites again found themselves in an active combat zone, with the same risk of serious damage if not outright destruction that they had run in 1940. Happily, the toll from the second battle of France and the renewed fighting in Belgium was similarly light. Rod's report from the end of October 1944, by which time the fighting had moved beyond all of the American memorial sites, listed only the monuments at Tours and Montsec, and the Romagne cemetery, as having suffered serious injury. "In all other establishments," the Frenchman wrote, "either war damage dates back to 1940, or is of minor importance."[107]

At Romagne, the bulk of the damage occurred September 1, 1944, as American planes attempted to bomb German troops and light tanks that were positioned in the cemetery near the chapel. Several bombs exploded just west of the chapel, a mere two hundred meters outside the perimeter, and some fragments landed in the burial grounds, piercing one of the stained glass windows and chipping more than a dozen stones from the cemetery's enclosing wall. A number of trees were damaged as well. The next day, French Forces of the Interior (resistance fighters) did incidental damage with rifle fire at the Romagne entrance to the cemetery. At Tours, the damage came from aerial bombardment on June 15 and fighting on the ground in the city during August, and consisted chiefly of chipped stones on the monument, cracked pavement, and injured trees and shrubs. The damage to the Montsec monument seemed most serious of all and was done during a firefight on September 2. The Germans had placed eight machine guns on the monument grounds and along the road leading to it, and the attacking Americans fired repeatedly at these positions. Rod estimated that nine shells, probably from a tank, had burst on the monument's columns or inside its entablature, taking splinters and chips out of the stone measuring from a foot to five feet in length or breadth and up to a foot deep. Falling stone had, in turn, damaged the table supporting the battle map. "Although the damage is relatively important," Rod reported, "the monument may remain in its present condition without harm."[108]

Apart from these three sites, the damage that was reported was almost trivial. The cemeteries at Belleau, Bony, Waregem, and Thiaucourt sustained no damage at all during the fight for liberation; one cross was chipped at Oise-Aisne; and twenty-three crosses were slightly damaged at Suresnes due to fragments from three years of German anti-aircraft guns firing from the nearby fort on Mont Valérien. The only other casualty of consequence among the monuments was that the Germans had carted off the commemorative plaque from Pershing's old AEF headquarters at Chaumont.[109] Major Charles B. Shaw, of the commission's headquarters staff, told the House Appropriations Committee in February 1945 that the cemeteries suffered so little damage in the 1944 fighting because "the Germans went by them so fast they made no stand."[110]

Pierre Rod noted in the final report he filed on November 1, 1944, that he had not been able to gain access to any of the cemeteries and monuments between August 15 and the end of September because of active hostilities all over northern France. The October circuit to all the sites came at the first opportunity he had had to make it. The wonder is that he had been able to maintain firsthand inspections on a regular basis throughout the war. Thomas North later wrote that on occasion during the 1941–44 period, when Rod had not been able to obtain gasoline to make such visits by car, he had traveled "station to station on foot, sometimes covering twenty kilometers a day." North went on to say that "the devotion and conscientiousness" of such employees "under these most trying conditions deserved our Country's deepest gratitude."[111]

As the battle for liberation in 1944 cleared the Germans out of the locations of the ABMC sites, other individuals were as eager as Pierre Rod to report on the condition of the cemeteries and memorials. The first of these, in fact, was General Dwight D. Eisenhower, who, as noted earlier, had served two different details with the commission in the late 1920s. The Supreme Commander cabled General Pershing on the latter's eighty-fourth birthday in September 1944 that the ABMC memorials "appear in wonderful state of preservation."[112] Eisenhower followed a month later with a fuller report based on recent visits to the sites by officers from his headquarters. This report, which was quickly forwarded to all seven members of the commission, expressed joy that "most of the sites have weathered the misfortunes of the past four years so well," and indicated that "normal depreciation [had been] only slightly accelerated." Eisenhower concluded with a hearty tribute to "the devotion of the caretakers," which he described as "admirable" and as having "contributed in high degree to the gratifying conditions which prevail."[113]

Yet another army officer with substantial ABMC service in earlier times filed a report as he passed through the recently liberated areas where cemeteries and memorials were located. Colonel Xenophon H. Price, commission secretary between 1923 and 1938, was serving in 1944 as president of the War Observers Board. His own path of travel with the American forces allowed him to inspect and photograph a number of the sites whose construction he had directly supervised. While obliged to submit his report to his immediate superiors in the army and the War

Department, Price requested that a copy be sent to his old boss at the ABMC as well.[114] Once this succession of communications reached Pershing, the aged chairman could be of good heart as he came to realize that almost all of the sites for which he cared so deeply had avoided the worst of the war's devastation.[115]

From the standpoint of the American Battle Monuments Commission, the Second World War had spared the entire contingent of American personnel and all but two or three of the European memorials serious harm. Nor is there evidence of any harm coming to locals because of their work at the sites. As has been shown, however, this was not because people and places had always remained out of harm's way. At various times the violence of the war had put individuals doing the work of the commission, and just about every memorial site, at risk. ABMC service had placed numerous employees and family members in the middle of active combat zones in 1940, and provided officers such as Charles Holle and T. Bentley Mott with the rarest and riskiest of vantage points from which to observe war-torn and occupied France. In moments of relative calm and dire peril, under constant wartime pressure and sometimes under fire, the officers-in-charge at the Paris headquarters, the corps of superintendents, and commission employees at all levels had performed loyally and responsibly, often imaginatively and heroically, in their assigned roles.

General Pershing, as he moved through his ninth decade and navigated the second global war of his lifetime, this time from the safety of home, had closely monitored the unfolding overseas drama and made the difficult decision to evacuate the commission's American personnel from occupied Europe in a timely enough manner to get all of them back to the United States unharmed. The chairman had also found a way to get his old friend T. Bentley Mott to undertake a daring and dangerous mission right in the middle of the war to check firsthand on how the American memorials were faring in French care on German-held territory. In the absence of normal on-site American supervision, furthermore, Pershing had set feasible guidelines for the preservation by friendly Europeans of the memorials into which he had poured so much of his own creative energies and administrative talents during the two preceding decades. The fact that the Germans generally confined their vandalism of the defenseless sites to residential and storage structures and respected the sanctity of the cemeteries and monuments themselves helped mightily to minimize the damage. Indeed, the only evidence this study has uncovered of willful vandalism of any of the American burial grounds during the German occupation is the breaking of some Jewish headstones in the Saint-Mihiel cemetery. According to Thomas North, when the local German commander learned of this, he "saw to it that there was no repetition." North's overall assessment in his memoir is that "the German troops treated the cemeteries with respect."[116] But, the diligent and faithful efforts of the responsible agencies of the French and Belgian governments and innumerable and largely anonymous ABMC personnel from the host countries had no doubt contributed the most toward ensuring that the necessary work of maintenance, preservation, and protection had gotten done throughout the war.

All in all, the story of the passage of these memorials from one war safely through the next is about big decisions rightly made and countless instances of courage, resourcefulness, devotion, and loyalty on the part of scores of citizens from both sides of the Atlantic. This same kind of collaboration would sustain and energize the next generation of the commission's work that began with the return of peace.

6

Reopening the European Office and New Leadership for a Renewed Mission, 1944–1948

When World War II ended in September 1945, four of the original members of the American Battle Monuments Commission—General Pershing, Vice Chairman Robert Woodside, Senator Reed, and D. John Markey—still held their posts. Judge Finis J. Garrett (who had replaced Thomas Miller in 1926), Mrs. Cora W. Baker (who had replaced Mrs. Josephine L. Bentley in 1929), and Leslie Biffle (who had replaced John Philip Clayton Hill in 1941) filled out the seven-member complement. The office of commission secretary had not been permanently filled since Xenophon Price left it in January 1938. Although James Mangum had served in that role on an "acting" basis during most of the war, he was no longer with the agency at the return of peace.

The Washington office had never ceased to function during the years of worldwide conflict. A trio of European employees—Pierre Rod, Madame Lundborg, and Madame Courtois-Suffitt—had kept the Paris office at least marginally operational, but the regular American personnel had not manned their posts there or in the cemeteries on the continent since 1941. While the continued preservation and, where necessary, the restoration of the World War I sites would be immediate priorities of the commission in the new postwar period, the need permanently to bury hundreds of thousands of American servicemen killed in the Second World War and the desire to commemorate the victorious deeds of American arms presented the ABMC with the prospect of greatly expanded tasks and challenges. The deaths of Paul Cret and General Pershing within three years of the war's end, the appointment of General Thomas North as secretary in April 1946, and the expansion of the commission to eleven members with the official renewal of its mandate meant that the agency would fulfill the second generation of its mission largely under the direction of new leaders. Before these transitions could fully take place, however, the commission and its elderly chairman once again called upon a tested and familiar figure to get their European headquarters prepared for the renewal of its operations.

As the dramatic liberation of Paris and the ABMC sites in northern France unfolded throughout the summer of 1944, General T. Bentley Mott was in the midst of his second forced repatriation to American soil from commission service in his adopted country. On October 12, at Pershing's request, Mott sailed once again for the still warring European continent. Nearing his eightieth birthday, Mott was under instructions to reopen the ABMC's Paris office and take charge of the maintenance of the World War I sites. The general's return would herald the reestablishment of an American presence at the commission headquarters in the old embassy building on Rue Gabriel. After a layover of several weeks in England, the indefatigable Mott crossed the channel in mid-November and joined his three erstwhile European colleagues in the French capital.[1]

Mott's most urgent priorities were finances and the condition of the ABMC's existing sites. The only funds formally allotted to the commission for European operations through the end of FY 1945 had been budgeted while no Americans were on station there and were meant for salaries of clerical staff in Paris and field personnel in France and Belgium. Mott was quick to report that these employees "are all underpaid and most of them have stuck to their jobs when they could have bettered themselves."[2] He was committed to increasing their salaries "as much as possible" from the commission's available funds, but had to acknowledge that no new funds would be available for nearly eight more months, until the start of FY 1946. In the meantime, the Graves Registration Service (GRS), then headquartered in London, was paying ABMC personnel at the Brookwood cemetery, while other agencies of the army—principally, the quartermaster general's office—were volunteering essential supplies and personnel that, in Mott's view, would not have been "obtainable otherwise."[3] There was not even funding to cover the costs of accommodations for Pershing's representative. Mott informed the Washington office in his end-of-the-year report that, since returning to France, he had been paying the costs of his own food and lodging out of personal funds.[4]

Of equally immediate concern to the American in Paris was the scarcity of money for upkeep and rehabilitation of the World War I sites. Mott was able to confirm what Pierre Rod and several US officers, including General Eisenhower, had earlier discovered: the American cemeteries and memorials were generally in good shape. More work needed to be done, however, to bring the sites back to the same high standard in which they had been kept before the war. Incidental damage awaited repair at most locations, the monument at Brest and the commemorative tablet at Chaumont needed to be completely replaced, and many of the marble crosses had developed stains as a result of reduced maintenance.[5]

Still, Mott reported that "crowds of our soldiers" were visiting the original cemeteries, "and I hear nothing but expressions of admiration coming from them." In the general's opinion, this added urgency to the quick retrieval of prewar standards of maintenance. The more beautiful the cemeteries could be made, the more likely that relatives of the World War II dead—whether soldiers or civilians visiting from the United States—might be influenced to entrust the remains of lost loved ones permanently to an overseas cemetery. "I feel certain," Mott wrote after six weeks in Paris, "that a few thousand dollars given us *now* [his emphasis] may well help in saving huge sums for the transfer of bodies home."[6]

Bereft of funds of its own, the Paris office received vital assistance from the army. General Robert M. Littlejohn, chief quartermaster for the European Theater of Operations (ETO), proved especially sympathetic to the ABMC's plight and, as Mott put it, "[went to] the legal limit to help us."[7] By July 1945 the army was providing aid at the rate of $100,000 a year to the ABMC operations in France and Belgium, Mott estimated, and had spent another $5,000 at the Brookwood site in England. The chief quartermaster had actually created a new unit, the 4278th Quartermaster Company, for the commission's use and staffed it with four officers and a dozen enlisted men. All office and maintenance supplies, food, and clothing for European field personnel, numerous vehicles, and over a hundred tons of coal needed to reactivate and sustain the ABMC's work during the early transition from war to peace had come from the army.[8]

As the fighting neared its end in Europe, another "serious and difficult question" developed: how to deal with requests by individual units to erect monuments in the battle zone. When Mott received a petition from the commander of the 6th Engineers Special Brigade for permission to put up a commemorative structure in Normandy, he sounded the alarm at ETO headquarters. "When the war is over," the ABMC representative confidently asserted, Congress would address the need for a new generation of national memorials. Surely "the new memorials will be no less splendid than those to whose perfecting General Pershing devoted his energy, his good taste and a very tender interest." In the meantime, he pleaded, the military command must intervene to prevent its own units from building the same spate of hastily designed structures, on ground for which legal title had not been secured, and without the means of properly preserving them, that had come in the wake of World War I.[9] Mott's presentation was so persuasive that at the end of June 1945 the ETO headquarters notified all commanding generals in the theater that the erection of battle monuments "by any military organization, or by groups of military personnel," was prohibited.[10] This measure offered some hope of preempting a repeat of the post-1918 situation, although Thomas North later observed that, whether "by oversight or disregard," this prohibition was "not strictly observed."[11]

A few months after V-E Day, General Mott's position as the ranking ABMC officer in Europe came up for review. Notwithstanding his incomparable experience with the commission, the army proved unwilling to keep an officer of his advanced years on active duty beyond a certain point. Vice Chairman Woodside notified the chairman's devoted deputy in August 1945 that the agency would not request his retention on active duty past the end of that calendar year.[12] Even so, Mott remained in the French capital as an informal "special assistant" to General Thomas North, President Truman's choice to be the new commission secretary, while a new officer-in-charge was found for the Paris bureau. North claimed to have benefited "from [Mott's] long experience in France and his friendly helpfulness" during those transitional months.[13] Vice Chairman Woodside had earlier commended Mott for his "exceptional service" to the commission, "under conditions that I dare say no other officer of our army has ever experienced."[14]

Before General Mott's final round of service at the Paris office ended, he had much to say to the Washington office about the need to formally secure the commission's place in the nation's effort to commemorate the service and sacrifices of its World War II soldiers. He was especially concerned that, in view of General Pershing's ill health, the agency had effectively lost its voice in the hurly-burly of intragovernmental politics. Without some timely and forceful assertion of the commission's standing, Mott feared, another federal agency might not only take charge of the new future program, but also usurp custody of the World War I sites, as had almost happened during the 1930s. "We have got to remember that very few men in Congress know anything about what took place after the last war or how ABMC was born," Mott declared in a May 1945 letter, "and it would be quite easy for them to forget its existence and the services it is now equipped to render on a wider scale."[15]

The commission's representative in Paris was equally anxious that the agency advocate to American families for the retention in European burial grounds of as many of the soldier dead as possible. "Naturally it is not for us to begin this defensive campaign," he insisted. "But, remembering what took place after the last war, I should think that an effort could be made to do some educational work before the undertakers' union or some other interested organization had already started a crusade to have the bodies returned to the United States."[16] In this connection, he raised a troublesome fact that continues to stalk the work of the ABMC—namely, "that the average American knows nothing whatever concerning the marvelous attention which the army dead received from [the] American Battle Monuments Commission." As possible advocates for the commission's role in the upcoming commemorative effort, Mott identified General Eisenhower ("it is worth remembering that [he] used to work in our organization") and General Marshall, whose immediate appointment as vice chairman of the commission Mott recommended.[17] Pershing's overseas deputy was still in Paris when President Truman issued an executive order confirming that the ABMC would retain its authority over the World War I sites and direct the nation's World War II memorial program. One of the general's final dispatches from the French capital, in July 1946, anticipated the imminent return of many of the same personnel who had held posts before the late war to the cemeteries of the earlier conflict, an action made possible by the funds made available to the ABMC for FY 1947.[18]

Mott was not the only principal in the prewar leadership of the commission whose service ended in the early aftermath of the conflict. On September 8, 1945, the ABMC's consulting architect, Dr. Paul Cret, died at age sixty-eight in Philadelphia. The reading of a letter of condolence signed by General Pershing to Mrs. Cret was the first item of business on the November 15, 1945, agenda when the seven-year interlude between the forty-fifth and forty-sixth meetings of the commission ended. Praising Cret's "professional genius and personal qualities," the chairman observed: "In his passing we feel the loss not only of a valued associate but of a dear friend."[19]

The letter to Mrs. Cret was one of Pershing's last official acts as leader of the ABMC. In May 1941, he had taken up full-time residence in a small suite at Walter Reed Hospital. His sister, his nurses, and his doctors controlled access to him there with increasing strictness.[20] Pershing attended none of the ten commission meetings between November 1945 and the end of his life, although he continued to hold the chairmanship. Robert Woodside presided over each of those meetings and served as acting chairman until George C. Marshall was formally elected to the commission's highest office at the fifty-seventh meeting on January 26, 1949.[21] The nation's first general of the armies died quietly on July 15, 1948.

Pershing's funeral drew three hundred thousand people into the streets of Washington as his body was carried to its final resting place in Arlington National Cemetery.[22] At a hastily organized meeting on the morning of the event, the American Battle Monuments Commission enacted a formal resolution of condolence and respect for the man who had led them since the agency's inception. The resolution recognized that Pershing's "intense interest and devotion to the work of the Commission was primarily responsible for the magnificent cemeteries overseas . . . , for the historic memorials commemorating the services of the American Armed Forces in . . . [the First World War], and for the collection, compilation and publication of important historical data relative to the operation of those forces." The resolution affirmed that the late general's "fellow-members of the Commission held for him the deepest esteem and admiration because of his superb leadership and sterling personal qualities and recall with prideful memory our association with him in these works."[23]

By the time Pershing died, the commission on which he had left such an indelible stamp was well into its next round of design, construction, and direction of the national effort to commemorate the courage and sacrifice of the World War II soldiers. Fourteen new cemetery sites had been selected in Europe, Africa, and Asia that would become the permanent resting places for more than ninety thousand of the American dead. Thomas North was well established as the ABMC secretary, a post he would hold until 1968—almost as many years as Pershing had been chairman. John Harbeson, selected from Paul Cret's Philadelphia firm, was also in his third year as the new consulting architect to the commission. Four new members, added to fulfill a mandate in the 1946 congressional reauthorization, were bringing their own experience and perspectives to the renewed labors and deliberations of the agency. The renowned General Marshall, finally, was poised to offer more than a decade of his own service to the commission.

7

Building the World War II Memorials, 1945–1960

The commission's work in the aftermath of World War II broadly followed the pattern that had unfolded after World War I. Thus, an already familiar sequence progressed from recouping the dead to the dedication of the new sites. Unlike the commemorative program after 1918, the World War II constructions did not include a large collection of monuments independently situated from the cemeteries. Because of decisions already made during the 1920s, moreover, lengthy debates regarding the basics of design or layout of the World War II cemeteries and chapels, headstones, inscriptions, or artwork generally did not occur. Land acquisition for the next generation of sites proved much easier because host governments donated practically all of the ground needed for the American memorials.

The army's Graves Registration Service (GRS) had already begun to collect, identify, and consolidate the remains of the fallen thousands in overseas cemeteries well before the formal cessation of hostilities. Upon being canvassed by the War Department in 1947 and 1948, the families of the dead made their decisions as to where the bodies of their loved ones would be permanently interred—in the United States, in an ABMC cemetery abroad, or at some other location of their own choosing. Within a year of the return of peace, the commission had worked out with the GRS a process for determining where the permanent sites would be located. Once architects were chosen and their design proposals were approved by the two relevant Washington commissions—the ABMC and the Commission of Fine Arts—construction could begin. Creation of the fourteen cemeteries took fifteen years, almost exactly as long as it had taken to complete the World War I sites. By the summer of 1960, all of the ABMC cemetery memorials had been formally dedicated.

General of the Army George C. Marshall served as chairman of the American Battle Monuments Commission throughout almost all of the years it took for the new generation of memorials to be built. John J. Pershing had been the most famous living American soldier when he became ABMC chairman in 1923, but Marshall was obliged to share that high distinction with wartime commanders such as Dwight D. Eisenhower, Omar Bradley, and Douglas MacArthur when he became Pershing's successor in January 1949. However, there was no denying the immense personal esteem and popularity Marshall enjoyed throughout the fourteen years he lived past the end of the war, nor any denying that he left a distinctive personal stamp on the commission's work. Pershing had directed the creation of nineteen sites in three European states, plus Gibraltar, to commemorate nineteen months of war, the loss of roughly one hundred thousand dead, and the service of 4 million soldiers. In Marshall's time the commission built memorials in eight countries on three continents to commemorate forty-five months of war, the loss of four hundred thousand dead, and the service of 16 million soldiers.

The new chairman directed the commission's work with a much lighter touch than his predecessor. For example, Marshall did not do yearly inspections of the overseas sites as they were being built. Pershing's successor visited the American memorials on only one occasion during that time—in 1952, when he presided over the dedication of the enlarged chapel and burial ground at Suresnes and looked in on a number of the other cemeteries under construction before returning home. He had already seen many of the World War I sites while on a European trip as secretary of state in November 1948.[1] Marshall never exercised the same power of approval over the smallest details of design that Pershing wielded, nor did he ever call a halt to the construction of a site until he was satisfied with how the memorial ultimately would look. Of the twenty-eight plenary meetings held during his membership on the commission, moreover, Marshall attended only thirteen, and of the eighteen meetings during his chairmanship, he presided over eleven, significantly below Pershing's level of participation. Finally, unlike Pershing, whose ABMC service was largely undistracted by other jobs, Marshall's term on the commission overlapped his two years as secretary of state (from January 1947 to January 1949), eleven months as chairman of the American Red Cross (October 1949–September 1950), and year as secretary of defense (from September 1950 to September 1951).

If the commission was not always Marshall's chief preoccupation, however, he still pursued his ABMC work with considerable depth of emotion. Ten years into his service, he referred to the "high task" of the commission and the "very great, if melancholy, satisfaction" he took from his involvement with it. When he recalled his own visits to the American cemeteries, he described himself as "an old soldier seeking fallen comrades." Americans, Marshall insisted, should think of the dead in our cemeteries as "the sons of every free man." In creating these sites, "we were keeping faith with the fallen . . . and taking to them all that we could of home, of beauty, and of remembrance."[2] Upon his death in October 1959, the commissioners praised Marshall "for his always tactful but nevertheless positive direction of our deliberations," and they recalled "with prideful memory our association with him."[3] As the account below will attest, the general, like his predecessor, was a consistently effective advocate for the work of the commission.

With the return of peace in 1945, the commission had to gain reauthorization to take up its mission of remembrance. A month after Japan capitulated, Secretary of War Henry Stimson and Secretary of the Navy James Forrestal coauthored a letter to President Truman urging him to renew the ABMC's mandate to direct the program of national memorials abroad. The most immediate concern of the two secretaries was to vest some agency with the power to forestall the building of private and unauthorized monuments on the American battlefields. "It is our opinion," they wrote, "that similar controls [to those after World War I] should be exercised over memorial projects arising from World War II." They argued that the "American Battle Monuments Commission, with certain revisions in its authority and composition, is the body which can appropriately be charged with this responsibility."[4] Because Stimson and Forrestal further believed that the established prestige of the ABMC "derives in large measure from that of its individual members," they advised the president to expand the commission membership from seven to eleven citizens to open spots for veterans of the 1941–45 conflict.[5]

In March 1946, President Truman issued an executive order that conformed to the counsel of his two secretaries.[6] Truman reinforced his endorsement of the ABMC's renewed mandate a month later with the appointment of General North, whom he had detailed to the agency at the end of the war, as commission secretary.[7] North served in that important post until his retirement in 1968, just as General Jacob Devers's term as the third chairman was about to end.

The earliest meetings of the newly constituted commission addressed topics ranging from repair and ongoing maintenance of the World War I sites to decisions about the new memorials. Two of the Pershing era sites—the commemorative plaque at the general's Chaumont headquarters and the naval memorial at Brest—had not survived the German occupation of France. The commissioners quickly approved an inscription General Mott suggested for the replacement plaque at Chaumont and agreed to seek funding for the rebuilding of the Brest memorial if the secretary of the navy approved the idea.[8] In time for the forty-seventh meeting in April 1946, Admiral Chester W. Nimitz signaled his department's desire to see the structure at Brest rebuilt, and the commission proceeded to investigate the cost.[9] Numerous obstacles delayed the actual reconstruction of the monument until the mid-1950s, however, one of which was the desire of the French city's leadership to see their own people's homes restored before an American monument from the Great War was replaced. By the time the ABMC structure was dedicated in 1960, the heavily damaged port city had itself been largely rebuilt.[10]

A new consulting architect was needed as well, and at the second meeting after the end of the war, the ABMC voted formally to seek from the Fine Arts Commission a list of people worthy of consideration.[11] In July 1946, John Harbeson, who had studied under Paul Cret and become a senior partner at the illustrious Frenchman's Philadelphia firm, was selected. "A more fortunate choice could hardly have been made," Secretary North later wrote. Harbeson held the position until 1979 and proved, in North's judgment, "a kindly critic yet firm; tactful; modest; inventive," and "a priceless aid to the Commission and to its Secretary."[12] Harbeson became a regular participant in commission meetings and was months past his ninetieth birthday when he retired.[13]

The chief architect immediately undertook the exploration of possible sites for the next generation of cemeteries and an inspection tour of the World War I memorials. He reported on the condition of the latter sites to the commission in November 1946. Of greatest concern was the Montsec monument, where damaged stones threatened to break loose and fall on people once the coming frost penetrated and dislodged them. Similar anxiety was expressed about shell damage at the Belleau chapel. More incidental harm was noted to scattered headstones and the monuments at Château-Thierry, Montfaucon, and Tours, from bombing and shelling and, in the case of some Stars of David, vandalism. The commission voted unanimously to authorize Secretary North to proceed with the smaller repairs, while deferring the more expensive projects at Montsec and Belleau until Congress approved the necessary funding.[14]

The recommendation in the Stimson-Forrestal letter to increase the commission's membership from seven to eleven became part of Public Law 456 passed by the 79th Congress on June 26, 1946. The measure confirmed additional provisions of the earlier executive order that had extended the ABMC's mission and assigned to the president of the United States the same untrammeled freedom contained in the founding statute of 1923 to select the members of the commission.[15] Truman added to the existing board a sitting member of the House of Representatives, Joseph C. Baldwin, a Republican from New York and a decorated veteran of service in France with the US Army in World War I; an incumbent senator, Burnet R. Maybank, a Democrat from South Carolina and a naval veteran from World War I; General Alexander Vandegrift, a Medal of Honor recipient for his service as commander of the 1st Marine Division in the Solomon Islands; and General Marshall.[16]

The expanded membership was immediately informed of how the War Department and the ABMC proposed to share responsibilities for the selection and development of permanent overseas cemeteries for the World War II dead. General George A. Horkan, head of the Memorial Division of the quartermaster general's office, had conferred with Secretary North in July 1946 on the delineation of such responsibilities. The agreement called for the War Department to select the sites for the permanent cemeteries and acquire the land for them in close consultation with the ABMC. The GRS was authorized to do all burials and reburials in each cemetery in a manner that conformed to the layout specified by the commission. The ABMC was to be "solely responsible for the permanent design and construction of the cemetery and all buildings incidental thereto," and would assume "complete control and responsibility" for each site once the War Department had finished with all of the interments.[17] North later recalled that "from first to last there was virtually no friction between the two organizations," and added that the GRS "proved to be consistently sympathetic and helpful" with the commission's concerns.[18]

As soon as the two agencies established how they would work together, they began to evaluate sites for the World War II memorials. Between June and October 1946, Secretary North had traveled to the Far East, Europe, North Africa, and Iceland to survey possible locations for permanent American cemeteries. John Harbeson and Commissioner Leslie Biffle had accompanied the secretary on his European travels. Reviewing reports on these travels was part of the crowded agenda for the commission's forty-eighth meeting in November.[19] Guidelines emerged by the end of the year for determining the location of the burial sites. Each cemetery should have "a pleasing site and surroundings" and be as free as possible from hazards "such as floods, drought, lack of water supply, [or] ledge rock." Existing temporary cemeteries should constitute the pool of possible sites for the permanent cemeteries; retaining the larger temporary grounds as permanent memorials would make for "economy of effort." The latter sites, moreover, should be "easily accessible," "bear an identifiable relationship to military operations [from the War]," and "preferably be on ground captured by American troops."[20]

Officials from the War Department impressed upon the ABMC the importance of completing the final disposition of the dead as quickly as possible. Congress had allotted five years for this process, but Colonel Ira K. Evans from the quartermaster general's Memorial Division told the commission in November 1946 that his department sought to complete it in two years.[21] In compliance with this desire, three ABMC subcommittees reported early in 1947 on their research into possible sites for the permanent cemeteries. General Vandegrift's Pacific Area Committee, which also included Judge Garrett and General Marshall, recommended the establishment of three such sites in its assigned region: the Punch Bowl Crater in Hawaii; Manila (Republic of the Philippines); and somewhere in the Marianas Islands (Guam, Tinian, Saipan). Vandegrift's group observed that "the ideal situation would be to establish a cemetery on each Pacific Island where our men fought and fell," but conceded that "many considerations would . . . make that inadvisable."[22] The Pacific subcommittee drew heavily from the report of Secretary North's visits to twenty-four temporary cemeteries on twelve different islands the previous June, and also from recommendations solicited directly from General MacArthur, the theater commander in the late war. For practical reasons of cost and ease of accessibility, MacArthur had counseled that there be only one Pacific cemetery, in the Hawaiian Islands. If more burial space were needed, he suggested that, in order of priority, Guam and Manila should be considered.[23]

Commissioner Markey's subcommittee, which also included Senator Maybank and Mrs. Cora Baker, evaluated permanent sites as far afield as India and Trinidad. Proposals for burial grounds in Italy at Paestum, Anzio, and Florence came with the concurrence of General Mark W. Clark and were supposed to commemorate, respectively, the Salerno beaches, the Volturno-Anzio region, and the Arno and Po valley, where Clark's Fifth US Army had seen its most important combats. Markey's group recommended a fourth Italian cemetery near Messina (Sicily) in the event that sufficient dead to justify it were to remain on the island. A Trinidad cemetery was proposed in spite of the quartermaster general's insistence that a site he envisioned for Puerto Rico would have room for all of the dead from the Caribbean and South Atlantic Theater. But Secretary North countered that without a site on non-American soil in that region, next-of-kin desiring burial of their loved ones in a permanent *overseas* cemetery could not be satisfied. Two sites were proposed for North Africa, one in Tunisia and another farther west in either Oran or Casablanca, despite a recommendation from General Eisenhower that the latter cemetery not be built because any Americans buried there would likely have died at the hands of Frenchmen. The ABMC also proposed a permanent location outside of Calcutta for the American dead of the China-Burma-India Theater. A possible site in Iran, however, was ruled out because it was deemed too remote for potential visitors, and because General Horkan reported that American bodies then buried in Teheran were already being transferred elsewhere.[24]

Senator Reed, who worked with Leslie Biffle and Congressman Baldwin on European sites, relied largely on the findings documented by Biffle the previous November. Generals Bradley, Devers, Lawton Collins, and Wade Haislip were also consulted and broadly concurred with the earlier report. At the end of 1946 there were 150,340 Americans buried in thirty-six temporary cemeteries in six European countries. Reed's group recommended that nine of those sites be made permanent: five in France and one each in the Netherlands, Belgium, Luxembourg, and the United Kingdom. In France, a site near Saint-Laurent was to be principally for those who died in the landings at Omaha Beach and in operations immediately thereafter. Blosville was for those who died at Utah Beach, in the airborne landings and fighting in the Cotentin Peninsula, and in the breakout from Normandy. Saint-Avold was for those who died in Lorraine or Germany; Épinal for those who died in Alsace or Germany; and Draguignan for the dead from Operation Anvil and the advance up the Rhône valley. Cambridge was to contain those who died in the United Kingdom, largely from injuries suffered on bombing missions or in fighting on the continent. Margraten, Henri-Chapelle, and Hamm, finally, were for those who died, respectively, in Holland, Belgium, and Luxembourg or in nearby Germany. The commission also recommended retaining temporary cemeteries at Limey and Saint-James (both in France) and Neuville-en-Condroz (in Belgium), subject to seeing how many bodies were to remain overseas permanently. At the same time, the commissioners decided to study further the possibility of enlarging the Brookwood site if Cambridge became inadequate for the contingent to be left in England. After determining that a suggestion by General Eisenhower to expand the Suresnes cemetery to accommodate large numbers of World War II dead was not feasible, the commission unanimously resolved to enlarge the chapel at that site into a shrine for the dead of both world wars.[25]

With the ABMC findings on permanent sites a matter of record, the quartermaster general's office and the commission worked together to reduce the list, mainly in an effort to limit costs. Both groups had recommended overseas cemeteries at Cambridge, Margraten, Henri-Chapelle, Hamm, Saint-Laurent, Épinal, Anzio, Tunis, and the Philippines, as well as Hawaii and Puerto Rico on US soil. General Horkan and members of his staff appeared at a meeting again in mid-May 1947 to address the proposed sites about which the two agencies disagreed.

Horkan observed that the quartermaster general would not oppose expanding the Brookwood site if the British and the commission wanted it, although he continued to maintain that Cambridge would be large enough to accommodate all the graves likely to remain in the UK. As for Normandy, the general would favor a second cemetery, either at Blosville or Saint-James, if more than 25 percent of the American dead from that campaign were to remain in France. Of those two sites, Saint-James was the preference because of more favorable water table conditions, a viewpoint John Harbeson shared. Horkan's office agreed to drop its recommendation for an additional memorial in the Paris area (at Villeneuve-sur-Auvers) in view of the commission's decision to add a World War II shrine to the chapel at Suresnes. The quartermaster general's representative agreed that the Neuville-en-Condroz cemetery, which then contained more than 14,500 bodies and was still growing with the influx of remains from Germany, should become a permanent site. Horkan also indicated his readiness to withdraw any objection to keeping the Draguignan site, on the grounds that it was simply too small, if the commission wanted to make it permanent "for historical reasons." He spoke similarly about a second permanent cemetery in Italy, even though his agency continued to believe that the Anzio site would be large enough to hold all the bodies likely to remain in that country. Horkan repeated his advocacy of a single cemetery in North Africa, at Tunis, and observed that "the lack of respect of the people of India for their own dead," and the inaccessibility of such a site to visitors from the United States, would negate the effect of an American cemetery in that country. Finally, if three cemeteries in the Pacific were deemed necessary, the general would concur with the commission's recommendations for that region.[26]

The ABMC members accepted the War Department's judgment on all of the points that General Horkan had addressed. The commissioners reaffirmed their commitment to permanent burial grounds at Saint-James, Neuville-en-Condroz, Saint-Avold, Draguignan, and Florence, but agreed to abandon sites proposed earlier for Blosville, Villeneuve-sur-Auvers, Limey, Paestum, Oran, Casablanca, and Calcutta. It was also agreed that any of the World War II dead remaining in the temporarily expanded Brookwood cemetery *after* repatriation should be moved to Cambridge, thus returning the original ABMC cemetery in the UK to its uniquely World War I character.[27]

The commission made an extremely important decision at the May 1947 meeting regarding the overall scope of its commemorative project for World War II: "that the permanent cemeteries, with their memorial chapels and museums would constitute monuments to the military operations as well as memorials to the dead, and that duplication by the erection nearby of large monuments is, in general, unnecessary." Secretary North told the commissioners that his office was receiving an "increasing number of privately sponsored memorial projects" for possible approval. Presumably many of the privately generated monument projects could be forestalled, as had happened during the 1920s and 1930s, on the grounds of redundancy with the commission's plans once the latter were clarified. At the same time, North reiterated the importance of keeping the total cost of the ABMC program as low as possible, which could be more easily accomplished by not building a collection of monuments outside of the cemeteries.[28]

General Marshall, still in his term as the nation's top diplomat and not yet ABMC chairman, was on hand for most of the important decisions relating to site selection of the permanent cemeteries. At the February 1947 meeting, Marshall strongly endorsed the idea of a cemetery in the Philippines for the "psychological effect . . . such permanent evidence of American sacrifice" would have on the islands' inhabitants. (The United States had granted the Filipinos their independence less than a year earlier.) The general also observed that the US government should have been quicker to promise Gold Star pilgrimages after World War I in order to make it easier for next-of-kin to decide that it was acceptable to leave their soldier dead buried thousands of miles from home. He told the commission that he had witnessed "too many mass interments [in Arlington National Cemetery] unattended by next-of-kin" of soldiers killed in the Great War whose families might have decided to leave them abroad if they had not been intimidated by the prospect of never being able to visit their graves. The general even suggested that the government should commit right now to such publicly funded visits while families were being asked again to decide where their loved ones should be permanently interred, intimating that such a timely commitment would multiply the number of soldiers allowed to rest in overseas sites—which was, to him, a good thing.[29]

Marshall also encouraged the commission's European office to leave some of the scars of the 1940–45 war unrepaired on the World War I memorials for "psychological effect and added interest." Such a policy, he said at the May 1947 meeting, would highlight the degree to which "action in the second war fell into the same pattern as the first war." Secretary North was quick to inform him that the commission "had already resolved to leave war damage untouched if it would not endanger the structural integrity of the buildings."[30] Visitors to such structures as the Belleau chapel can attest that this resolve was indeed followed.[31]

By the fifty-first commission meeting in June 1947, the decision to build fourteen permanent cemeteries had been confirmed, and the quartermaster general's office had projected, on the basis of a retention rate for overseas burial of 25 percent, the following numbers of interments for each site: Cambridge (2,451), Saint-Laurent (6,347), Saint-James (2,782), Margraten (5,352), Henri-Chapelle (5,677), Neuville-en-Condroz (7,568), Hamm (2,254), Saint-Avold (8,459), Épinal (4,112), Draguignan (598), Anzio (5,866), Florence (4,832), Tunis (2,101), and the

Philippines (13,423).[32] John Harbeson announced at that same meeting the architects chosen for each of the sites, based on recommendations from the Fine Arts Commission and his own consultations with Secretary North.[33] Thirteen of the architectural firms on his original list actually completed the work at their assigned cemeteries. The most difficult site to match with a designer turned out to be Luxembourg. When the New York City agency of Keally and Patterson wound up securing that assignment, the geographical distribution was three sites to Boston firms, one each to agencies from Philadelphia, Chicago, Atlanta, Washington, D.C., and San Francisco, and six from the nation's largest city.[34]

By the end of 1947, plans for the general layout of all of the cemeteries had won ABMC approval. Eleven of the fourteen had also passed muster with the CFA.[35] Designs for Tunis, Florence, and Manila took longer to prepare because final site selection at each place proved more challenging. At Tunis, the principal difficulty lay with the abundance of ancient ruins beneath the most desirable sites. The French government, Tunisia's colonial masters until 1955, ultimately granted the Americans a location several hundred yards removed from their first choice, which had turned out to be in the midst of a particularly heavy concentration of Punic and Roman relics. In the course of excavating for the cemetery at its present location, numerous ancient artifacts were still unearthed. Shortly after Tunisia gained its independence, and as the US memorial neared its completion, President Habib Bourguiba presented a Roman mosaic that had been retrieved in perfect condition from this digging as a gift to the Americans. They have displayed it since 1959 in the visitors' room at the cemetery.[36] The site originally preferred for the Florence cemetery, twenty miles southeast of the city near the town of Castelfiorentino, was discovered to be prone to flooding. Today's cemetery occupies a new location less vulnerable to this danger and closer to the city.[37]

In the Philippines, the major concern was finding a site that would be easily accessible to the public but also capable of housing what ultimately became the largest of the overseas cemeteries. According to Secretary North, the two large temporary burial grounds established at the end of World War II (Manila #1 and #2) simply were not suitable as permanent sites. When North and a member of Harbeson's firm traveled to the islands early in 1948, they liked a location at the southeastern edge of the city on the grounds of the former US Army Reservation of Fort McKinley (renamed Fort Bonifacio by the Filipinos). Upon hearing of this choice, the country's President Manuel Roxas sought to redirect the Americans to a potential site in the Corregidor-Bataan region famous from the initial round of fighting in 1941–42. The ABMC secretary recalled that travel to Corregidor was so taxing, and the wartime devastation in both areas still so widespread, that it would have been impossible to establish the cemetery there. When they reported back to President Roxas, the Filipino head of state agreed in a pact signed on April 1 to cede more than 150 acres within the Fort McKinley domain as earlier requested. Two weeks later the president died.[38] The development of the Manila site still posed formidable challenges, one of which was rock so close to the surface as to prohibit burials in wide areas of the cemetery that are merely grassed over to this day.[39]

The location of each of the fourteen permanent cemeteries closely conformed to the original guidelines in the Biffle report of November 1946. All of them are in places accessible to the general public, even though many are in rural locations. The most urban memorials are Cambridge, Luxembourg, Florence, North Africa, and Manila, all of which are within, at most, seven to eight miles of cities. Nine of them occupy the exact sites of temporary cemeteries that had been established before the fighting stopped, and three more (Henri-Chapelle, Normandy, and Lorraine) are within a mile of such earlier burial grounds. Florence and North Africa are the only exceptions to both of these standards. Twelve of the fourteen sites, furthermore, occupy ground liberated by US troops.[40] Three of the cemetery sites—Normandy, Henri-Chapelle, and Ardennes (Neuville-en-Condroz)—were taken by the 1st Infantry Division between June and September 1944. The forces that liberated the remaining locations are indicated in parentheses as follows: Saint-James (8th Infantry Division), Lorraine (80th Infantry Division), Anzio/Nettuno (3rd Infantry Division), Florence (Fifth US Army), Rhône (36th Infantry Division), Luxembourg (5th Armored Division), Épinal (45th Infantry Division), Margraten (30th Infantry Division), and Manila (Sixth US Army).[41] It can indeed be said of most of the American cemeteries from World War II, as the superintendent at Normandy once explained, that "the battle came right through here."[42]

Under prodding from the quartermaster general, the ABMC gave the cemeteries their "official names" in February 1948. Each cemetery would effectively be known within the agency by two names—that of the community in or near which it was located, and the newly established "official" designation. In the case of the Cambridge, Henri-Chapelle, Épinal, Florence, and Manila sites, the name of the community became the formal name of the American memorial—e.g., "Cambridge American Cemetery." The cemetery between Saint-Laurent and Colleville became the "Normandy American Cemetery," while Saint-James hosted the "Brittany American Cemetery." Margraten was home to the "Netherlands American Cemetery"; the Neuville-en-Condroz site became the "Ardennes American Cemetery"; Hamm became the "Luxembourg American Cemetery"; Saint-Avold, the "Lorraine American Cemetery"; and Draguignan, the "Rhone American Cemetery." At the northern edge of Nettuno, Italy, a half-mile behind Anzio beach, lies the "Sicily-Rome American Cemetery," and the Carthage site became the "North Africa American Cemetery."[43]

By the time the fourteen permanent sites were selected and named, the ground to be occupied had been formally acquired by either the War Department or the commission through agreements with the host governments. Unlike so many instances after World War I, in which the US government was required to purchase sites for its cemeteries and monuments from private owners, the World War II sites all rest on ground acquired by the host governments or, in the case of the Cambridge cemetery, given outright by a private donor (the University of Cambridge) and ceded to the United States for use as a cemetery. In no case after 1945 did the American government have to purchase land for an overseas military cemetery from a private landowner. Regardless of how the ground may have been acquired, the Americans asked that the host government retain title to it. The US, in turn, was given complete freedom to use and develop the ground as war memorials without taxes, rents, or fees of any sort. As General North later observed: "This arrangement has many advantages and no apparent drawbacks for our government." If local police assistance were needed for any reason, there would be no issue with regard to their right to enter the grounds. For the sites not considered American soil, moreover, the commission would be spared the "embarrassment" of becoming a potential sanctuary for fugitives or asylum-seekers.[44]

In at least one instance, the positioning of the fourteen cemeteries left wounded feelings on the part of a local community that wished to have American dead permanently interred in its soil. Sainte-Mère-Église, the first town behind Utah Beach to be liberated on D-Day by soldiers of the 82nd Airborne Division, was originally home to two temporary American cemeteries. A third one was at nearby Blosville. The latter was among the last sites cut by the ABMC and the GRS when the decision was made to concentrate at Saint-Laurent all of the dead from the initial stage of the Normandy campaign. Mayor Alexandre Renaud, who along with the citizens of his community is much celebrated for stalwart support of the Americans on D-Day, requested repeatedly after the war that the US authorities make permanent at least one of the local temporary cemeteries. When it became clear that these requests would not be granted, the mayor asked the Americans "to let Sainte-Mère-Église have the body of an Unknown . . . to care for, to go and visit him and pray, and care for his grave, as a symbol of the hundreds and thousands of Heroes who would be moved from our soil." There were so many unknowns "in our cemetery," Renaud recalled, and his citizens had grown so accustomed to decorating their graves with flowers, that it would be painful to see them all removed to other places. The Americans denied his requests, however, and Renaud was left to recount his story eight years later in a mood of lingering bitterness and disappointment.[45]

As the decisions of the affected families were duly reported to the War Department throughout 1947 and 1948, thousands of bodies were exhumed from the temporary cemeteries for repatriation to the United States or for reburial in one of the fourteen soon-to-be ABMC memorials. When the canvassing of families began in 1947, there were 209 cemeteries all over the world in which 240,483 identified and 12,572 unidentified American dead were interred. An additional 19,215, of which 10,810 were identified and 8,405 were unidentified, rested in isolated graves that had been located. An estimated 19,625 remained in unlocated isolated graves worldwide, making for a total number of 291,895 known dead, roughly four times the number at the end of World War I.[46]

Happily, the same sort of acrimonious public debate that had developed after World War I over what the families ought to do with their loved ones' remains did not materialize after 1945. The War Department claimed to have no preference of its own regarding the choice the families should make. The question of final burial was "of such a personal nature," according to one high-ranking officer in the quartermaster general's office, that those entrusted with it "must not be subjected to undue pressure."[47] Colonel Ira K. Evans had told the ABMC in November 1946 that he knew of "no evidence of attempts by outside interests to influence the next-of-kin."[48] That is not to say, however, that government officials always spoke or behaved as if they were entirely neutral about the issue.

Colonel Evans had also briefed the ABMC members on the literature to be sent to each family to be canvassed. The packet contained pamphlets that pictured and described the national cemeteries at home and the ABMC sites abroad. The all-important form for the respondents to communicate their burial choice to the government accompanied the explanatory material. Commissioner Markey observed that it would be "preferable" if the first option mentioned on the form could be "interment in permanent military cemeteries overseas, rather than interment in National cemeteries in the United States." Colonel Evans balked at this request, citing his department's wish not to influence the next-of-kin's decision. When Vice Chairman Woodside pressed the point, a higher-ranking member of the visiting delegation, General Aaron Bradshaw of the War Department General Staff, intervened. Affirming the desire of the secretary of war "to cooperate completely with the Commission," Bradshaw ruled that "the order of presentation of the options" would be changed in accordance with the ABMC's desires.[49]

The War Department's decision to give such priority listing to leaving bodies of the soldier dead in overseas cemeteries seemed a concession to the commission's desire to persuade the families to make that choice. One scholar has even employed this evidence as the basis of a claim that the "ABMC led the counteroffensive against repatriation."[50] Another scholar has offered selected statements by President Truman urging that "the boys" should be allowed to rest where they had fallen, and various press accounts about families who had recently visited a son's grave in a temporary cemetery and reacted favorably, as evidence of a more "blatant" effort by agents of the government to promote the option of overseas burial.[51] Material in the ABMC files, however, does not sustain such a strong charge against the commission. The ABMC's unconcealed preference for leaving the dead in cemeteries abroad simply did not translate into an organized, overt effort of much magnitude to steer families that way.

While the families were responding to the War Department canvas during 1947 and 1948, the GRS proceeded with the collection and sorting of bodies for repatriation or for permanent burial in an overseas cemetery. When the final disposition of the bodies in a particular cemetery became known, the grounds were closed to the public until all of the exhumations and permanent interments could be completed. At the Margraten site, where more than seventeen thousand American soldiers had been buried within a year of the end of the war, the Memorial Day ceremony in May

1948 marked the last time the general public would be allowed on the grounds until March 1951. The ABMC took full control of this cemetery in "a simple religious ceremony" on December 28, 1949, upon completion of the eighty-three hundred permanent burials. By the time the grounds were reopened for general visitation, the "architectural embellishment" of the site was just beginning and none of the marble headstones had been delivered. The reverential local citizenry flocked back to the grounds as quickly as they could, in any case, and eagerly tracked which of their beloved American dead would forever rest in Dutch soil.[52]

As the reburials at all fourteen of the sites were completed by mid-1951, the GRS ceded full control of each cemetery in its turn to the commission.[53] Vice Chairman Woodside attended ceremonies at Carthage and Cambridge in July 1949 marking the first two hand-overs.[54] The final cemetery to come completely under ABMC control, and to have its dead permanently in place, was the Ardennes site on June 30, 1951. A memorandum from the army secretary to Chairman Marshall on that occasion acknowledged that "the operational mission of the Department of the Army with respect to the cemeteries" was now complete.[55]

When the burials were all done, the construction of chapels and service buildings, the commissioning and creation of artwork, and the placement of permanent headstones could proceed apace—with the qualifier, in North's words, "as funds became available."[56] Chapel and memorial designs had been approved for eleven of the sites at the two commission meetings in 1948. The remainder were approved by March 1950.[57] Designs for individual sculptures and other artistic features (such as mosaics and stained glass), the work of artists selected by the architects, were also approved by the commission as they were submitted, generally without much controversy.

The end of the War Department canvas of families and the completion of burials in the overseas cemeteries also meant that the ABMC occasionally had to confront petitions for the removal of bodies. Secretary North told the commission that the War Department had sometimes granted such requests if the body in question was not yet permanently buried, or if the cemetery had not yet been turned over to the ABMC. Supported by the commission's ruling in the Dyer J. Bird case from 1935, however, North insisted that, once made by the legal next-of-kin, the decision permanently to bury a soldier in an overseas cemetery could not be reversed. "Future exhumations from our overseas cemeteries will leave conspicuous gaps which will mar the beauty and destroy the unity of the cemetery blocks," the secretary observed, and would give relatives of the other dead soldiers "cause for complaint."⁵⁸ When this issue came before the full commission at the sixtieth meeting, with General Marshall in the chair, the vote (with two dissents) upheld the precedent from fifteen years earlier.⁵⁹

In his memoir, Thomas North identified a number of obstacles encountered during the construction of the new sites. Finding people for the ABMC overseas staff who were qualified to supervise contractors and workmen in the language of the host countries was a particularly difficult challenge. Although a sufficient number of "project officers" were found, North and John Harbeson were obliged to monitor construction as closely as they could from the United States and to make frequent inspection trips to the sites. Such visits inevitably involved each of these officials in decisions on a range of problems that demanded "instant solution."⁶⁰ Each American architect, moreover, was contractually bound to engage an architect in the country where the memorial was to be constructed through whom the details of cemetery design could be translated into action. This, in North's words, proved "quite a job."⁶¹ Designing systems to provide adequate water for the acres of grass, plants, and trees adorning the memorials was an equally persistent difficulty that was solved in a manner unique to each site.⁶²

Secretary North also cited problems with construction that did not typically occur. Ample quantities and varieties of building stone for the memorial structures, walls of the missing, and perimeter walls were locally available at most of the sites, especially those in France, Italy, and England. Portland stone had to be imported from England to compose the memorials in the Netherlands and Ardennes cemeteries, and medium-hard limestone from Burgundy was dispatched to the Normandy and Henri-Chapelle sites. The Manila and Honolulu Memorials chiefly contain Roman travertine. But structures in the other cemeteries largely utilized products from the host regions.⁶³

Personnel problems rarely surfaced either. One of the rare ones developed late in 1954 when the longest-serving military officer in the Paris office, Major George M. ver Hulst of the US Air Force, came under investigation by his service for a variety of alleged misdeeds. Ver Hulst had been detailed to the commission since April 1948. In the end, the air force dropped the action, having accomplished little more than to irritate General Marshall by blindsiding him with the proceedings against his Paris officer. Ver Hulst was honorably relieved from his post in March 1956.[64] Only at Luxembourg was there a change in architect once construction had begun, the result of a disagreement with the commission over details in the design of the memorial structure.[65] Friction between the ABMC and the Fine Arts Commission on design issues, moreover, tended to be minimal. According to North, such criticism proffered by the CFA was "sympathetic and constructive."[66] Work at all the sites proceeded generally in an accident-free environment as well.

The choice of material for the permanent headstones touched off another quarrel, but of less intensity and of a different sort from the one two decades earlier. The commission decided in May 1948 to solicit bids from potential suppliers in accordance with procedures used after World War I.[67] No doubt remembering their bitter failure to secure bids for the World War I cemeteries, no American quarry answered the commission's request for bids for the next generation of cemeteries.[68] After 1945 the rivalry erupted between competing Italian quarries. Firms that harvested and supplied Carrara marble bid upwards of $46.00 per headstone this time around, while a Lasa company submitted the lowest bid, ranging between $26.95 and $29.15, depending on the distance between quarry and cemetery. When Secretary North visited the Lasa quarry, he noticed markers made of the local product that had stood along a narrow-gauge railway for more than twenty years and showed no signs of weathering.[69] His somewhat unscientific "study" of the properties of Lasa marble, along with the appealing price, was enough to persuade the secretary that this material was suitable. Provided that the Bureau of Standards ruled favorably on its durability, the commission agreed to choose the Lasa product.[70] The purity of its whiteness, even to the point of lacking the silvery vein that ran through the Carrara stone, also recommended it.

Stung by this rebuff from the Americans and suffering already from "disastrous unemployment conditions," however, the partisans of Carrara marble took their complaints to politicians in both Rome and Washington, though to no avail.[71] Initial inadequacies with the quality of workmanship on the cutting and engraving of the headstones, along with inefficiencies of production, were overcome, and the Lasa quarries fulfilled their contract satisfactorily. As it happened, the Carrara firms were not completely excluded from the project. When the one designated non-Italian supplier of marble, a local firm in the Philippines, asked to be excused from its contract to furnish the seventeen thousand-plus headstones for the Manila cemetery, about half of those crosses and Stars of David wound up coming from Carrara, and half from Lasa.[72]

The commission made important additional decisions early on about the headstones. In May 1948, Secretary North gained the group's concurrence with recommendations from an inter-services board that the data displayed on the individual grave markers—name, rank, service number (on the back of the headstone), military unit, state, and date of death—should essentially match how it had been done in the World War I cemeteries.[73] In January 1949, the commissioners decided that families would not be invited to propose personalized inscriptions on the back of the headstones. In the latter case, the commission concluded that "the difficulties and expense involved would be incommensurate with the satisfaction given to the very few" likely to request such inscriptions.[74] Finally, in May 1949, a new inscription was chosen for the headstones of the Unknowns: "Here rests in honored glory a comrade in arms known but to God."[75] "Comrade in arms" replaced "an American soldier" that was on the World War I headstones because it was thought to be more inclusive of all the services in the nation's military.

Scarcity of funds was the most consistent impediment to the pace of construction at the World War II commemorative sites. Once it was determined in 1947 that there would be fourteen new cemeteries, plus an expansion of the Suresnes memorial to make it a shrine to both world wars, the commission unanimously ratified Secretary North's total cost estimate of $30.5 million for chapels, artwork, headstones, landscaping, walls and other infrastructure, and outbuildings. North had calculated this sum by applying a multiple to the known cost of the World War I cemeteries, and by estimating the number of dead to remain overseas.[76] The estimate of total cost was increased a decade later to nearly $35 million, but this figure covered four major projects not part of the original program—namely, the reconstruction of the Brest monument and the construction of new ABMC monuments in the Honolulu cemetery and on both coasts of the US mainland.[77] A document compiled in 1962 praised the "economical operation" of the commission and put the total cost of all the new construction since 1947, including the projected price tag of the unfinished East and West Coast Memorials, back at $30 million.[78] Along the way, in any case, Congress did not part easily with the funding necessary to accomplish the commission's program.

The outbreak of the Korean War in June 1950 coincided with the beginning of the construction of the new overseas memorials and had an immediate effect on funding priorities within the national government. The mere suggestion that compulsory economies might indefinitely delay the commission's construction program evoked a forceful resolution from the commissioners at their October 24 meeting.[79] Chairman Marshall, who was also the secretary of defense at the time, received notice from Secretary North at the end of November that the Bureau of the Budget had indeed acted to reduce ABMC funding.[80] Such limitations, it was feared, could delay the efforts to eliminate the unsightly disruptions of recently completed burials at some cemeteries, not to mention jeopardize the timely fulfillment of the entire construction program at the memorial sites. Marshall immediately put the budget director on notice regarding the "very serious reaction" that likely would come from the families whose loved ones were buried in cemeteries consigned to remain unfinished for an indeterminate period of time.[81]

Before the end of 1950, North had come to an agreement with the Budget Bureau that all work at all cemeteries would proceed, *except* for the construction of the more costly edifices—namely, chapels and accompanying adornments, to include walls of the missing. This meant that remaining burials could go forward, as could placement of headstones, landscaping, and construction of reception facilities and service buildings. But North was obliged to set up a two-tiered schedule for work on the chapels and related parts of the various sites. Such construction at Margraten, Henri-Chapelle, Neuvillé-en-Condroz, Saint-Avold, Hamm, and Manila was put on hold for at least two years, until after FY 1952. While the secretary expressed his own concerns about the adverse effects on relatives of the dead, especially those without graves who awaited commemoration by other means within the cemeteries, neither he nor the chairman seemed able to change things.[82]

The next round of budgeting, in the summer of 1951, brought more restrictions and more objections from ABMC officials. General Marshall received instructions from the acting budget director at the end of June that all programs of his agency "should be reviewed in the light of their direct contribution to the defense effort and to essential civilian need." No new construction, or even "additional features of going projects," should be started, and building already under way should be pursued "only to provide for protection of investments already made."[83] The budget office, furthermore, reduced the commission's request for FY 1952 from $12.5

million to $4 million. This action came on the heels of a cut to the previous year's request from $8.5 million to $5.5 million.⁸⁴

North saw grim consequences in these limitations: any money saved from cuts today would be more than consumed by rising costs of construction later; construction already begun on eight memorials would have to stop, and suspensions already in place would continue; building stoppages would leave trained project managers with nothing to do and probably mean they would leave the service of the commission; and plaster models of proposed sculptures would deteriorate in storage. Worst of all, the secretary predicted, the commission's reputation would be damaged, "and probably [that of] our Government" as well.⁸⁵ Marshall took these concerns to President Truman in a face-to-face meeting on August 28. "I merely stated to the President," he wrote later, "what is my firm conviction, that he cannot afford politically to have a series of uncompleted cemeteries abroad with others completed and thousands of visitors going over there each year to visit the graves of their sons or husbands."⁸⁶

In a follow-up letter to the army chief of staff, the ABMC chairman enclosed a copy of the report submitted from Brussels a month earlier by Illinois congressman Fred Busbey, a member of the House Appropriations Committee, which had sounded similar notes. Marshall sent the same report to Harry Truman a few weeks later.⁸⁷ Busbey, who claimed to have traveled fourteen hundred miles to inspect memorial sites from Normandy to the border of Germany, had recounted that "words could not possibly describe the sickening feeling that would come over me to witness a mother, father, or a brother come to visit a soldier's grave to find the permanent headstone not as yet placed on his grave, or dirt from construction work going on piled high upon it, and the memorial and chapel, where one might go and commune with God according to the dictates of his soul, not completed." The congressman acknowledged that everything cannot be accomplished "over night," but urged that his colleagues on Capitol Hill do whatever they could to support completion of the construction "at the earliest possible date."⁸⁸

Economies mandated by the national government also threatened staffing levels at the ABMC offices and construction sites. The first notice in February 1951 of cutbacks in the number of military officers detailed to the commission prompted Secretary North to sound the alarm. After he was unable to persuade the secretary of the army to rescind a recently issued personnel authorization, North informed the commission that five of the ten army officers detailed to the agency would have to be let go by June 30. This would mean significant reductions in staffing at each of the commission's overseas offices—Paris, Rome, and Manila—and would also mean that a single army officer, not the current two, would be posted at the Lasa quarry to inspect the quality of headstones streaming out of Italy to the new cemeteries. "The load on our Paris office is now considerably heavier than the peak load of World War I construction," North told his fellow commissioners,[89] having failed to convince the secretary of the army that the envisioned personnel cuts would "cripple the activities of this Commission."[90]

On the same day that North broke this particular news to his eleven-member board, General Marshall contacted his wartime subordinate, General Omar Bradley, then serving as chairman of the Joint Chiefs of Staff. "My personal concern," Marshall explained, "has mainly to do with the possible adverse reaction in the event this reduction in officer personnel creates conditions of poor maintenance in the existing cemeteries and poor supervision of construction work on our new cemeteries." The ABMC chairman reiterated his warning about the likelihood that the increasing number of relatives crossing the Atlantic to visit the graves of their soldier dead would be disappointed with the lagging state of completion at the sites.[91]

At the urging of Bradley's staff, Marshall next took his case to General Joseph T. McNarney, the man from whose office the proposed personnel reductions had directly come. While deftly declaring that he was "naturally hesitant to become personally involved," Marshall expressed concern "about the overall morale factor if our foreign national cemeteries are not adequately maintained, and if the long-range program for construction at and improvement in our World War II cemeteries is postponed or otherwise interfered with." Still preserving his air of hesitancy and restraint, the chairman concluded: "Offhand, I am inclined to think that we should, if anything, increase the personnel assigned to the Battle Monuments Commission overseas."[92] Five days later, General McNarney wrote back that he had reviewed the matter, determined that the allotment of military officers to the ABMC could indeed be increased, and informed each of the service chiefs that the new numbers would be sixteen army officers, four from the air force, and two from the navy—"all to be deployed in a manner determined by General North."[93] Plainly, it did not hurt the commission's fortunes to have George C. Marshall as its chairman.

Still, the war against the cost cutters continued on other fronts. Secretary North wired from Paris at the beginning of October 1951 that half of the "field supervision force" would need to be released in order to comply with the most recent budgetary guidelines from the comptroller general's office. If the commission were to adhere to this latest directive, North calculated, it would be possible to maintain only six active construction sites.[94] Fortunately, the most crippling of the personnel restrictions were eased in the new year. Marshall's new complaint was that the forced discharge of "many tried men in connection with the engineering and the cemetery work generally" made it hard for the commission to refill the vacancies. The chairman wrote Army Chief of Staff Lawton Collins in October 1952 that the ABMC was "very much under-staffed, particularly on the technical side."[95]

For all of the difficulties with budgetary constraints, there was still significant progress to report from the various sites by the spring of 1953. All of the permanent headstones had been placed at seven cemeteries—Épinal, Draguignan, Saint-Avold, Brittany, Cambridge, North Africa, and Sicily-Rome—and two-thirds were in position at Normandy. Stone work on the memorial chapel complexes was substantially completed at Épinal, Brittany, Normandy, Cambridge, and Sicily-Rome, though barely under way elsewhere. At Margraten and Florence, the bidding process was still ongoing; at North Africa, contracts had been awarded but no construction begun; at Ardennes, Saint-Avold, and Henri-Chapelle, planning had not gotten beyond the paper stage. At Manila, finally, the site was three-quarters graded and the sprinkler system was 85 percent installed, but not one headstone was in place and no progress was recorded toward construction of the memorial.[96]

The first of the post–World War II constructions to be completed was at Suresnes, the World War I cemetery in suburban Paris originally dedicated by President Wilson on Memorial Day 1919. The ABMC had decided to convert this site into a memorial to the dead from both world wars by adding loggias and chambers on each side of the chapel and by creating an additional burial plot for twenty-four "Unknowns" from the 1941–45 conflict. The overall price tag for the project was between $500,000 and $600,000. Its small scale relative to the fourteen new cemeteries and its prominent location in the suburbs of the French capital likely gave it a measure of insulation from the budgetary strictures that slowed construction elsewhere. Strikes had nonetheless been a problem at this site, and the targeted date of completion was pushed back several times.[97]

The expanded chapel at this unique site extended sixty-four feet from each of the original side walls to provide space enough to commemorate both wars and honor the dead. Special attention is paid to the missing, with inscriptions and sculptured panels on the inner walls of each loggia and in the memorial chambers. At the end of each wing is a white figure in Carrara marble mourning the soldiers, sailors, marines, and airmen who lost their lives in all theaters of the worldwide fighting. Each loggia is covered and enclosed on three sides, but open to the graves area below and to the stunning, panoramic view of Paris in the distance. The architects for the enlarged memorial were sons William and Geoffrey of the designer of the original structure a generation earlier, Charles A. Platt.[98]

The commission had decided in November 1951 that the inaugural ceremony at Suresnes the following year should be regarded as "the general dedication of all World War II memorials since it constitutes a shrine to all of our overseas Dead." Later dedications, as each memorial was completed, would be "less elaborate ceremonies."[99] As early as February 1952, Secretary North communicated ideas to General Marshall for the dedication of the Suresnes site and urged the chairman to deliver the principal address—unless, of course, President Truman decided to attend. North believed that the ceremony should be of comparable importance to the one at Montfaucon in August 1937, when heads of state and the highest-ranking generals from France and the United States participated in the dedication of the principal American World War I monument.[100] Marshall saw it the same way and emphasized that the ceremony should be "international in scope." It was later determined that President Truman would send a message to be read in his absence; France's Premier Antoine Pinay would read a message from the president of the republic, Vincent Auriol; General Marshall would preside and deliver introductory remarks; and at Marshall's invitation, General Matthew Ridgway would deliver the dedicatory address.[101] The September 13 date ultimately chosen for the event happened to be the ninety-second anniversary of General Pershing's birth.

The Suresnes dedication unfolded in a fashion quite similar to its counterparts at the World War I cemeteries and monuments a mere fifteen years earlier. Like those of 1937, the speeches highlighted the long-standing friendship between the United States and France and the shared commitment of the two peoples to defend freedom. As Marshal Alphonse Juin, the senior French soldier at the event, put it: "I think there could be no better evidence of French-American friendship than this cemetery and monument erected and maintained by reverent hands and for the inauguration of which so many distinguished American guests crossed the Atlantic." President Auriol's message noted, "Twice the sons of generous America have come over to shed their blood, side by side with our soldiers, in the battle for Freedom, Justice, and Peace." General Ridgway said that "we stand not only on the soil of France, but on the soil of freedom; and our words go not to America alone, but to all people of all lands to whom life without freedom is worse than death." Reverence for the American dead was repeatedly expressed as well. The French president addressed those permanently interred in the cemetery with particular poignancy: "American brothers-in-arms, France does not forget you. She guards your graves with reverence; she faithfully honors your memory."[102]

General Marshall was especially keen, at this early stage of the Cold War, to reaffirm America's determination to stand with France and the Atlantic community in the defense of freedom. At his own request weeks earlier, the State Department had given him suggestions regarding what he should emphasize in his Suresnes speech. The ABMC chairman incorporated some of this counsel almost word-for-word into his remarks. Referencing the American dead in the cemetery and the current political discourse in the host country, especially the steady cry from French Communists that Americans should "go home," Marshall said that "these soldiers can never go home."[103] He further assured his audience that "Americans will not go home until our friends here feel that our presence is no longer essential to their security, when we can leave a land free of terror, a land where the dignity of the individual is supreme."[104]

Marshall's report to the commission on his European travels was the highlight of the December 5, 1952, meeting, the board's first in thirteen months. The chairman called the memorials he had seen, even in their unfinished state, "a remarkable artistic display," and he expressed the hope that they would become centers of tourism. Europeans in particular, he imagined, were "apt to respond to the great artistic triumph which the memorials constitute."[105]

The general's appreciation of the new sites, and his persistent concern for how relatives of the dead would react to them—especially in their incomplete condition—were never devoid of intimately personal feeling.

Mrs. Katherine Marshall's youngest son (from a previous marriage) was buried in the Sicily-Rome cemetery behind Anzio beach, near where he had died in action in 1944. When Marshall and his wife traveled Europe during the month after the Suresnes dedication, they visited the young man's grave. In a letter years later, the general wrote that they had found the site "a very beautiful cemetery in layout, buildings, statuary, and mosaics."[106] Sadly, he would never see the memorial in its completed state. Marshall was not healthy enough to attend when the cemetery was dedicated in July 1956.

At the December 1952 meeting, Secretary North also presented very encouraging budgetary news. The Budget Bureau seemed "sympathetic" to his request that the commission receive in FY 1954 the entire balance of the funds needed to complete its full construction program. When this appropriation was not granted for the next fiscal year, North received assurances that the remainder would be authorized for FY 1955. These developments meant that the commission could proceed with "all work at all cemeteries" as quickly as it could make necessary preparations.[107]

January 1953 saw the inauguration of a new president, and with him came major turnover in the membership of the commission. This was the first change of administration since the ABMC had received its expanded mandate and four additional members in 1946. Eisenhower initially informed Marshall that only he and Leslie Biffle would remain from the old commission.[108] The new members ultimately chosen were Admiral Thomas Kinkaid (US Navy, ret.); General Carl Spaatz (US Army, ret.); General Benjamin Oliver Davis (US Air Force, ret.), former commander of the Tuskegee Airmen and the first African American general officer in the air force; General Joseph J. Foss (US Marine Corps, ret.), a fighter ace who received the Medal of Honor as a captain for his heroism at Guadalcanal; Senator Charles E. Potter of Michigan; Congressman John Phillips of California; and the widows of General Theodore Roosevelt Jr. and 1940 Republican presidential nominee Wendell Willkie. General Vandegrift was also kept on from the Truman board.[109]

Within a year of the change in the commission's membership, the secretary of defense decided that the Medal of Freedom should be awarded to Robert Woodside, one of the original appointees to the ABMC whose work as vice chairman had been particularly valuable during the relatively long period of General Pershing's inactive service. When Secretary North learned that Marshall would not be able to make the presentation in Washington on the date appointed for it, he advised that the medal and accompanying citation simply be mailed to Woodside. But the chairman would have none of that, and advised his own aide to ask the president to do it, "as a favor to me?"[110] On the date of the presentation, Eisenhower sent Marshall a note confirming that he had indeed presented the award, adding: "We missed you."[111]

The president's willingness to present Woodside's award had been a relatively easy solution to the brief dilemma of how to formalize the honor to one of the commission's hitherto unsung heroes. For almost a decade following the end of the war, the question of how to properly honor the remains of one of the nation's most celebrated wartime heroes nagged at both the military establishment and the ABMC. General George S. Patton Jr. had died in December 1945 from injuries received in an automobile accident in occupied Germany. At the request of his family, he was buried on December 24, 1945, in the midst of thousands of his soldiers in what was then a temporary cemetery in Luxembourg, in soil his troops had liberated in the campaigning of 1944–45.

The family's choice of cemetery proved far easier than the decision of where to place the body *within* the cemetery. At first, Patton's remains lay deep within the graves area, requiring those who wished to visit it to traverse numerous rows of other graves along the way. Such a placement accorded completely with established policy in overseas cemeteries that no favor of marking or location should be shown to any grave based on rank. When Secretary of War Robert P. Patterson visited Patton's original grave early in 1946, he made much in public of the fact that the general's body lay in one of the long rows in the middle of the cemetery, marked by "a simple cross," just like all the other graves. "That is the way he [Patton] would want it," the secretary had said. "That is George Patton."[112] For the very large numbers of people anxious to visit it, however, getting to the grave remained an arduous, often muddy trek.

In mid-1947, consequently, the GRS moved Patton's remains to the first row of the cemetery, between the two flagpoles. There it rested for the next two years, during which time the more than five thousand permanent interments were determined and the ABMC developed its own designs for the final beautification of the site. The GRS ceded full control of the cemetery to the commission on December 16, 1949, upon the completion of all burials and reburials. Before that moment came, Patton's widow had requested that Secretary of Defense Louis Johnson order her husband's grave to be isolated in front of the rows of other graves so that it would stand out more. In keeping with established patterns of cooperation with the ABMC, Secretary Johnson sought the commission's approval for this new idea even though the GRS still controlled the final positioning of all graves within the Luxembourg cemetery.[113]

At its May 4, 1949, meeting, the commission voted unanimously to reject Secretary Johnson's proposal. From its first consideration of this question, as far back as February 1948, the commissioners had opposed giving "preferential treatment" to Patton's grave.[114] Three months after that, they had effectively reaffirmed the same decision out of a desire to follow "exactly" the architect's design for the grave plots at Luxembourg.[115] General Marshall's explanation to Secretary Johnson emphasized the commission's devotion to the principle of equal treatment for all graves, recalling that such a policy had won strong and unequivocal support from the American Legion and the Congress. Marshall also worried that yielding to the special request for Patton would make it impossible to turn down any other petition by a dead soldier's family for a variance in the presentation of the grave.[116]

Neither the family nor the secretary of defense, however, would drop the idea of moving Patton's grave to a more prominent position. In August 1949, while the GRS still controlled the cemetery, Johnson proposed the addition of an entirely new row of graves in front of the center section so that Patton's remains could be placed in the middle of it. The ABMC, with General Marshall presiding, again stood unanimously against this idea.[117] During the final days of GRS custody over the cemetery, heedless of the unrelenting objections of the commission, Patton's grave was moved to its current position, isolated and solo in front of the other plots.

The matter was still not settled, however. In June 1950, General Patton's wife learned of a proposal from the ABMC, now the custodian of the Luxembourg site, to move her husband's grave out of its "present isolated position" and back to the center grave block. The widow told General Thomas Handy that she would never accept such a "demotion" for her spouse's remains. Handy responded with a stiff warning to Thomas North. Patton was "a national hero," he said, and "growing in stature as he drops farther into the past." Especially in Luxembourg, "no other American commander is held in anything like the same veneration." To deny Patton's grave its privileged place, Handy suggested, would be nothing less than putting US relations with western Europe at risk.[118] Apparently in response to this adverse reaction, the ABMC left the latest positioning undisturbed.

Nine months later, R. Warren Davis, superintendent at the Luxembourg cemetery, reported that during a recent visit Mrs. Patton and her son, an army lieutenant, took note that the grave, still where the GRS had placed it in late 1949, was off the center axis of the cemetery. While the widow seemed willing to accept this placement, the son was not. He urged his mother, in fact, to "start a crusade to have the grave moved here to the center line." Superintendent Davis acknowledged that he felt "petty" reporting on this encounter, and found the whole matter "distasteful," but told his superiors in Paris that he felt obliged to keep them informed "of such incidents."[119]

Nothing further came of these murmurings. In December 1954, however, the commission seemed prepared to move the remains back to the position it had believed right for them all along. In a new design under consideration for the cemetery's central memorial, the steps leading to it from the graves area threatened to encroach on the Patton burial site. Of all the graves in the cemetery at that moment, moreover, Patton's was the only one without a permanent headstone, as if to confirm the commission's belief that the placement of the general's remains was still not final. With Chairman Marshall presiding, the commissioners formally directed Secretary North "to take no steps to move the grave, and to install its permanent headstone."[120] It continues to be the only burial in any of the ABMC cemeteries from either war to be set off in such a manner.

There remains to recount a second, though less controversial, story about a particularly famous interment in one of the World War II cemeteries. Since July 1918, the body of Theodore Roosevelt's youngest son, Quentin, an army lieutenant killed by the Germans in aerial combat, had lain in an isolated grave in the Champagne region of France. As already noted in an earlier chapter, the former president had expressed emphatically to the head of the GRS the family's wish for Quentin's tomb to remain undisturbed where the Germans had placed it and marked it.[121] In making this choice, the Roosevelts undertook full and perpetual responsibility for the upkeep of Quentin's grave and absolved the US government of any obligations regarding the current or future disposition of the young man's remains. The family contracted with a local woman to care for the grave. To honor the young pilot further, the American Red Cross, to which the president had donated a substantial portion of the proceeds from his Nobel Peace Prize in 1906, financed a memorial fountain designed by Paul Cret in the nearby village of Chamery.[122]

Two things about this situation changed with the end of World War II. After the passage of nearly three decades, the French woman who had cared for Quentin's burial site was no longer able to fulfill that task. In response to an October 1946 inquiry about the condition of the grave, Secretary of War Patterson reminded Archibald Roosevelt that his parents had "released the United States Government of all future responsibility" for its upkeep, and advised the family to contact the State Department for any assistance it might be able to provide toward finding a new caretaker.[123]

Sometime during the next eighteen months, secondly, the widow of Quentin's oldest brother, Theodore Jr., who had died of a heart attack while on active duty as an army general in July 1944, decided to have her husband's remains permanently interred in the new Normandy American Cemetery. This prompted a formal request in March 1948 by Archibald Roosevelt to the quartermaster general to have Quentin's remains transferred from his original grave to lie alongside Theodore Jr. But the secretary of the army was constrained to deny the request. Citing "existing law" and "established policy" of his department as his reasons, the secretary reiterated to the Roosevelt brother: "I cannot break faith with the expressed desire of your esteemed father."[124]

Here matters rested for more than five years, with official Washington dug in behind the idea that the next-of-kin's original decision about an overseas burial was irrevocable, and the Roosevelt family grudgingly consigned to Quentin's body remaining where it was. The appointment of Mrs. Theodore (Eleanor B.) Roosevelt Jr. to a seat on the American Battle Monuments Commission in 1953, and the ABMC's assumption of full jurisdiction over the Normandy cemetery by the end of 1951, evidently stirred the family's desire to try again for a ruling more to its liking.

After Commissioner Roosevelt raised the issue with Thomas North in a June 1954 letter, her brother-in-law Archibald formally petitioned the ABMC in March 1955 to have Quentin's body moved to Normandy, at the family's expense.[125] At its sixty-eighth meeting the following month, the commission voted unanimously to grant the request.[126] Both Secretary North and the GRS insisted, however, that there could be no official involvement of either government agency in the transfer of the remains to their new burial site.[127] Private labor and family money had to be employed in the exhumation of the body, the removal to New York of the memorial stone that had covered the original grave, and the transfer of the filled casket to the new burial site.

The ABMC still had observers at the disinterment of Quentin's body, of which only bones remained, on September 22, 1955, and at the reinterment the next afternoon.[128] No ceremony attended either stage of this process, in keeping with Secretary North's counsel that publicity should be avoided out of respect for the family.[129] The two Roosevelt brothers side by side are one of forty-five pairs of brothers at the Normandy site. They rest at the corner of one of the ten lettered plots, and large numbers of visitors seek out their graves. Unlike the Patton grave, however, their headstones enjoy no privilege of place. The inscription on General Roosevelt's grave is accentuated in gold, but this is because he was awarded the Medal of Honor. No such special adornment of any kind is on Quentin's headstone.[130]

The commission resolved several additional issues relating to burials as the cemeteries began to take shape. One pertained to the interment of "general prisoners," or those American soldiers put to death during the war for military crimes. The World War I cemeteries contain only six such men, all buried without distinction among the other dead. In January 1949, the quartermaster general sent several officers to appear before the commission and determine what to do with the ninety-four such dead from the European and Mediterranean theaters of World War II.[131]

Secretary North was ready with a proposal to have these men sent to a special plot, now known as "Plot E," on the grounds of the Oise-Aisne cemetery. This particular space is across the road from the main burial grounds and well screened from general view by vegetation. General K. L. Hastings, the ranking officer from the quartermaster general, told the ABMC that his agency could transport these remains, some of which had been temporarily interred at Brookwood, to the new site and complete the reburial. Hastings noted that the next-of-kin had been told that the men had died by execution, but had been given no option regarding their final burial. With the unanimous support of the commission,[132] this arrangement was effectuated, and Plot E for many years was kept a tightly held secret.

At the Margraten site, the commission encountered a host population devoutly eager to involve itself in the life of the cemetery by "adopting" graves. During the final months of the war, local families had housed and often formed strong friendships with American G.I.s, for whom the

Limburg province was a staging area for deeper and deeper forays into Germany. Many of the American dead in the Margraten cemetery, therefore, were personally known to the Dutch inhabitants, and the interest in adopting graves dated as far back as 1945, when the site was still deemed temporary.

In March 1950, a request from the Netherlands War Graves Commission came before the ABMC that the names of those interred at Margraten be released to the Dutch public in order to facilitate the adoption of the permanent graves. Such a commitment meant that the volunteer agreed to visit the designated grave and also to decorate it periodically. At its sixtieth meeting, the commission agreed to release the names of the Margraten burials, but not of the next-of-kin back home. Given the ongoing commitment of the US government to care for the graves, moreover, no outside organizations were to consider themselves charged with sharing this obligation in any way.[133]

Five years later, a poorly informed officer in the commission's Paris office instructed the superintendent at Margraten to actively discourage the adoption of graves. The American ambassador to the Netherlands immediately alerted General Marshall about the damage this directive threatened to do, and the chairman told Secretary North to put the issue on the agenda of the sixty-eighth meeting. Meanwhile, Marshall's aide, Colonel C. J. George, reminded his boss that the upset locals had once made the general an "honorary citizen" of their province and that "this sort of thing [adoption of graves] can do more good toward the cordial relationship between countries than any other thing I know." The commission soon reiterated its support for the practice, and confirmed that "correcting instructions" should be dispatched to all concerned.[134] Marshall, moreover, sent an emphatic assurance to the US ambassador: "The Commission appreciates the sympathy which has moved the citizens of the Province of Limburg who have adopted graves of our World War II Dead, as well as the importance of these reactions to our international relations."[135]

Even so, the commission unanimously reaffirmed "its instructions to refrain from releasing the names and addresses of the next-of-kin."[136] As it has happened over the years, however, American families and Dutch locals found ways to make contact. Some of these relationships date from the time when G.I.s lived with Dutch hosts, told their folks back home about them, and the two groups starting writing to each other. For many years, not only all of the 8,301 graves at Margraten have been adopted, but also each one of the 1,722 names on the cemetery's Wall of the Missing. When American family members come to the Netherlands to pay homage to their dead loved ones, the adopters of the graves are frequently present to welcome them. During the 1960s, the Netherlands War Graves Commission sponsored travel and arranged lodging in private Dutch homes for mothers of the American dead to visit their sons' graves in the Margraten cemetery. Grave adoptions routinely become multigenerational commitments as well.[137]

At the beginning of 1949, the commission addressed two remaining issues relating to its overall memorial program: a second permanent cemetery for the dead of the Asia-Pacific Theater and a structure to commemorate the dead of the Pearl Harbor attack. Because both of these sites would be in Hawaii, there were jurisdictional complications stemming from the fact that the ABMC mandate was to build memorials on territory *outside* of the United States. The cemetery at Honolulu, in the Puowaina or "Punchbowl" Crater, was designated a permanent site over possible alternatives on another central or south Pacific island because it afforded greater accessibility to potential visitors. Since Hawaii was not foreign territory, however, the burial ground would remain under the authority of the army quartermaster general.

By the time of the fifty-seventh ABMC meeting in January 1949, a division of the dead between the two Pacific cemeteries had been worked out. Those from fighting in the Philippines, New Guinea, and Peleliu, along with some "Unknowns" from other regions, would lie in the Manila cemetery, while dead from the China-Burma-India Theater, Australia, Okinawa, the Marianas and the Bonins (including Iwo Jima), and other islands of the central and southern Pacific, would lie in Hawaii. With two different jurisdictions involved in handling the memorialization of dead from the same theater of war, disagreement arose over whether a chapel would be erected and what kind of grave markers would be used at the Hawaii site. General K. L. Hastings from the quartermaster general's office told the ABMC, in fact, that no chapel was planned for the latter cemetery because national cemeteries under army control did not have such buildings. Quartermaster general–type headstones would mark the graves, moreover, to be consistent with other national cemeteries, and to satisfy local residents, who wished to preserve "a park-like appearance" for the cemetery. The ABMC commissioners, however, unanimously expressed the view that the Hawaii site should look like their own cemeteries and persuaded General Hastings to postpone ordering headstones until the difference of opinions between the two agencies could be resolved.[138]

When the question of a memorial at Pearl Harbor—specifically, a commemorative edifice built over the wreck of the USS *Arizona*—came before the same meeting, the ABMC unanimously rejected the idea. Removing bodies from the submerged hull of the battleship to accommodate such a structure would be "repugnant," in the estimation of the commission, and the whole project would be "prohibitively expensive." In addition, "the thought of constructing a garden or memorial over these bodies so that sightseers might walk above them would be distasteful to many."[139]

The final disposition of both Hawaii projects took years. The commission clung to its desire to build a chapel-memorial at the Punchbowl in the face of the army's insistence that no such edifice was necessary and that the ABMC could not build it on US territory in any event. Not until December 1953 was the ABMC's subcommittee on Pacific memorials, chaired all the while by General Vandegrift, able to report that the army had dropped its opposition to a memorial at the Punchbowl built by the commission.[140] Within a year of this breakthrough, the commissioners had recommended to congressional appropriators an allotment of $1.7 million for the project, selected an architectural firm, and authorized it to make recommendations as to the design and the siting of the memorial. Although the agency unanimously favored the use of cross-type headstones in the Hawaii cemetery, the army ultimately carried the day with its insistence that the markers there match those of other national cemeteries within the United States.[141]

The commission's design for the Honolulu Memorial consisted of a chapel as the centerpiece, with eight tree-shaded squares lining a mall descending a slope toward the graves area, and steles bearing the names of the missing surrounding each square.[142] Nearly thirteen thousand dead from the Second World War are interred in the cemetery, with additional burials from the Korean and Vietnam conflicts. On tablets in the "Courts of the Missing" are roughly eighteen thousand names from World War II, eighty-two hundred from Korea, and twenty-five hundred from Vietnam. Map galleries, moreover, extend from the two sides of the chapel, with instructional panels recounting more than a dozen individual operations from the 1941–45 and Korean conflicts.[143] The memorial was formally dedicated on May 1, 1966, in a ceremony presided over by the commission's chairman at the time, General Jacob Devers.[144]

The commission never withdrew its opposition to a memorial above the grave of the USS *Arizona*. In May 1949, in response to news that the Hawaii territorial legislature had passed a resolution that federal funds should be employed to realize such a monument, the ABMC reiterated its determination not to undertake this project.[145] Notwithstanding the commission's "disapproval," a naval veterans group dedicated a small monument on Ford Island to the Pearl Harbor dead at the end of 1955.[146] Two years later, the Navy Department was poised to secure congressional approval for the larger project that the ABMC had so consistently refused to build.

The navy had never been satisfied that the memorial the commission was building at the Punchbowl cemetery adequately commemorated the dead from Pearl Harbor—more specifically, the 1,102 dead from the *Arizona*. Early in 1957, when Secretary North learned of the navy's intention to pursue a memorial over the battleship independently of the ABMC, he wrote the director of the Bureau of the Budget in an attempt to kill the project. Under federal statute, North reminded the budget director, only the ABMC was authorized to build war memorials.[147] North seemed particularly irritated that the secretary of the navy was promoting the *Arizona* memorial even though, a year earlier, he had conceded to North that the project resided solely "within the purview of the American Battle Monuments Commission."[148] At the end of 1957, the House of Representatives passed a bill authorizing the navy to build the long-sought monument over the hull of the *Arizona*, and the commission was left to fume in futile opposition. The fact that the people of Hawaii, not the Navy Department, had sponsored the House measure was of little consolation to Secretary North, who saw a real danger that the ABMC's unique authority had been permanently compromised. In his memoirs, North commented caustically that the *Arizona* memorial was "the sole monument that I can recall which this nation or any other had built to commemorate a defeat."[149]

At the commission's seventy-third meeting, Admiral Kinkaid "reiterated his own conviction against the erection" of the *Arizona* memorial, and the other members instructed Senator Potter to "take appropriate action," presumably to thwart Senate endorsement of the plan.[150] Whatever Potter may ultimately have done in this regard, the project went forward to completion with funding from a mix of public and private sources and was dedicated on Memorial Day, 1962. The *Arizona* memorial remains under the shared authority of the Navy Department and the National Park Service.

The ABMC was ready officially to dedicate six of its European cemeteries—Cambridge, Normandy, Brittany, Épinal, Rhône, and Sicily-Rome—during the second half of July 1956. A discussion at the December 1955 commission meeting confirmed that these ceremonies would be "less elaborate than that of Suresnes," and that expenses should be kept so low that a special appropriation from Congress might not be required.[151] At the April 1956 meeting, the commissioners decided that they would play "prominent parts" in the ceremonies, along with the respective American ambassadors, but that the dedicatory addresses should be made by high-ranking representatives of the military or combat veterans currently seated on the ABMC.[152] As it happened, the principal addresses were delivered by General Carl Spaatz (Cambridge) and Senator Charles Potter (Épinal) from the commission; the current secretaries of the army, air force, and navy at Normandy, Brittany, and Sicily-Rome, respectively; and General Jacob Devers, future ABMC chairman and army group commander in the late war, at the Rhône site.[153]

The formal report delivered to General Marshall after the events indicated that the audiences numbered between twelve hundred and two thousand at each site, and that Americans comprised only 10 to 15 percent of each crowd.[154] Medal of Honor recipients, high government officials or their representatives (no heads of state from the United States or any of the host countries attended these dedications), and leaders from each of the patriotic organizations chartered by Congress—the Veterans of Foreign Wars, American War Mothers, American Legion, Disabled American Veterans, and American Veterans of World War II (AMVETS)—also participated in each ceremony. One of the most poignant moments came when Mrs. Theodore Roosevelt Jr., an ABMC commissioner, laid a wreath on her husband's grave in the Normandy cemetery. President Eisenhower sent personal messages to be read at each ceremony.[155] Admiral Thomas Kinkaid, vice chairman of the commission and author of the report to General Marshall, largely credited "the zealous and efficient work of the Secretary of the commission and his staff" for the "impressiveness of the ceremonies."[156] At the December 1956 meeting, the last one attended by General Marshall, the ABMC chairman observed that he had received "nothing but compliments" about the ceremonies, and that President Eisenhower had also expressed "his appreciation of the Commission's conduct of those ceremonies."[157]

The remaining eight cemeteries were dedicated in 1960, beginning with Luxembourg on July 4 and culminating with Manila on December 8. The rebuilt tower at Brest was dedicated on July 16, and a monument to the missing off the West Coast was formally inaugurated in San Francisco on November 29 as the ABMC delegation made its way to the Philippines. Members of the commission presided at each cemetery, with newly installed Chairman Jacob Devers serving in this capacity at three of the sites (Henri-Chapelle, Florence, and the West Coast Memorial). The most prominent figures to deliver dedicatory addresses were Secretary of the Navy William B. Franke at Brest, Fleet Admiral Chester Nimitz at the West Coast Memorial, and Admiral Raymond Spruance, former commander of the US Fifth Fleet, at Manila. Admiral Kinkaid, former commander of the Seventh Fleet, presided at the ceremony in the Philippines. Two heads of state, Queen Juliana of the Netherlands and President Carlos Garcia of the Philippines, spoke at their respective events, and the grand duchess of Luxembourg attended the ceremony there. President Eisenhower, as he had done in 1956, sent personal messages to be read at each of the 1960 ceremonies.[158] On July 1, 1960, the commission had met in Paris, primarily to consider points relating to the upcoming dedications in Europe. It was the first time the ABMC had convened outside the United States since August 1937, when General Pershing held the forty-fourth meeting in Paris during the spate of World War I dedications.[159]

The group convened again in Manila the day after the largest of the ABMC cemeteries had been dedicated in the Philippines capital. Amid expressions of deep satisfaction with the ceremony just conducted, as well as with the San Francisco event eleven days earlier, the commissioners took stock of the entire collection of memorials now officially inaugurated into service. It was agreed that the new generation of sites would create "a psychological impression in recording the sacrifices of the American people so favorable as to outweigh the relatively insignificant demands which they make upon the national budget." The panel also resolved to make a "positive effort" to spread knowledge of the cemeteries and memorials among the American and foreign peoples alike. "The Commission is rendering a great service to the cause of the free world," the minutes recorded, "by showing that the American people not only do not forget, but revere, the memory of these to whom all who love liberty owe so much."[160]

As the products of a conflict that killed roughly four hundred thousand Americans, the World War II cemeteries are generally larger than those of the earlier generation. Only the Draguignan site contains fewer than one thousand burials, but it is still larger than the two smallest of the eight World War I cemeteries. Nine of the fourteen burial grounds from the second global struggle numbered more than five thousand dead, while only two of the eight earlier sites (Meuse-Argonne and Oise-Aisne) had been that large.

The World War II cemeteries, for being all-inclusive memorials from a costlier conflict, also required more space for things other than burials. Walls of the missing honor nearly twenty times the number memorialized in this manner at the World War I cemeteries. Large, impressively artistic battle maps, and expanded museum buildings are part of these sites. More numerous sculptures adorn them as well. Indeed, the work of twenty different sculptors fills the fourteen cemeteries, and each site includes a particularly notable piece of statuary or a major work sculpted into or otherwise attached to the exterior of the chapel. "Youth Triumphing over Evil," a limestone statue, dominates the rear facade of the Brittany chapel, for example.[161] Two limestone bas-reliefs, one depicting "Crusade in Europe" and the other "Resurrection," welcome visitors to Épinal at the entrance to the chapel-museum complex.[162] An "Angel of Peace" rises twenty-three feet in granite above the bronze doors of the chapel at Luxembourg.[163] "Spirit of American Youth, Rising from the Waves," a statue twenty-two feet tall, is the centerpiece of the memorial colonnade that opens toward the burial plots at Normandy.[164] Free-standing depictions of an "Angel of Peace with Olive Branch" at Henri-Chapelle, of "The Gallant, the Brave, and the Beloved" at Ardennes, of "Honor" at Tunis, and of "Brothers in Arms" at Sicily-Rome further exemplify the outstanding sculptures. General Eisenhower offered especially strong praise for the sculptors, "whose genius is responsible in so conspicuous a measure for the beauty and dignity of these testimonials of a nation's gratitude."[165]

The chapels, frequently but not always decorated with mosaics, offer their own artistic highlights to each cemetery. Only at Normandy and Manila are the chapels situated in the center of the graves area. At the other sites, these structures are centrally located at some point along the periphery of the cemetery, often in a manner that requires visitors to pass by them on their way to the graves. Generally speaking, the World War II chapels do not fall into traditional categories such as Gothic, Romanesque, or classical; rather, they tend to be more modern rectangular or circular designs or, in the case of Luxembourg, Florence, and the Netherlands, towers ranging in height from fifty to a hundred feet. The chapel at Brittany, built of local granite, is uniquely constructed in the style of a village church.[166]

While the ABMC continues its stated mission of honoring and preserving the memory of the "courage, competence, and sacrifice" of American soldiers in foreign wars, it has built no new cemeteries since the aftermath of the Second World War. Responsibility for the maintenance of four additional overseas burial grounds—Mexico City, Panama, Clark Veterans Cemetery (in the Philippines), and, most recently, the memorial to the Lafayette Escadrille in Paris—has been assigned to the commission during the past seventy years, but the only cemeteries it helped to construct hold those who died in the two World Wars. The government's policy for the 1917–18 and 1941–45 wars was to leave no soldier's remains on "unfriendly soil." For those Americans who have died in wars abroad since the end of World War II, all of the bodies recovered from the field of combat or from overseas hospitals have been brought home for burial. As a consequence, former ABMC commissioner Victor Davis Hanson has remarked that the creation of the twenty-two cemeteries abroad will stand as an altogether unique achievement of the American government, never to be replicated.[167]

General Pershing's expressed wish for all of the ABMC sites was that they would "outlast time itself" and inspire all who visited them, or merely saw them in the distance, with their beauty and their strength. General Eisenhower observed that the building of the ABMC memorials may well stand as "the greatest collaboration in the arts ever undertaken by this country."[168] In July 1949, at the beginning of the construction of the World War II sites, Robert Woodside addressed a memorandum to the employees of the commission "in Europe and the Mediterranean areas," in which he presented the work before them as a challenge. "The people of our country and the spirits of the brave Americans who lie in these cemeteries," he wrote, "look to us to see that their sacrifices are fittingly commemorated."[169] Within a bit more than a very eventful decade thereafter, that challenge was met.

Conclusion

The ABMC Story Goes On, 1960–Present

For the nearly sixty years since the last of the World War II cemeteries was dedicated, the work of the commission has been more about preservation than creation. The 1965 annual report, the first of two compiled by the third chairman, General Jacob Devers, observed that the commission "lays great stress upon a high standard of maintenance."[1] A half-century later, Secretary Max Cleland emphasized the same point. "Throughout the year [2016], as always, our highest priority was ensuring that our commemorative cemeteries and memorials remain among the most beautiful shrines of their nature in the world—the service and sacrifice they honor deserve nothing less."[2] The lion's share of the agency's annual budget covers the cost of this maintenance and the personnel necessary to perform it. Showing hospitality and kindness to visitors on a day-to-day basis has always been another high priority for the commission staff. The 1965 document attached special importance to maintaining "a sympathetic, helpful attitude towards bereaved relatives."[3] While the passage of years has inevitably diminished the number of actively grieving next-of-kin coming to the cemeteries, visitors of all kinds have learned that this "sympathetic, helpful attitude" is a vital part of the agency's ethos.

But properly welcoming visitors to the sites and keeping the grass cut, the trees trimmed, the headstones polished, and the stonework well pointed will never represent the totality of the commission's ongoing importance or value to the country. The mission of remembrance since 1960 continues to entail the hosting of commemorative ceremonies and observances, especially at the cemeteries, on Memorial Days, Armistice Days, and anniversaries of wartime events of particular significance to the individual memorials. If the dedication of the East Coast Memorial in 1963 and the Honolulu Memorial in 1966 marked the definitive completion of the generation of construction conceived during the Marshall years, new monuments continue to become part of the ABMC's commemorative program. Because of its impressive accomplishments in earlier years, the commission directed the construction of perhaps the grandest and best known of all the war monuments in the American homeland, the World War II Memorial on the National Mall in Washington, D.C., although another government agency has had administrative authority over this site since its dedication in 2004. During the past decade, well-designed, highly informative "interpretive centers" have begun to supplement the presentation at both the World War I and World War II cemeteries. An ever-expanding educational effort, enhanced constantly by the agency website (www.abmc.gov), seeks to bring to life the service and sacrifices of American soldiers abroad for successive generations of the nation's schoolchildren as well as the general public. Since 1978, finally, a number of the ABMC sites have gained additional measures of public awareness from high-profile presidential visits. The Normandy cemetery, in particular, has enjoyed notably increased fame in the past twenty years because a very successful and popular Hollywood movie featured it both at the beginning and the ending of the picture. Limitations of space will not permit the fullest examination of each of the foregoing topics, but this conclusion will endeavor to identify highlights of the past five to six decades.

General Jacob Devers's appointment to the ABMC by President Eisenhower, and his election as chairman in time for the seventy-seventh meeting of the commission in March 1960, filled the vacancy created by General Marshall's death. In choosing Devers for this position, Ike honored one of the most revered soldiers in the country, but one with whom he shared a relationship characterized in a recent biography as "sometimes toxic."[4] In any event, the third chairman never missed any of the ten commission meetings during the near-decade that he served, and was a couple of years past his eightieth birthday when President Nixon replaced him in 1969.

Devers presided over the dedication of all three of the large memorials built by the ABMC on American soil to complete the post–World War II commemorative program. The November 1960 ceremony for the

West Coast Memorial, which honors 413 of those in uniform or merchant mariners who perished in Pacific coastal waters during the war, was mentioned in the previous chapter. The East Coast Memorial, which honors 4,611 who perished without a trace in Atlantic coastal waters, was dedicated in May 1963. The idea of building memorials for these lost appeared for the first time in the minutes of the sixty-sixth commission meeting in March 1954. On that occasion, Chairman Marshall proposed that the structures be placed where they are today, and where he imagined that they would be most readily seen—on "the sea front" south of the Golden Gate in San Francisco, and in Battery Park, New York City.[5] President John F. Kennedy, a navy veteran from World War II, delivered the dedicatory address at the latter site on May 23, 1963, while he was in town to celebrate his forty-sixth birthday. The Honolulu Memorial, whose story was also recounted in the previous chapter, was dedicated on May 1, 1966.[6]

Before Devers's own service to the ABMC ended, he artfully employed his connection with Eisenhower to ward off a threat to the agency's independence. Such perils had surfaced before, and would come again, but the one in question seemed especially urgent. During the latter stage of Lyndon Johnson's term, the idea arose in Congress and found support in the executive branch that all cemeteries administered by the federal government should be under the jurisdiction of the Veterans Administration. Had this reform been implemented, it would have meant the extinction of the ABMC.

In March 1968, General Devers sought the help of former President Eisenhower in protecting the commission against the possibility that its most important function would be reassigned to another agency. The ABMC chairman presented several arguments to his wartime boss for why the proposed reform should be stopped. First, the burial sites maintained by the commission are "in treatment monuments rather than cemeteries" and thus have nothing in common with "grave-sites for veterans." Devers also highlighted the fact that the work of the ABMC was largely overseas, a realm with which the Veterans Administration had little experience, and that the smaller agency had an "enviable reputation" for high standards of maintenance, public relations, and economical operations. "I have taken the liberty of presenting these views to you because of your service with the Commission as a junior officer," Devers explained, "and your great interest in the Commission as The President of the United States." If Ike sympathized with these concerns, Devers suggested, he should mention the matter to President Johnson.[7]

Within a week Ike had promised to write "promptly" to LBJ to encourage him to give Devers a hearing in the Oval Office.[8] The former president dutifully wrote his successor the same day,[9] and Johnson answered with equal dispatch. The latter insisted that his administration had taken no position on the pending action in Congress, but assured Eisenhower that "the expertise and the dedicated service of the Commission are well appreciated here, and I shall keep in touch with this matter personally."[10] Although there was divided opinion among the eleven commissioners themselves when this issue came before their June 7 meeting, and the chairman of the House Veterans Affairs Committee ultimately short-circuited action on Capitol Hill,[11] it is hard to resist concluding that President Johnson also helped to keep this particular proposal from carrying the day. It should be noted, further, that Ike had earned a large share of the president's goodwill in recent weeks from numerous sympathetic and supportive communications as Johnson sank deeper into the Vietnam morass. The Eisenhowers had hosted LBJ in mid-February at their vacation residence in southern California on his way back to Washington from an inspection visit to Southeast Asia, and Johnson had sent his predecessor an effusive letter of thanks just over a month before Ike asked for the president's help in preserving the ABMC's independence.[12]

These exchanges among the two retired generals and President Johnson happened to coincide with a particularly noteworthy transition in the leadership of the commission. In February 1968, General Thomas North announced his retirement after twenty-two years as ABMC secretary. His replacement was General Andrew J. Adams, who assumed the post in time for the next meeting of the commission in June and held it until 1992.[13] One source has suggested that North, "who simply loved his work and was reluctant to leave it," stepped down at the encouragement of General Devers, who wished to "revitalize the staff of ABMC."[14] As already recounted, North's service to the commission spanned five decades. Major George C. Marshall described him in 1920 as "a well educated and cultured man of pleasing personality," and "a very valuable officer."[15] More than thirty years later, General of the Army George C. Marshall praised North for his "character and integrity and . . . keen initiative," and ranked him "one of the most outstanding officers over whom I have had direct supervision."[16] Eisenhower, in a 1966 note that began with "Dear

Tommy," had told North: "Personally I don't see how the Battle Monuments organization would get along without you."[17]

North's legacy to the ABMC is prominent and undeniable, and virtually impossible to encapsulate fully. He established the commission's Paris office in the mid-1920s. As secretary throughout the period of post–World War II construction, North was primarily responsible for supervising the selection and performance of the architects and builders who created the overseas memorials. He had actually played a similar role as Xenophon Price's subordinate during the 1920s and 1930s, gaining valuable experience for his own service as secretary. "He [North] had every reason to be very proud of ABMC and his work with it," observed one of his own subordinates. "Its cemeteries and memorials were by far the most beautiful and meticulously maintained in the world,"[18] and he deserved no small credit for that achievement. Altogether, North spent fifty-one years in the army, was a veteran of both world wars, and was a recipient of the Distinguished Service Medal. He died in 1990 at ninety-seven years of age.[19]

During the year after North's retirement, Richard Nixon entered the White House, General Devers resigned as ABMC chairman, and General Mark Clark was appointed to the commission to replace him. At the eighty-seventh meeting, on February 16, 1970, Clark was unanimously elected chairman. Later that same afternoon, all eleven commissioners, eight of whom were attending their first meeting, plus the newly appointed secretary, met the president in the Oval Office. It was the first time since the 1920s that the commission had been received in its entirety in the executive mansion. During the course of the meeting Nixon expressed the belief that the ABMC members should visit the cemeteries and stated that the money to do so would be made available to them. According to Secretary Adams's report on the White House visit, "The President feels that these cemeteries and the sacrifices of those buried in them should be an inspiration to the people of America and give them a sense of pride in our national heritage and accomplishments."[20] Indeed, inspection trips to Europe and the Far East did follow within a year.

The relationship between Clark and Nixon was unusually close. The general had campaigned for the Nixon-Agnew ticket in 1968 and attended the inauguration the following January.[21] When Nixon announced a military incursion into Cambodia in May 1970, an event that coincided with the commission's European inspection trip, the general wired the president from Nancy, France, that he and the entire panel fully supported "the selfless and courageous action you have taken in the Cambodian situation in protecting our heroic men in Vietnam and preventing a communist take-over in South East Asia."[22] Fifty years of ABMC records reveal no precedent for this sort of unified expression by the commissioners on a matter of state. Nor did Clark shrink from appealing personally to the president when the commission desired special funding for its projects, although such appeals did not guarantee success. A letter to Nixon in November 1970 itemizing roughly a million dollars sought for FY 1972 to enable the creation of eight new memorials, one of which was to honor John J. Pershing in the heart of Washington, D.C., yielded no fruit with the Office of Management and Budget.[23] An important initiative Clark did successfully pursue early in his chairmanship was to have the headstones of Medal of Honor winners in the ABMC cemeteries engraved with a star and the words "Medal of Honor" in gold leafing.[24]

Pursuit of the new monument projects would take much longer. A memorial to General Pershing was the earliest idea for a monument beyond the original program for World War II cemeteries. Not surprisingly, this proposal originated within a year of his death. The commission addressed it at its fifty-eighth meeting in May 1949, the first one chaired by General Marshall. The new chairman appointed three commissioners to a committee to study the matter, and the stubbornly long gestation period for the monument to the nation's only general of the armies (as of that date) was under way.[25]

Acts of Congress in 1956 and 1966 authorized the monument, but provided no funding. The decision to construct the site in a park-like island along Pennsylvania Avenue between 14th and 15th Streets meant that, in addition to the two national commissions possessing the authority to approve designs for such memorials, the Pennsylvania Avenue Development Corporation and the National Capital Planning Commission would also have a say. Congress appropriated $100,000 to fund the design of the memorial in FY 1973,[26] and the ABMC requested $950,000 for its construction in the budget for FY 1975.[27] At this point, however, budgetary tightness and disagreements over details of design conspired to further delay progress. Finally, $300,000 was approved in FY 1978 for construction of what had now become the "Pershing AEF Memorial,"[28] although the site did not open until May 1981 and the statue of General Pershing was not mounted until the following year. What is now known as the "American Expeditionary Forces Memorial" is under the care of the

National Park Service, and the 2014 National Defense Authorization Act has mandated that the site be refashioned into the National World War I Memorial.[29]

Two additional ABMC memorials are in Normandy. In 1979, the French government turned over the Pointe du Hoc, with its Ranger monument perched atop a German bunker, to the United States, and the commission has since made substantial improvements to the site with expanded parking, a visitor center with interpretive exhibits, and numerous informational markers along the pathway to the cliffs. In 1984, as part of the fortieth anniversary of D-Day, President Reagan dedicated a red granite obelisk in the dunes fronting Utah Beach as a national memorial to the American forces who landed on that stretch of coastline and eventually liberated the Cotentin Peninsula. Smaller markers or structures at Dartmouth (England), Guadalcanal, Midway, Papua New Guinea, and Saipan round out the most recent collection of World War II monuments constructed by the ABMC.

The commission's track record of building war memorials earned it the challenge of creating two more for the National Mall in Washington, D.C.: the Korean War Veterans Memorial, dedicated in 1995, and the World War II Memorial, dedicated in 2004. The idea for both of these projects originated with the veterans' communities of each of the respective conflicts. Congress authorized the ABMC to establish the Korean War monument in 1986 and the one to the Second World War in 1993. As in the case of the AEF Memorial, administration and maintenance of both of these sites passed to the National Park Service upon their formal dedication. Sadly, a fuller recounting of the creation of these memorials is beyond the scope of this study.[30]

There is no denying that one of the fondest wishes of every generation of the commission's leadership has been for the sites to attract visitors. Annual reports prepared during General Mark Clark's chairmanship (1969–84) assert that such numbers did increase over time. In 1969, 2.5 million visitors called at the twenty-two ABMC cemeteries. By 1975 that number had doubled, and within a decade it had doubled again, to 11.7 million. During the first twenty-five years since the World War II cemeteries were officially inaugurated, the most visited among them were Normandy, the Netherlands, Henri-Chapelle, Luxembourg, and Manila. The first two of those sites began attracting 1 million visitors per year during the latter half of the 1970s. Europeans constituted the largest portion of visitors at all of the cemeteries; the highest percentage of American visitors tended to be at Normandy, Luxembourg, and Manila.[31]

By contrast, visitorship at the World War I sites during these same years lagged quite substantially. The highest individual totals were consistently reported at Meuse-Argonne and Aisne-Marne, but only in FY 1976 and 1977 (Meuse-Argonne both times) did any of the eight sites report more than one hundred thousand visitors. It was not uncommon for a World War I cemetery to fall short of ten thousand in a single year. By the same token, the number of Americans turning up at these memorials tended to constitute a much smaller percentage of the overall total than for the World War II sites. In similar fashion, attendance reported for Memorial Day ceremonies at the younger cemeteries routinely outpaced that of the older sites, with numbers at the latter rarely exceeding one thousand and the newer cemeteries rarely missing that marker. The Sicily-Rome cemetery recorded Memorial Day attendance each year between 1982 and 1984 at ten thousand or more. In 1982, Queen Beatrix of the Netherlands was among the twelve thousand who traveled to the Margraten cemetery for the annual commemoration.[32]

For the past forty years, presidents of the United States have been the most prominent visitors to the ABMC memorials. Jimmy Carter's appearance at the Normandy cemetery in January 1978 initiated an almost unbroken string of visits to that site by every American chief executive to this day. (President George H. W. Bush was the only one of that group not to make it to Normandy during his White House years, although he did visit as a private citizen the year after his term ended.) The nation's chief executives since Carter have visited the other overseas burial grounds much less frequently. While in office, President Clinton and both Bushes each called at Sicily-Rome; Clinton, George W. Bush, and Obama each visited Manila; the younger Bush also visited Suresnes and the Netherlands site; Clinton called at the Cambridge cemetery; and in March 2014, at the beginning of the current centennial of World War I, Obama met the king of Belgium at the Flanders Field cemetery.

Each of the decennial anniversaries of D-Day since the fortieth in 1984 has brought the American president and his French counterpart to Normandy. It is safe to say, however, that none of these occasions has surpassed President Reagan's visit in sheer drama or long-term significance. For one thing, 1984 was an election year, and the details of timing and backdrop for the president's first major address on June 6 at Pointe du Hoc in front of scores of US Ranger veterans who had seized that spot on the "Day of Days" forty years earlier were carefully orchestrated to embellish his reelection bid.[33] The profound emotional impact of the speech in front of the "boys of Pointe du Hoc" and the one later in the afternoon at the American cemetery has reverberated through all the years thereafter. One scholar has observed that Reagan's day in Normandy "played a seminal role in launching the great re-appreciation of World War II veterans that swept America in the 1980s and continues today largely unabated." But for "Reagan's two elegiac June 6, 1984 homilies," Douglas Brinkley continues, the seminal literary works of Stephen E. Ambrose (especially *Band of Brothers*) and Tom Brokaw (*The Greatest Generation*), the cinematic work of Stephen Spielberg (*Saving Private Ryan*), and memorials such as the National D-Day Museum (now the National World War II Museum) in New Orleans "may never have been."[34] When the president's voice cracked during the reference in his speech at the cemetery to Lisa Zanatta Henn, daughter of a deceased D-Day veteran, who was attending to honor her father and put flowers on his grave, millions got to see the power of these memorials to stir the deepest and most genuine senses of pride, gratitude, and sorrow.[35] Reagan's death at ninety-three years of age and one day shy of the sixtieth anniversary of D-Day in 2004 somehow seemed profoundly fitting, even if it distracted from the coverage of President Bush's participation in the commemorative program in Normandy.

The filming of Spielberg's *Saving Private Ryan* in 1997, and its release the following year, added significantly to the intensifying degree of remembrance focused upon the World War II generation. Two scenes filmed by a grave in the American cemetery above Omaha Beach and positioned at the beginning and the end of this powerful movie were the only ones done on location in Normandy. Spielberg shot them during a single day in September 1997 with the special permission of the ABMC's Paris office. Cemetery Superintendent Phil Rivers carefully monitored the filming and reported to a superior that the first segment was bothered by unfavorable wind conditions, but had gone well with "no damage so far."[36] Rivers was able to assure another superior when it was all finished that the Dream-Works Studio ensemble had done an "excellent job respecting the joint agreement between the company and the ABMC," whose essence had pledged the film crew to leave no blemishes on any part of the cemetery.[37]

In fact, the impact of the encounter between Spielberg's crew and the

American cemetery went well beyond the clean bill of health Rivers was able to convey to his superiors. Throughout the spate of interviews he gave on the occasion of the film's release, the celebrated director made no effort to hide the emotional effect the cemetery had had on him. The first time he saw it, Spielberg said, he was "overwhelmed," and immediately resolved that "we must preserve for our children the memory of the veterans."[38] Tom Hanks, who starred in the film, repeatedly echoed these sentiments. Upon his initial visit to the cemetery, Hanks had been "very moved by the crosses." As the filming concluded, the actor's thoughts had turned to "the men who lay beneath the crosses."[39] The strongly positive reception of the film, capped by the presentation of the American Legion's "Spirit of Normandy" award to Spielberg in September 1998, sealed the lasting effect it would leave on public sentiments. Phil Rivers reported at the end of that same month, for example, that visitors to the American cemetery had increased by one-third over September 1997.[40] The graves of the Niland brothers, after whom the story in Spielberg's movie is loosely based, continue to attract large numbers of visitors within the cemetery.

Indeed, the prospect of increased numbers of visitors to the Normandy cemetery, in particular, played an important part in creating the opportunity for the commission to embark upon its newly found emphasis on "interpretation." Early in the new century, Congressmen John Murtha and David Obey visited the burial grounds above Omaha Beach and were singularly unimpressed by the smallness of the existing visitor center and by the fact that there was little at the site to inform tourists of the history of the cemetery, the men buried there, or the fighting that cost them their lives.[41] Under the sponsorship of these two men, Congress soon thereafter made an initial appropriation of $5 million to fund construction of greatly expanded facilities for the reception and education of visitors to the Normandy site. Eventually, $30 million would be committed to this project. On August 28, 2004, ground was broken for the "Normandy American Visitor and Interpretive Center," a thirty thousand-square-foot structure nestled in the brush atop the bluffs at the eastern edge of the cemetery grounds, between the graves area and a monument to the US 1st Division.

There were three stated goals in building the Visitor and Interpretive Center, which was completed and formally dedicated in 2007: (1) "To design an effective and efficient facility that architecturally complements the cemetery landscape with style and dignity"; (2) "To develop appropriate messages that increase the visitor's appreciation of the magnitude and significance of the Normandy operations and the sacrifices involved in victory"; and (3) "To expand public awareness of the American Battle Monuments Commission (ABMC) services, facilities, and objectives with regard to honoring America's War Dead."[42] In short, the center was designed "to complement and enhance the experience of visiting the cemetery." An additional hope was that "the Center will inspire future generations to explore, understand and emulate the values for which these heroes gallantly fought." A final intention was to make the realization of the project "a truly Franco-American team effort."[43]

Over the past ten years, the ABMC has created interpretive facilities at a number of its other sites and deepened its commitment to this form of education. Dwight Anderson, then director of visitor services at Normandy, remarked in 2010 that, hitherto, the agency had not been "in the interpretive business"; rather, it had been "in the business of keeping cemeteries."[44] In mild rebuttal of this contention, it is worth remembering that General Pershing insisted on the inclusion of maps and historical inscriptions at the original ABMC sites to ensure that for visitors, at least, "time will not dim the glory of their deeds." But the scope of the commission's current effort, and its resort to the best technical means to reach audiences well beyond visitors to the sites, exceeds anything possible during Pershing's time. Further, the new emphasis on giving fuller, more personalized identities to the soldiers buried in the cemeteries is a means of giving voices to the dead in a manner capable of inspiring the living. This is especially important at a time when the World War I veterans are all gone, and the World War II generation is itself passing into immortality. For this reason, and as the ABMC's own centennial fast approaches, it is particularly fitting for the commission to have undertaken the high purpose of keeping the individual stories and the powerful example of America's citizen soldiers before ever larger portions of the public.

In the concluding chapter of his excellent book on the creation of the national World War II Memorial, Nicolaus Mills observed that the building of that edifice was an exercise in "constructing more than the eye can see." The parts of the monument that the eye could see, in other words, were meant somehow to represent and lead people to the values that constituted America's "civil religion" and were most widely held by Americans, despite the fact that they transcended the limits of physical sight.[45]

The same could surely be said of the overseas cemeteries and memorials built and maintained by the American Battle Monuments Commission.

To gaze upon the crosses and the Stars of David that mark the graves of the fallen in an ABMC site, to examine the architecture and the artwork, to read the inscriptions—all of this invites one into a realm beyond what the eyes can see, the realm of lives and values held dear. Dwight Anderson further observed at the Normandy site in October 2010: "When people leave here, we don't want them just to see crosses, we want them to see people."[46] While visiting a French military cemetery more than two decades ago, a student said something similar, that he was trying to imagine what it would be like if each fallen soldier could rise from the grave and stand by his own headstone. The principal thrust of the commission's emphasis on interpretation in recent years has been just that: to enable visitors to its sites to know more about the dead who will forever rest in the cemeteries in order to appreciate more fully the weight of the price paid for the defense of our ideals and way of life, and to inspire the current generation not just to venerate but, if need be, to repeat the same sacrifices earlier generations willingly made.

In his famous "Funeral Oration" from the fifth century B.C., the Athenian statesman Pericles bid his listeners not to concentrate on his words, but rather to see beyond them to the nobility and honor in the acts of the dead soldiers to whom he was paying tribute. Overshadowing the moment, Pericles said, were "our ancestors," with whom the men defending Athens were seeking to keep faith. In a speech better known to Americans, Abraham Lincoln bid his audience at Gettysburg in November 1863 to do the same thing, and under the same imperative. "Four score and seven years ago" referred to 1776, the year the country was founded by the sacrifices of an earlier generation. Lincoln's later observation that people would "little note nor long remember what we say here," but will "never forget what they did here," invited his hearers to see beyond what physical senses proper could allow, and to contemplate the heroism and spirit of sacrifice that defined the dead soldiers.

The overseas memorial sites, and the ongoing work of the ABMC, are of inestimable importance for what they bid Americans to "see" that transcends sight itself: that successive generations of our countrymen have answered the call, with "competence, courage, and sacrifice," and successfully defended the freedom, human decency, and sense of right that their countrymen have traditionally cherished. One can take issue with General

Pershing's association of such deeds with "glory," perhaps, but one would deny at great peril that such ideals are worth the best efforts of the American people to preserve. It is often said that, as a tangible reward for the nation's participation in two world wars, all the United States ever sought from the peoples whom it had helped to defend and liberate was a place to bury its own dead. The story of the cemeteries and the monuments on foreign soil represents what this country has done with such ground.

One of the inscriptions that greets visitors entering the Netherlands American Cemetery seems deserving of the last word of this study for what it conveys of the enduring mission of these overseas sites of remembrance and the agency that preserves them, and for the poignant idea it contains that the dead are indeed still serving their country: "Here we and all who shall hereafter live in freedom will be reminded that to these men and their comrades we owe a debt to be paid with grateful remembrance of their sacrifice and with the high resolve that the cause for which they died shall live."

Acknowledgments

Throughout the preparation of this book, I have been the beneficiary of wise counsel, continual encouragement, and countless acts of kindness from friends, family, colleagues, and strangers alike. It is a pleasure to acknowledge, with the most sincere gratitude, at least some of this support and assistance.

Sam Williamson and Gerhard Weinberg, the two scholars most responsible for my professional training at the University of North Carolina, each read chapters and never flagged in their enthusiasm for this project. Jim Leutze, the third of my most important and revered mentors from Chapel Hill days, made it possible for me and scores of other Carolina students to make our first trips to ABMC sites in France, Belgium, Luxembourg, the Netherlands, and Italy many years ago.

From my first encounter with an ABMC official nearly forty years ago—the late General John Donaldson, then the officer-in-charge of the commission's European bureau—agency personnel have been unfailingly welcoming and ready to share their wealth of knowledge and experiences. Every one of those named in the Selected Bibliography contributed in essential ways to the writing of this book. Dan Neese, Hans Hooker, and Anaelle Ferrand graciously provided me with access to archival material at the Normandy cemetery and in the European office. Jeffrey Aarnio spent one of his days off as superintendent of the Oise-Aisne cemetery in 2010 to show me additional monuments in the region and acquaint me more fully with the unique responsibilities of the chief curator of that site. In 2011, after transferring to the Brittany cemetery, Jeffrey and his children hosted me for lunch and an extended conversation on another of his days off. The late Phil Rivers was always willing to sit down and talk, even when I dropped in on the Meuse-Argonne cemetery unannounced. Phil's successor at Romagne, David Bedford, kindly supplied me with a digital copy of *History of the American Graves Registration Service in Europe* that was produced after World War I, a key source for the book's first chapter.

Shane Williams, Bobby Bell, Lou Aske, Craig Rahanian, Dwight Anderson, Alan Amelinckx, Michael Coonce, Keith Stadler, David Atkinson, Scott Desjardins, Walter Benjamin, Bruce Malone, and the late Horace Thompson, all from the corps of ABMC superintendents, provided especially helpful information and perspectives on their work.

My gratitude to Michael G. Conley and the headquarters office in Arlington, Virginia, is equally substantial and heartfelt. Historical consultant John S. Brown provided especially useful direction to me at the earliest stages of the project. In the final stages, Alec Bennett kindly explored the agency files in search of photographs and maps, all of which have found their way into the book's illustrations. From our first meeting in October 2008, Mike Conley has shown me the most gracious hospitality and has never missed a chance to arrange helpful contacts with other ABMC officials, or to facilitate my access to historical materials within his charge. The hours he and I have spent together during my numerous research trips to the nation's capital have not only been immensely helpful, but have established a friendship I will always cherish. Along the way, we have celebrated three World Series championships by our sports heroes-in-common, the San Francisco Giants.

Friends and colleagues closer to home have contributed greatly as well. President Larry P. Arnn and other members of the senior administration of Hillsdale College, most notably Provost David Whalen and Vice President John Cervini, have cheered the project from the start. A sabbatical leave in the fall of 2010 and travel monies furnished by the college helped facilitate my research. For decades, my History Department colleagues, led since 2002 by chairman and dear friend Dr. Mark Kalthoff, by word and example, have offered encouragement and inspiration to my work—no less so for this, my first real foray into scholarly publication. Whatever might be the legacy of this book, it will be modest compared to what many of them have already contributed to their own respective fields.

The students of Hillsdale College, with whom I also interact daily, have been similarly inspiring and encouraging, though perhaps less knowingly. No matter—they are like family to me, and in a number of instances I have enjoyed the privilege of visiting ABMC sites in their company. The Hillsdale Summer Study Abroad Program and its incomparable tour director, Al Philipp, have made possible more than a dozen such trips, most of which I have done in collaboration with Dr. Kalthoff. The presence of Kevin Meyers, Lieutenant Jack Shannon, Kyle Murnen,

Kirk Higgins, Zack Miller, John Flo, Aaron Tracey, and Johnny Quint on more private journeys to the overseas battle sites in recent years has been a source of much support and enjoyment as well. Johnny has since become my "agent," and he provided indispensable help with compiling the illustrations for publication.

Victor Davis Hanson, who served one year on the American Battle Monuments Commission in 2008, originally put me in touch with the headquarters office and has contributed advice and encouragement freely and generously at every stage of things. I can still remember when I first raised with Victor, while traveling with one of his tour groups in Brussels, the idea of undertaking a history of the ABMC. Without his enthusiastic endorsement, I probably would not have followed through with it. John Schneider, Esq., of Grand Rapids, Michigan, and Dr. Sam Webster, with whom I did particularly meaningful European trips in 2002 and 2006, respectively, read and critiqued chapters in a most helpful and encouraging manner.

Others whom I did not know before undertaking this project, and in some cases are still strangers, have also contributed in important ways to its completion. The staffs at the National Archives in Washington, D.C.; at NARA ("Archives II") in College Park, Maryland; at the Manuscripts Division of the Library of Congress; at the Military History Institute (MHI) in Carlisle, Pennsylvania; and at the Dwight D. Eisenhower Presidential Library in Abilene, Kansas, answered every request for assistance competently and courteously. At NARA, Paul Brown, of the Technical Reference Section, shared useful insights about archival research on several occasions and, at a particularly crucial moment when essential material could not be found, went into the shelves area on his own time to locate the misfiled boxes. Paul B. Barron and Jeffrey Kozak at the Marshall Library in Lexington, Virginia, were similarly hospitable during a delightful week spent there in December 2010. Dr. Richard J. Sommers, senior historian at the MHI, helped to make my research visit there in 2009 especially fruitful.

Dr. Roger Cirillo, director of the book program of the Association of the United States Army (AUSA), was instrumental in getting me together with the University Press of Kentucky in March 2016. Everyone at the press—from acquisitions editors Allison Webster and Melissa Hammer, to Jackie Wilson in the Marketing Department, to editor David L. Cobb and, I'm sure, many whose names are not known to me—has been graciously supportive, helpful, and enthusiastic about this project. Derik Shelor's editing of the manuscript was careful, impressively insightful, and extremely beneficial. As a first-time author, I was not accustomed to working with an editor, and Derik made this experience wonderfully fruitful. I am also grateful to the specialist readers who reviewed the book, and especially to James Scott Wheeler for contributing the foreword.

Finally, to Gene S. Dellinger, Chevalier in the French Legion of Honor, and honorably retired from more than twenty years in the US Air Force and more than thirty years with the ABMC, I owe an incalculable debt. For nearly forty years since our first meeting while he was an assistant superintendent at the Normandy cemetery, Gene has freely shared with me stories of his own work with the agency and exemplified the ideal of a capable, compassionate, and dutiful public servant and ambassador for his country. In service to the noble mission of the ABMC, Gene has done great honor to the soldiers whose graves he has tended and whose memory he has helped to perpetuate, and he has worked especially hard to keep ever vibrant the friendship between the people of France and the United States. Indeed, Gene's marriage of more than sixty years to his wife, Monique, is an enduring symbol of that most special relationship, and has been the source of dozens of unforgettable afternoons and evenings I have enjoyed with them in their home. It is an honor to dedicate this book to him, and also to the memory of my father, Norman H. Conner, a World War II veteran, with whom other members of my family and I made our first visit to the Normandy cemetery in 1978. Dad passed on to me his love of history and his particularly keen interest in the Second World War, and he also taught me that it was not unmanly to shed tears while walking among the sea of marble crosses and Stars of David that will forever hallow the heights above Omaha Beach.

Appendix

Text of President Roosevelt's Address, Broadcast by Radio, to the Dedication Ceremony at Montfaucon, France— August 1, 1937

Printed in the *New York Times*, August 2, 1937

MONSIEUR le Président de la République Française, Monsieur le Maréchal Pétain, Ambassador Bullitt, General Pershing, Ladies and Gentlemen:

Though the seas divide us, the people of France and the people of the United States find union today in common devotion to the ideal which the memorial at Montfaucon symbolizes. That ideal, to which both nations bear faithful witness, is the ideal of freedom under democracy—liberty attained by government founded in democratic institutions.

In a real sense this monument, which we have reared on the French hillside to commemorate the victory of our First Army in the Meuse-Argonne offensive, symbolizes that devotion.

Today we reaffirm our faith in the democratic ideal. It was in defense of that ideal that we entered the Great War twenty years ago. In the Meuse-Argonne, we fought as champions of the rights of mankind. Neither France nor the United States sought or seeks conquest—neither had nor has imperial designs. Both desire to live at peace with all nations. Both seek kinship with lovers of liberty wherever they are found.

France is carrying on in the tradition of a great civilization, a civilization with which our own culture has had full communion from our very beginnings as a nation. We, of this country, have not forgotten nor could we ever forget the aid given us by France in the dark days of the American Revolution.

Our historic friendship finds apt expression in the quotation from the letter which Washington wrote to Rochambeau, and which is inscribed on the base of our monument to the great Frenchman: "We have been contemporaries and fellow-laborers in the cause of liberty, and we have lived together as brothers should do, in harmonious friendship."

Many things have gone into the making of the France which we revere and with whose culture we find ourselves in close communion. All of the past speaks to us in the living present, and out of the shadows of a thousand years emerge the glory and the achievement which are France.

These things we remember today, nor do we forget the living France: the green fields around Montfaucon, with broad farms and contented dwellers on the soil; the villages and cities with their artists and artisans—all these make and preserve the France we hail today.

To the preservation of this civilization American soldiers and sailors contributed their lives and lie buried on this and other battlefields. They died brothers-in-arms with Frenchmen. And in their passing America and France gained deeper devotion to the ideals of democracy. In their name, for their sake, I pray God no hazard of the future may ever dissipate or destroy that common ideal.

I greet the Republic of France, firm in the confidence that a friendship as old as the American nation will never be suffered to grow less.

Notes

Introduction

1. Michael G. Conley, Chief of Staff, ABMC Headquarters, communication with the author, July 14, 2017.

2. Several superintendents said this to me during interviews conducted at twelve of the European cemeteries in October 2010.

3. ABMC Annual Report 2010, pages 38–40, www.abmc.gov. The first two cemeteries not of World War I or II origin are in Mexico City (with 1,563 interments from the Mexican War) and Panama City (with 5,500 interments from personnel associated with the building and defense of the Panama Canal). In 2013, a twenty-fifth cemetery was placed under ABMC's control north of Manila, the Philippines, with 8,600 interments from fighting dating back to 1900, and from among the veterans community while the United States maintained bases in that country. The twenty-sixth cemetery was entrusted to the commission's control in January 2017 with the acquisition of responsibility for the monument to the Lafayette Escadrille outside of Paris, which contains the remains of fifty-one World War I flyers. Since administrative authority over these additional sites was not part of ABMC's principal mandate established at the end of each of the world wars, however, they will not garner much attention in this study.

4. Michael G. Conley, communication with the author, July 14, 2017.

5. Among the twenty-two cemeteries for dead from the two world wars, only the Ardennes cemetery in Belgium is still open for new burials, but solely in cases where the remains of American soldiers hitherto unburied are discovered and, when identifiable, the next-of-kin choose to have them buried abroad.

6. As of 2017, seven of the chairmen have come from the army, one from the marines, and one from the air force.

7. President Harding appointed General John J. Pershing to the original commission in 1923, and the members elected him chairman at their first meeting. He served until his death in 1948. Robert G. Woodside and D. John Markey

held seats from the beginning of the commission until the early months of the Eisenhower administration in 1953.

8. See the "Record of Proceedings" (hereafter "ABMC Minutes"), Sixty-Third Meeting, December 5, 1952, and Sixty-Fourth Meeting, September 3, 1953, ABMC Records, Records Group 117, National Archives (hereafter "ABMC Records"), entry 49, box 1.

9. ABMC Minutes, Seventy-Eighth Meeting, October 14, 1960, and Eightieth Meeting, November 28, 1961, ABMC Records, entry 49, box 1.

10. ABMC Minutes, Eighty-Sixth Meeting, June 7, 1968, and Eighty-Seventh Meeting, February 16, 1970, ABMC Records, entry 49, box 1.

11. ABMC Minutes, One Hundred Seventeenth Meeting, April 1994, viewed at the agency's headquarters in Arlington, Virginia, in March 2009.

12. Some sources close to the 2009 events say that the incoming president's operatives demanded the resignation of the Bush appointees, while others insist that it was the outgoing president's agents who required the commissioners whom he had appointed to resign rather than serve his successor.

13. See Carlo D'Este, *Eisenhower: A Soldier's Life* (New York: Holt, 2002), 190. Frank E. VanDiver's *Black Jack: The Life and Times of John J. Pershing*, 2 vols. (College Station: Texas A&M Univ. Press, 1977) gives the most attention to the general's ABMC service.

14. For example, Forrest Pogue's *George C. Marshall: Statesman, 1945–1959* (New York: Viking, 1987), 494, notes only that Marshall accepted the "nonpaying chairmanship" of the ABMC from President Truman after World War II.

15. See "President Builds Reporters Up for Awful Letdown," *Washington Post*, October 11, 1946, ABMC Records, entry 49, box 1.

16. See ABMC Minutes, Seventy-Seventh Meeting, March 22, 1960, ABMC Records, entry 49, box 1.

17. See ABMC Minutes, Eighty-Seventh Meeting, February 16, 1970, ABMC Records, entry 49, box 1, for the record of Clark's unanimous election as chairman.

18. General Mark Clark to President Jimmy Carter, letter of April 3, 1978 (copy), ABMC Records, entry 49, box 1.

19. Frederick M. Franks Jr., in ABMC Annual Report 2005, 2.

20. ABMC Annual Report 2010, 5.

21. Ibid.

22. Superintendent Bobby Bell, interview with the author, Henri-Chapelle American Cemetery, October 26, 2010. Superintendent Bell confirmed during my visit to the cemetery on May 31, 2017, that the note is still safe, and unopened.

23. Assistant Superintendent Bruce Malone, interview with the author at Lorraine American Cemetery, October 27, 2010.

24. Dwight Anderson, Director of Visitor Services, interview with the author at the Normandy American Cemetery, October 2010. The subject of the story is Peggy Harris, whose husband, Billie, died at age twenty-two when his plane was shot down near the Norman village of Les Ventes on July 17, 1944. CBS News aired a moving account of this story, and how the villagers continue to remember and honor the Harrises, on June 6, 2012.

25. President Carter visited in January 1978; President Reagan visited for the fortieth anniversary of D-Day in 1984; Clinton for the fiftieth anniversary of D-Day in 1994; George W. Bush for Memorial Day in 2002 and the sixtieth anniversary of D-Day in 2004; and Obama for the sixty-fifth anniversary of D-Day in 2009 and the seventieth in 2014. President George H. W. Bush did not visit during his term in office.

26. I am indebted to retired superintendent Gene Dellinger for giving me copies of the survey of visitors conducted for the Normandy cemetery for the month of May 2003.

27. Patrick Thomines, mayor of Colleville-sur-Mer, speech of May 29, 2011, at the Normandy American Cemetery.

28. Mustafa Kemal ("Ataturk") quoted in Huseyin Uluaslan, *Gallipoli Campaign* (Istanbul: Keskin Color, 2000), 22.

29. Muriel Dufrenne, interview at Somme American Cemetery, May 2009.

30. Interview with the author at Margraten, the Netherlands, October 25, 2010.

31. The "Adopt-A-Graves" Program at Netherlands American Cemetery in Margraten will be treated more fully later in the book. Peter Schrijvers's *The Margraten Boys: How a European Village Kept America's Liberators Alive* (London: Palgrave Macmillan, 2012) is an impressive and moving account of the special relationship between the Dutch residents and this American cemetery.

32. See Pershing diary, entry for May 30, 1919, in John Joseph Pershing Papers, Manuscripts Division, Library of Congress (hereafter "JJP Papers"), carton 4.

33. John J. Pershing, "Speech at Suresnes Cemetery," 1927 (copy), JJP Papers, carton 344.

34. Superintendent Michael Coonce, interview with the author at Saint Mihiel American Cemetery, October 2010.

35. Superintendent Gene Dellinger, Normandy American Cemetery, June 2001; see also "Though Dead, They Can Still Serve," *New York Times,* December 19, 1919.

36. See "Statement of Major General Andrew J. Adams, Assistant to the Secretary [of the American Battle Monuments Commission], before the Committee on Veterans' Affairs, House of Representatives," March 27, 1968, Dwight D. Eisenhower, Post-Presidential Papers, Augusta-Walter Reed Series, box 1, Eisenhower Library, Abilene, Kansas.

37. ABMC Minutes, One Hundred First Meeting, May 21, 1980, viewed at the agency's headquarters in March 2009.

38. Derrick Odell, interview with the author at Brookwood American Cemetery, May 2011. Cemetery associates are senior staff members at the American sites, but are typically foreign nationals.

39. As of this writing (June 2017), brand new interpretive centers have been dedicated at Cambridge American Cemetery, Sicily-Rome American Cemetery, Pointe du Hoc, Meuse-Argonne American Cemetery, and Flanders Field American Cemetery. Additional centers are planned to "enhance visitor services" at the Honolulu Memorial in Hawaii, the Château-Thierry monument in France, and the Manila American Cemetery.

40. See Thomas North, *One Soldier's Job*, which he produced at the end of the forty-six years of his "on and off" service, as he put it, to the ABMC. The unpublished, undated memoir is in the possession of the ABMC headquarters.

41. See Lisa M. Budreau, *Bodies of War: World War I and the Politics of Commemoration in America, 1919–1933* (New York: New York Univ. Press, 2010).

42. See Steven Trout, *On the Battlefield of Memory: The First World War and American Remembrance, 1919–1941* (Tuscaloosa: Univ. of Alabama Press, 2010), especially xv–xxxiii.

43. See G. Kurt Piehler, *Remembering War the American Way* (Washington, D.C.: Smithsonian Institution Press, 1995).

44. See John W. Graham, *The Gold Star Mother Pilgrimages of the 1930s* (Jefferson, N.C.: McFarland, 2005).

45. See, for example, Jay Winter's pathbreaking work, *Sites of Memory, Sites of Mourning: The Great War in European Cultural History* (Cambridge, UK: Cambridge Univ. Press, 1995); George L. Mosse's *Fallen Soldiers: Reshaping the Memory of the World Wars* (Oxford, UK: Oxford Univ. Press, 1990); and David W. Lloyd's *Battlefield Tourism: Pilgrimage and the Commemoration of the Great War in Britain, Australia, and Canada, 1919–1939* (Oxford, UK: Berg, 1998).

46. John A. Adams, *General Jacob Devers: World War II's Forgotten Four-Star* (Bloomington: Indiana Univ. Press, 2015), makes at least two erroneous claims about Devers's service on the ABMC.

47. See, for example, the aforementioned work of Carlo D'Este. Also see Stephen E. Ambrose, *Eisenhower: Soldier, General of the Army, President-Elect, 1890–1952* (New York: Simon and Schuster, 1983), 82–84, 87, and Ike's autobiographical account of his ABMC service in Dwight D. Eisenhower, *At Ease: Stories I Tell to Friends* (New York: Doubleday, 1967), 204–7.

48. I am indebted to Superintendents Dan Neese and Hans Hooker for kindly permitting my access to the historical files at the Normandy American Cemetery in May and October 2010. These same archives have provided impor-

tant support for a history, in French, of the cemetery and its ongoing work. See Constant Lebastard, *Le Cimitière Américain de Colleville-sur-Mer: Une Commission Américaine en Normandie* (Bayeux, France: OREP Éditions, 2012).

49. The records of this agency are housed in the National Archives in downtown Washington (Records Group 66).

1. Remembrance Begins, 1919–1923

1. It is very difficult, in the vast literature on the First World War, to find two sets of casualty figures that agree. The numbers cited here are from Meirion and Susie Harries, *The Last Days of Innocence: America at War, 1917–1918* (New York: Vintage Books, 1998), 451, 455. The number of American dead in this source is given as 75,558, with deaths in battle or from wounds being 47,940, deaths from disease numbering 23,937, and deaths from suicide, murder, or accident listed at 3,681.

2. Budreau, *Bodies of War*, 22.

3. Newton Baker, "To Bring Back Our Dead: Burials in France during War Will Be Only Temporary," *New York Times*, September 5, 1918. On the return of the dead from the Spanish-American War, an undertaking described as "probably without precedent in history," see Monro MacCloskey, *Hallowed Ground: Our National Cemeteries* (New York: Richards Rosen Press, 1968), 46–47.

4. US Army Graves Registration Service, *History of the American Graves Registration Service*, 3 vols. (Washington, D.C.: US Army Graves Registration Service, 1921), 1:7.

5. Ibid., 1:8; see also Piehler, *Remembering War the American Way*, 95.

6. Budreau, *Bodies of War*, 43–44.

7. Ibid.

8. Ibid., 13–16, 69–71; US Army Graves Registration Service, *History of the American Graves Registration Service*, 1:10; and Piehler, *Remembering War the American Way*, 94–97.

9. Piehler, *Remembering War the American Way*, 95; Budreau, *Bodies of War*, 69. One report has the Bring Home the Soldier Dead League forming out of a meeting in Pittsburgh of three hundred parents and next-of-kin of deceased soldiers in November 1919; see "Plans to Bring Back Hero Dead Abroad," *Washington Times*, November 26, 1919, Records of the Fine Arts Commission, RG 66, National Archives (hereafter "CFA Records"), entry 17, box 73.

10. See "Plans to Bring Back Hero Dead Abroad," CFA Records, entry 17, box 73; also Ralph Hayes, *The Care of the Fallen: A Report to the Secretary of War on American Military Dead Overseas* (Washington, D.C.: Government Printing Office, 1920), 14–19, CFA Records, entry 17, box 3.

11. Piehler, *Remembering War the American Way*, 95–96; Budreau, *Bodies of War*, 69.

12. Quoted from Edmund Morris, *Colonel Roosevelt* (New York: Random House, 2011), 538–39. Within three weeks of Quentin Roosevelt's death, American troops had occupied the ground near the village of Chamery where his body lay. See the ABMC guidebook *American Armies and Battlefields in Europe* (Washington, D.C.: Government Printing Office, 1938), 76–77, for an account of the arrival of Pershing's troops at the grave on August 2, 1918.

13. Quoted in Budreau, *Bodies of War*, 70. The relocation of Quentin's remains to the Normandy American Cemetery in 1955 will be recounted later in this book.

14. John J. Pershing, quoted from "Leave Our Dead in France, Advises General Pershing," *New York Times*, August 21, 1919.

15. "Though Dead, They Can Still Serve," *New York Times*, December 19, 1919.

16. Major H. R. Lemly to Charles Moore, letter of May 28, 1919 (original), CFA Records, entry 17, box 4.

17. Budreau, *Bodies of War*, 39–51; also see Hayes, *The Care of the Fallen*, 22–23.

18. Hayes, *The Care of the Fallen*, 22–23; also see Budreau, *Bodies of War*, 39–51. A summary of this matter that was surprisingly sympathetic to the French position appeared as "Americans Buried in France," in *New York Times Current History*, August 1919, CFA Records, entry 17, box 4.

19. White's remarks are quoted from a letter he addressed to Charles Moore on July 22, 1919, cited in a nine-page digest of minutes from Fine Arts Commission meetings held between August 1919 and January 1921. See "Minutes of Meeting August 20, 1919," in "American Cemeteries in France," undated document, CFA Records, entry 17, box 4.

20. See H. R. Lemly, "Memorandum for the Quartermaster General," August 11, 1919 (original), CFA Records, entry 17, box 4.

21. "Would Keep Our Dead: Pétain Offers His Services to Establish Cemeteries in France," *New York Times*, May 30, 1919.

22. Budreau, *Bodies of War*, 48; Hayes, *The Care of the Fallen*, 24–30; US Army Graves Registration Service, *History of the American Graves Registration Service*, 1:115–26.

23. US Army Graves Registration Service, *History of the American Graves Registration Service*, 3:101. ABMC literature currently reports that 30,973 bodies rest in its World War I cemeteries, including fifty-two in the crypt of the monument to the Lafayette Escadrille recently incorporated into the commission's permanent care. The remaining 1,656 of the American dead interred in Europe are "unknowns." As will be confirmed later in the book, the final proportions of 61 percent sent home, 39 percent left overseas exactly matched the ratio for the

American dead from World War II once their families had exercised the same free choice given at the end of World War I.

24. US Army Graves Registration Service, *History of the American Graves Registration Service,* 3:100–101. See also "Last of Heroes' Bodies on Way to Home Graves," *Evening World* (New York City), March 11, 1922, CFA Records, entry 17, box 4, for a report on the departure of the final shipment of fifteen hundred bodies from the French port of Brest in March 1922.

25. Lisa Budreau devotes almost the entire first third of her monograph to the story of the repatriation of the American dead; see Budreau, *Bodies of War,* 27–81. Large sections of the GRS's *History of the American Graves Registration Service* recount in fuller detail the organizational structure, policies and procedures, and actions of that agency throughout the process of final disposition of the dead. See especially 1:41–113 and 138–206; 2:3–116; and 3:passim.

26. Budreau, *Bodies of War,* 42–43. One of the best works on the history of the British cemeteries is Philip Longworth's *The Unending Vigil: A History of the Commonwealth War Graves Commission, 1917–1967* (London: Constable, 1967).

27. US Army Graves Registration Service, *History of the American Graves Registration Service,* 2:27–29.

28. See "Minutes of Meeting September 20, 1920," and "Minutes of Meeting November 13, 1920," in "American Cemeteries in France," undated document, CFA Records, entry 17, box 4.

29. US Army Graves Registration Service, *History of the American Graves Registration Service,* 2:28–29.

30. Ibid., 2:27.

31. Budreau, *Bodies of War,* 67.

32. The quoted passage is from US Army Graves Registration Service, *History of the American Graves Registration Service,* 2:28. The information about burials in the cemetery comes from a document, dated February 23, 1929, in the "Meuse-Argonne Cemetery" file in box 8 of the archives of the ABMC Overseas Operations Office (hereafter "ABMC Archives, Garches"), formerly the European office, in Garches, France.

33. US Army Graves Registration Service, *History of the American Graves Registration Service,* 2:28; also "Aisne-Marne Cemetery" file, ABMC Archives, Garches, box 8.

34. US Army Graves Registration Service, *History of the American Graves Registration Service,* 2:28; also see "Somme Cemetery" file, ABMC Archives, Garches, box 8. Mitchell A. Yockelson's *Borrowed Soldiers: Americans under British Command, 1918* (Norman: Univ. of Oklahoma Press, 2008) chronicles the story of the 27th and 30th Divisions that fought in the Somme sector during the late stages of the war.

35. US Army Graves Registration Service, *History of the American Graves Registration Service,* 2:29; also see "Oise-Aisne Cemetery" file, ABMC Archives, Garches, box 8.

36. US Army Graves Registration Service, *History of the American Graves Registration Service,* 2:29; also see "Saint Mihiel Cemetery" file, ABMC Archives, Garches, box 8.

37. US Army Graves Registration Service, *History of the American Graves Registration Service,* 2:29; also see "Flanders Field Cemetery" file, ABMC Archives, Garches, box 8.

38. On the establishment of the Fine Arts Commission, see the founding statute of May 17, 1910, in the Charles Moore Papers, CFA Records, entry 13, box 3, and *The Autobiography of Charles Moore* (an unpublished work that Moore composed in three volumes during the 1930s), volume 2, chapter 11, in the Moore Papers, CFA Records, entry 13, box 2.

39. Moore, *The Autobiography of Charles Moore,* in the Moore Papers, CFA Records, entry 13, box 2.

40. See "Minutes of [CFA] Meeting September 20, 1920," in "American Cemeteries in France," undated document, CFA Records, entry 17, box 4.

41. See "Minutes of Meeting October 9, 1920," in "American Cemeteries in France," undated document, CFA Records, entry 17, box 4.

42. Moore, *The Autobiography of Charles Moore,* 2:251–66, in the Moore Papers, CFA Records, entry 13, box 2.

43. Ibid.; see also "The American Cemeteries in Europe," undated, unsigned report of Moore's 1921 European visit, in Moore Papers, CFA Records, entry 13, box 1.

44. "The American Cemeteries in France," CFA Records, entry 17, box 4; see also "Resumé of Decisions, War Memorials Council," November 8, 1920, CFA Records, entry 17, box 73. The War Memorials Council was established by the War Department and was advisory to the secretary of war. The purview of the council was not confined to overseas sites, but also included the entire collection of national cemeteries within the United States.

45. Moore, *The Autobiography of Charles Moore,* 2:253, in the Moore Papers, CFA Records, entry 13, box 2.

46. Ibid.

47. "The American Cemeteries in Europe," undated, unsigned report in the Moore Papers, CFA Records, entry 13, box 1.

48. Moore, *The Autobiography of Charles Moore,* 2:255, in the Moore Papers, CFA Records, entry 13, box 2.

49. Ibid., 2:258.

50. Ibid., 2:264.

51. "Plans for Military Cemeteries: Charles Moore Home after Two Months' Trip to Europe," *New York Times,* May 11, 1921, CFA Records, entry 17, box 4.

52. Moore, *The Autobiography of Charles Moore,* 2:264–65, in the Moore Papers, CFA Records, entry 13, box 2. See the detailed report of Moore's encounter with the president, and the summary of the report he delivered to the chief executive, in "Plan Six Cemeteries for A.E.F. Abroad: Proposal of Commission of Fine Arts is Given to Harding for His Approval," *New York Times,* August 23, 1921, CFA Records, entry 17, box 4.

53. Moore, *The Autobiography of Charles Moore,* 2:265–66, in the Moore Papers, CFA Records, entry 13, box 2.

54. See H. P. Caemmerer, Secretary of the Fine Arts Commission, "Statement of Mr. Moore as he left the White House," Memorandum for the Commission of Fine Arts, December 14, 1921 (original), in Moore Papers, CFA Records, entry 17, box 4.

55. See Charles Moore to The Rt. Rev. Charles H. Brent, letter of December 9, 1921 (copy), in Moore Papers, CFA Records, entry 17, box 4.

56. President Warren G. Harding, quoted, from "Statement of Mr. Moore as he left the White House," Memorandum for the Commission of Fine Arts, December 14, 1921 (original), in Moore Papers, CFA Records, entry 17, box 4.

57. See the text of H. J. Resolution 263, February 3, 1922, CFA Records, entry 17, box 4.

58. See "Meuse-Argonne Cemetery" and "Suresnes Cemetery" files in ABMC Archives, Garches. The main part of the Suresnes cemetery consists of land on the Mont Valérien military reservation owned by the Commune of Suresnes and given to the United States for use as a military cemetery. Our government paid $8,970 in 1922 to reimburse France for land east of the Boulevard Washington that the Paris government acquired and then ceded to us as an increment to the cemetery.

59. A copy of the agreement of July 27, 1922, signed by Colonel Rethers, chief of the Graves Registration Service, is appended to John T. Knight, assistant to the quartermaster general, "Agreement, Statement, Receipts and descriptions of land acquired for permanent cemeterial sites in France," memorandum to the Judge Advocate General, October 11, 1923, ABMC Records, box 178.

60. This figure was reached by adding the following sums reimbursed to France for acquisition of land for US cemeteries: $8,970 for additions to Suresnes; $5,233 for thirty-two additional acres at Oise-Aisne; $7,803 for thirty-four additional acres at Aisne-Marne; $2,825 for thirty additional acres at Saint-Mihiel; and $1,975 for thirteen additional acres at Bony. Documentation of these transactions is in ABMC Archives, Garches, box 8.

61. See "Flanders Field Cemetery" file, in ABMC Archives, Garches, box 8.

62. See "Brookwood Cemetery" file, in ABMC Archives, Garches, box 8. The formal agreement establishing this cemetery dates from September 12, 1922.

63. The most detailed accounts of Wilson's participation in the 1919 Memorial Day observance at Suresnes are in the diary entries of several of the president's intimates—Dr. Cary T. Grayson, Edith Benham, and Ray Stannard Baker—who shared the occasion with him. See Arthur S. Link, ed., *The Papers of Woodrow Wilson,* 69 vols. (Princeton: Princeton Univ. Press, 1966–94), 59:605–6, 620–23.

64. Only on January 26, 1919, did the president agree to take a day to visit battle sites between Paris and Reims. While motoring through the Aisne-Marne area on that snowy Sunday, Wilson saw in the distance an American cemetery (Belleau) for the first time. See diary of Dr. Grayson, January 26, 1919, in Link, ed., *The Papers of Woodrow Wilson,* 54:278–81, and Charles L. Mee Jr., *The End of Order: Versailles, 1919* (New York: Dutton, 1980), 68–70, for a brief summary of that day's events.

65. Diary of Edith Benham, May 30, 1919, in Link, ed., *The Papers of Woodrow Wilson,* 59:621.

66. Woodrow Wilson, remarks at Suresnes Cemetery, May 30, 1919, in Link, ed., *The Papers of Woodrow Wilson,* 59:607. Benham described the cemetery as "new and bare and brown, but very well kept" and foresaw that "it will be lovely in time." (Link, ed., *The Papers of Woodrow Wilson,* 59:621.) Dr. Grayson recorded that six thousand were buried there at that time. (Link, ed., *The Papers of Woodrow Wilson,* 59:605.)

67. Diary of Dr. Grayson, May 30, 1919, in Link, ed., *The Papers of Woodrow Wilson,* 59:605–6.

68. Pershing noted in his diary that day that ten thousand were buried at Romagne. The general anticipated—wrongly, as it turned out—that "upon completion it will contain over 30,000 bodies." See diary of John J. Pershing, May 30, 1919 (original), JJP Papers, carton 4.

69. The best single volume on this battle is Edward G. Lengel, *To Conquer Hell: The Meuse-Argonne, 1918* (New York: Holt, 2008).

70. Pershing diary, May 30, 1919, JJP Papers, carton 4.

71. John J. Pershing, speech at Romagne Cemetery, May 30, 1919 (copy), JJP Papers, carton 4.

72. US Army Graves Registration Service, *History of the American Graves Registration Service,* 1:127–28.

73. "Honor 70,000 Heroes: US Flags Decorate Graves of America's Dead in France," *Washington Post,* May 30, 1920, CFA Records, entry 17, box 4. The GRS provides a full account of Memorial Day 1920 in US Army Graves Registration Service, *History of the American Graves Registration Service,* 1:127–37. Both the

American Legion, chartered by Congress in 1919, and the American Overseas Memorial Day Association, founded in 1920, continue to play active roles in annual Memorial Day observances at the ABMC sites.

74. "All France Unites in Paying Honor to American Dead: Marshal Pétain Salutes Them and Expresses the Gratitude of His Country," *New York Times*, May 31, 1920.

75. Henri-Philippe Pétain, speech at Suresnes cemetery, May 30, 1920, quoted from ibid.

76. Ambassador Hugh Wallace, speech at Suresnes cemetery, May 30, 1921, quoted from "France Decorates Our Heroes' Graves," *New York Times*, May 31, 1921.

77. Henri-Philippe Pétain, speech at Suresnes cemetery, May 30, 1921, quoted from "France Decorates Our Heroes' Graves," *New York Times*, May 31, 1921. A biography of Wallace's successor as US ambassador to France draws additional attention to the centrality of the Suresnes cemetery in the ongoing expression of Franco-American friendship, especially on Memorial Days. See T. Bentley Mott, *Myron T. Herrick, Friend of France: An Autobiographical Biography* (Garden City, N.Y.: Doubleday, Doran, 1929), 294. Herrick served as the ambassador in Paris from 1921 to 1929.

78. US Army Graves Registration Service, *History of the American Graves Registration Service*, 2:87–89.

79. Quoted in ibid., 2:94.

80. Pershing to the Adjutant General, cablegram No. 2770, June 17, 1919 (copy), ABMC Records, box 1.

81. Ibid.

82. These developments are recounted in "Memorandum for the Chief of Staff," War Plans Division 14675, May 16, 1921 (copy), in ibid.

83. This village is five miles east of Chateau-Thierry, on the southern side of the Marne, and was at the center of the 3rd Division's defense against a major German attack on July 15, 1918. For more on the engagement this particular memorial association wished to commemorate, see ABMC, *American Armies and Battlefields in Europe*, 60–61.

84. H. N. Gilbert to US Ambassador to France, letter of February 23, 1921 (copy), ABMC Records, box 1.

85. T. Bentley Mott to the Director of Military Intelligence, General Staff, letter of March 18, 1921 (copy), ABMC Records, box 1.

86. "Memorandum for the Chief of Staff," May 16, 1921. Pershing's appointment as army chief of staff took effect on July 1, 1921. The recipient of the important memorandum cited here, therefore, was General Peyton C. March.

87. "Special Orders," No. 134-0, War Department, June 11, 1921 (copy),

and "Marking American Battlefields in Europe," memorandum from J. A. Ulio, Adjutant General's Department, to Colonel John McA. Palmer, June 11, 1921 (copy), ABMC Records, box 1.

88. The members, coming from each of the five army departments (in the order listed in the chapter text) were Colonel John McAuley Palmer, Colonel George M. Hoffman, Colonel Oliver L. Spaulding Jr., Major James A. Ulio, and Captain Logan N. Rock.

89. Budreau, *Bodies of War,* 108.

90. See John J. Pershing to Henry Cabot Lodge, letter of June 15, 1942 (copy), in JJP Papers, carton 157. Colonel Palmer served overseas in 1917 and 1918 as assistant chief of staff for operations and commanded a brigade during the Meuse-Argonne offensive, for which he received the Distinguished Service Medal. In July 1948, Palmer was an honorary pallbearer at Pershing's funeral, and the two men are buried within a hundred yards of each other on "Pershing Hill" in Arlington National Cemetery. (Palmer died in 1955.)

91. See "Decisions to Be Made by Board," preliminary agenda for the Battle Monuments Board, September 21, 1921 (original), ABMC Records, box 1; also see "Proceedings of the Board" (hereafter "BMB Minutes"), meeting of September 22, 1921, ABMC Records, box 1.

92. See "Notes on Trip to Antietam Battlefield," October 13, 1921, ABMC Records, box 1.

93. BMB Minutes, meeting of October 18, 1921, ABMC Records, box 1.

94. BMB Minutes, meeting of November 9, 1921, ABMC Records, box 1.

95. X. H. Price, "Questions Pending Decision by the Board," memorandum of October 19, 1921 (original), in ABMC Records, box 1. As will be shown, Price went on from his service to the Battle Monuments Board to become the first secretary of the American Battle Monuments Commission. In 1921 he was a major in the Corps of Engineers; he would leave his ABMC post in 1938 as a colonel.

96. BMB Minutes, meeting of December 7, 1921, ABMC Records, box 1.

97. Ibid.

98. Ibid.

99. Colonel John McA. Palmer, "Plans of the Battle Monuments Board," memorandum of January 16, 1922 (copy), ABMC Records, box 1.

100. Ibid.

101. BMB Minutes, meeting of March 27, 1922, ABMC Records, box 1.

102. See "Communication from the President of the United States, transmitting Correspondence from the Secretary of War and the Director of the Bureau of the Budget concerning Proposed Legislation to Create a Commission to Erect Suitable Memorials Commemorating the Services of the American Soldier in

Europe . . . ," House of Representatives, 67th Cong., 2nd Sess., document no. 197, 1–6, ABMC Records, box 1.

103. See "History of Legislation," an undated, unsigned six-page document recounting the path through Congress of the bill that created the American Battle Monuments Commission. This informative piece, submitted as "Appendix III" of the final report of the Battle Monuments Board, is in ABMC Records, box 1.

104. Ibid.; also see Budreau, *Bodies of War,* 108–10.

105. "History of Legislation," ABMC Records, box 1.

106. Hearings before the Committee on Foreign Affairs, House of Representatives, 67th Cong., 2nd and 3rd Sessions, on "H.R. 9634 and H.R. 10801 for the Creation of an American Battle Monuments Commission to Erect Suitable Memorials Commemorating the Services of the American Soldier in Europe," 1–2, ABMC Records, box 1.

107. The text of H.R. 10801 is contained in ibid., 2–3.

108. At the beginning of the congressional review, consistent with the aforementioned "Plans of the Battle Monuments Board," H.R. 10801 called for roughly eighty relief maps, fifty outline sketch maps, twelve special monuments, and ten tablets to be fashioned and sited in Europe. The estimated total cost for their construction was $540,000. An additional $125,000 would be required for the first two years, and by the time the entire project was completed within five years, the bill estimated the annual cost of upkeep and maintenance at $5,000. See "Communication from the President of the United States, transmitting Correspondence from the Secretary of War and the Director of the Bureau of the Budget concerning Proposed Legislation to Create a Commission to Erect Suitable Memorials Commemorating the Services of the American Soldier in Europe . . . ," House of Representatives, 67th Cong., 2nd Sess., document no. 197, 7–10, ABMC Records, box 1.

109. Ibid., 2–6.

110. Weeks to Dawes, letter of February 18, 1922, ibid.

111. Ibid., 5.

112. Budreau, *Bodies of War,* 110–11; also "History of Legislation," Appendix III to the final report of the Battle Monuments Board.

113. Ibid.

114. "Hearings before the Committee on Foreign Affairs, House of Representatives," November 28, 1922, pages 19–23, ABMC Records, box 1.

115. Ibid., 29–58; also see "History of Legislation," Appendix III to the final report of the Battle Monuments Board. The Fine Arts Commission expressed its strong support for the bill in a letter from its secretary, H. P. Caemmerer, to Congressman Porter, dated November 28, 1922. See CFA Records, entry 17, box 3.

116. "History of Legislation," in ABMC Records, box 1. The page from the

Congressional Record containing Congressman Porter's defense of the bill on the House floor is in CFA Records, entry 17, box 4. Porter was not challenged on any provisions of the bill; rather, he only had to defend placement of H.R. 14087 on the "unanimous consent" calendar.

117. A published copy of H.R. 14087, "An Act for the Creation of an American Battle Monuments Commission to erect suitable memorials commemorating the services of the American soldier in Europe, and for other purposes," was Exhibit E with Appendix III to the final report of the Battle Monuments Board, in ABMC Records, box 1.

118. H.R. 14087, especially sections 1, 2, 3, and 4, Exhibit E with Appendix III to the final report of the Battle Monuments Board, ABMC Records, box 1.

119. Ibid., section 2.

120. Ibid., especially sections 5 and 8.

121. Ibid., section 2.

122. "U.S. Memorial Body Created: Battle Monuments Commission Created by Congress and O.K.'d by Harding," *Detroit News,* April 1, 1923, CFA Records, entry 17, box 4.

123. See "Report of Board," from General John McAuley Palmer to the Secretary of War, August 3, 1923 (original), ABMC Records, box 1.

124. Ibid.

125. "Memorandum for the Chief of Staff," undated document signed by General Palmer and attached to the BMB Minutes, meeting of March 9, 1923, ABMC Records, box 1.

126. Ibid.

127. John J. Pershing, "Memorandum for the Deputy Chief of Staff," March 29, 1923 (original), ABMC Records, entry 49, box 1.

128. See George B. Christian Jr., Secretary to the President, to Honorable John W. Weeks, letter of June 20, 1923 (original), ABMC Records, entry 49, box 1. Three pages of biographical information about the seven new appointees are enclosed with this document and serve as the source for the additional information about each one that is recounted below.

129. Pershing would retire from active duty and his position as army chief of staff on his sixty-fourth birthday, September 13, 1924. He held the rank of general of the armies until his death.

130. Mrs. Bentley was described as an "active club woman of Chicago," a "prominent" Republican, and president of the American Legion auxiliary in Chicago composed entirely of Gold Star Mothers. As already noted, she and her husband had given testimony to the Porter committee during its consideration of H.R. 10801. The Bentleys' son, Paul Cody Bentley, was killed in September 1917 and rests in the Oise-Aisne American cemetery.

131. In support of this latter claim, see "Appendix III, History of Legislation." Budreau briefly profiles Reed and analyzes why he might have been attractive to Harding as a potential ABMC member. See Budreau, *Bodies of War,* 113–15.

132. Hill spent six years in the House, beginning in 1921, and served on the ABMC until his death in 1941.

133. Despite being the youngest member of the original commission, Miller was actually the first to leave it. The last meeting he attended was on October 18, 1926. (See ABMC Minutes, Twenty-First Meeting, October 18, 1926, ABMC Records, entry 2, box 1A.) Finis J. Garrett, a Democratic congressman, was President Coolidge's choice to replace Miller. (See ABMC Minutes, Twenty-Second Meeting, December 21, 1926, ABMC Records, entry 2, box 1A.) In 1927 Miller was convicted and imprisoned on charges of defrauding the government while serving in the Harding administration.

134. See pages 24–26 of the published hearing from November 28, 1922.

135. Woodside was the first vice chairman of the ABMC and contributed especially valuable service in that role when the commission resumed its work after World War II, while Chairman Pershing was too infirm to preside over the meetings.

136. Budreau described General Palmer's attitude as "dismayed"; see Budreau, *Bodies of War,* 111. While Budreau was no doubt right to claim that President Harding's choices for the commission were politically motivated, she was wrong to assert that Pennsylvania was "overwhelmingly represented on the commission" (112). The Keystone State, along with Maryland, each had two on the commission, and Delaware, Illinois, and whichever state Pershing claimed as his residence after the War had one apiece.

137. See "Memorandum for the Chief of Staff," appended to BMB minutes of March 9, 1923, in which General Palmer wrote: "The only way to secure passage of the legislation at the last session of Congress was not to mention individuals but to leave the matter to the judgment of the President," ABMC Records, box 1.

138. See ABMC Minutes, First Meeting, September 21, 1923, ABMC Records, entry 2, box 1A. General Pershing's first meeting with the full commission came on April 15, 1924. Lisa Budreau's sweeping assertion (*Bodies of War,* 134) that Pershing "rarely attended meetings" was misleading for the sixteen meetings between 1923 and 1925 (he missed exactly half of them), and grossly inaccurate for the twenty-nine meetings between 1926 and 1938, of which the chairman missed only three.

139. Pershing diary, entries for June 25, 28, and July 4, 14, 1919, JJP Papers, carton 4.

140. Vandiver, *Black Jack,* 1035–51.

141. John J. Pershing, speech of July 10, 1921, Hoboken, New Jersey, JJP

Papers, carton 343. Biographer Frank Vandiver reports in *Black Jack* that Pershing "stood mute and sad" (1058) as the bodies of the 7,160 American soldiers were unloaded for eventual burial in their home soil.

142. Pershing diary, entries for October 1, 2, 5, 11, 12, 13, 16, 17, 1921, JJP Papers, carton 5. Texts of the remarks he made on October 2 at the French Tomb of the Unknown Soldier, and at the tomb in Westminster Abbey on October 17, 1921, are in JJP Papers, carton 329. Ambassador Herrick, who witnessed Pershing's presentation of the Medal of Honor to the Unknown Soldier of France, called the general "the very symbol of America." See Mott, *Myron T. Herrick, Friend of France*, 286.

143. Pershing diary, entries for November 1–5, 9, 10, 1921, JJP Papers, carton 5.

144. John J. Pershing, speech of April 15, 1920, New York City, JJP Papers, carton 343.

2. The New Commission Goes to Work, 1923–1938

1. American Battle Monuments Commission, Annual Report for 1924, ABMC Records, entry 3, box 2. This report was signed by Pershing, dated November 20, 1924, and submitted to the president of the United States. It numbered a mere twelve pages and was typewritten, not printed. The practice of filing such reports each year continued through 1926 and has resumed, but only since the 1970s.

2. ABMC Minutes, First Meeting, September 21, 1923, ABMC Records, entry 2, box 1A.

3. ABMC Minutes, Second Meeting, October 2, 1923, ABMC Records, entry 2, box 1A.

4. ABMC Minutes, Third Meeting, November 8, 1923, ABMC Records, entry 2, box 1A.

5. Budreau, *Bodies of War*, 115.

6. ABMC Annual Report for 1925, page 54, ABMC Records, entry 3, box 2. See also North, *One Soldier's Job*, 1:26.

7. ABMC Minutes, First Meeting, September 21, 1923.

8. "Address of Mr. Charles Moore, Chairman, Commission of Fine Arts, before the American Battle Monuments Commission, October 2, 1923," page 1, ABMC Records, entry 49, box 1. This document is actually an eleven-page typed transcript of the commission's conversation with Moore.

9. Ibid., 1, 7.

10. Ibid., 2–3, 5, 6, 9, 10.

11. See Memorandum from W. H. Hart, the Quartermaster General, to the Assistant Secretary of War, April 27, 1924 (copy), ABMC Records, entry 4, box

4. This memo is part of a "Memorandum for the Commission" that Secretary Price distributed on May 2, 1924, to acquaint members with the larger history of the discussion of headstones.

12. "Address of Mr. Charles Moore before the ABMC," October 2, 1923, 6.

13. Ibid., 10.

14. Senator David Reed, quoted from ibid.

15. ABMC Minutes, Third Meeting, November 8, 1923.

16. ABMC Annual Report for 1924, 8, 11; ABMC Minutes, Fourth Meeting, January 30, 1924, ABMC Records, entry 2, box 1A; North, *One Soldier's Job*, 1:3–4.

17. ABMC Minutes, Fourth Meeting, January 30, 1924.

18. Such resolutions had been enacted at the Third and Fourth ABMC Meetings; see also Budreau, *Bodies of War*, 123.

19. See Elizabeth G. Grossman, "Architecture for a Public Client: The Monuments and Chapels of the American Battle Monuments Commission," *Journal of the Society of Architectural Historians* 43, no. 2 (May 1984), 120, for a fuller discussion of the Fine Arts chairman's early thinking about cemetery and headstone design.

20. Charles Moore to Major Xenophon Price, letter of January 12, 1924 (copy), ABMC Records, entry 4, box 4; see also Budreau, *Bodies of War*, 122.

21. Moore to Price, letter of January 12, 1924 (copy), ABMC Records, entry 4, box 4.

22. Ibid.

23. X. H. Price to John J. Pershing, letter of February 1, 1924 (copy), ABMC Records, box 7.

24. Quoted in ibid. The McCrae poem from 1915, one of the most celebrated to come out of the war, actually reads: "In Flanders Fields the poppies blow Between the crosses row on row . . ."; see Herwig Verleyen, *In Flanders Fields: The Story of John McCrae, His Poem, and the Poppy* (Kortrijk, Belgium: Groeninghe Printing, 1995), 24.

25. John J. Pershing to Major Price, letter of February 18, 1924 (copy), ABMC Records, entry 4, box 4.

26. Major George C. Marshall Jr. to Charles Moore, letter of July 30, 1921 (original), in CFA Records, entry 17, box 73. At this time, the future chairman of the ABMC was Pershing's aide at the War Department.

27. See Major General Rogers, Quartermaster General, to Colonel George H. Penrose, Chief, Cemeterial Division, letter of October 14, 1921, quoted from Chief, Cemeterial Division, to Mr. Charles Moore, memorandum of November 29, 1921, CFA Records, entry 17, box 73; also see Charles Moore to General Pershing, letter of January 1922 (copy, exact date not specified), and Charles Moore to Colonel George H. Penrose, Chief, Graves Registration Service, letter of January 31, 1922 (copy), CFA Records, entry 17, box 73.

28. "Resolution Adopted by National Executive Committee [of the American Legion] Meeting in Session," January 14–15, 1924, contained in a Memorandum to the ABMC initialed by Major Price, February 11, 1924 (copy), ABMC Records, entry 4, box 4.

29. "Resolution Adopted at the Annual Armistice Meeting, November 1923," Gold Star Fathers Association, attached to a letter from A. S. McCaskey, President, to Secretary, Battle Monuments Commission, December 15, 1923 (original), ABMC Records, entry 4, box 4.

30. ABMC Annual Report for 1924, 8; also see ABMC Minutes, Fifth Meeting, April 15, 1924, ABMC Records, entry 2, box 1A.

31. ABMC Minutes, Tenth Meeting, November 21, 1924, ABMC Records, entry 2, box 1A.

32. ABMC Minutes, Fourteenth Meeting, November 4, 1925, ABMC Records, entry 2, box 1A.

33. Quoted in "Memorandum for the Commission of Fine Arts," by H. P. Caemmerer, Secretary, October 14, 1926 (copy), CFA Records, entry 17, box 4.

34. Ibid.

35. The full ABMC entourage included "spouses, children, valets, and maids," and many stayed in Europe until mid-August—even though the official business of the trip concluded on July 22 in Paris. See Budreau, *Bodies of War*, 115–16; also see "Official Schedule of the American Battle Monuments Commission in Europe, June–July 1924," compiled by Secretary Price, and enclosed with a "Memorandum to the Commission" sent by Price on August 18, 1924, ABMC Records, entry 4, box 4. Thomas North's brief recollections of the trip are found in *One Soldier's Job*, 1:4–6.

36. ABMC Minutes, Eighth Meeting, July 15, 1924, ABMC Records, entry 2, box 1A.

37. See "Official Schedule," June–July 1924, 14–15.

38. Ibid., 1–15; also see North, *One Soldier's Job*, 1:5.

39. "Official Schedule," 2–15.

40. ABMC Annual Report for 1925, 17. This lengthy report is, in large part, a digest of the 1924 inspection trip.

41. Ibid.

42. Ibid.; see also ABMC Minutes, Tenth Meeting, November 21, 1924.

43. ABMC Annual Report for 1925, 17, 21. The names of 4,452 missing were later engraved on the walls of the eight chapels. See North, *One Soldier's Job*, 1:6.

44. See "Information Obtained at Conference with Chief of Imperial War Graves Commission in London," June 23, 1924, ABMC Records, entry 4, box 4. North claims in *One Soldier's Job*, 1:5, that although the ABMC commis-

sioners also met with French, Belgian, and Italian officials responsible for war memorials, they attached the greatest importance to what they gleaned from the British.

45. ABMC Annual Report for 1925, 23, 25, 27.

46. On the emergence of the basic design of the British cemeteries, see Longworth, *The Unending Vigil,* 56–72; Julie Summers, *Remembered: The History of the Commonwealth War Graves Commission* (London: Merrell, 2007), 18–21; and the ABMC Annual Report for 1925, 25.

47. ABMC Annual Report for 1925, 49.

48. "To Limit Monuments Abroad: American Commission Favors Government Approval—Would Avoid Gettysburg Plan," *New York Times,* July 24, 1924.

49. ABMC Minutes, Ninth Meeting, September 4, 1924, ABMC Records, entry 2, box 1A.

50. Ibid.

51. Ibid.

52. ABMC Minutes, Tenth Meeting, November 21, 1924.

53. Ibid.

54. ABMC Minutes, Eleventh Meeting, November 22, 1924, ABMC Records, entry 2, box 1A.

55. One of the best published assessments of Dr. Cret's work for the ABMC is Grossman's "Architecture for a Public Client: The Monuments and Chapels of the American Battle Monuments Commission," 119–43. See X. H. Price, "Memorandum for the Commission," September 30, 1925, ABMC Records, entry 4, box 4, for the terms of the architect's initial contract with the ABMC.

56. ABMC Minutes, Eleventh Meeting, November 22, 1924.

57. ABMC Minutes, Third Meeting, November 8, 1923.

58. ABMC Minutes, Twelfth Meeting, March 17, 1925, ABMC Records, entry 2, box 1A.

59. Ibid.

60. Ibid.

61. ABMC Annual Report for 1925, 60.

62. See a report in the *Washington Star,* December 6, 1924, ABMC Records, entry 3, box 2.

63. ABMC Minutes, Thirteenth Meeting, May 12, 1925, ABMC Records, entry 2, box 1A.

64. President Coolidge dispatched Pershing to mediate efforts by the Peruvians and Chileans to schedule a plebiscite to resolve a boundary dispute. Pershing's undertaking did not succeed, and while in South America he experienced serious health problems. See Vandiver, *Black Jack,* 1074–83. For evidence of the mounting frustration on the commission over Pershing's extended absence, see

Major Price to John J. Pershing, letter of October 7, 1925 (copy), and Major Price to Pershing, letter of November 11, 1925 (copy), ABMC Records, box 7.

65. ABMC Minutes, Fourteenth Meeting, November 4, 1925.

66. ABMC Minutes, Fifteenth Meeting, November 16, 1925, ABMC Records, entry 2, box 1A. The architects chosen for each memorial site will be detailed in the next chapter.

67. ABMC Minutes, Thirteenth Meeting, May 12, 1925. This same inscription was later adopted for the monument erected over the Tomb of the Unknown Soldier in Arlington National Cemetery; see Thomas North, *One Soldier's Job*, 1:8–9.

68. ABMC Minutes, Fourteenth Meeting, November 4, 1925. Davis served in this important cabinet office for the duration of Calvin Coolidge's presidency. John Weeks, whom President Coolidge had carried over in the post from President Harding's administration upon the latter's death in August 1923, worked his last day at the War Department on October 13, 1925.

69. ABMC Minutes, Sixteenth Meeting, December 14, 1925, ABMC Records, entry 2, box 1A.

70. See X. H. Price, "Inscription for Headstones of Unknown Dead," Memorandum for Colonel Markey, February 4, 1926 (copy), ABMC Records, entry 4, box 4.

71. See ABMC Minutes, Thirteenth Meeting, May 12, 1925.

72. ABMC Minutes, Seventeenth Meeting, March 29, 1926, ABMC Records, entry 2, box 1A.

73. ABMC Minutes, Fifteenth Meeting, November 16, 1925; also see Oliver McKee Jr., "May Employ New England Granite in A.E.F. Memorials: Only Obstacle is that European Would Cost Less," *Boston Transcript*, November 23, 1925, CFA Records, entry 17, box 3.

74. See X. H. Price, "Memorandum for the Commission, No. 51, Award of Contract for Headstones," September 23, 1926 (original), ABMC Records, entry 4, box 4, for a summary account of the bidding process.

75. ABMC Minutes, Nineteenth Meeting, June 3/4, 1926, ABMC Records, entry 2, box 1A.

76. Ibid.

77. Ibid.

78. See X. H. Price, "Memorandum for the Commission, No. 46, Material for Overseas Headstones," July 17, 1926 (original), ABMC Records, entry 4, box 4.

79. Major Price to Lieutenant Thomas North, letter no. 287-W, June 28, 1926 (copy), ABMC Records, box 132.

80. See letter from Lucian O. Holman, Secretary of the American Granite

Association, dated May 19, 1926, that Price transmitted in "Memorandum for the Commission, No. 38, Material to be used for crosses and other monuments in France," May 24, 1926 (original), ABMC Records, box 132.

81. See "Comments by Mr. André Ventre, Architect-in-Chief of the French Government and Inspector of *Vestiges de Guerre,* on the proper stone for use in the headstones," undated, sent with X. H. Price, "Memorandum for the Commission, No. 39, Stone for use in headstones in Europe," May 28, 1926 (original), ABMC Records, box 132. On the authority of two of the most knowledgeable and experienced ABMC officials on such matters—Jeffrey Aarnio and Lou Aske—it must be noted here that Monsieur Ventre's worst fears for the durability of marble headstones in the harsh climate of the north and east of France have not been confirmed. Aarnio, who served more than a decade at the Meuse-Argonne, Oise-Aisne, and Brittany sites, writes that "with careful maintenance by the dedicated crews at ABMC cemeteries, the marble headstones have stood the test of time remarkably well." The bulk of Aske's experience has been with the Lasa marble of the World War II cemeteries (principally at the Sicily-Rome and Henri-Chapelle sites), but he echoes Aarnio's assessment. Breakage of the stone has never been a serious problem, and the ABMC has developed special procedures over the years to polish and clean the headstones in order to remove tarnishing and maintain a smooth surface. At both the World War I and II cemeteries, the overwhelming majority of the headstones are originals. See Jeffrey Aarnio and Lou Aske, communications with the author, March 9 and 11, 2018.

82. X. H. Price, "Memorandum for the Commission, No. 39," ABMC Records, box 132.

83. Price shared the content of Pershing's telegram in "Memorandum for the Commission, No. 52, Headstones," September 24, 1926 (original), ABMC Records, entry 4, box 4.

84. See X. H. Price to Thomas North (in Paris), letter no. 333-W, September 14, 1926 (copy), ABMC Records, box 132.

85. See Price, "Memorandum for the Commission, No. 46," July 17, 1926.

86. See Price to Thomas North (in Paris), letter no. 353-W, October 26, 1926 (copy), in ABMC Records, box 132; also see Thomas North, *One Soldier's Job,* 1:8. North cites cost as the chief determinant in the choice of Carrara marble.

87. ABMC Minutes, Twentieth Meeting, October 7, 1926, ABMC Records, entry 2, box 1A.

88. ABMC Minutes, Twenty-Seventh Meeting, January 4, 1928, ABMC Records, entry 2, box 1A.

89. Ibid.

90. North, *One Soldier's Job,* 1:8.

91. Ten of these special inscriptions are on headstones in the Somme Ameri-

can Cemetery. Only four of the 14,236 headstones in the Meuse-Argonne American Cemetery have such inscriptions. Two more are in the Saint-Mihiel burial ground, and one each in Aisne-Marne, Oise-Aisne, and Flanders Field.

92. North, *One Soldier's Job,* 1:8. This account is also standard among the ABMC officials with whom I have discussed the matter in recent years. Examples of some of the inscriptions on the back of headstones are: "How could a man die better than for his country"; "To live in hearts we leave behind is not to die"; and "It is not life that matters but the courage we bring to it."

93. ABMC Minutes, Twenty-First Meeting, October 18, 1926, ABMC Records, entry 2, box 1A.

94. With this situation in mind, and at the request of the British government, the commission voted in October 1926 to postpone for one year consideration of a naval monument in England. See ABMC Minutes, Twentieth Meeting, October 7, 1926.

95. Ibid.

96. ABMC Minutes, Thirty-Second Meeting, October 28, 1930, ABMC Records, entry 2, box 1A.

97. See ABMC Minutes, Twenty-Fifth Meeting, July 20, 1927, and Twenty-Ninth Meeting, June 26, 1928, ABMC Records, entry 2, box 1A.

98. Thomas North to X. H. Price, letter 348-P of June 10, 1926 (original), ABMC Records, box 21. The new schedule of debt payments from France to the United States was contained in the Mellon-Beranger agreement of April 1926, which called for the retirement of the obligation after sixty-two more installments.

99. Price to North, letter of June 23, 1926 (copy), ABMC Records, box 21.

100. ABMC Minutes, Twenty-First Meeting, October 18, 1926, and Twenty-Second Meeting, December 21, 1926, ABMC Records, entry 2, box 1A.

101. Price to North, letter of February 23, 1927 (extracts), ABMC Records, box 21.

102. ABMC Minutes, Seventeenth Meeting, March 29, 1926; see also "Pershing Blocks Marking of World War Sites with Merely Ornate American Memorials," *New York Times,* April 26, 1926.

103. ABMC Minutes, Seventeenth Meeting, ABMC Records, entry 2, box 1A.

104. "Pershing Blocks Marking of World War Sites with Merely Ornate American Memorials," *New York Times,* April 26, 1926.

105. ABMC Minutes, Twenty-Third Meeting, February 8, 1927, ABMC Records, entry 2, box 1A.

106. The original list of proposed sites is in the ABMC Annual Report for 1925, 63.

107. ABMC Minutes, Thirty-Second Meeting, October 28, 1930.

108. ABMC Minutes, Twentieth Meeting, October 7, 1926.

109. ABMC Minutes, Twenty-Fourth Meeting, March 7, 1927, ABMC Records, entry 2, box 1A.

110. Ibid.

111. See ABMC Minutes, Twelfth Meeting, March 17, 1925.

112. North, *One Soldier's Job,* 1:28–29.

113. Ibid.; see also ABMC Minutes, Thirty-First Meeting, December 20, 1929, ABMC Records, entry 2, box 1A, for the report from Eisenhower that the completed monument was indeed in place, and "French Group Resists Pershing on Memorial: Village of Sivry-sur-Meuse Makes Counter Request to Government to Keep American Monument," *New York Times,* August 12, 1930.

114. North, *One Soldier's Job,* 1:28–30. The 1938 ABMC guidebook acknowledges the existence of the controversial monument, but also notes that it is small, that it commemorates all of the American soldiers who fought in that vicinity, and that "no road runs near it." See ABMC, *American Armies and Battlefields in Europe,* 262.

115. North, *One Soldier's Job,* 1:27; also see ABMC Minutes, Thirty-Second Meeting, October 28, 1930.

116. ABMC Minutes, Thirty-Second Meeting, October 28, 1930.

117. North, *One Soldier's Job,* 1:27–28.

118. Charles Magny, prefect of the Meuse, quoted from ibid, 1:28.

119. See Budreau, *Bodies of War,* 154–57, for a thorough account of this episode.

120. Ibid.

121. ABMC Minutes, Twelfth Meeting, March 17, 1925.

122. Hamilton Fish and Senator David Aiken Reed, Hearings before the House of Representatives Committee on Foreign Affairs, March 3, 4, 5, 1926, quoted from Budreau, *Bodies of War,* 155. See also Hamilton Fish, "Monument in France to Colored American Infantry Regiments Attached to the French Army," Report to the House of Representatives, March 24, 1926, quoted from Jennifer D. Keene, "The Memory of the Great War in the African American Community," in *Unknown Soldiers: The American Expeditionary Forces in Memory and Remembrance,* ed. Mark A. Snell (Kent, Ohio: Kent State Univ. Press, 2008), 69–70.

123. The 93rd Division is one of four, along with the 2nd, 36th, and 42nd, cited on stones circling the four sides of the base of the ABMC monument at Sommepy, on Blanc Mont ridge in the Champagne region of France. The edifice was dedicated in 1937. An inscription inside the tower of the monument reads: "Three infantry regiments of the 93rd American Division [presumably the ones Congressman Fish wanted to be commemorated on their own monument], serving with the 157th and 161st French Divisions, engaged in intermittent fighting during September and October [1918] taking part in the capture of

Ripont, Sechault, and Trières Farm." See "Meuse-Argonne American Cemetery and Memorial," ABMC pamphlet, 23–24. The ABMC issues individual pamphlets on each of its World War I cemeteries. They are available digitally on the ABMC website, or as hard copies at the commission headquarters and the individual sites. A monument to the 369th Regiment was dedicated in 2001 in the French village of Sechault; see Budreau, *Bodies of War*, 272 n 32.

124. Upon the presentation of its budget estimates for FY 1926, for example, Budget Director General Herbert Lord had mocked the commission for having not so much as one completed design for any of its proposed monuments "after 27 months of existence"; see Budreau, *Bodies of War*, 154.

125. ABMC, *American Armies and Battlefields in Europe*, 522.

126. ABMC Annual Report for 1924, 10.

127. ABMC Annual Report for 1925, 72.

128. Lieutenant R. W. Hubbell to X. H. Price, letter of July 7, 1931 (copy), ABMC Records, entry 29, box 183, cited the "most cordial reciprocity" between the Historical Sections of the ABMC and Army War College.

129. See X. H. Price, Report for the Period July 1, 1926 to June 30, 1938 (hereafter "Final Report, 1938"), 27, attached to Price to General Pershing, letter of January 25, 1938 (original), ABMC Records, entry 3, box 3.

130. These volumes serve as the closest thing there is to an "official" (i.e., government-directed) history of the American effort in the First World War. As Thomas North notes in *One Soldier's Job*, 1:9, while the War Department compiled such a history for the Second World War, it did not do so for the First.

131. X. H. Price to Thomas North, letter no. 391-W (copy), December 29, 1926, ABMC Records, box 132.

132. North, *One Soldier's Job*, 1:20.

133. Trout, *On the Battlefield of Memory*, xvii.

134. See Mangum to Price, letter no. 629-W (copy), January 2, 1928, ABMC Records, box 132, for confirmation that the superintendent of documents had sold all available copies of the guidebook.

135. Trout, *On the Battlefield of Memory*, xviii.

136. See John J. Pershing to Major General Robert H. Allen, Chief of Infantry, letter of August 15, 1927 (original), in Dwight D. Eisenhower Pre-Presidential Papers, Eisenhower Library, box 92. Pershing observed in the letter that Ike's important contribution to the guidebook project could only have been achieved "by the exercise of unusual intelligence and constant devotion to duty."

137. Trout, *On the Battlefield of Memory*, xix–xx; also see Eisenhower, *At Ease*, 204–10.

138. Trout, *On the Battlefield of Memory*, xxviii. Although work on the revised guidebook began many years ahead of the twentieth anniversary of America's

entry into the world war, the publication was not on the market in time for the 1937 "Third AEF" in Paris.

139. North, *One Soldier's Job*, 1:22.

140. Trout, *On the Battlefield of Memory*, xxv–xxviii.

141. "Legion Trip to Europe a Marvel of System: 18,224 Made the Pilgrimage to France," *New York Times*, October 16, 1927. See also Budreau, *Bodies of War*, 190–91, and Graham, *The Gold Star Mother Pilgrimages of the 1930s*, 78–81, for useful information on the 1927 Legion event.

142. Gilbert Bettman, a Legionnaire from Cincinnati, recounted that 2 million Parisians had turned out for the AEF parade. See "Legion Pilgrimage Called Peace Bond," *New York Times*, October 12, 1927.

143. "Pershing Returns from Trip Abroad: Here on *Leviathan*, Delayed by Storms—Praises Reception to Legionnaires in Paris," *New York Times*, November 9, 1927.

144. "Pershing Says Legion Binds Us to France: He Declares that Paris Convention is a Great Pilgrimage of Good-Will," *New York Times*, June 24, 1927.

145. The fullest account of the Gold Star Mother pilgrimages is Graham, *The Gold Star Mother Pilgrimages of the 1930s*. Other accounts are to be found in Budreau, *Bodies of War*, 198–241, and Piehler, *Remembering War the American Way*, 101–7.

146. Graham, *The Gold Star Mother Pilgrimages of the 1930s*, 67; also see North, *One Soldier's Job*, 1:31.

147. Pershing's remarks are quoted from an account in the Paris edition of the *Chicago Tribune*, June 9, 1931, in Graham, *The Gold Star Mother Pilgrimages of the 1930s*, 132. One of the saddest aspects of the story of the Gold Star Mother pilgrimages is that white and black women never traveled together. The rigid segregation of these trips mirrored the segregation of the army and of much of American life at that time. Such separation of the races was not observed, it should be added, in the placement of bodies in the overseas cemeteries.

3. Building the American Memorials in Europe, 1925–1933

1. See John J. Pershing, "Our National War Memorials in Europe," *National Geographic Magazine* 65, no. 1 (January 1934), 1–36.

2. Price, "Final Report, 1938," 14.

3. See ABMC Minutes, Eleventh Meeting, November 24, 1924; Witold Rybczynski, "The Late, Great Paul Cret," *New York Times Style Magazine*, October 21, 2014, www.nytimes.com/2014/10/21/t-magazine/the-late-great-paul-cret.html; Budreau, *Bodies of War*, 149; and Charles E. Moore to Honorable David A. Reed, letter of January 17, 1925 (copy), CFA Records, entry 17, box 3.

4. X. H. Price to Charles E. Moore, letter of March 23, 1925 (original), CFA Records, entry 17, box 3.

5. X. H. Price, "Memorandum for the Commission (No. 12)," September 30, 1925 (original), ABMC Records, entry 4, box 4.

6. ABMC Annual Report for 1925, 75.

7. See ABMC Minutes, Fourteenth Meeting, November 4, 1925.

8. See ABMC Minutes, Fifteenth Meeting, November 16, 1925, for a complete list of the initial project assignments for fourteen different architects. This list does not reflect the later winnowing down of the original projection for the monuments that the ABMC would build.

9. Price, "Final Report, 1938," 14–16.

10. See ABMC Annual Report for 1926, 37–39, for a full list of the architects and architectural firms assigned to the ABMC sites, along with a representation of their best known accomplishments to date.

11. See "Addendum" attached to Paul Cret to Cram and Ferguson, letter of April 29, 1926 (copy), ABMC Records, box 31.

12. Designs for seven of the eight chapels were approved at the twenty-third meeting of the commission; the final design, for the Suresnes chapel, won approval at the twenty-fourth meeting a month later. See ABMC Minutes, Twenty-Third Meeting, February 8, 1927, and Twenty-Fourth Meeting, March 7, 1927, ABMC Records, entry 2, box 1A.

13. ABMC Minutes, Twenty-Third Meeting, ABMC Records, entry 2, box 1A.

14. ABMC Minutes, Twenty-Fourth Meeting, ABMC Records, entry 2, box 1A.

15. ABMC Minutes, Twenty-Fifth Meeting, July 20, 1927, ABMC Records, entry 2, box 1A.

16. ABMC Minutes, Thirty-Fourth Meeting, November 16, 1931, ABMC Records, entry 2, box 1A.

17. The descriptive details of the Aisne-Marne cemetery are drawn from material in the ABMC's pamphlet "Aisne-Marne American Cemetery and Memorial," 7.

18. See Charles Moore to Secretary X. H. Price, letter of October 18, 1926 (original), ABMC Records, box 31.

19. Secretary Price informed the Cram and Ferguson firm in early February 1927 that their design for the chapel had won the approval of both the ABMC and the CFA. See X. H. Price to Messrs. Cram and Ferguson, letter of February 9, 1927 (copy), ABMC Records, box 31.

20. ABMC Minutes, Twenty-Sixth Meeting, November 18, 1927, ABMC Records, entry 2, box 1A.

21. Ibid.

22. Chester Godfrey to Major X. H. Price, letter of November 26, 1927 (original), ABMC Records, box 31.

23. X. H. Price, "Memorandum for the Chairman," December 19, 1927 (original), ABMC Records, box 7.

24. Ibid.

25. Ralph Adams Cram to General John J. Pershing, letter of December 20, 1927 (original), ABMC Records, box 31.

26. Ibid.

27. ABMC Minutes, Twenty-Seventh Meeting, January 4, 1928, ABMC Records, entry 2, box 1A.

28. John J. Pershing to Ralph Adams Cram, letter of January 9, 1928 (copy), ABMC Records, box 31.

29. Captain Harris Jones, memorandum for Secretary Price, August 28, 1928 (original), and Pershing to Ralph Cram, letter of September 12, 1928, ABMC Records, box 31.

30. Paul Cret to John J. Pershing, letter of November 12, 1928 (original), ABMC Records, box 31.

31. ABMC Minutes, Twenty-Sixth Meeting, November 18, 1927.

32. Ibid.

33. ABMC Minutes, Twenty-Eighth Meeting, February 15, 1928.

34. ABMC Minutes, Twenty-Sixth Meeting, November 18, 1927.

35. ABMC Minutes, Twenty-Seventh Meeting, January 4, 1928.

36. These details are drawn from the complete collection of published pamphlets compiled about each cemetery by the American Battle Monuments Commission.

37. "Somme American Cemetery and Memorial," ABMC pamphlet, 10.

38. "Aisne-Marne American Cemetery and Memorial," ABMC pamphlet, 14.

39. "Oise-Aisne American Cemetery and Memorial," ABMC pamphlet, 10.

40. Aisne-Marne pamphlet, 14; "Suresnes American Cemetery and Memorial," ABMC pamphlet, 6; Somme pamphlet, 10; Oise-Aisne pamphlet, 10; "Flanders Field American Cemetery and Memorial," ABMC pamphlet, 11.

41. Suresnes pamphlet, 6.

42. Flanders Field pamphlet, 8; "Saint Mihiel American Cemetery and Memorial," ABMC pamphlet, 10.

43. Aisne-Marne pamphlet, 12.

44. "Meuse-Argonne American Cemetery and Memorial," ABMC pamphlet, 13.

45. Somme pamphlet, 10–11.

46. American Battle Monuments Commission, "Brookwood American Cemetery and Memorial," information sheet; Aisne-Marne pamphlet, 12; Somme pamphlet, 10; Oise-Aisne pamphlet, 10; Flanders Field pamphlet, 11.

47. Suresnes pamphlet, 6.

48. Saint Mihiel pamphlet, 10.

49. Meuse-Argonne pamphlet, 13–14.

50. Ibid., 14; Oise-Aisne pamphlet, 11.

51. Suresnes pamphlet, 6; Meuse-Argonne pamphlet, 13; Flanders Field pamphlet, 8; Somme pamphlet, 10; Oise-Aisne pamphlet, 11; and Saint Mihiel pamphlet, 9.

52. Oise-Aisne pamphlet, 9.

53. Aisne-Marne pamphlet, 10.

54. At Saint-Mihiel, the map is of the local region and is inlaid with various colored pieces of marble. See "Saint Mihiel" pamphlet, 10. At Oise-Aisne, an entire wall in the museum is covered by a map of the Aisne-Marne region that traces the lines of advance of numerous American divisions during the Aisne-Marne offensive and the Second Battle of the Marne of 1918. See Oise-Aisne pamphlet, 11–12.

55. Somme pamphlet, 3, 8.

56. Meuse-Argonne pamphlet, 3.

57. "Brookwood American Cemetery and Memorial," ABMC pamphlet, 13–14.

58. ABMC Minutes, Twenty-Fourth Meeting, March 7, 1927.

59. ABMC Minutes, Twenty-Eighth Meeting, February 15, 1928.

60. Saint Mihiel pamphlet, 7–13.

61. Paul Manship, who died in 1966, was officially commissioned by the ABMC after World War II to design panels, with the themes of "Remembrance" and "Resurrection," respectively, for the east facades of the chapel and the museum, as well as a statue depicting "Brothers in Arms," at the Sicily-Rome cemetery in Nettuno, Italy. See "Sicily-Rome American Cemetery and Memorial," ABMC pamphlet, 8–9.

62. See X. H. Price, "Memorandum to the Commission," August 6, 1930 (copy), ABMC Records, entry 4, box 4; also see ABMC Minutes, Twenty-Ninth Meeting, June 26, 1928, for a reference to Ellett's letter of March 1, 1928.

63. ABMC Minutes, Twenty-Ninth Meeting, June 26, 1928.

64. Price, "Memorandum to the Commission," August 6, 1930.

65. The first meeting after the decision was made to accept the statue from Mrs. Beale came in October 1930, but no formal action on the matter was recorded then or at any time thereafter. See ABMC Minutes, Thirty-Second Meeting, October 28, 1930, ABMC Records, entry 2, box 1A.

66. X. H. Price to General Pershing (in Tucson, Arizona), letter of March 22, 1935 (copy), ABMC Records, box 7.

67. The summary in this paragraph is informed by a letter from the War Department to Douglas Despard, dated June 25, 1926, found in ABMC Records, entry 4, box 4. A major in the 27th Division during the war, Despard had complained to Assistant Secretary of War Hanford MacNider after a visit to the

Somme cemetery of the effect of the unevenly arranged graves. Despard's solution, which was for the War Department to place a headstone above every one of the emptied graves, was rejected. But the War Department's letter provided the inquiring major with a thorough summary of the situation.

68. Ibid.

69. ABMC Annual Report for 1925, 13.

70. David A. Reed to Major X. H. Price, letter of September 22, 1925 (original), ABMC Records, entry 3, box 2.

71. Robert Woodside, "To the Chairman and members of the American Battle Monuments Commission," report of August 23, 1926 (copy), ABMC Records, entry 3, box 3.

72. Major X. H. Price to Lieutenant Thomas North, letter no. 306-W of July 21, 1926 (copy), ABMC Records, box 132.

73. Price to North, letter no. 333-W of September 14, 1926 (copy), ABMC Records, box 132.

74. ABMC Minutes, Twenty-First Meeting, October 18, 1926.

75. Woodside, Report to the Commission of August 23, 1926.

76. Earl L. Holliday, Chaplain, Dyer J. Bird Post of Rainbow Veterans, to General John J. Pershing, letter of June 2, 1934 (copy), ABMC Records, entry 4, box 4.

77. General Douglas MacArthur to Honorable George White, Governor of Ohio, letter of May 25, 1934 (copy), ABMC Records, entry 4, box 4.

78. Mrs. Mathilda Burling to Honorable George Dern, Secretary of War, letter of June 11, 1934 (copy), ABMC Records, entry 4, box 4.

79. Commander E. A. Hayes to Mrs. Mathilda Burling, letter of June 18, 1934 (copy), ABMC Records, entry 4, box 4.

80. ABMC Minutes, Thirty-Seventh Meeting, May 14, 1935, ABMC Records, entry 2, box 1A.

81. North, *One Soldier's Job*, 1:9–10.

82. Ibid., 1:12.

83. See ABMC Minutes, Fourteenth Meeting, November 4, 1925; Fifteenth Meeting, November 16, 1925; and Sixteenth Meeting, December 14, 1925, ABMC Records, entry 2, box 1A.

84. See ABMC Minutes, Nineteenth Meeting, June 3, 1926, and Twenty-Eighth Meeting, February 15, 1928, ABMC Records, entry 2, box 1A.

85. ABMC Minutes, Twentieth Meeting, October 7, 1926, ABMC Records, entry 2, box 1A.

86. ABMC Minutes, Thirty-First Meeting, December 20, 1929, ABMC Records, entry 2, box 1A.

87. ABMC Minutes, Eighteenth Meeting, May 5, 1926, ABMC Records, entry 2, box 1A.

88. The complete list of original architectural assignments is in ABMC Minutes, Fifteenth Meeting, November 16, 1925. The commission's annual report for 1926 lists the architects and their most prominent achievements to date (pages 37–39).

89. North and Secretary Price were both authorized to make contracts on behalf of the commission. See ABMC Minutes, Sixteenth Meeting, December 14, 1925.

90. North, *One Soldier's Job,* 1:18–19.

91. Ibid.

92. Ibid., 1:12–15.

93. Ibid., 1:16.

94. Ibid., 1:16–17. Sacco and Vanzetti were Italian immigrants to the United States. The avowed anarchists were convicted by a Massachusetts jury of robbery and murder in 1921. After a second conviction and the exhaustion of a string of appeals, both men were executed in 1927. The high possibility of a miscarriage of justice in their case agitated working class people, especially, on both sides of the Atlantic.

95. Ibid., 1:17–18.

96. The commission had earlier accepted from a private donor forty acres of land adjoining the Aisne-Marne cemetery. See ABMC Minutes, Thirty-Second Meeting, October 28, 1930.

97. "Report by Mr. Charles Moore, Chairman of the Commission of Fine Arts, as to Permanent American Cemeteries in Europe, after a Tour of Inspection July–September 1923," September 27, 1923, CFA Records, entry 17, box 4; "Belleau Wood Today," *New York Herald* (Christmas supplement, 1925), CFA Records, entry 17, box 4.

98. John J. Pershing to Mrs. Elizabeth Van Rensselaer Frazer, letter of May 13, 1926 (copy), in ABMC Records, box 10.

99. ABMC Minutes, Thirty-First Meeting, December 20, 1929.

100. James G. Harbord to John J. Pershing, letter of March 10, 1931 (original), ABMC Records, box 10.

101. See ABMC Records, box 10, for the newspaper article dated April 23, 1931.

102. See Mrs. Henry Fenimore Baker to General Pershing, letter of March 26, 1931 (original), ABMC Records, box 10. President Hoover appointed Mrs. Baker to replace Mrs. Bentley on the commission after the latter had died in September 1929.

103. X. H. Price to General Pershing, letter of October 23, 1931 (original), ABMC Records, box 10.

104. See Price to Pershing, letter of December 12, 1931 (extract), ABMC Records, box 10.

105. Aisne-Marne pamphlet, 17.

106. General Lemmel C. Shepherd Jr., Commandant of the United States Marine Corps, to Admiral Thomas Kinkaid, Vice Chairman of the American Battle Monuments Commission, letter of December 21, 1953 (original), in ABMC Records, box 10.

107. See General North to General Shepherd, letter of March 19, 1954 (copy), ABMC Records, box 10, for confirmation of the ABMC's approval of the marine corps' request to erect a monument in Belleau Wood; and see Colonel Jack D. Mage, Officer-in-Charge, ABMC European office, to ABMC Secretary (General North), letter no. 127-P, November 25, 1955 (original), ABMC Records, box 10, for a lengthy description of the dedication ceremony for the marine monument.

108. See Egerton Swartwout, "A Description of the Scheme submitted for the Memorial at Montsec, St. Mihiel, France," December 17, 1926 (original), ABMC Records, box 20.

109. Ibid.; also see ABMC Minutes, Twenty-Second Meeting, December 21, 1926.

110. Charles Moore to X. H. Price, letter of January 8, 1927 (original), ABMC Records, box 20.

111. Egerton Swartwout to Major X. H. Price, one-page letter of January 17, 1927 (original), ABMC Records, box 20; X. H. Price to Egerton Swartwout, letter of January 19, 1927 (copy), ABMC Records, box 20.

112. Swartwout to Price, five-page letter of January 17, 1927 (original), ABMC Records, box 20.

113. See Egerton Swartwout to Secretary Price, letter of February 7, 1927 (original), ABMC Records, box 20, for the architect's report of his day-long encounter with the CFA in New York City.

114. Charles Moore to Major Price, letter of February 7, 1927 (original), ABMC Records, box 20. The architect's conception of how "Design B" would have looked was actually published in the 1927 ABMC guidebook; see ABMC, *A Guide to the American Battle Fields in Europe*, 259.

115. ABMC Minutes, Twenty-Sixth Meeting, November 18, 1927; and Egerton Swartwout to General Pershing, letter of December 10, 1927 (original), in ABMC Records, box 20.

116. Swartwout to Pershing, letter of December 10, 1927, ABMC Records, box 20.

117. ABMC Minutes, Twenty-Seventh Meeting, January 4, 1928; Charles Moore to the American Battle Monuments Commission, letter of January 9, 1928 (original), in ABMC Records, box 20.

118. Swartwout to Pershing, letter of December 10, 1927, ABMC Records, box 20.

119. Price to Pershing, letter of January 15, 1932 (extract), ABMC Records, box 20.

120. Aisne-Marne pamphlet, 19.

121. ABMC Minutes, Twentieth Meeting, October 9, 1926. This meeting began on Thursday, October 7, and resumed two days later.

122. See Charles Moore to X. H. Price, letter of October 16, 1926 (original), ABMC Records, box 13.

123. ABMC Minutes, Twenty-Second Meeting, December 21, 1926.

124. Charles Moore to the American Battle Monuments Commission, letter of January 11, 1927 (original), ABMC Records, box 13.

125. ABMC Minutes, Twenty-Third Meeting, February 8, 1927.

126. See Price to Cret, letter of November 30, 1928 (copy), ABMC Records, box 13, for a reference to the architect's proposed wording for the inscription.

127. Price to Cret, letter of May 10, 1929 (copy), ABMC Records, box 13.

128. Major X. H. Price to General Pershing, letter of June 19, 1928 (extracts), ABMC Records, box 13.

129. Pershing to Price, letter of July 7, 1928 (extracts), ABMC Records, box 13. As will be shown below, the commission in fact spent only $251,000 more on its monuments than the original appropriation envisioned. While each of the three large structures cost considerably more than originally budgeted (Montfaucon $655,757 vs. $400,000; Montsec $433,057 vs. $230,000; and Aisne-Marne $412,964 vs. $230,000), the reduction from the original plan in the total number of monuments almost covered these additional costs.

130. Paul Cret to John Russell Pope, letter of April 28, 1926 (copy), ABMC Records, box 18.

131. ABMC Minutes, Twenty-Second Meeting, December 21, 1926; Charles Moore to Major Price, letter of January 8, 1927 (original), ABMC Records, box 18.

132. ABMC Minutes, Twenty-Sixth Meeting, November 18, 1927.

133. See the fuller account of the twenty-sixth meeting contained in extracts of a letter from ABMC Commissioner D. John Markey to Major Price, then in Paris, dated November 22, 1927, ABMC Records, box 18.

134. Ibid.; also see ABMC Minutes, Twenty-Sixth Meeting, November 18, 1927.

135. ABMC Minutes, Twenty-Eighth Meeting, February 15, 1928.

136. See the pertinent reference in *Le Sous-Secretaire D'Etat des Finances, Regions Libérées, à Monsieur le Lieutenant Thomas North,* letter of January 7, 1926 (copy), ABMC Records, box 16.

137. Thomas North to Secretary Price, letter no. 339-P, May 25, 1926 (original), ABMC Records, box 18.

138. Ibid.

139. Thomas North to Secretary Price, letter no. 403-P, September 21, 1926 (original), ABMC Records, box 18.

140. X. H. Price to John Russell Pope, letter of February 9, 1927 (copy), ABMC Records, box 18.

141. Dr. Paul Cret to John Russell Pope, letter of March 14, 1927 (copy), ABMC Records, box 18.

142. Prefect of the Meuse to Lieutenant Thomas North, letter of July 30, 1927 (copy), ABMC Records, box 16.

143. See "*Procès-verbal de remise par l'Etat à la Commission Américaine des Monuments de Guerre des terrains de la zone rouge de Montfaucon,*" August 17, 1938 (copy), ABMC Records, box 17.

144. See Charles Moore to Major Price, letter of February 14, 1931 (original), ABMC Records, box 18.

145. This description is taken from photographs contained in ABMC Records, box 18.

146. Pershing to Secretary Price, telegram of June 3, 1931 (copy), ABMC Records, box 18.

147. John Russell Pope to John J. Pershing, letter of June 9, 1931 (copy), ABMC Records, box 18.

148. Secretary Price to James E. Mangum, letter no. 1183-P, July 6, 1931 (extracts), and Dr. Paul Cret to Major X. H. Price, letter of July 10, 1931 (copy), ABMC Records, box 18.

149. Pope to Price, letter of July 29, 1931 (copy), ABMC Records, box 18.

150. Dr. Cret to Price, letter of July 31, 1931 (copy), ABMC Records, box 18.

151. Charles Moore to the American Battle Monuments Commission, letter of August 13, 1931 (original), ABMC Records, box 18. A. A. Weinman was at the time a member of the Fine Arts Commission, but Moore was quick to point out that he had not been when he was first engaged to do the Montfaucon statue, and that the sculptor had not taken part in the CFA's decision to approve the revised model. Dr. Cret and Mangum had represented the ABMC throughout the meeting of the Fine Arts Commission in Weinman's studio on August 5.

152. Price to Cret, letter of August 28, 1931 (copy), ABMC Records, box 18.

153. Mangum to Price, letter no. 1463-W, October 7, 1931 (copy), ABMC Records, box 18.

154. Cret to Price, letter of September 26, 1932 (extracts), ABMC Records, box 19.

155. Price to Pope, letter of October 22, 1932 (copy); Price to Pershing, letter of December 6, 1932 (extracts); and Price to Pope, letter of January 3, 1933, ABMC Records, box 19.

156. Price to A. A. Weinman, letter of January 3, 1933 (copy), ABMC Records, box 19.

157. Pope to Price, letter of January 16, 1933 (original), ABMC Records, box 19.

158. Montsec mentions the First and Second US Armies, but no individual divisions; the Château-Thierry monument names eight divisions and two corps; Bellicourt's inscriptions mention four divisions (27th, 30th, 33rd, and 80th), the II Corps, and the 6th and 11th Engineers; Sommepy specifically honors the 2nd, 36th, 42nd, and 93rd Divisions; Cantigny highlights the 1st Division and the X French Corps; Audenarde mentions the 37th and 91st Divisions; and Kemmel honors specifically the 27th and 30th Divisions.

159. Price hints in a March 1932 letter to Senator David Aiken Reed that the rush "to get in new plantings at the various cemeteries and monuments before the planting season is over, about April 15," had delayed progress on the Montfaucon inscriptions; see Price to Honorable David Aiken Reed, letter of March 29, 1932 (copy), in ABMC Records, box 18.

160. John Russell Pope to Secretary Price, letter of November 25, 1932 (copy), ABMC Records, box 19.

161. See Paul Cret to James Mangum, letter of January 30, 1933 (original), ABMC Records, box 19.

162. Price to Pershing, memorandum of February 27, 1933 (original), ABMC Records, box 19.

163. ABMC Minutes, Thirty-Fifth Meeting, May 25, 1933, ABMC Records, entry 2, box 1A.

164. Price to Pershing, letter of May 19, 1933 (extracts), ABMC Records, box 19.

165. Price to Pershing, letter of June 9, 1933 (extracts), ABMC Records, box 19.

166. Meuse-Argonne pamphlet, 19–22. A similar map, along with two others of the Aisne-Marne and Saint-Mihiel battlefields, accompanied the 1938 ABMC guidebook.

167. X. H. Price, "Final Report, 1938," 16–18.

168. Pershing, "Our National War Memorials in Europe," 36.

169. ABMC Minutes, Thirty-Sixth Meeting, December 21, 1933, ABMC Records, entry 2, box 1A.

4. The Completion of the ABMC's Original Mission and Looking toward an Uncertain Future, 1937–1938

1. See "Commission to Disband: American Work on War Monuments in France Nearly Finished," *New York Times,* August 13, 1933.

2. The fuller quotation of Pershing's remarks to Brigadier General Henry J. Reilly, from an interview that appeared in the *New York Sunday American* on July 4, 1937, reads: "With the cemeteries of the dead completed, the dedication of the battlefields monuments commemorating in stone the accomplishment of its war mission by the A.E.F. will complete my work." An original copy of the article is preserved in the second of six bound volumes of newspaper clippings on the dedi-

cations collected and compiled on Pershing's orders by ABMC's European office. See ABMC Records, boxes 172 and 173.

3. See "Schedule of Ceremonies: Dedications, American War Memorials in Europe, 1937," December 1937, ABMC Records, box 162, for a complete list of the major participants in each of the dedicatory ceremonies.

4. X. H. Price, "Memorandum for the Chairman of the Commission," August 22, 1930 (copy), ABMC Records, box 163.

5. ABMC Minutes, Thirty-Third Meeting, December 1, 1930, ABMC Records, entry 2, box 1A.

6. X. H. Price, "A Study concerning the Dates of Dedication for the Memorials Constructed by the American Battle Monuments Commission," attached to the letter from Price to Pershing, October 21, 1931 (original), ABMC Records, box 163.

7. James E. Mangum, "Some Statements, Personal Opinions, Questions and Comments for Consideration in Connection with Plans for Dedicating Memorials Erected by the American Battle Monuments Commission," November 12, 1931 (original), ABMC Records, box 163. A handwritten notation on this document indicated that General Pershing had read it on November 13, 1931, and that a copy of it was forwarded to Major Price a week later.

8. "Digest of Discussion which Took Place during the Thirty-Fourth Meeting of the American Battle Monuments Commission [November 16, 1931] regarding Dedication of the Commission's Memorials," prepared by James E. Mangum, November 21, 1931 (original), ABMC Records, box 163.

9. Ibid.

10. Pershing to Price, letter of November 28, 1931 (extracts), ABMC Records, box 162.

11. Price to Mangum, letter of December 14, 1931 (original), ABMC Records, box 162.

12. John J. Pershing, "Memorandum for the Commission (No. 78)," December 31, 1931 (copy), ABMC Records, box 162.

13. See Mangum to Pershing, letter of January 4, 1932 (original), ABMC Records, box 162.

14. ABMC Minutes, Thirty-Fifth Meeting, May 25, 1933, ABMC Records, entry 2, box 1A.

15. Pershing and Reed were quoted by Mangum in a "Memorandum for the Commission," dated March 18, 1933 (original), ABMC Records, box 162.

16. ABMC Minutes, Thirty-Sixth Meeting, December 21, 1933, ABMC Records, entry 2, box 1A.

17. ABMC Minutes, Thirty-Seventh Meeting, May 14, 1935, ABMC Records, entry 2, box 1A.

18. See Boatner to ABMC secretary, memorandum of October 20, 1936 (original), ABMC Records, box 162. Attached to this document are two memoranda of July 30 and August 24, 1936, addressed by Captain Boatner to General Pershing, which enumerated a host of issues that would need to be taken into account in the planning of the dedication ceremonies.

19. See pertinent references in the expanded digest of the discussion at the November 16, 1936, meeting of the commission that was prepared by James Mangum as a "memorandum for the files," and dated November 18, 1936, ABMC Records, box 162. An excellent account of the 1936 Vimy Ridge dedication can be found in Lloyd, *Battlefield Tourism,* 198–207.

20. This correspondence began with a letter dated September 30, 1936, from James Mangum to the Canadian Legion in Ottawa (copy), and concluded with a letter from Colonel H. C. Osborne of the Canadian Battlefields Memorial Commission to Secretary Price, dated December 8, 1936. See ABMC Records, box 162. The Canadians were extremely forthcoming about their own experience with the Vimy Ridge event and made every effort to accommodate the ABMC's inquiries, but the final response from Ottawa made clear that the respective dedication projects of the two countries were not altogether comparable because no fewer than four different agencies of the Canadian administration had contributed to the planning and execution of the Vimy Ridge event.

21. ABMC Minutes, Thirty-Eighth Meeting, November 16, 1936, ABMC Records, entry 2, box 1A. Xenophon Price was promoted from major to lieutenant colonel sometime between the thirty-seventh and thirty-eighth meetings of the commission.

22. Price to Pershing, letter of January 3, 1937 (original), ABMC Records, box 7.

23. Mangum to Captain Mark M. Boatner Jr., Officer-in-Charge, European office of the ABMC, letter of November 24, 1936 (copy), ABMC Records, box 162.

24. See Mangum's digest of the November 16, 1936, meeting of the commission, ABMC Records, box 162.

25. Ibid.

26. Boatner to Pershing, memorandum of December 15, 1936 (copy), ABMC Records, box 162.

27. Pershing to Boatner, memorandum of January 2, 1937 (extracts), ABMC Records, box 162.

28. This extended exposé of Captain Boatner's thinking—his memorandum and the cover letter—was dated February 20, 1937, and traveled from Paris to Tucson, where Pershing was wintering. See ABMC Records, box 162.

29. Boatner to ABMC chairman, letter no. 2025-P, March 23, 1937 (original), ABMC Records, box 162.

30. See ABMC Minutes, Thirty-Ninth Meeting, April 14, 1937, ABMC

Records, entry 2, box 1A. Also see the digest of the discussion at that meeting recorded by Mangum in a memorandum for the files, dated April 20, 1937 (original), ABMC Records, box 162.

31. ABMC Minutes, Fortieth Meeting, April 21, 1937, ABMC Records, entry 2, box 1A.

32. Pershing to Daniel Bell, Acting Director, Bureau of the Budget, letter of April 24, 1937 (copy), ABMC Records, box 164.

33. One of Pershing's biographers reports that the general was frequently troubled by poor health during his extended 1937 trip and experienced a "slight heart seizure" while in London. Pershing turned seventy-seven in September of that year. See Vandiver, *Black Jack*, 1088–89.

34. See the undated press release from the commission about the Memorial Day dedications, which paid special attention to this notable "first," in ABMC Records, box 162.

35. John J. Pershing, address at Meuse-Argonne American Cemetery, May 30, 1937 (copy), ABMC Records, box 161. Upon the completion of Pershing's address, the prefect of the Meuse conferred upon Walter Shield, superintendent of the cemetery, one of France's highest decorations, *Chevalier de la Légion d'Honneur*. At least one other superintendent of the ABMC's largest cemetery in Europe, Gene S. Dellinger, received the same honor in 1999.

36. Édouard Daladier, address at Suresnes American Cemetery, May 30, 1937 (copy), ABMC Records, box 161.

37. Mrs. Florence Becker, address at Somme American Cemetery, May 30, 1937 (copy), ABMC Records, box 161.

38. John J. Pershing, address of May 30, 1937, ABMC Records, box 161.

39. Alvin Mansfield Owsley, address at Saint Mihiel American Cemetery, May 30, 1937 (copy), ABMC Records, box 161.

40. John J. Pershing, address of May 30, 1937, ABMC Records, box 161.

41. Alvin Mansfield Owsley, address of May 30, 1937, ABMC Records, box 161.

42. William C. Bullitt, address at Suresnes American Cemetery, May 30, 1937 (copy), ABMC Records, box 161.

43. Pershing to Ambassador Bullitt, letter of June 8, 1937 (copy), ABMC Records, box 162.

44. ABMC Minutes, Forty-First Meeting, June 9, 1937, ABMC Records, entry 2, box 1A.

45. An undated copy of Roosevelt's letter is in ABMC Records, box 164.

46. See the report accompanying Joint Resolution No. 415, by Representative Clifton Woodrum of Virginia, dated June 18, 1937, part of Report No. 1064, House of Representatives, 75th Congress, in ABMC Records, box 164.

47. See "Final Statement of Cost of Dedication of Memorials Erected in Europe by the American Battle Monuments Commission," memorandum for the files signed by James E. Mangum, March 21, 1940 (original), ABMC Records, box 164. Mangum indicated that, of the $175,000 appropriated in June 1937, the commission returned $84,784 to the Treasury.

48. See, for example, X. H. Price to Honorable Newton D. Baker, letter of June 24, 1937 (copy), ABMC Records, box 164. As it happened, Baker, the wartime secretary of war, chose not to make the trip. His alternate was General Benedict Crowell, an assistant secretary of war while the AEF was in combat.

49. The names of those already selected for the official delegation were released to the press on July 12. See ABMC Records, box 172, for the relevant story in the Paris edition of the *New York Herald Tribune,* July 13, 1937.

50. See ABMC Records, box 173, for the relevant story in the Paris edition of the *New York Herald Tribune,* August 5, 1937. See "Heroes at the Meuse-Argonne," *Time* 30, no. 6 (August 9, 1937), 11–12, for a photo of Duffy, Gibson, and Russell, along with a story on the Montfaucon dedication and an explanation of why the senators were not present for it.

51. See Captain William W. Bessell's report, a copy of which was attached to Bessell to ABMC secretary, letter no. 2117-P, November 16, 1937 (original), ABMC Records, box 162; Naomi Lucille Lisle, "An American Girl in France," a memoir of her attendance at the Montfaucon ceremony published in *Lutheran Youth* 26, no. 23 (June 5, 1938), 4–6. A copy of the latter piece was sent to the commission's Washington office with a handwritten note addressed to James Mangum by Miss Lisle, dated June 5, 1938 (original), ABMC Records, box 161.

52. Ibid. See also the account from *Éclair de l'Est* (Nancy, France), August 2, 1937, ABMC Records, box 172.

53. Vandiver, *Black Jack,* 1088.

54. Lisle, "An American Girl in France," 5. Thomas North called Roosevelt's long-distance radio message "an uncommon feat for the epoch," but wrongly reported that the president had spoken from the White House. See North, *One Soldier's Job,* 1:32.

55. The headlines cited came from August 2 editions of newspapers in Clermont-Ferrand and Mulhouse, France, ABMC Records, box 172.

56. John J. Pershing, address at Montfaucon, August 1, 1937, quoted from *Éclair de l'Est* (Nancy), August 2, 1937, ABMC Records, box 172; Lisle, "An American Girl in France," 5.

57. Franklin D. Roosevelt, address to the ceremony at Montfaucon, August 1, 1937. The full text of Roosevelt's address, quoted from the August 2, 1937, edition of the *New York Times,* appears as an appendix at the end of this book.

58. Albert Lebrun, address at Montfaucon, August 1, 1937, quoted from *Éclair de l'Est* (Nancy), August 2, 1937, ABMC Records, box 172.

59. See Lisle, "An American Girl in France," 5, for the account of the raising of the flag and also the quote from President Lebrun; and see *Éclair de l'Est* (Nancy), August 2, 1937, ABMC Records, box 172, for the Colmery and Pershing quotes. For fuller references to Pershing's friendship with Baruch, see Vandiver, *Black Jack,* 1086, and Gene Smith, *Until the Last Trumpet Sounds: The Life of General of the Armies John J. Pershing* (New York: Wiley and Sons, 1998), 266, 287.

60. Quoted from Lisle, "An American Girl in France."

61. A copy of this news bulletin, dated July 28, 1937, was attached to Katherine P. O'Donnell (National Geographic Society's School and News Services) to James E. Mangum, letter of July 30, 1937, ABMC Records, box 164.

62. For a fuller account of the postwar recovery effort in the ten most affected of the French departments, see Hugh Clout, *After the Ruins: Restoring the Countryside of Northern France after the Great War* (Exeter, UK: Univ. of Exeter Press, 1996), especially 267–300.

63. See William Bessell's report on the dedications, November 16, 1937, ABMC Records, box 162.

64. The foregoing account is drawn from the summary of the American Legion pilgrimage by Alexander Gardiner, entitled "Pilgrims—but Not Strangers," in the December 1937 issue of *American Legion* magazine, found in ABMC Records, box 162. The *New York Times* had previewed the "Third A.E.F." several months earlier. See Bernhard Ragner, "Third A.E.F. off to France: Legion Pilgrimage Will Take Thousands of Ex-Doughboys over to Tour 1917–18 Battlefields as Guests of the Republic," *New York Times,* September 19, 1937.

65. Harry Colmery, address at the dedication of the Aisne-Marne monument, October 7, 1937, quoted from Gardiner, "Pilgrims—but Not Strangers."

66. See "Americans in France to Honor War Victims," *New York Times,* May 29, 1937, and "U.S. Will Dedicate 13 War Memorials," *New York Times,* July 4, 1937.

67. See "Group Sails to Honor War Dead in Europe," *New York Times,* July 15, 1937; "Americans in Paris Honor War Dead," *New York Times,* July 22, 1937; and "Speeches at U.S. War Shrine at Montfaucon," *New York Times,* August 2, 1937.

68. See "Heroes at the Meuse-Argonne," *Time* 30, no. 6 (August 9, 1937), 11–12.

69. See "Montfaucon Shaft Dedicated Today," *New York Times,* August 1, 1937.

70. "To Those We Left in France," *New York Times,* August 2, 1937.

71. See, for example, "Pershing May Retire after the Work Is Completed,"

New York Times, July 22, 1937, and "Heroes at the Meuse-Argonne," *Time* 30, no. 6 (August 9, 1937), 11–12, which declared that Pershing was "expected to retire now" (11).

72. ABMC Minutes, Thirty-Fourth Meeting, November 16, 1931, ABMC Records, entry 2, box 1A.

73. See X. H. Price, "Memorandum for the Chairman," November 21, 1932 (original), ABMC Records, entry 49, box 1.

74. The quoted passage comes from Roosevelt's Executive Order No. 6614, issued February 26, 1934, and cited in Garry D. Ryan, "Preliminary Inventory of the Textual Records of the American Battle Monuments Commission, RG 117," an in-house inventory and brief administrative history of the ABMC in the National Archives and Records Administration (College Park).

75. Pershing to Price, letter of February 15, 1934 (copy), "Personal and Confidential," ABMC Records, entry 49, box 1; see also Budreau, *Bodies of War,* 161, and MacCloskey, *Hallowed Ground,* 51.

76. For a fuller treatment of the Roosevelt administration's effort to reorganize the government, see Richard Polenberg, *Reorganizing Roosevelt's Government, 1936–1939: The Controversy over Executive Reorganization* (Cambridge, Mass.: Harvard Univ. Press, 1966).

77. X. H. Price, "Memorandum for the Chairman," November 20, 1937 (original), ABMC Records, entry 49, box 1.

78. Pershing to Secretary of War Harry Woodring, letter of January 5, 1938 (copy), ABMC Records, box 7.

79. Secretary of War Harry Woodring to Pershing, letter of January 18, 1938 (copy), ABMC Records, box 7.

80. Franklin D. Roosevelt to Pershing, letter of January 18, 1938 (copy), ABMC Records, box 7.

81. See Vandiver, *Black Jack,* 1089–91, and Gene Smith, *Until the Last Trumpet Sounds,* 276–79. Smith's account makes clearer how widespread was the expectation all over the country in February 1938 that Pershing was not going to survive this medical crisis. The *New York Times* reported both Pershing's April departure from Tucson for New York City (see photo caption "As Pershing left Tucson for New York," *New York Times,* April 19, 1938) and his August arrival in Paris (see "Pershing Reaches Paris," *New York Times,* August 18, 1938).

82. Polenberg, *Reorganizing Roosevelt's Government,* 162–88. The original bill failed in the House by a vote of 204–196.

83. ABMC Minutes, Forty-Fifth Meeting, November 12, 1938, ABMC Records, entry 2, box 1A.

84. Polenberg, *Reorganizing Roosevelt's Government,* 10, 216. The author

identified as his source for the claim that FDR intended to allow the commission its independence while Pershing lived (page 216) the transcript of a presidential news conference on October 31, 1939, found in the Roosevelt Papers. Polenberg was of the opinion that the ABMC was "unnecessary" (10).

85. See X. H. Price, "Final Report, 1938," ABMC Records, entry 3, box 3.

86. See undated note from James Mangum on Price's letter of January 25, 1938, ABMC Records, entry 3, box 3, confirming that Pershing had seen the full draft of the report and ordered it filed.

87. Price, "Final Report, 1938," 34–35.

88. Ibid., 8, 13, 35, 41.

89. Price to Pershing, letter of June 30, 1938 (copy), ABMC Records, box 7. There would be no permanent replacement for Price as secretary to the commission until President Truman appointed Thomas North to the position in April 1946. James Mangum, who had begun his ABMC employment in the 1920s as clerk in the Washington office, would hold the title "acting secretary" throughout the 1938–46 interim.

90. This summary of Price's career comes from the obituary published in the *Washington Star* on July 17, 1979, and found in ABMC Records, entry 49, box 1. Price was laid to rest in Arlington National Cemetery on July 18, 1979, one day shy of the thirty-first anniversary of General Pershing's interment in the same burial ground.

91. Price to Pershing, letter of May 10, 1937 (copy), ABMC Records, box 7.

92. Price to Pershing, letter of October 26, 1937 (copy), ABMC Records, box 7.

93. Price to Pershing, letter of April 29, 1939 (copy), ABMC Records, box 7. See also "Government Book on A.E.F. Is Ready," *New York Times,* April 24, 1939, for news of the guidebook's release for public sale.

94. William Bessell to Pershing, letter of May 9, 1939 (copy), ABMC Records, box 7.

5. The American Battle Monuments Commission and World War II, 1939–1945

1. See "American Officers and Employees (and Dependents) of the American Battle Monuments Commission Stationed in Europe," a document reported to the US Department of State on August 9, 1940, ABMC Records, box 132. The document enumerated twenty-one American employees of the commission in France, along with thirty-six dependents; two in England, along with five dependents; and one in Belgium, along with one dependent. In addition, two army officers were detailed full-time to the commission in the European office in Paris. This made for a total of sixty-eight employees and dependents, sixty-one of whom were serving on the continent.

2. Captain William W. Bessell Jr. to General John J. Pershing, letter of March 28, 1939 (copy), ABMC Records, box 8. Pershing was wintering in Tucson, Arizona, at this time. Bessell, whose service to the ABMC ended in June 1939, became a brigadier general by the end of World War II, won the Army Distinguished Service Medal for his wartime service, and became dean of the Academic Board at West Point in July 1947.

3. Ibid.

4. See "Field Memorandum No. 15," attached to Bessell to Pershing, letter of March 28, 1939 (copy), ABMC Records, box 8. The notices to be posted on the evacuated sites bore the official seal of the European office of the American Battle Monuments Commission and were to be written in English and French. One wonders why they were not also rendered in German.

5. See "Pershing Stands Voyage Well," *New York Times,* June 8, 1939, and Bessell to Mangum, letter of June 9, 1939 (original), ABMC Records, box 132.

6. See "Captain Back from Paris: Bessell Decorated by France for Monuments Service," *New York Times,* July 2, 1939.

7. Captain Charles G. Holle to Mangum, August 10, 1939, ABMC Records, box 132. Holle was, like Bessell, a member of the West Point graduating class of 1920. He retired as a brigadier general. He served in the office of the chief of engineers for most of his nearly two decades of active duty after his detail to ABMC ended in 1941.

8. Captain Holle described the move to Dreux in "Field Memorandum No. 22," October 19, 1939 (copy), ABMC Records, box 132.

9. See Holle, "Circular No. 15," December 1, 1939, ABMC Records, box 132.

10. Captain Holle, "Report to General Pershing on the Armistice Day Ceremony at Romagne," December 9, 1939, ABMC Records, box 8.

11. Holle to Pershing, letter of October 11, 1939 (copy), ABMC Records, box 8.

12. Holle to Mangum, letter no. 2537-P (original), September 29, 1939, ABMC Records, box 132.

13. Holle to Mangum, letter no. 2548-P (original), November 13, 1939, ABMC Records, box 132.

14. Mangum to Holle, letter of June 21, 1940 (copy), ABMC Records, box 132.

15. Holle to Mangum, cable of April 10, 1940 (original), ABMC Records, box 132.

16. Holle to Pershing, letter of April 16, 1940 (extracts), ABMC Records, box 132.

17. Mangum to Holle, cable of April 11, 1940 (copy), and cable of April 13, 1940 (copy), ABMC Records, box 132. Mangum told Pershing, but not Holle,

that the secretary of war would use funds in this instance that had originally been appropriated for "Military Intelligence Activities," and which could be disbursed at the secretary's discretion. See Mangum to Pershing, letter of April 13, 1940 (copy), ABMC Records, box 132.

18. Accounts of the fighting of May–June 1940 abound. Brief but excellent summations are in Martin Gilbert, *The Second World War: A Complete History*, rev. ed. (New York: Holt, 1989), 61–102, and John Keegan, *The Second World War* (New York: Viking, 1989), 60–87.

19. The foregoing paragraph was entirely based on the four-page report Superintendent Kaess submitted to the officer-in-charge of the European office, entitled "Evacuation of Personnel—Romagne Cemetery," dated May 16, 1940. This and similar reports from the superintendents at Oise-Aisne (Fère), Somme (Bony), and Saint-Mihiel (Thiaucourt) cemeteries accompanied Holle to ABMC chairman, letter no. 2592-P (original), May 22, 1940, ABMC Records, box 135.

20. Orlando Overstake, "Evacuation of Personnel from Bony Cemetery," report of May 18, 1940 (original), ABMC Records, box 135.

21. George C. Gorham, "Evacuation of Personnel from the St. Mihiel Cemetery," report of May 20, 1940 (original), ABMC Records, box 135.

22. John J. Dillon, "Evacuation of Personnel from the Fère Cemetery," report of May 20, 1940 (original), ABMC Records, box 135.

23. See Holle, "Report to General Pershing for the period May 10–21, 1940," entry for May 18, 1940, ABMC Records, box 135.

24. Ibid., entry for May 19, 1940. In a cable sent to the Washington office the same day, Holle reported that fifteen employees and thirty immediate family members departed Dreux for the Bordeaux area in two official cars, six personal cars, and four trucks, all under the supervision of Captain Hertford. See Holle to ABMC, Washington, telegram of May 19, 1940 (original), ABMC Records, box 135.

25. Holle to Pershing, letter of May 23, 1940 (original), ABMC Records, box 135.

26. Kaess's report of May 16, 1940, ABMC Records, box 135.

27. Overstake's report of May 18, 1940, ABMC Records, box 135.

28. Holle to Pershing, letter no. 2592-P, May 22, 1940, ABMC Records, box 135.

29. Holle to Pershing, letter of May 23, 1940, ABMC Records, box 135.

30. This reality did not prevent at least one report to the contrary from running in the *New York Times*. On May 17 the paper contained an article based on unconfirmed reports passed along by the American Legion headquarters in Paris that the Germans had attacked an unspecified cemetery in eastern France and "completely destroyed the chapel and many graves." See "U.S. War Graves in France Reported Bombed by Nazis," *New York Times*, May 17, 1940.

31. Captain Holle, "Special Report of Activities," entry for June 9, 1940. This was a daily log for the period May 22 to June 30 that was enclosed with Holle to Pershing, letter no. 2599-P (copy), July 1, 1940, ABMC Records, box 135.

32. Ibid., entry for June 10, 1940.

33. Ibid., entry for June 11, 1940.

34. Ibid., entries of June 14, 15, 17, 18, 20, 21, 22, 25, 1940.

35. Ibid., entry of June 26, 1940.

36. Ibid., entry of June 30, 1940.

37. The foregoing paragraph and the one to follow are drawn from sixteen pages of "Diary Notes" for the period July 1–29, 1940, which Holle compiled and enclosed with letter no. 2601-P to Pershing, dated July 29, 1940, under the heading "Special Report of Activities, July 1 to 29, 1940." A copy of these documents is in ABMC Records, box 134. The original, which Pershing returned after seeing it to the Washington office on September 6, 1940, is in box 135.

38. Holle, "Diary Notes," ibid.

39. Some of the damage that did occur will be detailed later. In a report to Pershing, Holle estimated that it would cost $3,100 to replace damaged headstones, $3,316 to repair damage to buildings, and $2,500 to replace damaged and stolen tools and equipment, for a total of $8,916. See Holle to Pershing, letter of October 17, 1940 (original), ABMC Records, box 8.

40. See Holle, "Diary Notes," entry of July 5, 1940.

41. Ibid., entries of July 6 and 7, 8, 9, 10, 11, 12, 1940.

42. Ibid., entry of July 8, 1940.

43. Ibid., entry of July 10, 1940.

44. Ibid., entry of July 8, 1940. The buried soldiers were later removed.

45. Ibid., entry of July 12, 1940.

46. Holle to Pershing, letter of July 14, 1940 (copy), ABMC Records, box 8.

47. Holle to Pershing, letter of August 24, 1940 (original), ABMC Records, box 8.

48. Ibid.

49. "Report of Condition of American World War Memorials erected by agencies other than the U.S. Government," in Holle to Pershing, letter no. 2612-P (original), August 29, 1940, ABMC Records, box 134.

50. Holle to Pershing, letter no. 2623-P (original), September 12, 1940, and Holle to Pershing, letter no. 2655-P (original), November 20, 1940, ABMC Records, box 134.

51. Holle to Pershing, letter of November 25, 1940 (original), ABMC Records, box 8.

52. On Ambassador Bullitt's departure from Paris, see Herbert R. Lottman,

The Fall of Paris, June 1940 (New York: Harper Collins, 1992), 382–83, and Charles Glass, *Americans in Paris: Life and Death Under Nazi Occupation* (New York: Penguin Press, 2010), 174. On the offer of the ambassadorial appointment to Pershing, see "Memorandum by Bullitt," November 9, 1940, in *For the President, Personal and Secret: Correspondence between Franklin D. Roosevelt and William C. Bullitt,* ed. Orville H. Bullitt (Boston: Houghton Mifflin, 1972), 505. See also William L. Langer, *Our Vichy Gamble* (New York: Knopf, 1947), 118. Admiral William D. Leahy eventually accepted the post and arrived in Vichy in January 1941. See Robert O. Paxton, *Vichy France: Old Guard and New Order* (1972; reprint, New York: Columbia Univ. Press, 2001), 85, 91.

53. See Holle to Pershing, letter of October 17, 1940 (original), ABMC Records, box 8.

54. See Holle's memorandum of October 5, 1940 (original), for the German authorities, appended to letter no. 2638-P to the ABMC chairman of October 21, 1940 (original), ABMC Records, box 132. The cemeteries in restricted zones were Flanders Field, Somme, Meuse-Argonne, and Saint-Mihiel. Monuments in the same zones were Audenarde, Kemmel, Bellicourt, Montfaucon, and Montsec. It was out of the question to get ABMC officials from occupied Europe to Brookwood at this time.

55. The High Army Commander, Chief of the Military Direction in France, to ABMC, letter of October 16, 1940 (translated copy), appended to letter no. 2638-P, October 21, 1940, ABMC Records, box 132.

56. Holle to ABMC Headquarters, telegram of October 23, 1940 (copy), ABMC Records, box 132.

57. Holle to Pershing, letter of October 17, 1940, ABMC Records, box 8.

58. Holle to Pershing, letter of November 25, 1940, ABMC Records, box 8.

59. Ibid.

60. Ibid.

61. The hard fate of the British cemetery personnel is recounted in Longworth, *The Unending Vigil*, 161–72.

62. Holle to Pershing, letter of November 25, 1940, ABMC Records, box 8.

63. Special Order No. 18, December 23, 1940 (copy), ABMC Records, box 132. After a few more months of availability to the commission in the United States, Holle served the balance of the war in various capacities with the army engineers.

64. Mott recounted the final months of the contingent of Americans posted to ABMC sites in Europe, starting with his own assignment as officer-in-charge on January 8, 1941, in a letter to Mangum that he wrote upon his own return to the United States seven months later. See T. Bentley Mott to James E. Mangum, letter of August 8, 1941 (original), ABMC Records, box 133. He had published

a memoir in 1937, unfortunately too soon to encompass his important service to ABMC. See T. Bentley Mott, *Twenty Years as Military Attaché* (New York: Oxford Univ. Press, 1937).

65. See Breckenridge Long to General Pershing, letter of January 17, 1941 (original), ABMC Records, box 135.

66. Pershing to Mangum, telegram of March 18, 1941 (original), ABMC Records, box 135.

67. Holle to Pershing, memorandum of March 20, 1941 (copy), enclosed with Mangum to Pershing, letter of March 20, 1941 (original), ABMC Records, box 135.

68. Pershing to the Secretary of State, letter of March 24, 1941 (copy), ABMC Records, box 135.

69. Sumner Welles to Pershing, letter of March 28, 1941 (original), ABMC Records, box 135.

70. Hull to Pershing, letter of April 28, 1941 (original), ABMC Records, box 135.

71. Mott (in Paris) to Pershing, telegram of April 29, 1941 (copy), dispatched over the signature of Ambassador William D. Leahy (in Vichy), ABMC Records, box 135.

72. See Gilbert, *The Second World War*, 153–76, for an account of additional developments at this time that portended a broadening of the war.

73. Hull to Pershing, letter of May 9, 1941 (original), ABMC Records, box 135.

74. The foregoing account, and the account to follow, are drawn from Mott to Mangum, letter of August 8, 1941, ABMC Records, box 133.

75. See Cordell Hull to General Pershing, letter of May 19, 1941 (original), ABMC Records, box 135. It was noted on this document that Pershing had seen it on May 21. Obviously, the aged general was monitoring closely the unfolding of this particular drama.

76. See clipping from the *Evening Star* (Washington, D.C.), June 13, 1941, and memorandum by Mangum, July 30, 1941 (original), ABMC Records, box 135; also see Mott to Mangum, letter of August 8, 1941, ABMC Records, box 133. A one-page "Note concerning Journey of Employees from Paris to Washington," authored by Colonel Mott, accompanied his August 8 letter to Mangum.

77. Mott to Mangum, August 8, 1941, ABMC Records, box 133.

78. See Secretary General G. Romsee, Belgian Ministry of the Interior and Public Health, to the Minister of the Interior and Public Health, letter of May 6, 1942 (translated copy), ABMC Records, box 132.

79. See "Arrangements with General Vincensini and Reports from Vichy, France, regarding Maintenance and Conditions of Cemeteries and Memorials in France," ABMC Records, box 133.

80. Pershing to the Secretary of the Treasury, letter of February 13, 1942 (copy), ABMC Records, box 8.

81. Ryan's report, addressed to Captain Hertford in Dreux, was dispatched on June 8, 1940. It can be found in ABMC Records, box 161.

82. "Services Curtailed in Occupied France," *New York Times,* May 31, 1941.

83. Reverend Spencer's prayer was entitled in the program for the ceremony "Prayer for Unity between English-Speaking Lands." See Ryan's "Report on Memorial Day Ceremony," June 3, 1941 (original), ABMC Records, box 161.

84. ABMC Minutes, Forty-Fifth Meeting, November 12, 1938, ABMC Records, entry 2, box 1A.

85. Pershing to Mangum, letter of March 7, 1941 (original), ABMC Records, box 8.

86. Within a month, President Roosevelt had appointed Mr. Leslie Biffle, secretary to the Democratic majority in the US Senate, to fill the vacancy. Pershing communicated this and other news, including word of the evacuation order for American personnel, to the commission in memo no. 106, June 24, 1941, ABMC Records, box 8.

87. Pershing to Secretary of the Treasury, letter of February 13, 1942, ABMC Records, box 8.

88. T. Bentley Mott to Pershing, letter of August 16, 1941 (original), JJP Papers, box 141.

89. Mott to Pershing, letters of November 3, 8, 14, and December 4, 1941 (originals), JJP Papers, box 141.

90. Mott to Pershing, letter of December 12, 1941 (original), JJP Papers, box 141.

91. Mott to Pershing, letter of January 3, 1942 (original), JJP Papers, box 141.

92. See Mott to Pershing, letters of May 15 and 21, 1942 (originals), JJP Papers, box 141, for an account of the rigors of the transatlantic voyage and details of his arrival in Lisbon.

93. Mott first referred to Pershing's request that he attend to matters relating to property Madame Resco owned in Paris, and also that he communicate with her family, three months before he and his wife sailed for Europe. See Mott to Pershing, letter of February 14, 1942 (original), JJP Papers, box 141. Mott made frequent reference in later letters to his efforts on her behalf. See, for example, Mott to Pershing, letters of May 31 and July 1, 1942 (originals), JJP Papers, box 141. For a more thorough perspective on this relationship, see Vandiver, *Black Jack,* 814–16, 995, 1007–8, 1084–85; and see Donald Smythe, *Pershing: General of the Armies* (Bloomington: Indiana Univ. Press, 1986), 296–301.

94. Mott to Pershing, letter of June 20, 1942 (original), JJP Papers, box 141.

95. Ibid.

96. Ibid. Mott encapsulated the arrangements he had made after his 1941 exit from Paris for the continuation of the commission's operations out of Suresnes, and what he was later able to discern about the operation of the rump ABMC office, in a six-page report he prepared for Pershing upon his return from Europe in 1944. See Mott to Pershing, letter of May 5, 1944 (original), ABMC Records, box 133. General North's memoir also mentions Mott's wartime mission, but only briefly, and several details in the latter account do not square with Mott's own. See North, *One Soldier's Job*, 1:34.

97. Mott to Pershing, letter of July 1, 1942 (original), JJP Papers, box 141.

98. Mott to Pershing, letter of August 21, 1942 (original), JJP Papers, box 141.

99. Mott to Pershing, letter of September 18, 1942 (original), JJP Papers, box 141.

100. Mott to Pershing, letter of May 5, 1944, ABMC Records, box 133.

101. See translated copy of a note, dated October 20, 1943, from the Swiss Foreign Office to the American legation at Bern, regarding General Mott, in JJP Papers, box 141.

102. Mott to Pershing, letter of May 5, 1944, ABMC Records, box 133. See also Breckenridge Long, Assistant Secretary of State, to Pershing, memorandum of November 26, 1943 (copy), JJP Papers, box 141, which conveyed news of Mott's condition and whereabouts furnished by the American legation in Bern.

103. Mott to Pershing, letter of May 5, 1944, ABMC Records, box 133. See also Pierre Rod, "Report on War Damage in Cemeteries and Monuments since the Combats of 1940," October 25, 1944 (copy), ABMC Records, box 134. Rod was one of three Europeans attached to the Suresnes office for the duration of the German occupation.

104. Mott to Pershing, letter of May 5, 1944, ABMC Records, box 133.

105. Ibid. Mott did comment at some length about weather staining on the headstones, but conceded that this had always been a problem and noted that it was being controlled for the time being by simple washing.

106. Ibid. Prior to this letter/report that Mott prepared for General Pershing upon the former's return to Washington, the younger officer had gotten a letter out of Paris to the chairman, dated January 28, 1944, through the good offices of the Swiss. The letter reached Pershing more than two months later and came with a cover letter from the State Department, dated April 4, 1944, and the last two quarterly reports from Pierre Rod from 1943 on the condition of ABMC sites. See Mott to Pershing, letter of January 28, 1944 (original), ABMC Records, box 133; and State Department to ABMC Headquarters, unsigned letter of April

4, 1944 (original), ABMC Records, box 133. Mott's message in the January 1944 letter was, in short: "As a whole our establishments are in good condition."

107. Rod's "Report on War Damage," October 25, 1944, was prepared after he had inspected the Tours monument on October 5 and all of the other European monuments—except for Brest—and cemeteries between October 12 and 18.

108. Rod, "Report on War Damage," October 25, 1944.

109. Ibid. Oddly enough, Rod's report did not mention the Saint-Mihiel cemetery, but an earlier press release from the War Department confirmed that this site was in "excellent condition." See War Department, Bureau of Public Relations, "Most U.S. World War Cemeteries in France, Belgium in Good Condition," press release of October 20, 1944 (copy), ABMC Records, box 134.

110. Quoted in "Army Graves Untouched: Congress Assured Germans Did Not Desecrate Our Cemeteries," *New York Times*, February 6, 1945.

111. North, *One Soldier's Job*, 1:35.

112. General Dwight D. Eisenhower, SHAEF Headquarters, to General of the Armies John J. Pershing, cable of September 13, 1944 (copy), ABMC Records, box 133.

113. Eisenhower's "Report on Conditions of World War I Cemeteries and Monuments in France and Belgium, September 1944," along with an undated cover letter by him, was received at the ABMC headquarters in Washington on October 11, 1944; see ABMC Records, box 133. The five-page document, which reported individually on each cemetery and monument, was forwarded to members of the commission two days later.

114. Price's four-page report, with photographs, covered the condition of the Brookwood, Suresnes, Aisne-Marne, and Oise-Aisne cemeteries and the Château-Thierry monument. See Colonel X. H. Price, President, War Observers Board, to Brigadier General L. D. Worsham, Commanding General, Army Service Forces, Washington, D.C., October 7, 1944 (original), ABMC Records, box 133.

115. There is evidence that Pershing's health deteriorated seriously at this very moment, probably because of some sort of stroke. See unsigned letter (most likely from Colonel George Adamson, Pershing's secretary) to General John McAuley Palmer, September 15, 1944 (copy), JJP Papers, box 157.

116. North, *One Soldier's Job*, 1:34–35.

6. Reopening the European Office and New Leadership for a Renewed Mission, 1944–1948

1. T. Bentley Mott to the chairman of the American Battle Monuments Commission, letter no. 2703-P (copy), November 15, 1944, ABMC Records, entry 39, box 15.

2. Ibid.

3. Ibid. The Graves Registration Service within the quartermaster general's office of the army had been paying the salary of Brookwood superintendent John T. Ryan since November 1942 and would continue to do so until the cemetery was returned to ABMC administration on July 1, 1948. See G. M. ver Hulst, Executive Officer (in Paris), to the ABMC secretary, letter no. 3968-P of January 12, 1949 (copy), ABMC Records, entry 39, box 16.

4. Mott to Major Charles B. Shaw (ABMC, Washington), letter of December 26, 1944 (copy), ABMC Records, entry 39, box 15.

5. Ibid.

6. Mott to General Pershing, letter of December 26, 1944 (original), ABMC Records, box 8.

7. Ibid.

8. Mott to Major Shaw, letter no. 2760-P (copy), July 19, 1945, ABMC Records, entry 39, box 15.

9. Mott to commanding general, European Theater of Operations, letter of May 2, 1945 (copy), ABMC Records, entry 39, box 15.

10. See "Erection of Battle Monuments in the European Theater," unsigned memorandum to all commanding generals, from Headquarters, European Theater of Operations, June 29, 1945 (copy), ABMC Records, entry 39, box 15.

11. North, *One Soldier's Job*, 2:2.

12. Robert Woodside to T. Bentley Mott, letter of August 10, 1945 (copy), ABMC Records, box 133.

13. North, *One Soldier's Job*, 2:4.

14. Woodside to Mott, letter of August 10, 1945, ABMC Records, box 133. In May 1947 it was announced that, on the recommendation of the Pershing board, the War Department had awarded General Mott with the Legion of Merit for his wartime service to the ABMC. See ABMC Minutes, Fiftieth Meeting, May 15, 1947, ABMC Records, entry 49, box 1.

15. Mott to Major Shaw, letter no. 2747-P (copy), May 20, 1945, ABMC Records, entry 39, box 15.

16. Ibid.

17. Ibid.

18. Mott to the secretary (General Thomas North), American Battle Monuments Commission, letter no. 2845-P (copy), July 3, 1946, ABMC Records, entry 39, box 15. The same five men who had superintended the American cemeteries in the actual battle zones of the First World War in France—Orlando Overstake at the Somme, Arthur Revoir at Belleau Wood, George C. Gorham at Saint-Mihiel, John J. Dillon at Oise-Aisne, and Adolph Kaess at Meuse-Argonne—all came back to their pre-1941 posts.

19. John J. Pershing to Mrs. Paul P. Cret, letter of September 10, 1945, in ABMC Minutes, Forty-Sixth Meeting, November 15, 1945, ABMC Records, entry 49, box 1. See *New York Times,* September 9, 1945, for Dr. Cret's obituary, which appeared under the title "Dr. Paul Cret Dies: A Noted Architect, Designer of War Memorials in Europe."

20. The final years of Pershing's life are covered especially thoroughly in Smith, *Until the Last Trumpet Sounds,* 284–310.

21. See ABMC Minutes, Fifty-Seventh Meeting, January 26, 1949, ABMC Records, entry 49, box 1, for the notice of Marshall's election as chairman.

22. The best description of Pershing's funeral is in Smythe, *Pershing,* 308–9, including photos of the body lying in state in the Capitol Rotunda on July 18, 1948, and sixteen army generals, including Eisenhower, Marshall, Bradley, Devers, and Clark, marching in the rain-soaked procession from Capitol Hill to Arlington the next day.

23. For the full text of the resolution, see ABMC Minutes, Fifty-Sixth Meeting, July 19, 1948, ABMC Records, entry 49, box 1.

7. Building the World War II Memorials, 1945–1960

1. General Marshall referred to his earlier visit to the World War I sites in a letter to Secretary Thomas North explaining why he did not intend to revisit them during his 1952 trip. See George C. Marshall to Thomas North, letter of July 31, 1952 (copy), in Papers of George C. Marshall (hereafter "GCM Papers"), Marshall Library, Lexington, Virginia, box 161, file 46.

2. George C. Marshall, "Our War Memorials Abroad: A Faith Kept," *National Geographic Magazine* 111, no. 6 (June 1957), 731, 733.

3. The American Battle Monuments Commission, "Resolution of Sympathy for Mrs. Katherine Marshall," in ABMC Minutes, Seventy-Sixth Meeting, October 21, 1959, ABMC Records, entry 49, box 1. Marshall had died five days earlier.

4. Henry Stimson and James Forrestal to President Harry S. Truman, letter of September 20, 1945 (copy), in ABMC Records, entry 49, box 1.

5. Ibid.

6. North, *One Soldier's Job,* 2:1–2.

7. Ibid., 2:2–3. See also ABMC Minutes, Forty-Sixth Meeting, November 15, 1945, ABMC Records, entry 49, box 1.

8. ABMC Minutes, Forty-Sixth Meeting, ABMC Records, entry 49, box 1.

9. ABMC Minutes, Forty-Seventh Meeting, April 5, 1946, ABMC Records, entry 49, box 1.

10. North, *One Soldier's Job,* 2:16–17, 21. See also ABMC Minutes, Sixty-Ninth Meeting, December 15, 1955, ABMC Records, entry 49, box 1, for the commission's approval of an inscription on the rebuilt monument confirming

that it was "an exact replica of the original" built on the same site in 1932 and destroyed "by the Enemy" on July 4, 1941.

11. ABMC Minutes, Forty-Seventh Meeting, April 5, 1946.

12. North, *One Soldier's Job*, 2:4–5.

13. Commission minutes reveal that Harbeson missed no more than five of the fifty-three meetings held between November 1946 and April 1979. He died in December 1986 at the age of ninety-eight.

14. ABMC Minutes, Forty-Eighth Meeting, November 19, 1946, ABMC Records, entry 49, box 1.

15. North, *One Soldier's Job*, 2:3.

16. ABMC Minutes, Forty-Eighth Meeting, November 19, 1946.

17. General George A. Horkan, "Delineation of Responsibility between the War Department and the American Battle Monuments Commission," memorandum of July 29, 1946 (copy), appended to ABMC Minutes, Forty-Eighth Meeting, November 19, 1946. At this meeting the ABMC formally approved the foregoing terms.

18. North, *One Soldier's Job*, 2:4.

19. See memoranda from Secretary North to Vice Chairman Robert Woodside, one dated July 29, 1946, and the other dated November 1, 1946, and another memorandum from Leslie Biffle to Woodside, dated November 1, 1946 (hereafter "Biffle Report"), copies of which are in the GCM Papers, box 12, folder 26.

20. See ABMC Minutes, Forty-Eighth Meeting, November 19, 1946, ABMC Records, entry 49, box 1; see also "Biffle Report," GCM Papers, box 12, folder 26.

21. ABMC Minutes, Forty-Eighth Meeting, November 19, 1946.

22. Alexander A. Vandegrift, "Report of Pacific Area Committee," January 3, 1947 (copy), appended to ABMC Minutes, Forty-Ninth Meeting, February 13, 1947, ABMC Records, entry 49, box 1.

23. Ibid.

24. ABMC Minutes, Forty-Ninth Meeting, February 13, 1947; also see D. John Markey, "Report of Meeting concerning Permanent Cemeteries in Tropical Region," January 21, 1947 (copy), appended to ABMC Minutes, Forty-Ninth Meeting, February 13, 1947.

25. ABMC Minutes, Forty-Ninth Meeting, February 13, 1947; also see the "Biffle Report," November 1, 1946, and Thomas North to General Thomas B. Larkin, Quartermaster General, letter of February 21, 1947 (copy), appended to ABMC Minutes, Forty-Ninth Meeting, February 13, 1947. In May 1947, General Eisenhower submitted to the War Department a comprehensive summary of his own views regarding where monuments should be placed. See Dwight D. Eisenhower, "Memorandum for the Director, Plans and Operations Division,

WDGS," May 7, 1947 (copy), in Eisenhower Pre-Presidential Papers, Eisenhower Library, Abilene, Kansas, box 128. Ike expressed the belief that monuments erected by the United States "should be few in number and should be erected only in territories either owned by the United States or in countries where a history of friendship gives reasonable assurance of permanent respect." While the foregoing sentiments pertained to monuments, they were not wholly irrelevant to the planning for overseas cemeteries.

26. ABMC Minutes, Fiftieth Meeting, May 15, 1947, ABMC Records, entry 49, box 1.

27. Ibid.

28. Ibid.

29. ABMC Minutes, Forty-Ninth Meeting, February 13, 1947. When it became clear that there would be no government-funded Gold Star pilgrimages after World War II, Congress did agree to designate money so that each family, on request, could receive a photograph of their loved one's grave or listing on a wall of the missing, as well as an aerial photograph of the appropriate ABMC cemetery. This program, established in 1956, became known as "the Andrews Project" after the Alabama congressman who conceived the idea. To prepare for the fulfillment of individual requests, the overseas offices of the ABMC were instructed to make photographs of every World War II headstone and every section of the walls of the missing, and send them to a master file at the commission headquarters in Washington, D.C. See North, *One Soldier's Job*, 3:14–16.

30. ABMC Minutes, Fiftieth Meeting, May 15, 1947.

31. "To the right of the chapel entrance," notes the official ABMC pamphlet on the Aisne-Marne Cemetery and Memorial, "is a hole in the stonework made in 1940 by a German anti-tank gun which was firing at French tanks passing in the vicinity of the cemetery" (10–12).

32. ABMC Minutes, Fifty-First Meeting, June 5, 1947, ABMC Records, entry 49, box 1, and Appendix I, prepared by John Harbeson for this meeting. In all but two cases, Neuville-en-Condroz (at 5,328 burials) and Florence (at 4,402 burials), the quartermaster general's projections for the eventual number of burials at each site proved too conservative.

33. Ibid. For the Cambridge cemetery, Perry, Shaw, and Hepburn (Boston) was the firm chosen; for Saint-Laurent, Harbeson, Hough, Livingston, and Larson (Philadelphia); for Saint-James, William T. Aldrich (Boston); for Margraten, Coolidge, Shepley, Bulfinch, and Abbott (Boston); for Henri-Chapelle, Holabird and Root (Chicago); for Neuville-en-Condroz, Reinhard and Hofmeister (New York); for Saint-Avold, Murphy and Locraft (Washington, D.C.); for Épinal, Delano and Aldrich (New York); for Draguignan, Toombs and Creighton (Atlanta); for Anzio, Gugler, Kimball, and Husted (New York); for Florence,

McKim, Meade, and White (New York); for Tunis, Moore and Hutchins (New York); and for the Philippines, Gardner Dailey (San Francisco). In the latter instance, Arthur Brown of San Francisco was listed as the first choice, but Gardner Dailey was to be the selection, as Harbeson put it, "if Mr. Brown is unable to undertake this work." For Luxembourg, Frohman, Robb, and Little of Boston was the firm originally named, but, as indicated in the text, the job ultimately went to Keally and Patterson of New York City.

34. ABMC Minutes, Fifty-First Meeting, June 5, 1947, ABMC Records, entry 49, box 1, and Appendix I, prepared by John Harbeson for this meeting; also see North, *One Soldier's Job,* 2:10–11.

35. ABMC Minutes, Fifty-Second Meeting, October 20, 1947, and Fifty-Third Meeting, December 10, 1947, ABMC Records, entry 49, box 1.

36. ABMC Minutes, Fifty-Second Meeting, October 20, 1947; also see North, *One Soldier's Job,* 2:6–7, and ABMC pamphlet, "North African American Cemetery and Memorial," 19–20.

37. North, *One Soldier's Job,* 2:6.

38. Ibid., 2:7–8.

39. ABMC pamphlet, "Manila American Cemetery and Memorial," 9–10.

40. The North African American Cemetery rests on ground taken by British troops in 1943. The site of the Cambridge American Cemetery did not require liberation.

41. This information comes from the individual pamphlets on each cemetery published by the American Battle Monuments Commission.

42. Gene S. Dellinger, superintendent of Normandy American Cemetery, June 2001.

43. ABMC Minutes, Fifty-Fourth Meeting, February 16, 1948, ABMC Records, entry 49, box 1. Although the minutes did not indicate this, the commission now formally refers to all of its cemeteries as "American Cemetery and Memorial."

44. North, *One Soldier's Job,* 2:8.

45. Alexandre Renaud to Mrs. Theodore Roosevelt Jr., letter of May 30, 1954 (original), ABMC Records, entry 24, box 180. At the time Renaud wrote to Mrs. Roosevelt, she was a member of the American Battle Monuments Commission, appointed by President Eisenhower.

46. Joseph J. Shomon, *Crosses in the Wind: The Unheralded Saga of the Men in the American Graves Registration Service in World War Two* (New York: Stratford House, 1947), 149, available online at www.hathitrust. org.

47. General Larkin, quoted from Shomon, *Crosses in the Wind,* 154.

48. ABMC Minutes, Forty-Eighth Meeting, November 19, 1946.

49. Ibid.

50. Ron Robin, *Enclaves of America: The Rhetoric of American Political Architecture Abroad, 1965* (Princeton: Princeton Univ. Press, 1992), 110. Robin takes pains to argue that making burial in a permanent military cemetery overseas "Option 1" on the War Department questionnaire "blatantly suggested" to the families that this was "the most appropriate form for final rites." His charge that the "ABMC and its allies applied moral pressure on bereaved families" (111) is seriously weakened, however, by a string of factual errors and oversights in his account.

51. Schrijvers, *The Margraten Boys,* 63–68.

52. Ibid., 68–75.

53. North, *One Soldier's Job,* 4:1.

54. See "Report of Robert G. Woodside, Vice-Chairman," undated (original), enclosed with memorandum from Secretary North to General Marshall, GCM Papers, box 161, file 2.

55. See Secretary of the Army Frank Pace Jr. to George C. Marshall, memorandum of June 26, 1951 (copy), GCM Papers, box 197, file 27.

56. North, *One Soldier's Job,* 4:1.

57. See ABMC Minutes, Fifty-Fourth Meeting, February 16, 1948; Fifty-Fifth Meeting, May 24, 1948; Fifty-Seventh Meeting, January 26, 1949; Fifty-Eighth Meeting, May 4, 1949; and Sixtieth Meeting, March 29, 1950, ABMC Records, entry 49, box 1.

58. Thomas North, "Memorandum No. 138 to the Commission," March 24, 1950 (original), GCM Papers, box 164, file 17.

59. ABMC Minutes, Sixtieth Meeting, March 29, 1950.

60. North, *One Soldier's Job,* 4:2.

61. Ibid., 4:9.

62. Ibid., 4:3–7.

63. Ibid., 4:12–14.

64. See General George C. Marshall to General Nathan F. Twining, Air Force Chief of Staff, letter of December 10, 1954, GCM Papers, box 161, file 21; Twining to Marshall, letter and summary memorandum of April 5, 1955, GCM Papers, box 161, file 23; and Twining to Admiral Thomas C. Kinkaid, Vice Chairman of ABMC, letter of February 16, 1956, GCM Papers, box 161, file 26.

65. North, *One Soldier's Job,* 4:19.

66. Ibid., 4:11.

67. ABMC Minutes, Fifty-Fifth Meeting, May 24, 1948.

68. North, *One Soldier's Job,* 3:2.

69. Ibid., 3:1a–2; see also ABMC Minutes, Fifty-Eighth Meeting, May 4, 1949.

70. ABMC Minutes, Fifty-Eighth Meeting, May 4, 1949.

71. North, *One Soldier's Job,* 3:1a.

72. Ibid., 3:5–7.

73. ABMC Minutes, Fifty-Fifth Meeting, May 24, 1948.

74. ABMC Minutes, Fifty-Seventh Meeting, January 26, 1949.

75. ABMC Minutes, Fifty-Eighth Meeting, May 4, 1949.

76. ABMC Minutes, Fifty-First Meeting, June 5, 1947. See also "Rough Estimate of Cost of Cemeteries and Chapels, World War II," a memorandum Secretary North prepared for the fifty-first meeting, found in the archives of the ABMC headquarters, Arlington, Virginia, during a visit by the author on January 11, 2017.

77. See "Secretary's Report," November 21, 1956, which contained a list of the projected costs for each site, dated September 21, 1956, and reflecting funding authorized through FY 1957, also found in the headquarters archives.

78. See "Brief History of the American Battle Monuments Commission," undated and unsigned, but citing figures of appropriations authorized through FY 1962, also found in the ABMC headquarters archives.

79. ABMC Minutes, Sixty-First Meeting, October 24, 1950, ABMC Records, entry 49, box 1.

80. Thomas North, "Curtailment of ABMC Program by Budget Bureau," confidential memo for General Marshall, November 27, 1950 (original), GCM Papers, box 197, file 24.

81. George C. Marshall to F. J. Lawton, memorandum of December 7, 1950 (copy), GCM Papers, box 197, file 24.

82. Thomas North to George C. Marshall, confidential memo of December 13, 1950 (copy), GCM Papers, box 197, file 24.

83. Elmer B. Staats, Acting Director, Bureau of the Budget, to George C. Marshall, memorandum of June 26, 1951 (copy), GCM Papers, box 197, file 27.

84. Figures contained in Thomas North, "Memorandum to the Commission," July 18, 1951, GCM Papers, box 197, file 28.

85. Ibid.

86. George C. Marshall, "Memorandum for the Budget Director," September 6, 1951 (copy), GCM Papers, box 197, file 30.

87. See George C. Marshall to Harry Truman, letter of September 25, 1951 (with enclosure), GCM Papers, box 197, file 30.

88. Fred E. Busbey, "Report on Inspection of ABMC Sites" (copy), August 18, 1951, found in the ABMC headquarters archives.

89. Thomas North, "Memorandum for Members of the Commission," no. 147, March 13, 1951 (original), GCM Papers, box 161, file 3.

90. North to the Secretary of the Army, letter of February 14, 1951 (copy), GCM Papers, box 161, file 3.

91. Marshall to General Omar Bradley, letter of March 13, 1951 (original), GCM Papers, box 161, file 3.

92. Marshall to General Joseph T. McNarney, letter of March 16, 1951 (original), GCM Papers, box 161, file 3.

93. McNarney to Marshall, memorandum of March 21, 1951, GCM Papers, box 161, file 3.

94. Thomas North to ABMC Headquarters, Washington, D.C., telegram of October 1, 1951, GCM Papers, box 197, file 31.

95. George C. Marshall to Lawton Collins, letter of October 30, 1952 (copy), GCM Papers, box 236, file 45.

96. See Lieutenant Colonel Charles B. Shaw, Officer-in-Charge, Paris Office, "Memorandum for Major George," April 1, 1953 (original), GCM Papers, box 161, file 11.

97. See "Secretary's Report," November 21, 1956; also see ABMC Minutes, Sixty-First Meeting, October 24, 1950, and Sixty-Second Meeting, November 8, 1951, ABMC Records, entry 49, box 1.

98. See "Dedication of First World War II Memorial," undated memorandum by Thomas North, in GCM Papers, box 161, file 45; also see "Suresnes American Cemetery and Memorial," ABMC pamphlet, 5–12.

99. ABMC Minutes, Sixty-Second Meeting, November 8, 1951.

100. North to Marshall, memo of February 6, 1952 (original), GCM Papers, box 164, file 1.

101. Marshall to Major General James L. Bennett, Army Chief of Chaplains, letter of July 28, 1952 (copy), GCM Papers, box 161, file 42.

102. All of these quotes come from the elaborate and thorough album of press reports and other memorabilia of the Suresnes ceremony compiled for the ABMC archives at General Marshall's direction, exactly as General Pershing had instructed for the 1937 dedications. See ABMC Records, box 174.

103. Quoted in "Marshall: U.S. Will Not 'Go Home' until Freedom Abroad Is Secure," *New York Herald Tribune* (European edition), September 15, 1952, ABMC Records, box 174. The State Department communicated its counsel for the general's speech in "Suggestions for General Marshall's Statement at Dedication of Suresnes Cemetery," with cover letter from Acting Secretary David Bruce, August 13, 1952, GCM Papers, box 161, file 43.

104. Quoted from the text of the speech in *Stars and Stripes,* September 14, 1952.

105. ABMC Minutes, Sixty-Third Meeting, December 5, 1952, ABMC Records, entry 49, box 1. Another highlight of Marshall's participation in the Suresnes dedication was his presentation of the "Medal of Freedom" to a number of European employees of the Paris office who had served so courageously during the years of German occupation. See the relevant reference in ABMC Minutes, Sixty-Fourth Meeting, September 3, 1953.

106. George C. Marshall to Mrs. Mary McConnell Addington, letter of January 16, 1956 (copy), GCM Papers, box 161, file 26.

107. ABMC Minutes, Sixty-Third Meeting, December 5, 1952.

108. Eisenhower to George C. Marshall, letter of April 27, 1953 (original), GCM Papers, box 161, file 12.

109. The new members, save one, were presented at the sixty-fourth meeting of the commission on September 3, 1953. See ABMC Records, entry 49, box 1. Joseph Foss was not present on that occasion, and never did attend any meetings. His resignation from the commission was announced at the sixty-seventh meeting on December 9, 1954.

110. Marshall had noted this direction to his aide on the letter from North, dated January 7, 1954 (original), informing him of the secretary of defense's intention. See GCM Papers, box 161, file 18.

111. Eisenhower to Marshall, letter of February 4, 1954 (original), GCM Papers, box 161, file 18.

112. Secretary of War Robert P. Patterson, speech of April 4, 1946, quoted from ABMC chairman to the Secretary of Defense, letter of May 16, 1949 (copy), GCM Papers, box 161, file 1.

113. Louis Johnson, memorandum to the American Battle Monuments Commission, April 30, 1949 (copy), GCM Papers, box 161, file 1.

114. ABMC Minutes, Fifty-Fourth Meeting, February 16, 1948.

115. ABMC Minutes, Fifty-Fifth Meeting, May 24, 1948.

116. Marshall to Johnson, letter of May 16, 1949.

117. ABMC Minutes, Fifty-Ninth Meeting, November 9, 1949, ABMC Records, entry 49, box 1.

118. Thomas North to General Marshall, letter of June 5, 1950 (copy), GCM Papers, box 161, file 3.

119. R. Warren Davis to Officer-in-Charge, Paris Office, March 9, 1951 (original), GCM Papers, box 197, file 25.

120. ABMC Minutes, Sixty-Seventh Meeting, December 9, 1954, ABMC Records, entry 49, box 1.

121. Theodore Roosevelt to Colonel Charles G. Pierce, letter of November 2, 1918 (copy), ABMC Records, entry 24, box 180.

122. Ethel R. Derby (Quentin Roosevelt's sister) to General Thomas North, letter of February 1959 (original), ABMC Records, entry 24, box 180.

123. Robert P. Patterson to Archibald Roosevelt, letter of October 16, 1946 (copy), ABMC Records, entry 24, box 180.

124. Kenneth C. Royall, Secretary of the Army, to Archibald Roosevelt, letter of March 25, 1948 (copy), ABMC Records, entry 24, box 180.

125. Mrs. Eleanor B. Roosevelt to General North, letter of June 4, 1954 (orig-

inal), and Archibald Roosevelt to General North, letter of March 17, 1955 (original), ABMC Records, entry 24, box 180.

126. ABMC Minutes, Sixty-Eighth Meeting, April 6, 1955, ABMC Records, entry 49, box 1.

127. Thomas North to Archibald Roosevelt, letter of July 27, 1955 (copy), ABMC Records, entry 24, box 180.

128. Mr. Daniel Gibbs, "Report on Transfer of Body of Lt. Quentin Roosevelt from Coulonges-en-Tardenois (Aisne) to the Normandy Cemetery," September 1955, ABMC Records, entry 24, box 180. Contrary to an erroneous claim in a recent biography of General Theodore Roosevelt Jr., Quentin's body never rested side by side with his brother in a cemetery in Sainte-Mère-Église. See Tim Brady, *His Father's Son: The Life of General Ted Roosevelt, Jr.* (New York: New American Library, 2017), 305–6.

129. General North to Colonel Jack Mage, Officer-in-Charge, ABMC Paris Office, confidential letter of April 12, 1955 (copy), ABMC Records, entry 24, box 180.

130. "Normandy American Cemetery and Memorial," ABMC pamphlet, 8–10.

131. ABMC Minutes, Fifty-Seventh Meeting, January 26, 1949.

132. Ibid.

133. ABMC Minutes, Sixtieth Meeting, March 29, 1950.

134. George C. Marshall to Ambassador H. Freeman Matthews, letter of March 10, 1955 (copy), and Colonel C. J. George to General Marshall, letter of March 2, 1955 (original), GCM Papers, box 161, file 23. See also ABMC Minutes, Sixty-Eighth Meeting, April 6, 1955.

135. Marshall to H. Freeman Matthews, letter of April 15, 1955 (copy), GCM Papers, box 161, file 23.

136. ABMC Minutes, Sixty-Eighth Meeting, April 6, 1955.

137. North, *One Soldier's Job,* 3:12–13. For information about the history of graves adoption at Margraten and stories of the innumerable transatlantic relationships that have grown out of it, see the website of the Dutch organization that administers the program: www.adoptiegraven-margraten.nl.

138. ABMC Minutes, Fifty-Seventh Meeting, January 26, 1949.

139. Ibid.

140. ABMC Minutes, Sixty-Fifth Meeting, December 11, 1953, ABMC Records, entry 49, box 1.

141. ABMC Minutes, Sixty-Seventh Meeting, December 9, 1954.

142. ABMC Minutes, Sixty-Eighth Meeting, April 6, 1955.

143. "Honolulu Memorial, National Memorial Cemetery of the Pacific," ABMC pamphlet, 4–5, 12–24.

144. Ibid., 3. Also see the souvenir album of the dedications, ABMC Records, box 176.

145. ABMC Minutes, Fifty-Eighth Meeting, May 4, 1949.

146. ABMC Minutes, Sixty-Ninth Meeting, December 15, 1955, ABMC Records, entry 49, box 1.

147. Thomas North to Percival Brundage, Director, Bureau of the Budget, letter of January 14, 1957, in "Secretary's Report [to the Commission]," November 26, 1957, in the ABMC headquarters archives.

148. Secretary of the Navy to Thomas North, letter of February 27, 1956, quoted from "Secretary's Report," November 26, 1957, in the ABMC headquarters archives.

149. "Secretary's Report," November 26, 1957, in the ABMC headquarters archives. Also see North, *One Soldier's Job*, 9:8.

150. ABMC Minutes, Seventy-Third Meeting, December 10, 1957, ABMC Records, entry 49, box 1.

151. ABMC Minutes, Sixty-Ninth Meeting, December 15, 1955.

152. ABMC Minutes, Seventieth Meeting, April 12, 1956, ABMC Records, entry 49, box 1.

153. See "Dedicatory Album" for 1956, ABMC Records, box 174.

154. Thomas Kinkaid to George C. Marshall, memorandum of September 25, 1956 (copy), ABMC Records, box 174.

155. "Our War Memorials Abroad," 747. This portion of the article was written by Howell Walker of the *National Geographic* staff, who attended all six dedications in 1956.

156. Quoted from Kinkaid to Marshall, memorandum of September 25, 1956.

157. ABMC Minutes, Seventy-First Meeting, December 18, 1956, ABMC Records, entry 49, box 1.

158. ABMC Records, box 175, contains the album of important memorabilia from each of the 1960 dedications.

159. See ABMC Minutes, Forty-Fourth Meeting, August 13, 1937, ABMC Records, entry 2, box 1A, and ABMC Minutes, Meeting of July 1, 1960 (unnumbered), ABMC Records, entry 49, box 1.

160. ABMC Minutes, Seventy-Ninth Meeting, December 9, 1960, ABMC Records, entry 49, box 1.

161. "In Proud Remembrance: American Memorials and Military Cemeteries of World War II," *National Sculpture Review* 14, no. 1 (1965): 9.

162. Ibid., 10.

163. Ibid., 12.

164. Ibid., 8.

165. Ibid., 6, 14, 15, 16, 17. Eisenhower's words are quoted from a foreword to the article entitled "A Salute from the Allied Supreme Commander."

166. Ibid., 7, 9, 12, 24.

167. Victor Davis Hanson, conversation with the author, Hillsdale, Michigan, September 1, 2017.

168. Eisenhower, quoted from "In Proud Remembrance," 6.

169. Robert Woodside, "Memorandum to Each officer and employee connected with the American Battle Monuments Commission in Europe and the Mediterranean areas," July 27, 1949 (copy), in ABMC Records, box 133.

Conclusion

1. ABMC Annual Report for 1965, ABMC Records, entry 48, box 1. Since the agency's founding, annual reports have appeared sporadically. After the first three years (1924–26), which saw a report for each, the habit of compiling such documents every year did not resume until 1969, when a report was issued during the final month of General Devers's service as chairman. The 1965 report numbered only four pages and was sent to the president of the United States on August 16 of that year.

2. "Secretary's Report," in ABMC Annual Report for 2016, page 1.

3. ABMC Annual Report for 1965.

4. James Scott Wheeler, *Jacob L. Devers: A General's Life* (Lexington: Univ. Press of Kentucky, 2015), 2.

5. ABMC Minutes, Sixty-Sixth Meeting, March 18, 1954, ABMC Records, entry 49, box 1.

6. The albums with photos, newspaper accounts, and memorabilia from all three of the large monument dedications are in ABMC Records, box 176.

7. Devers to Eisenhower, letter of March 26, 1968 (original), Eisenhower Post-Presidential Papers (hereafter "DDE Post-Presidential Papers"), Eisenhower Library, Abilene, Kansas, Augusta-Walter Reed Series, box 1.

8. Eisenhower to Devers, letter of April 3, 1968 (copy), DDE Post-Presidential Papers, Augusta-Walter Reed Series, box 1.

9. Eisenhower to Lyndon B. Johnson, letter of April 3, 1968 (copy), DDE Post-Presidential Papers, Augusta-Walter Reed Series, box 1.

10. Johnson to Eisenhower, letter of April 13, 1968 (original), DDE Post-Presidential Papers, Augusta-Walter Reed Series, box 1.

11. ABMC Minutes, Eighty-Sixth Meeting, June 7, 1968, ABMC Records, entry 49, box 1. Senator Charles Potter was the commissioner who expressed support for the idea that jurisdiction over the cemeteries abroad should be transferred to the Veterans Administration. Representative T. C. Connell, who had been sworn in earlier in the meeting to fill the vacancy created by General Vandegrift's resignation, observed presciently that Chairman Teague would work against final enactment of the legislation. A thorough summary of this episode

can be found in "History of the American Battle Monuments Commission during the Administration of President Lyndon B. Johnson," a draft report submitted to the White House under cover letter from Secretary Andrew J. Adams to Matthew Nimetz, August 29, 1968, in ABMC Records, entry 49, box 1.

12. See Johnson to Eisenhower, letter of February 22, 1968 (original), DDE Post-Presidential Papers, Augusta-Walter Reed Series, box 1, for LBJ's "thank you" note for the Eisenhowers' hospitality four days earlier.

13. See ABMC Minutes, Eighty-Sixth Meeting, June 7, 1968, for the formal introduction of Secretary Adams by General Devers. As it turned out, this would be Devers's final meeting, and the full commission would not reconvene until February 1970, more than a year into the Nixon administration.

14. William P. Jones Jr., "Service with the American Battle Monuments Commission, 1 April 1967 to 30 June 1974," page 3, William P. Jones Papers, Military History Institute (hereafter "MHI"), Carlisle, Pennsylvania. Jones served during the indicated years as assistant to the secretary of the commission, first under North, and ultimately under Adams, and left the cited document as a memoir.

15. Major George C. Marshall to Adjutant General of the Army, letter of July 1, 1920, Thomas North Papers, MHI. In this letter, Marshall was recommending North, a native of England, for a permanent commission as an officer in the US Army.

16. Marshall to Adjutant General of the Army, letter of June 24, 1953, Thomas North Papers, MHI. This document was Marshall's annual "Efficiency Report" for North.

17. Eisenhower to North, letter of June 13, 1966 (original), Thomas North Papers, MHI.

18. Jones, "Service with the American Battle Monuments Commission," 3.

19. Obituary for Major General Thomas North, *Washington Post,* June 28, 1990, enclosed with Jones to Richard Sommers, Archivist-Historian, US Army Military History Institute, letter of June 28, 1990, Thomas North Papers, MHI.

20. A. J. Adams, "Memorandum for the Record on President Nixon's meeting with the American Battle Monuments Commission 16 February 1970," February 17, 1970, ABMC Records, entry 49, box 1.

21. Martin Blumenson, *Mark Clark: The Last of the Great World War II Commanders* (New York: Congdon and Weed, 1984), 279.

22. Mark W. Clark to President Richard Nixon, telegram of May 4, 1970 (copy), ABMC Records, entry 49, box 1.

23. Clark to the president, letter of November 27, 1970 (copy), Annex D to the Minutes of the Eighty-Eighth Meeting, November 17, 1970, ABMC Records, entry 49, box 1.

24. See ABMC Minutes, Ninety-First Meeting, November 14, 1972, ABMC Records, entry 49, box 1, for a report that these engravings had been completed for the World War II headstones, at a cost of $9,000, and would be finished for the World War I headstones during FY 1973.

25. ABMC Minutes, Fifty-Eighth Meeting, May 4, 1949. George Washington was elevated posthumously to the exalted rank in 1976.

26. ABMC Minutes, Ninety-First Meeting, November 14, 1972.

27. See "Progress Report on the Pershing Memorial," no date, attached to the ABMC Minutes, Ninety-Second Meeting, May 1, 1973, ABMC Records, entry 49, box 1.

28. ABMC Minutes, Ninety-Ninth Meeting, November 30, 1977, ABMC Records, entry 49, box 1.

29. American Battle Monuments Commission, "Commemorative Sites Booklet" (August 2015), 40.

30. Happily, an excellent monograph tells the story of the World War II Memorial, and the role of the ABMC in it, in great depth, and also contains a substantive account of the creation of the Korean War Memorial. See Nicolaus Mills, *Their Last Battle: The Fight for the National World War II Memorial* (New York: Basic Books, 2004).

31. See ABMC Annual Report for 1969, page 16, and subsequent reports for each of the years between 1970 and 1984, in ABMC Records, entry 48, box 1.

32. The visitor figures began to be itemized for each of the cemeteries in the annual report for 1976. In the reports for 1982 and the two subsequent years the data ceased to be specific for total visitation and only gave figures for the Memorial Day attendance. While the data on visitorship in the annual reports of the Clark years is interesting, there is good reason to be skeptical of the accuracy of the numbers. The commission acknowledges today the difficulty of collecting such data and no longer publishes it.

33. See Lou Cannon, *President Reagan: The Role of a Lifetime* (New York: Simon and Schuster, 1991), 483–85. The text of the president's speech from June 6, 1984, is engraved on bronze tablets that now line the pathway to the Pointe du Hoc. A particularly memorable phrase from that speech is: "Soon, one by one, the Rangers pulled themselves over the top, and in seizing the firm land at the top of these cliffs, they began to seize back the continent of Europe."

34. Douglas Brinkley, *The Boys of Pointe du Hoc: Ronald Reagan, D-Day, and the U.S. Army 2nd Ranger Battalion* (New York: William Morrow, 2005), 7.

35. Cannon, *President Reagan*, 485. In my own experience, I know that I have seen more grown men shed tears in Normandy than anywhere else I have ever been.

36. Rivers to General Dickey, email of September 12, 1997, Archives of the Normandy American Cemetery (hereafter NOAC Archives).

37. Rivers to Walter Frankland, letter of September 22, 1997, NOAC Archives.

38. Steven Spielberg, quote in *Normandie Magazine* 148 (September–October 1998), NOAC Archives.

39. "Interviews with Tom Hanks and Steven Spielberg," *Ciné Live* magazine (September 1998), 48–49, NOAC Archives.

40. See Charles Truehart, "'Private Ryan' Launches New Normandy Invasion," *Washington Post,* October 21, 1998, NOAC Archives.

41. Gene S. Dellinger, then superintendent at the Normandy American Cemetery, provided me with this account during several conversations in 2001 and 2002.

42. "Program for the Groundbreaking Ceremony for the Normandy American Visitors and Interpretive Center," August 28, 2004, NOAC Archives.

43. Ibid.

44. Dwight Anderson, interview with the author at the Normandy American Cemetery, October 15, 2010.

45. Mills, *Their Last Battle,* 201.

46. Dwight Anderson, interview with the author at the Normandy American Cemetery, October 15, 2010.

Selected Bibliography

Archival Sources

American Battle Monuments Commission
Headquarters Archives, Arlington, Virginia
European Office Archives, Garches, France
Archives of the Normandy American Cemetery, Colleville-sur-Mer, France

Eisenhower Library, Abilene, Kansas

Eisenhower, Dwight David, Pre-Presidential Papers and Post-Presidential Papers.
Flemming, Arthur, Papers.
McCann, Kevin, Papers.

Library of Congress, Manuscripts Division, Washington, D.C.

Pershing, John Joseph, Papers.

Marshall Library, Lexington, Virginia

Goodpaster, Andrew, Papers.
Marshall, George C., Papers.

Military History Institute, Carlisle, Pennsylvania

Jones, William P., Jr., Papers.
North, Thomas, Papers.

National Archives and Records Administration, Washington, D.C.

RG 66, Records of the Commission of Fine Arts.

National Archives and Records Administration, College Park, Maryland

RG 92, Records of the Office of the Quartermaster General.
RG 117, Records of the American Battle Monuments Commission.

Interviews with ABMC Personnel

Aarnio, Jeffrey—May 2009 and October 2010 (Oise-Aisne American Cemetery); May 2011 (Brittany American Cemetery).

Amelinckx, Alan—May 2010 (Brittany American Cemetery); October 2010 (Ardennes American Cemetery); July 2014 (Normandy American Cemetery).

Anderson, Dwight—May 2010 (Normandy American Cemetery).

Aske, Lou—October 2010 (Flanders Field American Cemetery); May 2017 (Henri-Chapelle American Cemetery).

Atkinson, David—May 2009, October 2010, and July 2015 (Aisne-Marne Cemetery).

Bedford, David—May 2011 (Meuse-Argonne American Cemetery).

Bell, Bobby—May 2009 (Saint Mihiel American Cemetery); October 2010 and May 2017 (Henri-Chapelle American Cemetery).

Benjamin, Walter—May 2009 (Lorraine American Cemetery); October 2010 (Somme American Cemetery); July 2015 (Brittany American Cemetery).

Conley, Michael G.—At least once a year since October 2008 at ABMC Headquarters, Arlington, Virginia.

Coonce, Michael—October 2010 (Saint Mihiel American Cemetery).

Dellinger, Gene S.—At least once a year since 2000 at the Normandy American Cemetery, or in his home in Bayeux, France.

Desjardins, Scott—October 2010 (Luxembourg American Cemetery).

Didiot, Dominique—May 2009 (Meuse-Argonne American Cemetery).

Dufrenne (Castier), Murielle—May 2009, May 2010, and October 2010 (Somme American Cemetery).

Ezz-Eddine, Nadia—October 2010 and July 2013 (Saint Mihiel American Cemetery).

Ferrand, Anaele—May 2010 and July 2013 (European Office, Garches, France).

Green, Michael—May 2011 (Cambridge American Cemetery).

Hays, Jeffrey—June 2017 (Saint Mihiel American Cemetery).

Hooker, Hans—May 2009 (Luxembourg American Cemetery); October 2010 (Normandy American Cemetery).

Lahaye, Frenk—October 2010 (Netherlands American Cemetery).

Malone, Bruce—October 2010 (Lorraine American Cemetery); July 2015 (Brittany American Cemetery).

Neese, Dan—May 2010 (Normandy American Cemetery).

O'Dell, Derrick—May 2011 (Brookwood American Cemetery).

Rahanian, Craig—May 2009 (Somme American Cemetery); May 2011 (Brookwood American Cemetery).

Rivers, Joseph P. ("Phil")—October 2010 (Meuse-Argonne American Cemetery).

Sims, Chris—October 2010 (Flanders Field American Cemetery).
Stadler, Keith—October 2010 (Netherlands American Cemetery).
Thompson, Horace—May 2010 (Brittany American Cemetery).
Williams, Shane—October 2010 and May 2011 (Normandy American Cemetery).
Woolsey, James—May 2010 (European Office, Garches, France).

ABMC Sites Visited

World War I

Aisne-Marne Cemetery, May 2009; October 2010; July 2015; June 2017.
Brookwood Cemetery, May 2011.
Flanders Field Cemetery, October 2010.
Meuse-Argonne Cemetery, May 2009; October 2010; May 2012; July 2015; June 2017.
Oise-Aisne Cemetery, May 2009; October 2010; June 2013.
Saint-Mihiel Cemetery, May 2009; October 2010; May 2011; May 2012; July 2013; June 2017.
Somme Cemetery, May 2009; May 2010; October 2010.
Suresnes Cemetery, May 2008.

AEF Monument, Washington, D.C., January 2014; January 2015; March 2017.
Bellicourt Monument, May 2010; July 2013.
Brest Monument, July 2015.
Cantigny Monument, June 2012.
Château-Thierry Monument, May 2009; October 2010; July 2015.
Marine Corps Monument, Belleau Wood, June 2017.
Montfaucon Monument, May 2009; October 2010; May 2011.
Montsec Monument, October 2010; June 2017.
Sommepy Monument, October 2010; July 2015.
Tours Monument, July 2013.

World War II

Ardennes Cemetery, October 2010.
Brittany Cemetery, May 2011; July 2015.
Cambridge Cemetery, May 2011.
Épinal Cemetery, May 2011.
Henri-Chapelle Cemetery, October 2010; May 2017.
Lorraine Cemetery, May 2009; October 2010; May 2012.
Luxembourg Cemetery, May 2009; October 2010.

Netherlands Cemetery, October 2010; May 2017.
Normandy Cemetery, May 2009; July 2010; October 2010; May 2011; July 2011; July 2012; July 2013; July 2014; July 2015; July 2016; June 2017; July 2017.
Sicily-Rome Cemetery, May 2012.

East Coast Memorial, April 2015; April 2017.
Pointe du Hoc, at least once every year since 2004.
Utah Beach, at least once every year since 2004.

Books and Articles

Adams, John A. *General Jacob Devers: World War II's Forgotten Four Star*. Bloomington: Indiana Univ. Press, 2015.

Ambrose, Stephen E. *Eisenhower: Soldier, General of the Army, President-Elect, 1890–1952*. New York: Simon and Schuster, 1983.

American Battle Monuments Commission. *A Guide to the American Battle Fields of Europe*. Washington, D.C.: Government Printing Office, 1927.

———. *American Armies and Battlefields in Europe*. Washington, D.C.: Government Printing Office, 1938.

Bailey, Thomas A. *Woodrow Wilson and the Lost Peace*. New York: Macmillan, 1944.

Berg, A. Scott. *Wilson*. New York: G. P. Putnam's Sons, 2013.

Blumenson, Martin. *Mark Clark: The Last of the Great World War II Commanders*. New York: Congdon and Weed, 1984.

Bouchet, Ceil Miller. "Over There: A Hundred Years after the Start of World War I, the Yanks Are Coming Again." *National Geographic Traveler* (May 2014), 46–55.

Brady, Tim. *His Father's Son: The Life of General Ted Roosevelt, Jr.* New York: New American Library, 2017.

Brinkley, Douglas. *The Boys of Pointe du Hoc: Ronald Reagan, D-Day, and the U.S. Army 2nd Ranger Battalion*. New York: Morrow, 2005.

Brokaw, Tom. *The Greatest Generation*. New York: Random House, 1998.

Brownell, Will, and Richard N. Billings. *So Close to Greatness: A Biography of William C. Bullitt*. New York: Macmillan, 1987.

Budreau, Lisa M. *Bodies of War: World War I and the Politics of Commemoration in America, 1919–1933*. New York: New York Univ. Press, 2010.

Bullitt, Orville H., ed. *For the President, Personal and Secret: Correspondence between Franklin D. Roosevelt and William C. Bullitt*. Boston: Houghton Mifflin, 1972.

Cannon, Lou. *President Reagan: The Role of a Lifetime*. New York: Simon and Schuster, 1991.

Carroll, Andrew. *My Fellow Soldiers: General John Pershing and the Americans Who Helped Win the Great War*. New York: Penguin Press, 2017.

Clout, Hugh. *After the Ruins: Restoring the Countryside of Northern France after the Great War*. Exeter, UK: Univ. of Exeter Press, 1996.

Cooper, John Milton. *Woodrow Wilson: A Biography*. New York: Knopf, 2009.

Crane, David. *Empires of the Dead: How One Man's Vision Led to the Creation of WWI's War Graves*. London: William Collins, 2013.

Cray, Ed. *General of the Army: George C. Marshall, Soldier and Statesman*. New York: Norton, 1990.

Dessente, Ferdinand M. *Les Cimitières militaires de Neuville-en-Condroz*. Neupré, Belgium: Alpha and Omega, 1997.

D'Este, Carlo. *Eisenhower: A Soldier's Life*. New York: Holt, 2002.

Dodge, George W. *Arlington National Cemetery*. Charleston, S.C.: Arcadia Publishing, 2006.

Dupont, Karen Dellinger. *ABMC—American Memorials in France, in Particular that of Normandy*. Unpublished Thesis, University of Paris III, 1981.

Eisenhower, Dwight D. *At Ease: Stories I Tell to Friends*. New York: Doubleday, 1967.

Fussell, Paul. *The Great War and Modern Memory*. Oxford, UK: Oxford Univ. Press, 1975.

Gilbert, Martin. *The First World War: A Complete History*. New York: Holt, 1994.

———. *The Second World War: A Complete History*, rev. ed. New York: Holt, 1989.

Glass, Charles. *Americans in Paris: Life and Death under Nazi Occupation*. New York: Penguin Press, 2010.

Goldhurst, Richard. *Pipe Clay and Drill: John J. Pershing, the Classic American Soldier*. New York: Reader's Digest Press, 1977.

Graham, John W. *The Gold Star Mother Pilgrimages of the 1930s*. Jefferson, N.C.: McFarland, 2005.

Gregory, Adrian. *The Silence of Memory: Armistice Day, 1919–46*. Oxford, UK: Berg, 1994.

Griffiths, Richard. *Pétain: A Biography of Marshall Philippe Pétain of Vichy*. Garden City, N.Y.: Doubleday, 1972.

Grossman, Elizabeth G. "Architecture for a Public Client: The Monuments and Chapels of the American Battle Monuments Commission." *Journal of the Society of Architectural Historians* 43, no. 2 (May 1984): 119–43.

Hamilton, Nigel. *Bill Clinton: Mastering the Presidency*. New York: Perseus Books, 2007.

Hanson, Neil. *Unknown Soldiers: The Story of the Missing of the First World War*. New York: Knopf, 2006.

Harries, Meirion, and Susie Harries. *The Last Days of Innocence: America at War, 1917–1918.* New York: Vintage Books, 1998.

Hayes, Ralph. *The Care of the Fallen: A Report to the Secretary of War on American Military Dead Overseas.* Washington, D.C.: Government Printing Office, 1920.

Heckscher, August. *Woodrow Wilson: A Biography.* New York: Charles Scribner's Sons, 1991.

Hernon, Peter. *The Great Rescue: American Heroes, An Iconic Ship, and the Race to Save Europe in World War I.* New York: HarperCollins, 2017.

Hill, A. W. "Our Soldiers' Graves." Pamphlet. London: H.M. Stationery Office, 1920.

Horne, Alistair. *To Lose a Battle: France, 1940.* London: Penguin, 1979.

Keegan, John. *The Second World War.* New York: Viking, 1989.

Kent, George. "Not Far from God." *Readers Digest* 82, no. 494 (June 1963), 236–40.

Kolb, Richard K. "Keeping Alive the Memory of the Doughboy." *VFW Magazine* 95, no. 11 (August 2008), 18–26.

Langer, William L. *Our Vichy Gamble.* New York: Knopf, 1947.

Lebastard, Constant. *Le Cimitière Américain de Colleville-sur-Mer: Une Commission Américaine en Normandie.* Bayeux, France: OREP Editions, 2012.

Lengel, Edward G. *To Conquer Hell: The Meuse-Argonne, 1918.* New York: Holt, 2008.

Link, Arthur S., ed. *The Papers of Woodrow Wilson.* 69 vols. Princeton: Princeton Univ. Press, 1966–94.

Lisle, Naomi Lucille. "An American Girl in France." *Lutheran Youth* 26, no. 23 (June 5, 1938), 4–6.

Lloyd, David W. *Battlefield Tourism: Pilgrimage and the Commemoration of the Great War in Britain, Australia and Canada, 1919–1939.* Oxford, UK: Berg, 1998.

Longworth, Philip. *The Unending Vigil: A History of the Commonwealth War Graves Commission, 1917–1967.* London: Constable, 1967.

Lorcin, Patricia M. E., and Daniel Brewer, eds. *France and Its Spaces of War: Experience, Memory, Image.* New York: Palgrave Macmillan, 2009.

Lottman, Herbert R. *The Fall of Paris, June 1940.* New York: Harper Collins, 1992.

———. *Pétain: Hero or Traitor: The Untold Story.* New York: Morrow, 1985.

Lowdermilk, Jeffrey A. *Saluting America's World War I Heroes: Armistice Day, Meuse-Argonne (France).* Santa Fe, N.Mex.: J. Lowdermilk, 2008.

MacCloskey, Monro. *Hallowed Ground: Our National Cemeteries.* New York: Richards Rosen Press, 1968.

Macmillan, Margaret. *Paris 1919: Six Months that Changed the World*. New York: Random House, 2003.
Marshall, George C. "Our War Memorials Abroad: A Faith Kept." *National Geographic Magazine* 111, no. 6 (June 1957), 731–35.
Mayo, James M. *War Memorials as Political Landscape: The American Experience and Beyond*. New York: Praeger, 1988.
Mee, Charles L., Jr. *The End of Order: Versailles, 1919*. New York: Dutton, 1980.
Mills, Nicolaus. *Their Last Battle: The Fight for the National World War II Memorial*. New York: Basic Books, 2004.
Moore, Charles. "The American Cemeteries in Europe." *Daughters of the American Revolution Magazine* 57, no. 12 (December 1923), 728–34.
———. "War Memorials Bad and Good." *American Legion Weekly* 4, no. 36 (September 8, 1922), 14–16.
Morris, Edmund. *Colonel Roosevelt*. New York: Random House, 2011.
Mosse, George L. *Fallen Soldiers: Reshaping the Memory of the World Wars*. Oxford, UK: Oxford Univ. Press, 1990.
Mott, T. Bentley. *Myron T. Herrick, Friend of France: An Autobiographical Biography*. Garden City, N.Y.: Doubleday, Doran, 1929.
———. *Twenty Years as Military Attaché*. New York: Oxford Univ. Press, 1937.
Nicholson, J. W. "Off the Beaten Path." *Army: The Magazine of the Association of the United States Army* 55, no. 11 (November 2005), 40–42, 44.
North, Thomas. *One Soldier's Job*. Unpublished, undated memoir in the possession of the ABMC headquarters.
Palmer, Frederick. *John J. Pershing, General of the Armies: A Biography*. 1948. Reprint, Westport, Conn.: Greenwood Press, 1970.
Paxton, Robert O. *Vichy France: Old Guard and New Order*. 1972. Reprint, New York: Columbia Univ. Press, 2001.
Pershing, John J. "Our National War Memorials in Europe." *National Geographic Magazine* 65, no. 1 (January 1934), 1–36.
Piehler, G. Kurt. *Remembering War the American Way*. Washington, D.C.: Smithsonian Institution Press, 1995.
Pogue, Forrest C. *George C. Marshall: Education of a General, 1880–1939*. New York: Viking Press, 1963.
———. *George C. Marshall: Organizer of Victory, 1943–1945*. New York: Viking Press, 1973.
———. *George C. Marshall: Statesman, 1945–1959*. New York: Viking Press, 1987.
Polenberg, Richard. *Reorganizing Roosevelt's Government, 1936–1939: The Controversy over Executive Reorganization*. Cambridge, Mass.: Harvard Univ. Press, 1966.

Poole, Robert M. *On Hallowed Ground: The Story of Arlington National Cemetery.* New York: Walker, 2009.

Robin, Ron. *Enclaves of America: The Rhetoric of American Political Architecture Abroad, 1900–1965.* Princeton: Princeton Univ. Press, 1992.

Roze, Anne. *Fields of Memory: A Testimony to the Great War.* London: Cassell, 1999.

Schrijvers, Peter. *The Margraten Boys: How a European Village Kept America's Liberators Alive.* London: Palgrave Macmillan, 2012.

Shomon, Joseph J. *Crosses in the Wind: The Unheralded Saga of the Men in the American Graves Registration Service in World War Two.* New York: Stratford House, 1947. Available online at www.hathitrust. org.

Sledge, Michael. *Soldier Dead: How We Recover, Identify, Bury, and Honor Our Military Fallen.* New York: Columbia Univ. Press, 2005.

Smith, Gene. *Still Quiet on the Western Front Fifty Years Later.* New York: Morrow, 1965.

———. *Until the Last Trumpet Sounds: The Life of General of the Armies John J Pershing.* New York: Wiley and Sons, 1998.

Smythe, Donald. *Pershing: General of the Armies.* Bloomington: Indiana Univ. Press, 1986.

Snell, Mark A., ed. *Unknown Soldiers: The American Expeditionary Forces in Memory and Remembrance.* Kent, Ohio: Kent State Univ. Press, 2008.

Stamp, Gavin. *The Memorial to the Missing of the Somme.* London: Profile Books, 2006.

Steere, Edward, and Thayer M. Boardman. *Final Disposition of World War II Dead, 1945–51.* Washington, D.C.: Historical Branch Office of the Quartermaster General, 1957.

Summers, Julie. *Remembered: The History of the Commonwealth War Graves Commission.* London: Merrell, 2007.

Trout, Steven. *On the Battlefield of Memory: The First World War and American Remembrance, 1919–41.* Tuscaloosa: Univ. of Alabama Press, 2010.

Uluaslan, Huseyin. *Gallipoli Campaign.* Istanbul: Keskin Color, 2000.

US Army Graves Registration Service. *History of the American Graves Registration Service.* 3 vols. Washington, D.C.: US Army Graves Registration Service, 1921.

VanDiver, Frank E. *Black Jack: The Life and Times of John J. Pershing.* 2 vols. College Station: Texas A&M Univ. Press, 1977.

Van Duyne, Frederick W. "Erection of Permanent Headstones in the American Military Cemeteries in Europe." *Quartermaster Review* (January–February 1930).

Verleyen, Herwig. *In Flanders Fields: The Story of John McCrae, His Poem, and the Poppy.* Kortrijk, Belgium: Groeninghe Printing, 1995.

Walker, Howell. "Here Rest in Honored Glory: The United States Dedicates Six New Battle Monuments in Europe to Americans Who Gave Their Lives during World War II." *National Geographic Magazine* 111, no. 6 (June 1957), 739–68.

Ware, Fabian. *The Immortal Heritage: An Account of the Work and Policy of the Imperial War Graves Commission during Twenty Years, 1917–1937.* Cambridge, UK: Cambridge Univ. Press, 1937.

Wheeler, James Scott. *Jacob L. Devers: A General's Life.* Lexington: Univ. Press of Kentucky, 2015.

Winter, Jay. *Sites of Memory, Sites of Mourning: The Great War in European Cultural History.* Cambridge, UK: Cambridge Univ. Press, 1995.

Yockelson, Mitchell A. *Borrowed Soldiers: Americans under British Command, 1918.* Norman: Univ. of Oklahoma Press, 2008.

Index

Adams, Andrew J., 3, 9, 225, 301–2n11, 302nn13–14
AEF Memorial. *See* American Expeditionary Forces Memorial
Aisne-Marne battle, 88, 101, 105, 108, 268n54
Aisne-Marne cemetery, 250n64, 261–62n91, 270n96; chapel at, 85, 87–91, 92, 93, 94, 153–54, 156, 187, 192, 266n19, 293n31; chapel dedication and, 127; grave numbers at, 29, 87, 134; land acquisition for, 28, 249n60; location, 23, 24, 27; monument on grounds of, 62, 88, 95; visitors to, 81, 104–5, 192, 229; after World War II, 187, 290n18, 293n31; World War II and, 150, 153–54, 156, 157–58, 163, 172, 187, 289n114, 293n31. *See also* Belleau Wood, France; Château-Thierry monument
Aisne-Marne monument. *See* Château-Thierry monument
Aisne-Marne region, 18, 108, 250n64
Ambrose, Stephen E., 230
American Armies and Battlefields in Europe (ABMC), 141
American Battle Monuments Commission (ABMC) after World War I: annual reports and, 53, 98, 117, 256n1, 270n88, 301n1; architects and, 63, 66, 83–85, 86, 88–91, 95, 97, 102–3, 106, 107, 108–10, 113–16, 206, 226, 266n19, 270n88, 271n114; arrangement of graves and, 97–100, 265n147, 268–69n67; battlefield marking project and, 43, 46, 53, 56, 65; battle maps and, 94–95, 107, 108–9, 110, 115, 232, 268n54; Battle Monuments Board (BMB) and, 37, 39–40, 44, 45, 46–48, 49, 56, 61, 65, 140, 252n95, 254n117, 255n137; battle research and, 78–80, 264nn130, 136, 264–65n138; British World War I cemeteries and, 55, 60, 61, 70–71, 258–59n44; cemetery artwork and, 95–97, 268n65; cemetery superintendents and, 105, 277n35; chapels at cemeteries and, 52, 53, 60, 62, 64, 65, 66, 73, 83, 84, 85–94, 128, 206, 258n43, 266nn12, 19; commemorative plaques and, 52, 62, 85, 172, 178, 186; commissioners of, 2, 3, 13, 44, 45–46, 47–49, 52, 176, 241n6, 241–42n7, 254nn128, 130, 255nn131–133, 135–136, 270n102; congressional funding and, 58–59, 64–65, 81, 109, 123,

American Battle Monuments
Commission (ABMC) after World
War I *(cont.)*
125, 126, 129, 139, 264n124,
278n47; construction of sites and,
4, 33, 82, 85, 116, 117, 123, 136,
226; creation and, 1, 3, 15, 16,
25, 39–40, 42–48, 241–42n7,
253nn103, 108, 115, 253–54n116,
254n117; dedication of memorials
and, 83, 116, 117, 118–35, 139,
141, 206, 219, 274–75n2, 275n7,
276nn18, 20, 28, 277nn34–35,
278nn48–51, 297n102; design of
monuments and cemeteries and,
25, 53, 54–55, 60, 61, 62, 63–65,
66, 71, 84–85, 95, 260n66;
determination of memorial sites
and, 46, 56, 65, 66, 71–73, 83;
earlier agency of, 10, 16, 36;
European employees and, 52,
143–44, 177–78; European visits
and, 26, 56, 59–60, 65, 75, 79,
80–81, 89, 99, 102, 112, 116,
120, 128–30, 258n35; Gold Star
pilgrimages and, 81–82, 124,
192, 265n147; guidebooks and,
53, 79–80, 117, 118, 137, 140–41,
142, 263n114, 264nn130, 136,
264–65n138, 271n114; headstone
design and, 53, 55, 56–59, 61, 63,
66–71, 85, 99, 227, 256–57n11,
257n24, 261n81, 261–62n91,
262n92, 303n24; headstone
material and, 53, 56, 66–70, 99,
200, 261n81; Historical Section
and, 53, 74, 78–80, 114–15,
140–41, 264nn128, 130; Jewish
American dead and, 56, 57, 59,
86–87, 119; land acquisition for
monuments and, 100–101, 103–5,
111–12, 195, 270n96; literature
on, 11–12, 244nn40, 47; main
guidelines and, 62, 63, 65, 97;
main task of, 5, 12–13, 36, 51,
52, 53, 221, 256n1; maintenance
of memorials and, 76, 135–36,
142, 261n81; Medal of Honor
recipients and, 70, 227, 303n24;
memorial tablets and, 73, 74,
78, 120, 139; missing dead and,
2, 60, 86, 93–94, 220, 258n43;
monument-building program
and, 72–75, 77–78, 81–82,
83–84, 264n124; monument
construction costs and, 109,
272n129; monuments and, 10,
43–44, 46, 52, 64–65, 100–116,
139, 273n151, 274n158; museum
buildings and, 92, 94–95; naval
memorials and, 64, 65, 71,
73, 101–2, 262n94; overseas
liaison and, 53–54, 56; possible
reorganization/disbanding of, 118,
135–38, 142, 281n89; presidents'
involvement with, 1, 2–3, 45, 46,
47–49, 52, 78, 118, 129, 136–37,
138–39, 241–42n7, 255nn131,
133, 136–137, 256n1, 270n102,
280–81n84; private monuments
and, 52–53, 54, 60, 61–62,
63, 64, 72–78, 96–97, 211–13,
263n114, 263–64n123; secretary
of, 44, 45, 47, 252n95; total
cemeteries and monuments and,
1, 11, 52, 62, 64, 73, 78, 83, 118,
124, 139, 143, 184, 220, 241n5;
total costs of projects, 139, 201,
253n108; total dead in cemeteries
controlled by, 2, 184, 241n5;

Index 317

twentieth anniversary of US entry into World War I and, 118, 123; unknown dead and, 66, 86, 260n67; World War I cemeteries and, 20, 23–24, 33, 46, 52, 53, 60, 61, 64, 71, 88–96, 97–100, 135, 213, 246–47n23. *See also* Graves Registration Service (GRS) of the US Army; inscriptions; sculptures; stained glass

American Battle Monuments Commission (ABMC) after World War II, 119, 290n14; annual reports and, 222, 228, 301n1, 303n32; architects and, 182, 186, 193, 198, 200, 206, 210, 292n13, 293–94n33; archival material and, 12, 245n49; battle maps and, 94, 216, 220, 232; burials of American war dead and, 176, 183, 187, 188–91, 192–93, 196–98, 202, 209–13, 246–47n23, 293n29, 293n32, 295n50, 299n128; cemetery planning and, 4, 187, 188–92, 193–94, 198–99, 210, 211, 292–93n25, 294n40; cemetery superintendents and, 6, 9, 180, 194, 211, 230, 242n22, 290n18, 294n42; chapels at cemeteries and, 198, 202, 205, 206, 215, 216, 220–21; commemorating American WWII dead and, 176, 179–80, 181–82, 183–85, 188–92, 201, 222–24; commissioners of, 2–5, 13, 165, 176, 177, 182, 185, 187, 208, 226, 241n6, 241–42n7, 242n12, 255n135, 281n89, 294n45, 298n109; congressional funding and, 187, 201–3, 205, 208, 216, 218, 227, 228, 231; construction of sites and, 4, 199–203, 205–6, 208, 221, 226; damage to cemeteries and monuments and, 151, 152, 153–54, 186; dedication of memorials and, 105–6, 184, 186, 206–7, 208, 216–17, 218–20, 222, 223–24, 228, 297nn102–103, 105, 300n155; education programs and, 10, 223; European employees and, 2, 8, 177, 199, 204, 205, 221, 244n38; European visits and, 188, 199, 207–8, 226–27; funding and, 177–78, 180; Gold Star pilgrimages and, 192, 293n29; grave adoptions and, 8, 213–15, 243n31; headstone material and, 200–201, 204, 261n81; headstones and, 71, 198, 201, 202, 203, 205, 215–16, 227, 303n24; inspections of sites and, 177, 178; land acquisition for sites and, 183, 187, 195; later memorials and, 1–2, 221, 223, 227–28, 241n3, 303n30; low profile and, 1, 4, 5, 11, 180; main task of, 1, 5, 221, 233–34; maintenance and repair of WWI memorials and, 178, 186–87, 192, 201, 219, 291–92n10, 293n31; maintenance of memorials and, 176, 177, 222–23, 261n81; Medal of Honor recipients and, 213, 227, 303n24; missing dead and, 2, 206, 215, 216, 219, 220, 224, 293n29; monuments and, 105–6, 183, 191, 201, 223, 292–93n25; new burials and, 2, 221, 241n5; Pacific Area Committee and, 188–89; Pacific cemeteries and, 191,

American Battle Monuments
Commission (ABMC) after World
War II *(cont.)*
215–17; possible dissolution and,
224–25, 301–2n11; presidents'
involvement with, 5, 7, 179, 180,
185–86, 187, 208, 223, 224–25,
226–27, 228, 229–30, 242n12,
243n25, 281n89, 294n45, 301n1;
private monuments and, 178–79,
185, 191, 211–13; repatriating
bodies and, 183, 196–97, 198–
99, 221, 246–47n23, 295n50;
secretary of, 2, 3, 9, 11, 177, 179,
181, 186, 222, 225, 302nn13–14;
staffing levels and, 2, 203–4, 205,
222; total cemeteries and, 1, 181,
183–84, 190, 191, 192–93, 194–
96, 220, 241nn3, 5, 293–94n33,
294nn41, 43; unknown dead and,
196, 201, 205, 215; visitors to
sites and, 5–9, 10, 192, 194, 198,
203, 204, 215, 222, 228–32, 233,
234, 242n22, 243nn24–26, 31,
303n32; World War I cemeteries
and, 177, 184, 192, 223, 229,
261n81, 291n1, 293n31. *See also*
inscriptions; sculptures
American Battle Monuments
Commission (ABMC) during
World War II, 142, 143–55, 165–
66, 284n44, 288n96; American
employees in Europe and, 143–
44, 145, 146–50, 151–53, 154,
155, 158, 159–63, 165, 169–70,
174, 176, 281n1, 283n24, 285–
86n64, 287n86; British World
War I cemeteries and, 154, 158,
285n61; cemetery superintendents
and, 145, 148–50, 152, 154, 163,
164, 283n19; chapels at cemeteries
and, 154, 156; combat around
sites and, 148–50, 151, 154,
171–72; damage to cemeteries and
monuments and, 150, 170, 172,
174–75, 192, 283n30, 284n39;
European employees and, 148–50,
157–58, 163, 168, 170–71, 175,
176, 283n19, 285n54, 288n103,
290n3, 297n105; evacuation of
sites and, 145, 148–49, 282n4;
funding and, 164, 171, 282–
83n17; inspections of sites and,
12, 153–57, 158–59, 172–75, 178,
285n54, 288n105, 288–89n106,
289nn107, 109, 113–114; Jewish
American dead and, 175, 187;
maintenance of memorials and,
143, 144, 146, 147, 154–55, 156,
157, 163–64, 166, 168, 170–71,
288n105; private monuments and,
155–56; secretary of, 176, 281n89;
World War I commemorations
and, 146, 164–65
American Expeditionary Forces
(AEF), 93, 96, 102, 114, 140,
278n48; 1st Division, 78, 101;
3rd Division, 35, 44, 48, 78, 155,
251n83; 5th Division, 78, 155;
27th Division, 98, 268–69n67;
28th Division, 63, 78, 155; 30th
US Infantry (3rd Division),
35, 44; 37th Division, 24, 74,
78; 42nd Division, 99–100;
79th Division, 48, 74–75; 91st
Division, 24, 29; 93rd Division,
76–77, 263–64n123; 315th
Pennsylvania regiment, 75–76;
316th Pennsylvania regiment,
74–75, 76; African American

Index   319

troops and, 76–77, 82, 265n147; chaplaincy and, 18, 57; Gold Star Mothers European visits and, 81–82, 265n147; headstone design and, 57, 58; Meuse-Argonne battle and, 24, 31, 41, 48, 75, 101, 111–13, 115; most important battles and, 16, 21, 24, 29, 38, 40, 41, 43, 74–75, 88, 111, 115, 251n83; Pershing and, 3, 16, 19, 21, 24, 31, 34, 47, 49–51, 80–81, 88, 130–31, 146, 159, 181, 227; veteran visits to Europe and, 80–81, 265n142
American Expeditionary Forces Memorial, 2, 227–28
American Granite Association, 67, 68, 69, 70
American Institute of Architects, 57, 66
American Legion, 63, 100, 210, 231, 283n30; ABMC creation and, 39, 45, 47, 48, 254n130; dedication of memorials and, 129, 130, 134, 218; design of headstones for World War I cemeteries and, 57, 58; Memorial Days and, 32, 164, 250–51n73; tenth anniversary of US entry into World War I and, 8–9, 79, 80–81; twentieth anniversary pilgrimage to Europe and, 124, 125, 126, 128, 134, 279n64
American Memorial Highway Commission, 42
American Overseas Memorial Day Association, 32, 126, 164, 250–51n73
American Red Cross, 184–85, 211–12
American Unknown Soldier. *See* Tomb of the Unknown Soldier

American Veterans of World War II (AMVETS), 218
American War Mothers, 128, 218
Anderson, Dwight, 232, 233
Antietam battlefield, 38
Anzio beach, 189, 195, 208
Anzio Cemetery. *See* Sicily-Rome American Cemetery
Ardennes, Belgium, 194, 241n5
Ardennes American Cemetery, 190–91, 192, 194, 195, 198, 199, 202, 241n5, 293n32, 293–94n33
Argonne cemetery. *See* Meuse-Argonne American Cemetery
Argonne forest, 130, 133
Arizona, USS, 216, 217–18
Arlington National Cemetery, 19, 55, 57, 181, 192, 252n90, 260n67, 281n90, 291n22
Army War College, 79, 80, 124, 264n128
Arthur, Chester, 96
Audenarde monument, 95, 103, 133, 274n158; location, 63, 73, 101, 102; World War II and, 162, 285n54
Auriol, Vincent, 206, 207
Ayres, Louis, 91
Azores, 64, 65

Baker, Cora W., 176, 189, 270n102
Baker, Newton, 17, 21, 24, 25, 57, 278n48
Baldwin, Joseph C., 187, 189
Barnes, Maynard, 158, 159, 160, 161, 162
Barthou, Louis, 26, 28
Baruch, Bernard, 132
Battle Monuments Board (BMB), 140, 252nn88, 95; ABMC

Battle Monuments Board *(cont.)* creation and, 39–40, 44, 45, 46–48, 49, 254n117, 255n137; battlefield marking project and, 16, 36, 37, 40–42, 43, 46–47, 56, 65; dissolving of, 16, 39, 46–47; guidelines for monuments, 37–40, 41–42, 61

Beale, Harriet Blaine, 96, 268n65

Beale, Walker Blaine, 96

Beatrix (queen of the Netherlands), 229

Becker, Florence, 127

Belgium, 60, 194, 241n5; American dead from World War I and, 24, 28, 29, 33, 35, 52, 157, 178; commemorative highway and, 42, 43; World War II and, 144, 148, 155, 157, 163, 171–72, 175; World War I monuments and, 63, 65, 73, 100–101. *See also* Ardennes American Cemetery; Audenarde monument; Flanders Field American Cemetery; Kemmel monument

Belleau Wood, France, 24, 104, 130, 134, 165; Aisne-Marne Cemetery chapel at, 87, 88, 89, 90, 91, 153–54, 187, 192, 293n31; Marine Corps monument and, 1, 105–6; after World War II, 187, 192; World War II and, 149, 150, 153–54, 156, 157. *See also* Aisne-Marne Cemetery

Bellicourt monument, 95, 101, 274n158, 285n54; architect of, 85, 102; dedication of, 133

Bentley, Fred, 45

Bentley, Josephine L. Cody, 45, 48, 67, 176, 254n130, 270n102

Bessell, William W., 141, 144, 145, 282nn2, 7

Biddle, Anthony, 152

Biffle, Leslie, 176, 188, 189, 194, 208, 287n86

Bird, Dyer J., 100, 198

Blaine, James G., 96

Blanc Mont, Champagne. *See* Sommepy monument

Blosville site, 189, 190, 191, 195–96

Blum, Léon, 127

Boatner, Mark, 122, 124, 125, 276nn18, 28

Bony cemetery. *See* Somme American Cemetery

Bourguiba, Habib, 193

Bradley, Omar, 184, 189, 204, 291n22

Bradshaw, Aaron, 197

Brent, Charles, 18

Brest naval monument, 73, 101–2, 103, 170, 201; dedication of, 119, 121, 133; rededication after World War II, 219; after World War II, 178, 186, 291–92n10

Bring Home the Soldier Dead League, 18, 245n9

Brinkley, Douglas, 230

Brittany American Cemetery, 190, 191, 192, 194, 195, 202, 205, 218, 220, 221, 261n81, 293–94n33

Brokaw, Tom, 230

Brookwood American Cemetery, 27, 95, 250n62; chapel at, 85, 92, 93, 102; chapel dedication and, 121, 126, 133; grave numbers at, 10, 29; location, 23–24; after World War II, 177, 178, 190, 191, 213; World War II and, 143, 150, 164–65, 285n54, 289n114, 290n3

Budreau, Lisa, 11, 37, 44, 48
Bullitt, William, 127, 128, 130, 131, 144, 145, 156
Burling, Mathilda, 100
Busan, South Korea, 1
Busbey, Fred, 203
Bush, George H. W., 3, 5, 229, 243n25
Bush, George W., 5, 229, 230, 242n12, 243n25

Calcutta, 189, 191
Cambridge American Cemetery, 190, 191, 192, 194, 195, 198, 205, 218, 229, 244n39, 293–94n33, 294n40
Canada, 122–23, 276n20
Cantigny monument, 73, 95, 101, 102, 133, 274n158
Carrara marble, 67, 69–70, 99, 200–201, 206
Carter, Jimmy, 5, 229, 243n25
Carthage site. *See* North Africa American Cemetery
Casablanca, 189, 191
CFA. *See* National Commission of Fine Arts (CFA)
Chambrun, Adelbert de, 127
Château-Thierry monument, 73, 95, 101, 130, 187, 244n39, 251n83, 272n129, 274n158; architect of, 85, 102, 108; dedication of, 121, 126, 128, 133, 134; design, 107, 108–9, 111; land acquisition for, 103, 270n96; World War II and, 149, 154, 155, 289n114
Chaumont commemorative tablet, 62, 73, 85, 120, 139, 172, 178, 186
Chautemps, Camille, 130
China, 131, 189
Churchill, Clementine, 164

Clark, Mark W., 189, 291n22; ABMC service, 3, 4–5, 9, 11, 226–27, 228, 303n32
Clark Veterans Cemetery, 221
Cleland, Max, 3, 222
Clemenceau, Georges, 20, 30
Clichy cemetery, 171
Clinton, Bill, 3, 5, 229, 243n25
clock towers, 73, 74
Collins, Lawton, 189, 205
Colmery, Harry, 130, 132, 134
commemorative bridges, 72, 155
commemorative fountains, 72, 73, 212
"Committee on Memorials," 62, 63
"Committee on Naval Memorials," 64
Coolidge, Calvin, 78, 255n133, 259–60n64, 260n68
Cram, Ralph Adams, 85, 86, 87, 88, 90, 91
Cram and Ferguson, 88–89
Cret, Paul Philippe, 64, 67, 73, 82, 83, 84, 97, 182, 186, 212, 273n151; chapels at cemeteries and, 66, 85, 86, 87, 90, 91; Château-Thierry monument and, 102, 108, 109; death of, 176, 180–81; Montfaucon monument and, 110, 112, 113, 115; Pennsylvania monument and, 63, 155–56
Crezancy, France, 35, 251n83
Cuba, 1

Daladier, Édouard, 127
Dartmouth, England, 1, 228
Daughters of the American Revolution, 127
Davis, Benjamin Oliver, 208
Davis, Dwight Filley, 59, 66, 69, 99, 260n68

Davis, R. Warren, 211
Dawes, Charles G., 27, 42, 43
Delbos, Yvon, 130
D'Este, Carlo, 3
Devers, Jacob, 291n22; ABMC service, 3, 4, 11, 186, 189, 217, 218, 219, 222, 223–25, 226, 301n1, 302n13
Dillon, John J., 149, 290n18
Disabled American Veterans, 128, 218
Doumergue, Gaston, 81
Draguignan Cemetery. *See* Rhône American Cemetery
Drottningholm, SS, 167
Duffy, Ryan, 129–30
Dun-Sur-Meuse, 155

East Coast Memorial, 201, 223, 224
Eaton, Charles, 129
Eggers, Otto, 111
Eisenhower, Dwight D., 184, 291n22; ABMC service, 11, 12, 75, 79–80, 173, 178, 180, 189, 190, 220, 221, 224–26, 264n136, 289n113, 292–93n25; as president, ABMC and, 3, 4, 208, 209, 218, 219, 223, 241–42n7, 294n45
Ellett, Thomas Harlan, 85, 96, 97
Épinal cemetery, 190, 192, 194, 195, 205, 218, 220, 293–94n33
Evans, Ira K., 188, 196, 197
Executive Order 6614, 136

Fairfield, A. P., 134
Fère-en-Tardenois region, 23, 24, 89, 153. *See also* Oise-Aisne cemetery
Field of Honor Association, 18
Fish, Hamilton, 76–77, 263–64n123
Fismes, France, 63, 155

Flanders Field American Cemetery, 10, 23, 27, 95, 229, 244n39, 261–62n91; chapel at, 66, 85, 92, 93, 94; chapel dedication and, 121, 126, 133; construction costs, 139; grave numbers at, 29, 85; land acquisition for, 28, 29; World War II and, 150, 153, 154, 157, 162, 163, 172, 285n54. *See also* Audenarde monument; Kemmel monument
Florence cemetery, 189, 191, 192, 193, 194, 195, 205, 219, 221, 293n32, 293–94n33
Foch, Ferdinand, 30, 31, 51, 81, 130
Forrestal, James, 185, 187
Foss, Joseph J., 208, 298n109
France, 35–36; ABMC creation and, 43–44; ABMC design of headstones and, 68–69, 261n81; ABMC monuments and, 63, 65, 72, 100–101, 221; acquisition of land for American World War I cemeteries and, 21, 26, 28–29, 249nn58–60; American dead from World War I and, 20–21, 22, 26, 30, 31, 32–33, 51, 60, 241n3, 246n12, 246–47n23, 251n77, 299n128; American dead from World War II and, 189–91, 193, 195–96, 294n45, 299n128; Bastille Day commemorations and, 50, 125; commemorative highways and, 42, 43; debt payments to US, 72, 112, 262n98; total US World War I cemeteries and monuments, 52, 62; United States partnership, 8, 30–31, 44, 51, 81, 103–4, 111–12, 127, 128, 131–32, 134, 206–7,

Index 323

232, 251n77; US veteran visits and, 80–81, 265n142; Vichy France and, 151, 156, 161, 163, 164, 166, 167–68, 284–85n52; World War I and, 24, 256n142; World War II and, 144, 147, 151–58, 177. *See also specific World War I and World War II cemeteries and monuments*
Franco, Francisco, 131
Franke, William B., 219
Franks, Frederick M., Jr., 3, 5
Frazer, Elizabeth Van Rensselaer, 105
French Unknown Soldier, 125, 256n142

Gallipoli, 8
Garcia, Carlos, 219
Garfield, James, 96
Garrett, Finis J., 176, 188, 255n133
George, C. J., 214
Georges, Alphonse, 146
Germany, 34, 122, 131, 142, 146, 158, 160, 162, 165, 166, 167, 169, 190–91
Gettysburg Address, 165, 233
Gettysburg battlefield, 45, 61–62
Gibbs, George, 25
Gibraltar monument, 52, 64, 65, 73, 102, 184; dedication of, 120, 125, 133–34
Gibson, Ernest W., 130
Gilbert, Cass, 102
Gilbert, H. N., 35, 36, 44
Glucksman, H. L., 86
Godfrey, Chester N., 88–89
Gold Star Fathers Association, 45, 58, 67
Gold Star Mothers Association, 45, 48, 100, 254n130; pilgrimages and, 11, 81–82, 124, 192, 265n147, 293n29

Gompers, Samuel, 18
Goodpaster, Andrew, 5
Gorham, George C., 148–49, 290n18
Graham, John W., 11
Graves Registration Service (GRS) of the US Army, 69, 136, 177, 212, 290n3; burials of American World War I dead and, 16, 20, 22, 26–27, 63, 211; burials of American World War II dead and, 183, 187, 197, 209; exhuming bodies from World War I and, 22, 26–27, 31, 211, 247nn24–25; repatriating bodies from World War I and, 15, 16, 17, 22, 25, 26–27, 32–33, 247nn24–25; World War I cemeteries and, 1, 15, 20, 23, 24, 25, 26, 32, 46, 54, 57, 81, 139; World War I cemeteries' grave arrangements and, 98, 99; World War I cemetery grave numbers and, 29–30; World War II cemeteries and, 188, 196, 198, 210; World War II cemeteries' grave arrangements and, 209–11
Great Britain, 50, 126, 148, 162, 256n142; American dead from World War I and, 23–24, 29, 30, 164–65, 191; American dead from World War II and, 189, 190, 191, 195; British World War I cemeteries and, 22–23, 55, 60, 61, 70–71, 154, 158, 258–59n44, 285n61; US naval memorials and, 64, 65, 71, 262n94. *See also* Brookwood American Cemetery; Cambridge American Cemetery
Great Depression, 120, 121–22

Greece, 64, 65
Greenleaf, James L., 25
Guadalcanal, 228
Guam, 188, 189

Haislip, Wade, 189
Hamm Cemetery. *See* Luxembourg American Cemetery
Handy, Thomas, 210
Hanks, Tom, 231
Hanson, Victor Davis, 221
Harbeson, John, 182, 186, 188, 190, 193, 199, 292n13
Harbord, James, 105, 134
Harding, Warren G., 25, 27–28, 42, 44, 45, 47–49, 50, 241–42n7, 255nn131, 133, 136, 260n68
Harmon, Arthur Loomis, 102
Hastings, K. L., 213, 215, 216
Hawaii, 188, 190, 199, 201, 215–18, 223, 224, 244n39
Hayes, E. A., 100
Henn, Lisa Zanatta, 230
Henri-Chapelle cemetery, 190, 194, 195, 199, 220, 261n81, 293–94n33; construction of, 202, 205; dedication of, 219; grave numbers at, 192; visitors to, 6, 228, 242n22
Hertford, Kenner, 145, 147, 151, 152, 154, 155, 283n24
Hill, John Boynton Philip Clayton, 48, 58, 59, 64, 116, 165, 176, 255n132
Hill, Lister, 129
Hindenburg Line, 24, 101
History of the American Graves Registration Service (GRS), 23, 32, 33

Hitler, Adolf, 122, 127, 131, 142, 144, 151, 162, 169
Holle, Charles G., 145, 282n7, 282–83n17, 285n63; ABMC inspections during World War II and, 153–55, 156–57, 170, 284n39; American ABMC employees in Europe during World War II and, 146–48, 149, 150, 151–53, 158–59, 160–61, 174, 283nn19, 24
Honolulu Memorial, 188, 190, 199, 201, 215–17, 223, 224, 244n39
Hoover, Herbert, 75, 270n102
Horkan, George A., 187, 189, 190, 191
Howe, George, 85, 91
H.R. 9634, 42, 43, 44, 45
H.R. 10801, 42–45, 48, 253n108, 254n130
H.R. 14087, 45–46, 47, 253–54n116, 254n117
Hughes, Charles Evans, 54
Hull, Cordell, 160–61, 162
Husted, James W., 42, 44, 45

Imperial War Graves Commission, 23, 60; 61, 158, 164, 165. *See also* Great Britain
India, 189, 191
inscriptions, 10, 96, 183, 186; chapels at cemeteries and, 86, 92–94, 206; headstones and, 66, 70–71, 140, 201, 261–62n91, 262n92; Medal of Honor recipients and, 70, 213, 227, 303n24; monuments and, 108–9, 114–15, 274nn158–159, 291–92n10; World War II cemeteries and, 234
Iran, 189

Italian Unknown Soldier, 59
Italy, 59, 64, 71, 73, 131, 169, 189, 191

Japan, 131, 185
Jefferson Memorial, 110
Jewish Welfare Board, 86
Johnson, Louis, 209–10
Johnson, Lyndon B., 3, 224–25, 301–2n11
Jones, Harris, 90
Jones, William P., 302n14
Juin, Alphonse, 207
Juliana (queen of the Netherlands), 219
Juvigny site, 102

Kaess, Adolph, 105, 148, 149, 152, 163, 283n19, 290n18
Keally and Patterson, 193, 293–94n33
Kelley, P. X., 5
Kemal, Mustafa (Ataturk), 8
Kemmel monument, 73, 95, 133, 139, 274n158; location, 101, 103; World War II and, 162, 285n54
Kendall, William M., 25
Kennedy, John F., 3, 224
Kinkaid, Thomas, 208, 217, 218, 219
Korean War, 1, 201–2, 216
Korean War Veterans Memorial, 2, 228, 303n30

Lafayette Escadrille, France, 221, 241n3, 246–47n23
Lambeth, J. Walter, 129
Lasa marble, 200, 201, 204, 261n81
Lebrun, Albert, 128, 130, 132
Lemly, H. R., 19–21
Lend-Lease Act, 162

Liberty Memorial, 51
Limey cemetery, 190, 191
Lincoln, Abraham, 165, 233
Lincoln Memorial, 106
Lisle, Naomi, 133
Littlejohn, Robert M., 178
Lloyd George, David, 30
Long, Breckenridge, 159
Lord, Herbert Mayhew, 109, 264n124
Lorraine American Cemetery, 6, 189, 191, 192, 194, 195, 202, 205, 293–94n33
"Lost Battalion," 41
Luxembourg American Cemetery, 189, 190, 194, 195, 202, 219; architect of, 193, 200, 293–94n33; arrangement of graves at, 209–11; artwork and chapel at, 220, 221; grave numbers at, 192, 209; visitors to, 228, 229

MacArthur, Douglas, 100, 184, 188
Maginot, André, 21
Magny, Charles, 76
Mangum, James E.: ABMC service, 59, 120, 121, 129, 273n151, 275n7, 276n20, 278nn47, 51, 281n89; World War II ABMC service, 147, 159–60, 165, 176, 282–83n17
Manhattan, SS, 129, 145
Manila American Cemetery, 188, 189, 190, 192, 195, 215, 220, 293–94n33; construction of, 202, 205; dedication of, 219; grave numbers at, 193–94; material for headstones at, 199, 200–201; visitors to, 228, 229, 244n39
Manship, Paul, 96, 268n61

Margraten cemetery. *See* Netherlands American Cemetery
Marianas Islands, 188, 215
Marine Corps monument. *See* Belleau Wood, France
Markey, D. John, 48, 59, 64, 99, 116, 176, 189, 197, 241–42n7
Marshall, George C., Jr., 187, 225, 257n26, 291n22, 302n15; ABMC appointment and, 3–4, 180, 181; ABMC dedications and, 206, 207, 208, 218–19, 297nn102–103, 105; ABMC European visits and, 184, 207–8, 291n1; ABMC funding and, 202, 203, 204, 205; ABMC service, 11, 12, 182, 199–200, 207–9, 223, 224, 242n14; death of, 4, 185, 223, 291n3; other commitments and, 184–85; World War II cemeteries and, 188, 192, 198, 207–8, 210, 211, 214, 227
Massachusetts, 74
Maybank, Burnet R., 187, 189
McNarney, Joseph T., 204
McPeak, Merrill A., 3, 5
Mellor, Meigs, and Howe, 103
Memorial Association, 105
Memorial Days, 7–8, 222, 229, 243n25, 303n32; 1919, 8, 15, 21, 30–32, 50, 126, 205, 250nn63, 66; 1920, 32, 250–51n73; 1921, 32–33, 251n77; 1937, 124, 125–28, 131, 135, 277n34; 1948, 197–98; World War II and, 164–65
Messina cemetery, 189
Meuse-Argonne American Cemetery, 100, 261n81, 290n18; chapel at, 66, 85, 91, 92, 93, 94, 130; chapel dedication and, 119, 126, 127–28, 277n35; first Memorial Day and, 8, 30, 31–32, 50, 126; grave numbers at, 29, 220, 250n68, 261–62n91; land acquisition for, 28; monument on grounds of, 62, 88, 95, 124; as Romagne cemetery, 23, 24, 27, 28, 29, 30, 66, 91, 119, 126, 127, 130, 139, 141; visitors to, 81, 141, 229, 244n39; World War II and, 146, 148, 149, 150, 151, 153, 154, 156, 162, 163, 172, 283n19, 285n54. *See also* Montfaucon monument
Meuse-Argonne battle, 24, 31, 41, 48, 75, 88, 93, 101, 111–13, 115, 119, 132–33, 252n90
Meuse-Argonne battlefield, 8, 31, 37, 101, 111, 124
Meuse-Argonne monument. *See* Montfaucon monument
Meuse-Argonne region, 23, 76, 93, 132–33
Mexico City, 221, 241n3
Midway Island, 1, 228
Miller, Thomas W., 48, 64, 77, 176, 255n133
Millerand, Alexandre, 21
Mills, Nicolaus, 232
Montfaucon monument, 64, 95; architect of, 102, 110–11, 112; construction of, 83, 112–15, 274n159; construction costs, 139, 272n129; dedication of, 119, 121, 124, 125, 126, 128, 129, 130–33, 135, 206, 239–40, 278nn50–51, 54, 57; design, 107, 108, 109–11, 112–14, 273n151; land acquisition for, 111–12; location, 73, 101, 102, 111; World War II and, 156, 187, 285n54. *See also* Meuse-Argonne American Cemetery

Montfaucon village, 74
Montsec monument, 73, 133, 272n129, 274n158; architect of, 102, 106, 107, 271n114; design, 106–8, 111; land acquisition for, 103–4; location, 96, 101; World War II and, 146, 172, 186, 187, 285n54. *See also* Saint Mihiel American Cemetery
Moore, Charles, 25, 26–28, 29, 54–55, 56–57, 84, 88, 104–5, 107, 113, 273n151. *See also* National Commission of Fine Arts (CFA)
Morgenthau, Henry, 164
Moses, William, 154, 163
Mott, Georgette, 166–69
Mott, T. Bentley, 35–36, 44, 287n93; ABMC American employees during World War II and, 159, 161, 162, 163; ABMC inspections during World War II and, 177–78, 288nn96, 105; ABMC service, 12, 164, 166–71, 174, 177–80, 186, 285–86n64, 288–89n106, 290n14
Murtha, John, 231
Mussolini, Benito, 59, 71, 169

Nancy, France, 65, 72, 73
Nantillois, France, 63, 76
National Archives, 12, 78, 110, 245n49
National Commission of Fine Arts (CFA), 12; ABMC and, 53, 54–55, 56–58, 59, 63, 98; ABMC chapels at cemeteries and, 88, 90, 266n19; ABMC creation and, 25, 39, 45, 46, 253n115; ABMC monuments and, 46, 62, 84, 106, 107, 108, 110, 111, 112, 113, 273n151; ABMC work after World War II and, 183, 186, 193, 200; World War I cemeteries and, 16, 19, 24–28, 29, 46, 54–55, 56–58, 59, 98
National Defense Authorization Act of 2014, 228
National Geographic Magazine, 83, 97, 116, 300n155
National Geographic Society, 133
National Park Service, 2, 218, 228
National World War II Museum, 230
National World War I Memorial, 228. *See also* American Expeditionary Forces Memorial
Necropolis and Mausoleum Company (London), 29
Netherlands American Cemetery, 190, 194, 195, 199, 221; construction of, 202, 205, 293–94n33; grave adoptions and, 8, 213–15, 243n31; grave numbers at, 192, 197; Memorial Days and, 197–98; visitors to, 198, 219, 228–29, 234
Netherlands War Graves Commission, 214, 215
Neuville-en-Condroz cemetery. *See* Ardennes American Cemetery
New York City, 224
New York Sun, 66
New York Times, 9, 19, 27, 32, 135, 145, 164, 280n81, 283n30
Nicholson, John W., 3
Nimitz, Chester W., 186, 219
Nixon, Richard M., 3, 223, 226–27, 302n13
Normandy American Cemetery, 12, 218, 220, 293–94n33; burials of American war dead and, 189, 196, 212, 213, 246n13, 299n128; construction of, 199, 205;

Normandy American Cemetery *(cont.)* grave numbers at, 192; location, 194, 195; visitor and interpretive center at, 10, 231–32; visitors to, 3, 7, 8, 9, 223, 228–32, 243nn24–26, 303n35

North, Thomas, 76, 302n15; ABMC guidebooks and, 79, 80; ABMC memoir and, 11, 244n40, 258n35, 258–59n44, 264n130, 288n96; ABMC monuments and, 100, 103, 104, 111, 112; ABMC repairs after World War II and, 187, 192; ABMC service after World War I, 56, 68, 70, 72, 75, 82, 99, 173, 175, 226, 270n89, 278n54, 281n89; ABMC service after World War II, 3, 11, 177, 179, 181–82, 186, 206, 208–9, 217, 225–26, 281n89, 291n1, 302n14; ABMC World War II cemeteries and, 188–89, 191, 193–95, 198–99, 200–201, 202, 203–5, 210, 212–13, 214

North Africa American Cemetery, 190, 191, 192, 193, 194, 195, 198, 205, 220, 293–94n33, 294n40

Obama, Barack, 3, 229, 242n12, 243n25
Obey, David, 231
Ohio, 73, 74, 78, 99–100
Oise-Aisne cemetery, 81, 95, 254n130; arrangement of graves at, 98, 99; battle maps and, 94, 268n54; chapel at, 85, 91, 92–93, 94, 127; grave numbers at, 29, 134, 220; headstones at, 172, 261n81, 261–62n91; land acquisition for, 28, 249n60; location, 23, 24; Plot E, 213; World War II and, 149, 150, 153, 172, 283n19, 289n114, 290n18. *See also* Château-Thierry monument

Oise-Aisne region, 23, 24, 268n54
Omaha Beach, 7, 189, 230, 231, 238
Oran, 189, 191
O'Ryan, John F., 19
"Outline Sketch Map Monuments" (BMB), 40
Overstake, Orlando, 148, 149–50, 163, 290n18
Owsley, Alvin Mansfield, 127, 128

Paestum site, 189, 191
Palmer, John McAuley, 37, 38, 39–40, 41, 44–45, 46–47, 48, 65, 252nn88, 90, 255nn136–137
Panama City, 2, 221, 241n3
Papua New Guinea, 228
Paris Peace Conference, 20
Patterson, Robert P., 209, 212
Patton, George S., Jr., 209–11, 213
Pearl Harbor, 215, 216, 217
Pennsylvania, 155, 255n136
Pennsylvania Battle Monuments Commission, 63–64, 74, 84
Pericles, 233
Pershing, John J., 206, 233–34, 251n86, 257n26; ABMC and private monuments and, 75, 76, 78; ABMC and World War II and, 144, 147, 149, 150, 154, 155, 156, 158–63, 164, 165, 166–71, 173, 174, 282–83n17, 286n75, 287nn86, 93, 288n96, 288–89n106; ABMC and World War II end and, 176, 177, 179–81; ABMC chapels at cemeteries

and, 87, 88, 89, 90–91; ABMC creation and, 3, 47, 48; ABMC dedications and, 119, 120–25, 126–27, 128–32, 133, 134, 135, 219, 274–75n2, 275n7, 276nn18, 28, 277n35, 297n102; ABMC design of headstones and, 55, 58, 59, 69, 70; ABMC guidebooks and, 79, 80, 141, 264n136; ABMC monuments and, 62, 72, 102, 105, 106, 107, 108, 109–11, 112–14, 115; ABMC service after World War I, 5, 8–9, 52–53, 82, 83, 117–18, 136, 137, 140, 145–46, 181, 184, 208, 221, 241–42n7, 242n13, 255n138, 256n1, 281n86, 282n2; AEF service, 3, 16, 19, 21, 24, 31, 34, 47, 49–51, 80–81, 88, 130–31, 146, 159, 181, 227–28, 256n142; archival material and, 11, 12; death of, 4, 176–77, 181, 241–42n7, 252n90, 254n129, 281n90, 291n22; diplomatic work and, 66, 84, 102, 259–60n64; Eisenhower and, 79, 80, 173, 264n136, 291n22; European visits and, 51, 53, 60, 69, 80–81, 82, 88, 122, 123, 126–27, 138, 142, 145–46, 167, 277n33, 280n81; first Memorial Day and, 8, 21, 30, 31–32, 50, 126; as general of the armies, 37, 117, 144, 254n129, 303n25; Meuse-Argonne battle and, 31, 48, 112–13, 115; monument program start and, 34, 35, 36, 37; poor health, 118, 137–38, 141, 142, 208, 255n135, 259–60n64, 277n33, 280n81, 289n115; repatriating bodies from World War I, 18–19, 50, 255–56n141; retirement of, 117–18, 135, 279–80n71; World War I cemeteries and, 28, 30, 31–32, 60, 95, 96–97, 98, 99, 232, 250n68

Pétain, Henri-Philippe, 21, 125, 134, 145; Montfaucon monument dedication and, 130, 135; Suresnes cemetery, 1921 and, 32–33, 251n77; Vichy France and, 151, 163, 167, 169

Philippines, 2, 188, 192, 193–94, 219–20, 221, 241n3. *See also* Manila American Cemetery

Phillips, John, 208

Piehler, G. Kurt, 11

Pierce, Charles, 25, 26, 57

Pinay, Antoine, 206

"Plans of the Battle Monuments Board" (BMB), 40

Platt, Charles A., 56, 85, 206

Platt, Geoffrey, 206

Platt, William, 206

Poincaré, Raymond, 81

Pointe du Hoc, 228, 230, 244n39, 303n33

Pope, John Russell, 102, 110, 112, 113, 114–15

Porter, Stephen G., 42, 44, 45, 47, 48, 253–54n116, 254n130

Potter, Charles E., 208, 217, 218, 301–2n11

Price, William G., 63

Price, Xenophon H., 56, 141–42, 176, 226, 258n35, 270n89, 276n21, 281nn89–90; ABMC chapels at cemeteries and, 85, 88, 89–90, 266n19; ABMC creation and, 47, 49, 252n95; ABMC dedications and, 118, 119, 120, 121, 123, 124, 125, 129, 139, 275n7; ABMC

Price, Xenophon H. *(cont.)*
design of headstones and, 57, 59, 66, 256–57n11; ABMC future, 1938 and, 136, 137; ABMC guidebooks and, 79, 117, 118, 140, 141; ABMC material for headstones and, 68, 69, 70; ABMC monuments and, 53, 64, 72, 82, 83, 84, 85, 102, 106, 107, 108, 109, 112, 113, 114–16, 274n159; Battle Monuments Board (BMB) and, 38–39, 45, 47, 140, 252n95; World War I cemeteries and, 53, 82, 83, 96–97, 98–99, 105, 274n159; World War II and, 173–74, 289n114
Puerto Rico, 189, 190
Punchbowl Crater, Hawaii. *See* Honolulu Memorial

Raleigh, USS, 134
Reagan, Ronald, 228, 229–30, 243n25, 303n33
Reed, David Aiken, 48, 64, 77, 255n131; ABMC dedications and, 120–21, 122, 133; ABMC headstones and, 55, 57–58, 59, 67; ABMC monuments and, 84, 274n159; World War I cemeteries and, 99, 274n159; World War II cemeteries and, 176, 189
"Regulations Governing the Erection of World War Memorials in Europe by Americans" (ABMC), 62
"Relief Map Monuments" (BMB), 40
Renaud, Alexandre, 196, 294n45
Resco, Micheline, 167, 169, 287n93
Reserve Officers Association, 45
Rethers, Harry, 26, 27, 249n59
Rhône American Cemetery, 190, 191, 192, 194, 195, 205, 218, 220, 293–94n33
Ridgway, Matthew, 206, 207
Rivers, Phil, 230, 231
Rod, Pierre, 168, 170, 172, 173, 176, 178, 288n103, 288–89n106, 289nn107, 109
Romagne Cemetery. *See* Meuse-Argonne American Cemetery
Roosevelt, Archibald, 212
Roosevelt, Eleanor B. (Mrs. Theodore Roosevelt Jr.), 212, 218, 294n45
Roosevelt, Franklin D., 156; ABMC and, 118, 123, 126, 129, 136–37, 138–39, 165, 280n74, 280–81n84, 287n86; Montfaucon monument dedication and, 130, 131–32, 135, 239–40, 278nn54, 57
Roosevelt, Quentin, 18, 211–13, 246nn12–13, 299n128
Roosevelt, Theodore, 18, 19, 211–12
Roosevelt, Theodore, Jr., 208, 212, 218, 299n128
Roxas, Manuel, 194
Russell, Richard, 130
Russia, 93
Ryan, John T., 164

Sacco and Vanzetti, 104, 270n94
Saint-Avold cemetery. *See* Lorraine American Cemetery
Sainte-Mère-Église, 195, 196, 299n128
Saint-James cemetery. *See* Brittany American Cemetery
Saint-Laurent cemetery. *See* Normandy American Cemetery
Saint-Menehould, 130
Saint Mihiel American Cemetery, 81, 261–62n91, 268n54, 290n18;

Index   331

artwork at, 95–97; chapel at, 85, 92, 93, 94; chapel dedication and, 119, 127; grave numbers at, 9, 29; land acquisition for, 28, 249n60; location, 23, 24; monument on grounds of, 62, 73, 88; World War II and, 148–49, 150, 162, 172, 175, 283n19, 285n54, 289n109. *See also* Montsec monument

Saint-Mihiel battle, 24, 88, 96, 101

Saint-Mihiel battlefield, 37, 62, 107

Saint-Mihiel monument. *See* Montsec monument

Saint Quentin canal, 101

Saipan, 228

Salerno beaches, 189

San Francisco, 219, 224

Saving Private Ryan (film), 7, 230–31

sculptures, 95–97, 112–14, 220, 268nn61, 65, 273n151

Service Star Legion, 67

Shaw, Charles B., 172–73

Shaw, Howard Van Doren, 103

Shield, Walter, 141

Sicily-Rome American Cemetery, 189, 190, 191, 218, 293–94n33; artwork at, 220, 268n61; grave numbers at, 192; headstones at, 205, 261n81; location, 194, 195; visitors to, 208, 229, 244n39

Sims, Chris, 10

Soissons site, 102

Somme American Cemetery, 8, 127, 261–62n91, 290n18; arrangement of graves at, 98, 99, 268–69n67; Bony village and, 23, 24, 27, 148; chapel at, 85–86, 91, 92, 93, 94; grave numbers at, 29, 86, 91; land acquisition for, 28, 249n60; monument on grounds of, 73, 95, 162; World War II and, 148, 150, 151, 155, 162, 163, 172, 283n19, 285n54

Somme battle, 24, 101, 247n34

Somme monument. *See* Bellicourt monument

Sommepy monument, 133, 156, 263–64n123, 274n158; architect of, 102–3; location, 73, 101

Somme River, 155

Souilly commemorative tablet, 40, 62, 73, 85, 120, 139

Southampton, England, 64, 65, 73

Southard, Addison M., 127

Soviet Union, 165

Spaatz, Carl, 208, 218

Spain, 131

Spanish-American War, 1, 17, 48, 245n3

Spanish Civil War, 133

Spaulding, Oliver L., Jr., 38, 252n88

"Special Monuments" (BMB), 40

Spencer, Marcus A., 165

Spielberg, Steven, 7, 230–31

Spruance, Raymond, 219

stained glass, 78, 92, 93, 172, 198

Sternfield, Harry, 102, 103

Stimson, Henry, 185, 187

Summary Operations in the World War (ABMC Historical Section), 79, 264n130

Suresnes cemetery, 8–9, 20, 27, 95, 229; chapel at, 85, 92, 93, 94, 190, 205–7, 266n12; chapel dedication and, 127, 206–7, 208; dedication of after World War II, 184, 206–7, 208, 218, 297nn102–103, 105; first Memorial Day and, 30–31, 205, 250n63; grave numbers at, 29, 250n66; land

Suresnes cemetery *(cont.)*
    acquisition for, 28, 249nn58,
    60; location, 23–24; Memorial
    Days and, 32–33, 164, 251n77;
    World War II and, 143, 150, 164,
    168, 170, 172, 288nn96, 103,
    289n114; World War II dead and,
    92, 184, 190, 201, 205–7
Swartwout, Egerton, 85, 102, 106,
    107, 108

Taft, William Howard, 18
Tardieu, André, 75
Thiaucourt cemetery. *See* Saint Mihiel
    American Cemetery
Thiaucourt region, 23, 24
37th Division Battle Monuments
    Commission of Ohio, 74
Time magazine, 135
Tomb of the Unknown Soldier, 51,
    140, 260n67
Toul site, 62
Tours Services of Supply monument,
    62, 73, 101, 102, 104;
    construction costs, 65; dedication
    of, 119, 133; World War II and,
    152, 172, 187, 289n107
Treaty of Versailles, 50
Trinidad cemetery, 189
Trout, Steven, 11, 80
Truman, Harry S., 3, 4, 179, 180,
    185–86, 187, 197, 203, 206, 208,
    242n14, 281n89
Tunis cemetery. *See* North Africa
    American Cemetery
Tunisia, 189, 193

US Army Corps of Engineers, 90,
    140, 252n95
US Department of the Interior, 137

US Marine Corps, 1, 57, 87, 105–6, 134
US Navy, 64, 65, 102, 217, 219
US Rangers, 230, 303n33
Utah Beach, 189, 195
Utah Beach monument, 228

Vandegrift, Alexander, 187, 188, 208,
    216, 301–2n11
Vanderbilt, Cornelius, 18
Varennes, 63, 155
Ventre, André, 68, 261n81
Verdun, 74–75, 130, 132. *See also*
    Meuse-Argonne battle
ver Hulst, George M., 199–200
Vesle River, 24
Veterans Administration, 224,
    301–2n11
Veterans of Foreign Wars, 45, 48,
    126, 128, 129, 218
Vietnam War, 216, 225, 226–27
Villeneuve-sur-Auvers site, 191
Vimy Ridge Canadian memorial,
    122–23, 276n20
Vincensini, Pierre, 163, 166, 168, 171
Virginia Battle Monuments
    Commission, 74
Volturno-Anzio region, 189

Wainwright, J. Mayhew, 98
Wallace, Hugh, 32–33, 35
War Department, 264n130, 292–
    93n25; ABMC creation and, 42,
    43, 44, 45, 46, 48; battlefield
    marking project and, 16, 78;
    headstones and, 26, 56, 57, 67, 68,
    69, 70; monuments and, 33–34,
    35–36; plans to disband ABMC
    and, 136, 137; private makeshift
    monuments and, 26, 39; World
    War I cemeteries and, 23, 24,

Index   333

26, 27, 28–29, 56, 57, 70, 98, 99, 248n44, 249nn58–60, 268–69n67; World War I dead and, 19, 20–22, 23, 99; World War II and, 148, 173–74, 282–83n17; World War II dead and, 183, 187, 188, 195, 196, 197, 198, 295n50
Ware, Fabian, 23, 60, 165
Waregem region, 23, 24, 27, 154, 157. See also Flanders Field American Cemetery
Waregem site. See Flanders Field American Cemetery
War Observers Board, 173–74
Washington, D.C., 2, 110, 223, 227–28
Washington Post, 32, 105
Watson, Edwin "Pa," 156
Weeks, John, 25, 42, 43–44, 57, 59, 260n68
Weinman, A. A., 112, 113, 114, 273n151
Welles, Sumner, 161
West Coast Memorial, 201, 219, 223–24
White, Henry, 20
Willkie, Wendell, 208
Wilson, Herbert O., 134
Wilson, Woodrow, 20, 30–31, 32, 140, 205, 250nn63–64
Woerner, Fred, 5
Woodring, Harry, 137
Woodside, Robert G., 48, 84, 99, 133, 176, 179, 181, 197, 198, 208–9, 221, 241–42n7, 255n135
World War I, 8, 167, 187; Aisne-Marne battle, 88, 101, 105, 108, 268n54; American combat and, 16, 23, 24, 31, 34, 37–38, 40, 48, 65, 74–75, 88, 101, 108, 143;

American dead and, 2, 11, 15–19, 22, 31, 64, 184, 245n1, 246–47n23, 254n130; battle research and, 10, 16, 78–80, 264nn130, 136, 264–65n138; Belleau Wood, France, 1, 24, 87, 105, 134; commemorative highways and, 42, 43; desire for bodies to remain and, 18–21, 22, 23, 246–47n23; exhuming bodies to send home and, 98, 99–100, 247nn24–25; French debt payments to US and, 72, 112, 262n98; Meuse-Argonne battle, 24, 31, 41, 48, 75, 88, 93, 101, 111–13, 119, 132–33, 252n90; private makeshift monuments to, 34–36, 37, 38–39, 41, 43, 44, 52–53; repatriating bodies and, 15, 16, 17–19, 20–22, 50, 98, 245n9, 246–47n23, 255–56n141; Saint-Mihiel battle, 24, 88, 96, 101; Somme battle, 24, 101, 247n34; US memorials in United States and, 73. See also American Expeditionary Forces (AEF); Belgium; France; Great Britain
World War I cemeteries. See Aisne-Marne cemetery; Brookwood American Cemetery; Flanders Field American Cemetery; Meuse-Argonne American Cemetery; Oise-Aisne cemetery; Saint Mihiel American Cemetery; Somme American Cemetery; Suresnes cemetery
World War I monuments. See American Expeditionary Forces Memorial; Audenarde monument; Bellicourt monument; Brest naval monument; Cantigny monument;

World War I monuments *(cont.)*
Château-Thierry monument; Gibraltar monument; Kemmel monument; Lafayette Escadrille, France; Marine Corps monument; Montfaucon monument; Montsec monument; Sommepy monument; Tours Services of Supply monument

World War II, 4, 169, 177, 185, 194, 213–14, 215, 264n130; American dead and, 2, 6–7, 171, 176, 183, 184, 187, 188–89, 192–93, 196–98, 246–47n23, 293n29; beginnings of, 142, 143–51; D-Day landings, 3, 7, 140, 170, 171–72, 189–90, 195, 228, 229–30, 243n25; Dunkirk battle, 151, 164; Eisenhower and, 80, 173, 184; fall of France and, 144, 147, 151–58; private makeshift monuments to, 178–79, 185; repatriating American dead and, 178, 180; US entry into, 166–67; Vichy France and, 151, 156, 161, 163, 164, 166, 167–68, 284–85n52. *See also* American Battle Monuments Commission (ABMC) after World War II; American Battle Monuments Commission (ABMC) during World War II; Belgium; France; Great Britain; *specific World War I cemeteries and monuments*

World War II cemeteries. *See* Ardennes American Cemetery; Brittany American Cemetery; Cambridge American Cemetery; Épinal cemetery; Florence cemetery; Henri-Chapelle cemetery; Honolulu Memorial; Lorraine American Cemetery; Luxembourg American Cemetery; Manila American Cemetery; Netherlands American Cemetery; Normandy American Cemetery; North Africa American Cemetery; Rhône American Cemetery; Sicily-Rome American Cemetery

World War II Memorial, 2, 223, 228, 232, 303n30

World War II monuments. *See* East Coast Memorial; Pointe du Hoc; Utah Beach monument; West Coast Memorial

York and Sawyer, 91
Ypres monument. *See* Kemmel monument

CPSIA information can be obtained
at www.ICGtesting.com
Printed in the USA
BVHW040019130722
641979BV00002B/18